Global Migration beyond Limits

Global Migration beyond Limits

Ecology, Economics, and Political Economy

FRANKLIN OBENG-ODOOM

OXFORD
UNIVERSITY PRESS

Great Clarendon Street, Oxford, OX2 6DP,
United Kingdom

Oxford University Press is a department of the University of Oxford.
It furthers the University's objective of excellence in research, scholarship,
and education by publishing worldwide. Oxford is a registered trade mark of
Oxford University Press in the UK and in certain other countries

Published in the United States of America by Oxford University Press
198 Madison Avenue, New York, NY 10016, United States of America

British Library Cataloguing in Publication Data

Data available

Library of Congress Control Number: 2021941202

ISBN 978-0-19-886718-0

DOI: 10.1093/oso/9780198867180.001.0001

Printed and bound by
CPI Group (UK) Ltd, Croydon, CR0 4YY

Preface

The most wretched migrants had it easy, according to a fictionalised story I heard from a migrant (Balce, 2015). The neighbouring islands of Landen were terrible sites of economic stratification, social conflict, and deprivation. Northern Landen was recurrently hit by drought, while Southern Landen was almost always tortured by furious floods. Western Landen was filled with beaches, while Eastern Landen was full of rocks and mountain ranges. The limited arable lands on the islands were controlled by a few islandlords. What little those on the two islands could grow, they had to pay back to the islandlords as rent. Little or nothing of their labour remained after such rent was paid. Food was scarce. For a long time, the islanders would usually fight whenever one side could not find food. Not too long ago, they figured out that they could trade their limited surplus and co-operate. The beaches became sites for deliberations and occasional modest celebrations, during which the islandlords would usually have more food than was necessary.

One day, as the islanders reflected on their wretched lives on the beaches, a group of people appeared on the horizon of the sea facing them. The people looked shipwrecked, but as they got closer it was obvious they were rather boatwrecked. Most of these boat people were black, but there were other minority races as well. The single black women looked the most fatigued. The leaders of the group reached the shore first. They had little children on their backs. They all looked haunted and exhausted, young or old, women or men. Soon all the migrants reached the shore. The leaders of the boat people addressed the islanders, basically begging them for refuge. Where they had come from, most of them had been the target of systemic police violence. Their lands had been stolen from them. They had been enslaved, raped, tortured, exploited, and structurally impoverished. Some were better off than others, but they had all been subjected to the social forces of institutional oppression and uneven development. A major pandemic had killed most of their people, in part because they had no resources, but also because they were the most exposed, and the least cared for. First, they murmured and they tried to dialogue. Next, they protested. Then, they were persecuted. They had to leave. They loved their countries, counties, and cities. They wanted to stay, but they had finally been forced to leave on account of a range of interlocking pressures, including the monopolization of a vaccine in a few rich countries in the world. In the process, many lost their livelihoods, savings, friends, and family, while others had died at sea and elsewhere.

Touching, yes, but the islanders were in no mood to help them. Their leaders expressed sympathy, even empathy, but pointed out that they too were struggling with natural disasters and with a system in which few of them received all the earnings they were due. They had barely any food to eat, let alone to share. Population growth on their islands would amount to their brutal lynching. The leaders of these migrants continued to plead, promising to give them the little food they had because they preferred to die on land, rather than at sea. But the islanders refused to take their food. Their leaders would not budge, stressing that the strangers needed the food more than they did. The boat people consulted among themselves. They could offer themselves as slaves, but they might be seen as animals to be fed, imposing the cost of property management on the slavers. They could fight the islanders, but they were too weak to fight and, even if they fought and won, they would have compromised their core values of upholding the dignity of all women and men, the old, and the young. Having lived under slavery or slave-like conditions, they were resolved not to create such conditions for others, recognizing the indignity of slavery and the indignation that it causes.

The leaders of the castoff people consulted among themselves and with their people. They approached the islanders again, asking if they could inhabit the rocky parts of Landen. They could die there, but death ashore appeared preferable to them. This alternative was more acceptable to the islanders, who would become hosts. At least this alternative would mean that they would lose nothing and the discarded people would not be seen, nor would they influence their culture. The islanders made strict rules that the boat people should neither be seen nor be heard. With this agreement, the castaways moved on and were not heard from nor seen in a long time.

Meanwhile, however, the conditions of the hosts suddenly began to improve significantly. They still had serious problems with inequality and stratification, but they were much better off. The flooding in Southern Landen had stopped and the drought in Northern Landen had become less dire. Both the North and the South of Landen were doing quite well. Crops were greener and animals were healthier. Inequality was growing, but the people still had basic needs.

One fateful day, as the islanders relaxed while enjoying their changed conditions, they saw from afar a dancing and celebrating people approach them from the mountains. The strange people clearly did not mean war, but the islanders wondered who they were. As they came closer, the islanders recognized that they were the discarded people of yesteryear. The leaders of the boat people invited their hosts to follow them to the mountains. The hosts hesitated, but their children were curious, albeit cautious, as their parents had always tried to keep them safe from the boat people and their children.

Eventually, the hosts—both adults and children, women and men—decided to accept the invitation to go to the mountains. As they approached the mountains, greenery was everywhere, flourishing farms and thriving animals greeted them. Valleys of small-scale cooperative local farms and firms characterized the local economy, which was booming. Crucially, all the people seemed to be fairly represented in the governance of the mountain city. Wealth was spread quite evenly, not because they had progressive income taxes, but because land was held in common. Land rights were equal; not joint, and certainly not held individually nor privately. People were mostly self employed. Employed in co-operatives or by their city states. Where employed, they were paid just wages. To be sure, rent was evident, but it was redistributed through comprehensive social investment. Schools were inclusive. So were hospitals and work. The justice system was minimal, inclusive, and rarely used, with many conflicts addressed by socio-economic solutions.

The hosts were puzzled. They asked how the discarded people had created such conditions for progress and prosperity, sustainability and sovereignty. The migrants explained that they had constructed a canal to link the northern and southern parts of Landen. Flood water had been pooled in a way that the lake offered water to the boat people but also the water moved from flood to drought and from drought to pooled water whenever conditions demanded. Hence, there was no drought and no floods. People also worked on the land where they had equal rights. If rents were taken, they were socialized or used to develop the community and the environment that nourished it. No one privately appropriated commonly held land nor labour, through slavery, penalty wages, or public slave taxes.

This progress without environmental or social poverty became a philosophy of Landen, too, and instead of neighbouring islands, they became conjoined in a new system. The name 'Landen' was changed to Land and the boat people who were once discarded became the centre of Democratic Land. I return to this story at the end of the book but use it here partly to describe the kinds of migrants discussed in this book and particularly because the story captures the spirit and the features of contemporary global migration, including the complex institutional forces that shape why and how migrants leave their homeland, the contestable attitudes, assumptions, and interests of many receiving states or hosts generally, and the trans-formative contributions migrants can make, under particular conditions, to ecology, economy, and society.

I have adapted Balce's (2015) story for my own purposes. In many ways, the adaptation shows the nature of my own journey as a migrant from Ghana, West Africa. Like the story of Landen to Land, even though I take the broad ideas from others to whom I am grateful, I have reconfigured the advice. Like the migrants whose lives I am about to analyse and those in the story, I have, in my journey, many people to thank.

My gratitude goes to Ian Yeboah, Professor of Geography at the University of Miami, US, to Peter Waxman and Helen Gilbert, respectively former lecturers of economics and planning at the University of Technology Sydney, Australia, to Irene Browne, Associate Professor of Sociology at Emory University, US, to Kim Shanna Neverson of the Aboriginal Health Services Organisation, Montreal,

Canada, Alice Nicole Sindzingre, Member of the National Centre for Scientific Research, EconomiX, France, Frank Stilwell, Professor Emeritus of Political Economy and to Bill Dunn, Associate Professor of Political Economy, both at the University of Sydney, Australia. Tim Anderson, Director at the Centre for Counter Hegemonic Studies, also offered me excellent suggestions to sharpen the analysis in this book.

Others who also gave me excellent feedback on the book are Jock Collins, Professor of Social Economics at the University of Technology Sydney, Australia, and Hanson Nyantekyi-Frimpong, Assistant Professor of Geography at the University of Denver, US. Mark Shackleton, Docent Emeritus at the University of Helsinki, offered me detailed helpful feedback on all aspects of the book, for which I am very grateful.

I also appreciate the helpful feedback and support of my editor, Adam Swallow, and his team at Oxford University Press. Adam Swallow, in particular, was very kind in giving me detailed feedback on my proposal, which became significantly much stronger as a result. Thanks also to OUP anonymous reviewers, who offered additional substantive suggestions for improvement, and to Fiona Barry who worked on improving the clarity of my presentation, as did reviewers for, and editors and publishers of, the journals that published aspects of my work. These include *Forum for Social Economics, Journal of Higher Education Policy and Management, Land Use Policy, African Identities, Housing Studies,* and *International Critical Thought.* My colleagues in Global Development Studies, and the Helsinki Institute of Sustainability Science deserve special thanks for providing the research environment that enabled me to work on this book.

Four people also deserve special thanks. I single out Ha-Joon Obeng-Odoom because he has not only been a son, but also a companion. Born and raised in a multi-racial family in Australia, he has become an immigrant in Finland. From him, I have learnt that living a mixed-race life is complex and maneuvering complexity in a new country as a minority requires more than what is usually described in migration policies and politics. It has been a privilege for me to be part of, and to learn from, his experiences which have, among others, improved my own storytelling skills. Annie Herro, an Australian scholar of Lebanese heritage, based at the University of New South Wales in Australia, has been amazing for her unwavering support and encouragement. Apart from her abundant personal encouragement, professional insights, and feedback in many parts of this book, her teachings, philosophies, and great wisdom continue to act as a moderating influence in my life. Finally, my continuing friendship and conversations with Efua Amissah-Arthur and Joe Prempeh, two shrewd cosmopolitan Ghanaians who have been pivotal in shaping my own journey as a migrant from Ghana, including offering me practical support and insights too numerous to elaborate.

As I have noted, I have taken a broad range of ideas from others, but have attempted to adapt them for this book. In this journey of absorption, adaptation, and transformation, I am solely responsible for any errors that might have occurred along the way.

Franklin Obeng-Odoom

University of Helsinki, Finland

Contents

List of Figures

List of Tables

1

Unleashed

A New Normal

Migration is the new normal in the world. According to estimates by the International Organization for Migration (IOM), there are more than 1 billion migrants in the world today (IOM, 2015, 2020), being approximately 13% of the world's population. Almost one of every eight people in the world today is a migrant. Of this population, constituted by people born in areas other than those where they are now located, only about 27% are international migrants. Despite this prevalence of internal migration, it is international migration that gains most attention. International migration has not simply increased; it has soared. Initial estimates by the IOM in its *World Migration Report* of 2000 put the figure of total international migrants at 150 million. In 2020, it was estimated that the number nearly doubled to 272 million (IOM, 2020) and this figure is expected to increase further. Europe, North America, and Australia are the most likely places to host additional international migrants (IOM, 2015, 2020; Sata et al., 2020).

While pandemics such as the 2020–2021 COVID-19 outbreak could slow down the pace of migration, within the period of almost half a century examined in Table 1.1, the actual number of international migrants in 2019 was 3.5 times that of 1970, an increase in absolute terms of over 187 million people. These new migrants are not simply from all over the world, they are also made up of women and children. For instance, of the 5 million refugees in Turkey, Jordan, and Lebanon,

Table 1.1 The scale of global migration, 1970–2019

Year	Number of migrants	Percentage change	Migrants as a share of the world's population
1970	84,460,125	–	2.3
1980	101,983,149	20.8	2.3
1990	153,011,473	50.0	2.9
2000	173,588,441	13.4	2.8
2010	220,781,909	27.2	3.2
2019	271,642,105	23.0	3.5

Source: IOM, 2019, p. 21.

2 million (or 40%) are children (*The Economist*, 2016, p. 20). In 1960, the proportion of female migrants as a share of the total world population of women was only 2.4%, compared to the male migrant share of 2.7%. Research (Roose et al., 2020, p. 5) shows that, as of 2019, the share of female migrants had not only increased (3.4%), it was also nearly the same as that of male migrants (3.5%). In addition, more women are migrating independently. Together, this evidence suggests that migration has remained persistent, but has also become both quantitatively and qualitatively more widespread (Roose et al., 2020, p. 5).

Even more intriguing, a recent Gallup poll suggests that of all the world's adult population, 15% (or 750 million people) seek to migrate (*The Economist*, 2019d, p. 4), so mass migration is clearly on the rise and will no doubt continue to rise, barring further global pandemics. Since the outbreak of the COVID-19 pandemic, most countries have rapidly closed their borders. *The Economist* (2020p, p. 7) counts 65,000 restrictions on mobility which, according to this weekly newspaper, amounts to 'locking out' migrants. As recent systematic studies (Morris et al., 2020; 2021) show, remittances, student housing, and migrant livelihoods have all been significantly shaped by the COVID-19 pandemic.

The current situation has made the migration question even *more*, not *less*, pressing. If the growing pressure to restart the global economy after what advocates call 'its long weekend' persists, then, as *The Economist* (2020p, p. 7) newspaper puts it, the question is rather 'when and how to let migrants move again'. Regardless of orientation, however, whether more, less, or no economic growth, the history of humanity has been the history of migration. As Michael Fisher's authoritative analysis in *Migration: A World History* (2014) shows, no pandemic has ever permanently halted migration. Migration itself has historically been linked with pandemics. In modern times too, the migration–pandemic nexus has persisted. Donald Trump, for example, described migrants as 'a tremendous infectious disease … pouring across the border' (*The Economist*, 2020p, p. 45). COVID-19 has propelled migration to the centre of the global economy, not left it behind in the periphery. The pandemic has made most countries even more sensitive to migration, while highlighting the centrality of institutions and processes such as technological change, climate change, and social change. Increasingly, more migrants and migrant communities feel targeted, too. As authorities disproportionately blame them for the spread of COVID-19, and, hence, impose stricter curfews and lockdowns in migrant communities, the well-known problem of racial profiling and minority scapegoating could become endemic. Many of such cases have been discussed in the literature (Obeng-Odoom, 2020a). They appear to be worsening now that the pandemic and its effects appear to be borne disproportionately by migrants and their communities (see chapter 8).

Thus, there could be no better time to analyse the mass migration question. The related dramatic decisions and heated national and nationalist debates on mass migration also require further investigation (Somin, 2020; Sata et al., 2020;

Walia, 2021). Both the Brexit debates and the Donald Trump campaign were characterized by the denigration of particular migrant-sending countries, the rhetoric to build walls to exclude migrants, and the nostalgia of going back to past, so-called culturally homogeneous societies (Betts, 2019; Somin, 2020; Sata et al., 2020; Walia, 2021). The Biden-Harris administration's attempt to offer conditional aid to stay the migration trend may be subtle, but is similarly spirited. There are, as *The Economist* (2019c, pp. 13, 30–31, 35) puts it, 'growing barriers' not only in countries such as the UK or the US but also in regions such as the European Union (EU). In 2020, Switzerland voted in a referendum to reject a campaign by the Swiss People's Party to end free immigration between the EU and Switzerland, but xenophobia and Afrophobia, in particular, abound in these places and spaces. The politics of 'hate thy neighbour' (*The Economist* 2019c, p. 35) appears to be the new normal.

In more recent times, too, there have been new crises about migrants. 'Foremost', according to the IOM, 'have been the displacements of millions of people due to conflict (such as within and from the Syrian Arab Republic, Yemen, the Central African Republic, the Democratic Republic of the Congo, and South Sudan), extreme violence (such as inflicted upon Rohingya forced to seek safety in Bangladesh) or severe economic and political instability (such as faced by millions of Venezuelans). There has also been growing recognition of the impacts of environmental and climate change on human mobility (such as planned migration/relocation and displacement), including as part of global efforts and international policy mechanisms to address the broader impacts of climate change' (IOM, 2020, p. 2). Add the recent surge of migration from Afghanistan since the Taliban formed its government in 2021 and the situation indeed appears desperate. So dire is this 'migration crisis' that it has drawn extensive commentary in papal exhortations to the world. Pope Francis (Francis, 2020, p. 28) has described the trend of global migration as 'dramatic' and 'devastating' to all, destroying both families who migrate and those who stay behind (Francis, 2016, p. 36), as well as the familial 'transmission of values'.

Other accounts have been more graphic. Consider that of The Economist Intelligence Unit (2016, p. 6): 'We live in an era of unprecedented human mobility, in which over 244m international migrants worldwide are searching for economic opportunity, peace and security.' Although this figure is slightly lower than the IOM's estimate of 272m, earlier referenced (IOM, 2020), the point is that international migration is, indeed, a new normal.

Problematique

Nevertheless, the foregoing exposition must be problematized for three reasons. First, this description tends to emphasize *the number of people*, and how these additional bodies endanger society and the environment of the recipient country.

This depiction recalls the seminal contributions of Robert Malthus (1798/2004), Paul Ehrlich (1968), and Garrett Hardin (1974, 1993). In our current environmental age, this depiction is subtle, but settled in the 'limits to growth' arguments (Meadows et al., 1972, 2004) that dominate environmentalism today (for a review, see Obeng-Odoom, 2021). Social processes are considered, too, but such considerations still neglect the fact that internal migration, currently pegged at more than 70% of all human migration, is part of, not apart from, the story of human mobility. Second, most of the migration crisis is currently happening, and will continue, in cities. For instance, every day, an estimated 120,000 people migrate to cities in the Asia-Pacific region (IOM, 2015, pp. 2–3). Within such regions, the situation in India, for example (see Gollerkeri and Chhabra, 2016), tends to escape attention.

Third, global migration is commonly linked to 'growth', not inequality, and certainly not to social stratification. Kenneth Boulding (1964) was implicit about the issue in his proposal of marketable licences to have children. Addressing 'the population trap', as he called it (Boulding, 1964, pp. 121–136), would be a sure path to reducing or controlling growth. A few years later, in *The Limits to Growth,* Donella Meadows and her team were more explicit, noting that inequalities were only 'included implicitly in the data but they are not calculated explicitly nor graphed in the output'. Also, '… migration patterns … are not specifically treated' (Meadows et al., 1972, p. 102). Therein lies a serious problem: Although populationism is a recurrent point of emphasis for environmentalists, they have tended to treat migration superficially, at best using it as a synonym for growthism. Herman Daly, for instance, equates migration to growthism and how migration harms the planet through migration-led population growth, at least in the richer countries. In his words:

> Global population growth is of course entirely due to natural increase, and migration would hardly be the problem that it is today if the quadrupling of human numbers within one recent lifetime had not brought the world from two to nearly eight billion people. However, in the U.S., Western Europe, and Canada, recent population growth is mainly due to net immigration and higher average fertility of immigrants. So, it is hard to evade the increasingly difficult and divisive issue of immigration in discussing the already nearly taboo subject of population policy.
>
> (Daly, 2019, p. 3)

It is intriguing that Daly himself refers to a 'taboo subject', using the same expression which Garret Hardin (1993, see p. 4) adopts in his analysis in support of Thomas Malthus. For Daly (2019, p. 3), it is giving aid to address poverty and to 'help' the migrant-sending countries that is preferable, not what he calls 'borderless globalization'.

Research Questions

Taken together, these reasons show that the idea of a 'global migration crisis' must be problematized. The implication of doing so is that the three most important research questions that have intrigued scholars of migration for decades need to be revisited. First, what is the nature of global migration? Second, why does global migration occur? And third, what are the ramifications of migration for economy, society, and the environment?

Existing attempts to address these questions (see Chapters 2–9 for a detailed demonstration) are centred on nativist concerns, assumptions about the self-interest of migrants to seek more prosperous economic conditions of life else-where, claims related to dysfunctional states that create a humanist imperative for migration, and emphases on structural socio-economic processes that make migration a normal part of capitalism as an economic system. These positions reflect the conservative, mainstream, humanist, and radical positions in migration research, respectively.

Although simply stated, there are important subtleties in these four positions. For example, the mainstream story could start with a neoclassical analysis, but it quickly morphs into new institutional, and hence liberal and libertarian, concerns (e.g., Somin, 2020) that shape not just the analysis of the nature of migration, but also how its causes and effects, and hence possible solutions, are studied (for various schools of economic thought and their migration theories, see Abreu, 2012; Burnazoglu, 2017). Consider the idea that the 'tragedy of the commons'—implying, among other things, a lack of birth or population control—is a key driver of migration, hence enclosing land is a panacea, as argued by Garrett Hardin (Hardin, 1968, 1974, 1993). This Malthusian analysis of social problems percolates much of the nativist politics against migration. Still, not all mainstream analysis is anti-migration. In fact, much mainstream analysis is pro-migration. That is evidently the case for liberal analysis championed by various individual economists such as Kimberly Clausing (e.g., Clausing, 2019a, 2019b), policy makers (e.g., Gollerkeri and Chhabra, 2016), the world development agencies such as the World Bank, the IOM, and the media, led by *The Economist*. Perhaps, their case can simply be summarized in the trope of the 'triple win' because migration is said to benefit migrants, as well as both the sending and the receiving countries.

Humanists make similar win–win arguments, but they point to state dysfunction of political processes as drivers. Non-Governmental Organizations (NGOs), activists, and the sanctuary movements, including the Interfaith Movement for Human Integrity, seek to help migrants escape oppression, help them to assimilate, and help them to return when the dysfunction is resolved. Like liberals, they are keen to fix some cultural practices that might keep minorities backward or explain minority underdevelopment in terms of what they might have gone through historically, spatially, or socially. If these cultural issues are addressed through education and experience, such problems and inequalities can be dealt with, and migrants returned to their home countries. If not, migrants can continue to stay as an attempt to challenge the territorialization of the hosts. In this sense, much of the new field of border studies can be found in this theme, too.

These two positions are radically different, but they are also surprisingly similar. Both recognize that their case can be hamstrung by racism, but they seem to suggest that such racism is only temporary, is born out of ignorance, or is inspired by animus. So they both preach amity. Not only can racism be addressed by cultural fixes, it dissolves when human capital solidifies in terms of greater education, experience, and exposure. The greater forces of marketization in the Global North, or in host societies, work to drive out such racism, according to Garry Becker's theory of racism in the labour market (Becker, 1962, 1974). Historical marginalization does not seem to be that important here. What is needed is to help the current generation of migrants to integrate. These positions have most recently been articulated by *The Economist* in an issue with a lead story captioned, 'The New Ideology of Race and What Is Wrong with It' (*The Economist*, 2020n, p. 7).

To be sure, there is much critical research in the political economy of migration which investigates structural forces. This political economy approach is valuable because it challenges orthodoxy and provides alternatives to it (Burgess, 2019). For example, orthodox analysis presents refugee experiences as quite distinct from immigrant experiences on the grounds that the former are shaped by political and humanitarian considerations, while migrants pursue more economic refuge. Yet, experiences of refugees and asylum-seeking people in France (Burgess, 2019), for example, increasingly show that the treatment of refugees and migrants in the French public is similar; refugees live among immigrants. Therefore, it is not just political, or economic, analysis that we need, but rather political-economic investigations and interpretations of migration.

However, the existing political economy of migration must also be problematized. This political economy is mainly centred on a critique of the commodification of labour in the international migration process, typically pointing to labour–capital contradictions (see, e.g., Rosewarne, 2010, 2014, 2016, 2020a, 2020b), not migration resulting from the contradictions in monopolizing the land, for example. Even when land is mentioned, it is not seen as special or primary. Rather, it is considered to be mundane, a secondary product of capital, as in Marx's circuit of capital (for a commentary, see Fine, 1989, pp. 42–47). Leading feminists J. K. Gibson-Graham (1996/2006) famously called this body of work and its methodology 'capitalocentric'. There is a tradition in Marxian analysis centred on 'deagrarianization' and how landless peasants become migrants, but the analysis is typically left at the rural scale and the axis of contradiction located in the relationship between the class of capitalists and labour without carefully considering the relationship between landlords and other classes across scales (for a discussion, see Yaro, 2006; for a critique, see Bryceson and Jamal, 2019). Similar limitations apply in the use of dependency theory to explain the 'development of underdevelopment' and how that, in turn, drives migration.

Race and religion tend to be dismissed as mere symptoms of capitalism in much Marxist work. In turn, any systematic focus on race and religion tends to be denounced as mere 'identity politics' or the symbolic organization of backward groupings (Özkul, 2019). Historically, the power of such identity politics has typically been underestimated (Crenshaw, 1991). Analytically, critics fail to make the distinction between 'identity politics', which arises to challenge the oppression of certain identities, and identity politics, which simply excludes others for its own gain (Darity, 2021). These fundamental errors have had serious ramifications for research, policy, and practice.

The principal focus on class, as a secular concept, legitimizes the idea that power resides in class movements only. Yet, this denial is unfortunate. Going back to France, we find a country that actually promises asylum in the preamble of its 1946 Constitution. This Constitution has been amended a few times (notably in the 1958 Constitution and in the 1993 amendment), but fundamentally the promise and sometimes the institutionalization of asylum are still part of the republican status. Therefore, France would appear to be an example of a world power committed to ensuring freedom from suppression. However, the same country wavers when the asylum claims or applications are from black people, especially if they are Muslim (Burgess, 2019, pp. 1–11, 252–253; see also Özkul, 2019). The promise of asylum is highly marred by racism and sectarianism, and the case of France shows that race and religious discrimination cannot be reduced to the category of 'mere identity politics'.

As a highly institutionalized process (Burgess, 2019, pp. 8–10), involving the local (communities of migrants), the national (states and governments), the international (inter-state relations), the regional (including political economic blocks and institutions such as the African Union, AU, and the European Union, EU), and the global (highlighting institutions and organizations such as the United Nations, UN), migration is best studied in institutional economics. The emphasis on push–pull pomp and pageantry blinkers research to focus on source and destination only, overlooking the institutional processes that link the two and other intermediaries and assuming that push factors are in the origin, while pull factors are in the destination. Yet, evidence by Peter Tinti and Tuesday Reitano (2017) show that the push factors for non-European migrants moving to Europe is usually in Europe, whose policies compel migrants into becoming 'refugees, smugglers, and saviors' at different points in a journey that can be both uncertain and unchartered. Reverse remittances from the Global South to the Global North (Atiku, 2022, see also chapter 8 of this book) are usually overlooked, although they are quite commonly and consistently given in the process of migration. Accordingly, the social provisioning processes of migration is embroiled in multiple identities, some of which are made and formed during the journey, but others predate the journey, and many more are conferred on arrival, but persistent thereafter. Push–pull frameworks are, therefore, unhelpful.

The contributions of institutionalists greatly help to address many of these problems. For instance (see Nelson, 2016), they appreciate and draw attention to gender and what has been called 'the feminization of migration'. Currently, nearly half (48-49%) of all migrants are women (Government of Ghana, 2016, p. 91; Manuh, 2021). 'Women account for 47% of the 17 million immigrants in Africa' (Economic Community of West African States [ECOWAS] Commission, 2008, p.10). One manifestation of this 'feminization of migration' is the rise of female domestic workers from South-East Asia and Africa living and working in richer settlements such as Singapore, Hong Kong, and in Middle Eastern countries such as the United Arab Emirates (Kwok, 2017; Ho, 2021). The nature of the economy as socially connected within a web of relations also receives much-needed attention. So do very important forces of change such as 'circular and cumulative causation' (Myrdal, 1944) or exit, voice, and loyalty (Hirschman, 1970, see pp. 21-119 for a discussion of the concepts of 'exit', 'voice', and 'loyalty'), which help to addres the limitations of the rational individual-based push–pull gravity model of migration.

Yet the broader question of multiple identities eludes original institutional economists. Race, in particular, remains a difficult identity for institutionalists to analyse. Many institutionalist have been caught in the traps and trappings of racist or race-neutral theorizing. While putting the case for including all migrants, some minorities, notably blacks, are seen as underserving of inclusion because they are inferior races and groups (Leonard, 2016). Where, like Gunnar Myrdal, they have tried to theorize race (Myrdal, 1944), they have done so by emphasizing race to the neglect of its intersections with gender, class, and migrant status (e.g., Cox, 1945; Crenshaw, 1989, 1991), assumed that race and caste are respecters of borders, often ending at the national borders of India alone, for example (Gollerkeri and Chhabra, 2016), or caricatured the relationship between race and colour, not only among Indians but also between Indians and other nationalities.

As Eiman Zein-Elabdin (2016), Thomas Leonard (2016), and Tod Hamilton (2018) have carefully demonstrated, most institutionalists have advanced culturalist explanations of migration, cultural interpretations of social stratification, and cultural solutions to global socio-spatial and racial differences in income, wealth, and general indices of development and underdevelopment (Frank, 1966), regardless of whether they advocate more or less migration.

Stratification Economics

The subfield of stratification economics has arisen to address these problems and provide a coherent alternative explanation of the world (Darity, 2021). Much migration debate is centred on an uncritical acceptance of 'culture' (Hamilton,

2018), and, therefore, it is important to systematically ascertain the claims made in this cultural turn, along with existing contentions such as the irrationality of racism and how exposure and enlightenment provide lasting solutions to structural racism and discrimination (Hamilton, 2020). Stratification economics seeks to carefully engage these approaches and their claims about the nature, causes, and effects of migration, development, and underdevelopment on group-based wealth and power inequalities (Darity and Mullen, 2020; Hamilton, 2020; Darity, 2021). Developed mostly by black political economists associated with the National Economic Association founded in 1969 as the Caucus of Black Economists, notably William Darity Jr (see, e.g., Darity, 2009, 2021), the essence of stratification economics can be found on the pages of their journal, *The Review of Black Political Economy*.

Although broad in their intellectual influences and approaches, the specific stratification economics approach that is relevant for this book has been developed by a subgroup that has been keen to create a coherent alternative political economy. John Davis (2015, 2019) suggests that the economics of identity, identity economics, or the economics of exclusion would be theoretically sufficient to characterize this field, but an even wider approach is required.

Prominent among these influences and approaches are James Stewart, Major Coleman (Stewart and Coleman, 2005; Stewart, 2008), and William Darity Jr (e.g., Darity, 2009; Darity et al., 2015; Darity and Mullen, 2020). The specific application of stratification economics to migration has been developed by others, too, including Yale University political economist, Gerald Jaynes (2007). Younger, but promising, leaders include Darrick Hamilton (e.g., Hamilton, 2020). Stratification economics seeks to engage existing work positively because it does not cast away the best traditions of political economy. Like most political-economic approaches, it is historical, holistic, pluralist, and transdisciplinary (Obeng-Odoom, 2020a), and like institutional political economy, it takes institutions very seriously, significantly widening the ambit of such institutions as land laws to 'property interest in whiteness' or the laws of white privilege (Harris, 1993; Hamilton, 2020, pp. 334–335).

Yet, there are also important areas of new emphasis. While stratification economics describes its approach as 'political economy', its political economy cuts both ways. Unlike much Western political economy, which is critical mostly of the right and capitalism, stratification political economy, a strand of black political economy generally, is critical of capitalism, the left, and the right. Unlike much Western political economy, centred on mostly labour and capital, the stratification approach to migration strongly emphasizes land, along with labour, capital, and the state. Not only pluralism but also citizenship is central in its compass for sources of inspiration (Obeng-Odoom, 2020a, 2020b). As a consequence, the scholarship and knowledge systems of minorities, along with minority practices that seek to provide alternatives, are more carefully embraced.

Empirically (see, e.g., Hamilton, 2018), the stratification economics approach helps to identify the complex nature of migration, as well as provide more nuanced explanations of the causes and effects of migration. Theoretically, this approach critically scrutinizes—and develops alternative theories about—three key elements in the current literature: first, cultural explanations of stratification; second, human capital theories about race, ethnicity, and progress; and third, capitalocentric explanations. All these three are important in retheorizing socio-ecological crises nexus which, as I have argued elsewhere (Obeng-Odoom, 2021), more convincingly reflect global inequalities and stratification. These forces eschew narrow analysis of marginalization. They are, instead, intersectional, probing both discrimination and privilege in investigating the complex process of the nature, causes, and effects of migration. Such formulations can be challenged for being too broad, too open-ended. However, as Kimberlé Crenshaw suggests in another context, dismissing the approach only on this basis can be detrimental. She writes:

> Consider an analogy to traffic in an intersection, coming and going in all four directions. Discrimination, like traffic through an intersection, may flow in one direction, and it may flow in another. If an accident happens in an intersection, it can be caused by cars traveling from any number of directions and, sometimes, from all of them [...] [Insisting that only one driver must be proven to be complicit] is analogous to calling an ambulance for the victim only after the driver responsible for the injuries is identified. But it is not always easy to reconstruct an accident: Sometimes the skid marks and the injuries simply indicate that they occurred simultaneously, frustrating efforts to determine which driver caused the harm. In these cases the tendency seems to be that no driver is held responsible, no treatment is administered, and the involved parties simply get back in their cars and zoom away.
>
> (Crenshaw, 1989, p. 149)

Applying Crenshaw's notion of intersectionality (e.g., Crenshaw, 1989, 1991) means that complex and open-ended solutions need to be considered. A radical approach that seeks to decolonize existing methodologies, like Linda Tuhiwai Smith's seminal work (Smith, 1999), the foregoing is more holistic. However, the approach taken should not be a broad apolitical or non-political economic umbrella in which all forms of oppression are equivalized without historical and political-economic contexts (Wallis, 2018; Stache, 2019). Otherwise, we arrive at the confused criticisms such as those implied by the 'All lives matter movement' that seeks to undermine the historically specific contention that '# Black Lives Matter'. Indeed, the approach of intersectionality (e.g., Crenshaw, 1989, 1991) must itself be broadened to include cross-racial analysis and the more systematic untangling of which identities of the multiple intersectional ones carries the greatest explanatory power in a given context (Darity, 2021). Analyses of gender can be even more compelling when compared both within similar identity (e.g., racial, colour, and caste) groups and across different identity groups (e.g., black men and white women in Europe and the US), as Irene Browne's research (see, for example, Browne et al., 2003; Browne and Sullivan, 2022) has consistently demonstrated.

To date, the most extensive application of the stratification economics approach can be found in T.G. Hamilton's book, *Immigration and the Remaking of Black America* (Hamilton, 2018), although Crenshaw's work on immigration and migrant women is a valuable theoretical contribution (Crenshaw, 1991). These studies and many others (e.g., Browne et al., 2018), however, are focused on the US.

Even where there are clear overlaps between the concerns addressed in this book and the research that currently exists on similar themes, there are clear differences. First, I expand the focus from the US to the world, by analysing experiences elsewhere in the Global North, such as Australia. I consider the Global South, too, for example, China and Ghana, and elsewhere in the Middle East, such as Syria.

Second, I seek to salvage and critically develop relevant traditions of original institutional economics (see, for example, Myrdal, 1944; Polanyi, 1944/2001, 1957; Hirschman, 1970. Also, see, for a discussion of this history, Obeng-Odoom, 2018a; Chapter 3).

A third and final extension of existing research on stratification economics of migration is developing a specific point of departure that is also recurrently featured in the journey of the analysis, and at the point of arrival and beyond. For this book, that point is land, its role in producing and maintaining inequalities and stratification in income and wealth and in serving as a means of control, discrimination, and privilege. I place that point of entry within a universe of institutions. The choice of land is not arbitrary; it is central to the history of great migrations, such as those of the Irish. Land is also crucial to the formulation of the case for free movement of persons, as the history of *The Economist* shows, and land is at the heart of the political debates about walls and borders (Zevin, 2019), although land receives much less attention in the political-economic analysis of global migration. So, I have been developing a land-based analysis of global inequalities, stratification (Obeng-Odoom, 2020a), and global socio-ecological crises (Obeng-Odoom, 2021). This third extension into the question of global migration could, therefore, be understood within this context.

I have collected data from systematic interviews, longitudinal interviews, archives, documents, cemetery records, and local and global newspapers, such as *The Economist*. I have also relied on existing statistical compendiums, drawn on large surveys carried out by others, and utilized global datasets prepared by national governments and multilateral organisations such as the United Nations and other agencies. The decisions of courts of law, legislations, and policy documents also feed into my reservoir of data.

I have used several cases. They are from Africa, the Middle East, Asia, Australia, Europe, and the Americas. They range from migrant farmers to street workers, from refugees to international students, from Chinese workers in Africa to African workers in China, from Irish and other migrants in Australia to a wide range of migrants in the Middle East, from professional African migrants in the US to other types of Asian migrants in Australia, and many more.

These data and cases are analysed in various established ways in institutional and evolutionary social sciences (Holsti, 1969; Smith, 1999; Attride-Stirling, 2001; Bromley, 2019; Powell, 2021). Analytical strategies in these traditions include data reduction, presentation, and interpretation, data systematizing, content analysing, data contextualization, and data historicization from a broad critical realist standpoint. Within this tradition, these strategies are more abductive, rather than simply inductive or deductive, and, hence, far more open-ended than existing tools and modes of analyses. Utilising these strategies is justified because they help to address the serious methodological problems in migration research, briefly suggested but to which I shall return in chapters 2 and 3. Such limitations include the non-evolutionary nature of 'stylised facts', mono-scalar spatial analyses, and global scale analyses which are inattentive to space and time, as well as colonial, neo-colonial, and colonising frameworks of thought. More fundamentally, I utilise these approaches because, as I shall show, they are most effective in helping to address my three research questions about the nature, drivers, and consequences of migration.

Arguments

Based on my analysis of this evidence, using the methodology I have explained, my work shows multiple intersecting types of migration. The complexities of migration defy simple descriptions, but more categorical arguments can be made about causes and effects. Viewed from a diverse range of theoretical positions, including neoclassical economics, new institutional economics, humanistic border studies, and Marxist economics, it is hardly persuasive to contend that migration is driven by individual choices of migrants alone. Rather, however viewed, the evidence overwhelmingly shows that institutions shape all forms, forces, and functions of migration. Of these institutions, however, land is central, whether in internal migration, international migration, or global migration, class, caste, race, gender, or any other identity.

The evidence also clearly shows that migration and migrants transform both the sites, where migrants are resident and the places from which migrants travelled.

The change is more transformational than previous accounts have established, sometimes involving turning dead cities and towns into vibrant local economies and reconstructing food networks for entire regions and nations.

Portrayals of migrants as parasites neglect these contributions, but so do depictions of migrants as agents of transformation. More fundamentally, existing accounts downplay the extent to which migrants must go to become agents of change. Systemic discrimination and attacks aside, many migrants are overworked and overexploited, as they perform functions assigned to them.

This book also raises serious analytical questions about three bodies of literature, namely:

- conservative and nativist claims about conservation, population problems and alternatives to them;
- mainstream sustainability science and alternatives to it (e.g., ecological economics); and
- mainstream economics accounts of migration, environment, and inequality.

In nuancing political-economic accounts and substantially extending them, I argue that much of the crisis of migration *and* sustainability can be understood as a reflection of global *cumulative* stratification, reflected at different scales in the global system. The so-called migration crisis, therefore, seems quite routine and familiar. It is an expression of the political-economic system in which socially created value is privately appropriated as rents by a privileged few who use institutions such as land and property rights, race, ethnicity, class, and gender to keep others in their place.

The evidence shows that we can question the common narrative that (a) migration is entirely negative because migrants harm the environment and migrants reap where they have not sown through 'stealing' the jobs of locals or worsening labour conditions in the receiving countries, while draining the migrant-sending countries of vitally lacking skills; (b) migration is entirely aimed at opportunism and is a path for the convergence in wealth and incomes between migrants and residents and between the sending and receiving countries; and (c), more cautiously, migrants can be very useful if they are 'helped' in correcting their 'defects' in assimilating and are later sent back to enlighten their peoples.

The environmentalist argument about migration is typically made by nativists, but it is also made by some humanists, including some 'radicals'. Both contend that migration produces environmental stresses and, if not curbed, can also undermine both development and distribution. Other humanists overlook the migration question, but they need to respond to the nativist case against migration. Otherwise, it is the nativists who have the better arguments: that such global migration harms nature. I argue that, actually, on this issue, humanists and nativists converge. Whether degrowth, no growth, steady growth, or low growth, the key emphasis is what to do about 'growth'.

This book questions the dominant treatise that global migration is beyond limits, along with all its ecological, economic, and Western political-economic contentions. Because both migration and the sustainability crises are outward expressions within the circuit of global inequalities and social stratification, focusing on migration or sustainability itself is an exercise in futility. The book is, therefore, critical of freedom to move arguments canvassed by economists, humanists, political theorists, and political economists. Their reasons provided for open borders or migration for all differ radically; some are centred on individual opportunities for migrants, others on reducing the cost of production, and the rest on freedom for freedom's sake or on freedom for growth.

Yet, the evidence in this book shows that mere migration—whether it is of the conservative, mainstream, or humanistic hue—is not a panacea. The radical advocacy for replacing capitalism through socializing work goes further than existing approaches, but it also mistakes the form of social problems for their foundation.

For these reasons, this book puts emphasis on addressing the institutional drivers of socio-ecological crises and uneven global relations. These are not necessarily migration-related. Rather, they are long-term forces and currents of change that are global in scope and impact. Most of these crises arise from rules about land, whether in rural, urban, national, international, or global contexts, whether formal, informal, or formal-informal interactions.

Without equal access to and control of land in both origin and destination settlements, indeed at every point in between, migration cannot be called a panacea. Even with equal right to land guaranteed, it would be crucial to grant social protection to migrants, especially those in work relations, support self-employment, offer just wages, and grant permanent status to migrants, while enabling them to contribute to the common wealth in the destination settlement. Source problems need to be addressed directly, again, paying particular attention to the right to land and reconstructing other institutions to enable the flourishing of labour and the commons, rather than posit such commons as tragedies. Studying migration, then, could become another evidence-based approach to analysing, and possibly resolving, global long-term inequalities and socio-ecological stratification.

For these reasons, too, original institutional economics—the framework for much of my analysis—must be criticized for underestimating—indeed masking—and contributing to the pervasiveness and power of persistent privilege and discrimination. In all forms, forces, and functions of migration, such discrimination is widespread, shaping the migration experience in substantial ways. Therefore, institutional economics must embrace stratification economics. By analysing the global migration process in all its forms, this book shows how this holistic analysis can be undertaken.

These arguments are made in ten chapters of which this chapter, Chapter 1, sets the scene. The next section summarizes the remainder of the chapters.

Overview

Chapter 2: Problematic Explanations

This chapter accepts that there is substantial global migration, but it rejects as problematic the existing explanations of the mainstream conservative/nationalist/nativist, neoliberal, and humanist views, centred on various aspects of the thesis by Garrett Hardin and others whose approach develops the 'Chicago School of property rights' (Haila, 2016, p. 53). The chapter argues that the various proponents of dominant migration theories are theoretically inconsistent and lack empirical support. However, the existing alternatives to this orthodoxy, including Marxian analyses, are also problematic.

Chapter 3: Towards a New Framework

With the need for a new beginning established in Chapter 2, this chapter develops a more holistic framework for the analysis of migration. The framework draws on modified versions of the political economy of Henry George, the original institutional economics of J.R. Commons, among others, and the emerging subfield of stratification economics developed by black political economists, notably William Darity Jr. I call this synthesis a 'new' framework because what it enables the book to do is much bigger than (a) what, *relative to existing research* on migration, each of the parts does on its own; (b) what the various parts do by themselves; and (c) the sum total of the various analytical components. The chapter seeks to provide firmer theoretical foundations to answer questions raised in Chapter 1, which the frameworks I discuss in Chapter 2 struggle to address. Holistic and historical, this chapter prepares the ground for more theoretically informed empirical analyses in the rest of the book.

Chapter 4: Internal Migration

A much-neglected aspect of global migration is the increasing internal migration variegated along intersectional lines of ethnicity, migrant status, class, and gender. Internal displacement continues to receive attention, but other forms of internal migration remain relatively hidden. Using the experiences of urban farmers and street workers in Ghana as case studies, this chapter draws on, among other sources, census data to show that neither the decision to migrate nor the decision to return is based on individual calculations alone. Neither are these decisions a reflection of ecologically damaging 'over population' or migrant policies that create a moral hazard. Exit (that is, leaving or migrating), in fact, is not the only option available to migrants, but voice mechanisms (that is, opportunities to express grievances and have them addressed) are often compromised. That said, rural poverty does not provide a sufficient explanation for rural–urban migration, either. There are clearly circular and cumulative (Myrdal, 1944) factors that drive the process of migration, shaping exit instead of voice or loyalty to stay without exit (Hirschman, 1970). Clearly, the forces of migration are highly institutionalized, gendered, and ethnicized.

In contrast to the mainstream contentions that migration is win–win and all resulting problems are temporary or trivial compared to the benefits of migration, this chapter shows serious and systemic migrant challenges that are shaped by group, indeed institutional, rather than individual dynamics. Contentions about migrants exerting pressures on the environment neglect the fact that many of such migrants are displaced because of socioecological forces. Fundamentally, stereotypical views about migration and environment could more extensively engage migrant practices and institutions, such as food growing and making that enrich the local environment. Most migrants intend to return to their origins, but whether they do so, when, and how are conditioned by their gender, migrant and married status, ethnicity, and the class of migrants, and also by changing social institutions, such as property rights that pertain in both rural and urban contexts. For these reasons, policies framed around the assumptions in mainstream analyses of labour migration, such as removing urban bias and enhancing rural development—informed by stereotypical assumptions of the mainstream and its prevailing alternatives—have merely reinforced the process of uneven urban and regional development.

Chapter 5: Economic Crisis and Global Migration

If internal migration is complicated, global international migration is even more complex, raising questions such as, 'What are the causes of the current refugee crisis?', 'What about the causes of the 2008 global economic crisis?', and 'Are these crises interlinked and, if so, how can both be resolved?' Previous research has pointed to 'civil war' in refugee-sending countries and problematic practices or policies in the US as causal mechanisms of the refugee and economic crises, based on methodologies that considered these crises separately. Publicly available datasets published, among others, by the United Nations High Commissioner for Refugees (UNHCR), show, however, that neither war nor financial speculation is a sufficient explanation. Instead, both crises arise from a particular inequality-based rentier system of institutions aggressively pursued by a US-led West against a resistant Global South in the Middle East and North Africa (MENA) region. From this new explanation, existing proposals to address the so-called refugee 'problem', ranging from building and operating detention centres and instigating or engineering regime change to institutionalising sanctuary cities, are questionable.

Chapter 6: The Migrant Town

Consider the migrant town. Even when migrants are able to overcome the obstacles described in Chapter 5, the political economics I have so far described also shapes the migrant experience where migrants settle when they arrive at their destination. A major contributor to negative attitudes towards migrants is that they exert pressure on the infrastructure of the host communities without making any (substantial) contribution to the host economy and society. This negative sentiment is particularly acute in cities, where pressure on amenities is concentrated and more visible. In turn, migrant neighbourhoods are particularly despised. Coupled with the prevailing pervasive view that migrants are parasites, the migrant town is often dismissed. Drawing on multiple sources of evidence, including archival research at local libraries, and longitudinal interviews with long-time residents of Australia's largest necropolis, this chapter shows that, overall, migrants can, and often do, transform the spaces they occupy in ways that make a positive and lasting contribution to the host economy and to society more generally.

Contrary to the view that minorities need to mix with whites to learn the ways of civility (see, e.g., Ananat et al., 2018), migrants themselves bring along ways of life, labour, and innovation that are transforming and local food practices that can be sustainable in the local space. Yet, growing rent and affordability problems, along with systemic racism, are persistent, raising significant support for theories of stratification economics in ways hardly considered by countries facing the 'migrant crisis', which seek to wall out migrants to protect host economies and societies.

Chapter 7: Working with Hosts

A careful examination of local and national economies, however, shows such fears to be unwarranted. Working with hosts throws up revealing experiences and analytical ruptures. Take the example of Afro-Chinese interactions. This chapter shows that this specific migration experience is driven—or at least moulded— not so much by historical or personal factors, but by a process of combination and cumulation of several intersecting factors. Although Afro-Chinese migration and Afro-Chinese relations generally have contributed to economic growth, they have also accentuated much displacement and ecological degradation, particularly in Africa. While it is widely claimed that China—but not Africa—has a policy on Afro-Chinese relations, this chapter shows that the question is not so much whether policies exist; rather, it is about the effectiveness of the policy positions on the effects of Afro-Chinese labour migration.

Chapter 8: Education and Experience

The labour question can be viewed even more holistically by relating it to housing and land. International student migration is typically assumed using short-cuts such as the neoclassical economics theory of human capital, the most influential and most visible of all human capital theories. So, the lived experiences of such students are hardly empirically verified, except to be read off theory as win–win. Nevertheless, their increasing numbers and the ever-increasing pace of globalization in higher education, along with reports of international student stress, mean that this group of migrants can no longer be caricatured. What are the socio-economic characteristics of these migrants, how are they housed, where do they study, and what are their education and work experiences? Australia is one country where such migrants are central, so this chapter analyses the results of large surveys and official reports published by student associations, housing authorities, and universities, notably the University of Sydney and the Australian Government Department of Education, Employment and Workplace Relations in the country, complemented by additional interviews with international students, university support staff, and student unions.

The evidence questions the neoclassical human capital theory, as racism against students is persistent both in their encounters with housing providers and employers. The Australian authorities have not succeeded in providing an answer to the myriad of questions raised by international student migration generally, but to their housing question in particular. Students continue to depend on reverse financial and social remittances from their home countries to survive. In turn, accommodation remains a difficult issue for most international students and threatens to undermine the quality of their education and work experience, while extracting rent from poorer nations. Understood only as an accommodation problem, it may be argued that the situation could be improved if more affordable student housing was provided. However, this chapter argues that, until the problem is framed in socio-economic terms and analysed from a broad institutional, class, racial, and gendered perspective, a solution will remain elusive.

Chapter 9: Remittances and Return

On the flip side of the reverse remittances and rents problem is the question about migrant remittances and return. Is migration a spatial fix to socio-ecological problems? Migrationists tend to contend so, whether they are mainstream or humanist. Migrants themselves constantly dream of return. Sending remittances to build homes to which they can return is one concrete step towards this dream. So, this chapter examines the connection between source problems, destination challenges, and the dream of return. Data from sources such as interviews with migrants, large-scale surveys, and census reports are carefully analysed for this purpose. While mainstream economists claim that remittances generated from transnational, overseas work can be counted as aid to poorer nations, for example in terms of providing funding to improve housing conditions, this chapter shows that housing-based remittances can exacerbate the present housing conditions of migrants, as money that can help to ease their own housing conditions is sent overseas, while urban land contradictions intensify where they are presently located.

In theory, remittances used to develop gated housing can displace ordinary people in the settlement of origin, but often migrants are only struggling to survive. They are hardly speculators. Housing-related remittances and how they are generated show that remittances are contingent on working precariously. Remittances are not the silver bullet they are often portrayed to be, but they pave the way for return. What 'return' means, however, is complex. In contrast to the idea of permanent, one-off return, many migrants established in networks overseas, or involved in transnational and intergenerational families, become circular return migrants. The form of this circularity depends on the intermingling of institutions such as class, caste, race, colour, ethnicity, and gender.

Chapter 10: The Promised Land

This chapter summarizes the key arguments in this book, highlights their significance, and stresses their implications for present and future migration research, practice, and policy. The book's methodology, based on an amalgam of Georgist political economy (G), institutional economics (I), and stratification economics (S), questions both and deontological and consequentialist claims about migration. Yet, this GIS methodology does not lead only to questioning existing mainstream methodologies and their alternatives, but also provides the grounds for developing new pathways for exposition and explanation, based on which new migration policies, practices, and politics can be developed for the true promised land.

2

Problematic Explanations

The Orthodoxy: Conservatives, Neoliberals, and Humanists

Migration is a complex phenomenon. It is made up of several webs. To write of migration in the singular could be oversimplifying. It is possible to distinguish between multiple types of migration. Apart from pro-forma categories such as circular, seasonal, rural–urban, urban–urban, urban–rural, internal, regional, and global migration, there are other types of migration. Permanent migration is common for work or family reunion, temporary migration for school, work, or cohabiting with a family member for a limited time, or refugee migration for people escaping from or refusing to return to dangerous places. These migration types are moulded by national, regional, and global regulations, principles, policies and practices.

Like the types of migration, the orthodoxy on analysing and addressing the migration question is varied. So, it is important to understand this orthodoxy in its diversity. Understanding the orthodoxy in this more complex way is also important to order challenge and transcend conventional social sciences (Rosewarne, 2010; Piper et al., 2017). The text and the spirit of orthodoxy are constructed from a wide range of sources, including pioneering original research, existing meta and media accounts and reports by international organizations.

In contrast to existing simple characterization of the orthodoxy as one uniform viewpoint, this chapter develops a subtle taxonomy of the orthodoxy as conservative, neoliberal, and humanistic. Despite this plurality, the chapter argues that the orthodoxy shares similar conceptual frameworks and the multiple orthodoxies are increasingly converging. Whether divergence or convergence, however, both the orthodoxy and the alternatives to it constitute problematic explanations of migration.

To develop these arguments, I first examine various schools of thought ('Schools of Thought'). Next, I probe the 'laws of migration' ('The Laws of Migration'). Then, to pave the way for a new beginning, the chapter provides fundamental critiques of the orthodoxy ('Challenging the Orthodoxy').

Table 2.1 Analytical paradigms in economics

Analytical paradigms in economics	Neoclassical economics	New economics of labour migration	New institutional economics	Structuralism
Unit of analysis	Individual	The static household/ nuclear family	Transaction	Class
Outlook on migration	Positive	Cautiously positive	Contingent negative	Tolerance
Environment	Externalities	Externalities/ Population problem	Tragedy of the commons	Environment as capitalist crises

Source: author's taxonomy of existing orthodox schools of thought.

Schools of Thought

It is fiendishly difficult for any one school to grasp the complexity of global human mobility. So, even the most conventional school of thought on migration has become more diverse over the years. Three of such demand immediate attention because of their global influence. As suggested in Table 2.1, they are neoclassical economics, the new economics of labour migration (NELM), and new institutional economics. There are subtle differences between them in terms of their unit of analysis, outlook on migration, and construction of the environment. In new institutional economics, population size is seen as injurious to the environment. Hence, migration, particularly of certain populations perceived as typical 'breeders', is questioned.

This population focus is usually covert. White feminist economists are often proponents within the NELM school, in obtuse ways. As the critique by Linda Lammensalo (2021) shows, usually such feminists claim to be the defenders of the sexual and reproductive health rights of minority migrant women. In fact, much of what they seek is to curtail and control the number of children such women (particularly those from Sub-Saharan Africa) can have in order to reduce negative environmental pressure from 'population explosion'. Thus, under the guise of promoting sexual and reproductive health rights of minorities within the household, it is really a population-reducing theorizing that happens especially across NELM and new institutional economics. Neoclassical economics is quite different in this respect, as, for this economics, growth, whether of the economy or of the population is, all things being equal, a positive development, a path to scale and agglomeration economies. This is precisely the point of criticism by NELM and new institutional economics, heavily borrowing insights from Garrett Hardin's work on 'living within limits' (Hardin, 1993).

Hardin is vociferous in his objection to the critics of Malthus (see, e.g., Hardin, 1993, pp. 7–16, 94–101, 121–146, 276–293). For Hardin, there is, indeed, no point in accepting immigrants. Above all, accepting more migrants sets up positive incentives for migrant families to breed more. This dynamic, Hardin argues, undermines any gains from scale. More migration, for Hardin, creates diminishing returns. Hardin contends that Malthus was more than 95% right. If Malthus erred, it was because he reified his ratios and failed to accept economists' reinterpretation of his ratios as diminishing returns. Otherwise, the Malthusian analysis about limits to the population commons is, according to Hardin, right.

As I have shown elsewhere (Obeng-Odoom, 2021), concepts such as the 'tragedy of the commons' and 'transaction costs', typically used within the purview of new institutional economics, in which Hardin's ideas are so central, have become part of the intellectual armoury of neoclassical economics. So have neoclassical economics concepts of information asymmetry, risks, costs, and benefits seeped through the frameworks of new institutional economics (see, e.g., Betts et al., 2017). Therefore, the categories in Table 2.1 represent a continuum, not simple binaries. These interdependent influences have elevated the 'network' or 'pathway' analysis which assesses the benefits and costs of which rules can enhance or inhibit travel and at what cost. The role of migration agents becomes crucial in what is conceived of as 'migration industry' intended to facilitate migration. In this sense, information and communications technology (ICT) has also become a major point of interest because it apparently reduces transaction costs. Here, it is also commonly asserted that the state—whether in sending or receiving countries—exercises unfettered instrumentality or agency.

The convergence in the various orthodox schools of thought about migration can also be seen in terms of new alliances among the international organizations that govern global migration. According to recent research (Piper et al., 2017), the International Labour Organization (ILO), which sets the global standards for employing labour, is increasingly working with the World Bank to promote rights-based or decent-work-based labour migration, partly to promote 'migration for growth' and particularly to support 'migration for development'. In practice, players in this field, including the 'Global Commission of International Migration (GCIM) and its flamboyant child the Global Forum on Migration and Development (GFMD) have tread cautiously' (Gollerkeri and Chhabra, 2016, p. xx). The ILO's mandate and pre-commitments do not easily sit within neoclassical economics, but with the greater expansion of its approaches towards the 'middle' and its flourishing relationship with the World Bank, the ILO is beginning to resemble the World Bank or the International Monetary Fund (IMF).

If the orthodoxy of the ILO is growing, that of the International Organization for Migration (IOM) is soaring (Pécoud, 2018). Unconstrained by the United Nations (UN) human rights frameworks within which the ILO must work, and guided by its own approach to building market institutions, the IOM, a partial member of the UN system, is overt in its orthodoxy. Focused on facilitating migration for those who can lubricate the wheels of growth and development, the IOM often acts as an agency seeking to drive the economic agenda. The IOM seeks to address the needs of the global economy using migrants as key ingredients. In turn, the IOM evinces an entrepreneurial, growth-based orientation, commonly expressed in the work of new institutional economists (see, e.g., Betts et al., 2017. Like the other conventional schools of thought, new institutional economics is grounded in a particular orthodox framing of migration.

The Laws of Migration

A key idea in orthodox frameworks of migration is that it is individual choices that drive both exit and return. According to this view, individuals make an assessment of their current conditions, especially income, work out the prospects of migrating to new areas and, on balance, decide whether to migrate and, when they do, make similar rational calculations about when to return. If the conditions in the area of destination are better, they migrate; if they are worse, they remain at their place of origin. If the conditions at the destination become more costly, than the benefits at origin, they return.

It is this calculus that was formalized by E.G. Ravenstein (1885, 1889) as the 'laws of migration'. Later, these were organized into a 'push–pull' framework by E.S. Lee (1966, p. 52) who sees the 'conceptualization of migration as involving a set of factors at origin and destination, a set of intervening obstacles, and a series of personal factors'. These intervening factors are often discussed in terms of 'trans-action costs'; that is, the individual costs (especially monetary and informational) incurred in the process of migration (Obeng-Odoom, 2017b).

There are at least three important versions of this basic individual (for E.S. Lee, 'personal') rational choice framework. The first is usually attributed to John R. Harris and M.P. Todaro (Todaro 1969; Todaro and Smith 2006, pp. 344–345). Todaro, who famously used this framework to analyse rural–urban migration in the Global South, showed that in such countries the pull factors were typically expecta-tional. In other words, it is *expected* income differences, rather than *actual* income differences, that serve as the impetus for migration. Urban areas in developing countries, according to this view, do not play the same economic magnet role that richer cities in the West do. In turn, the movement towards such cities can only be expectational. In the second version of the rational choice framework, others (e.g., Tanis, 2020; Olarinde, 2021) look at demographic and geographical charac-teristics (age, race, ethnicity, gender, size of national versus urban population, for example) and how they impact on the rational choice model.

The third version of the rational choice framework emphasizes depressed conditions at the point of origin, rather than any pull factors that motivate the movement, although when the decision about *where* to go is made, individuals still make calculations about differential economic opportunities (for a discussion, see de Graft-Johnson, 1974; Mendoza, 2020). Whatever their form, their unit of analysis is either the individual (neoclassical economics model), the household (new economics of labour migration model), or some combination of the two (for a discussion, see Abreu, 2012; Obeng-Odoom, 2017b), which recalls the argument by the neoclassical economist, Charles Tiebout (1956), that individuals 'vote with their feet' if the cost of staying outweighs the benefit of doing so, a point recently defended and developed by Ilya Somin in *Free To Move: Foot Voting, Migration, and Political Freedom* (Somin, 2020).

There is a strong emphasis on the concept of rational choice in the application of this framework. *The Economist* notes that 'Europe is peaceful, rich and accessible. Most people would rather not abandon their homes and start again among strangers. But when the alternative is the threat of death from barrel-bombs and sabre-wielding fanatics, they make the only rational choice' (*The Economist*, 2016, p. 6). Even when the framework is based on the 'bounded rationality' of migrants' psychosocial and behavioural choices, rather than mere rationality, the unit of analysis in the 'laws of migration' remains the autonomous individual and the presumption that such individuals are driven by utility maximization.

Conservatives, neoliberals, and humanists draw different lessons from this framework of thought, as Table 2.2 shows. For conservatives and nationalists (see, e.g., Hardin, 1993, pp. 276–293), migration is parasitic. Coupled with population concerns and the discomfort about cultural mixing, especially of certain undesirable races, this pessimism leads them to reject migration. The strictest of border controls are advocated, together with the criminalization, witch-hunting, and scapegoating of migrants. At the international level, policies include 'turning back the boats', 'building walls', and distributing migrants across countries. Others emphasize border protection using the army and strict laws about granting visas.

In this conservative view, the biggest 'pull factor' is prosperity in 'destinations' such as Europe, laced with *willkommenskultur*, the intrinsic welcoming culture of the Europeans, especially Germans, so 'wave after wave' of 'migrants will keep coming' (La Guardia, 2016; see discussion in *The Economist*, 2016, p. 67). The preferred solution offered by this conservative stance is to manage the problem. Consequently, there are three top solutions, all geared towards stopping the push factors, first 'by beefing up aid to refugees', second to 'review asylum claims while refugees are still in centres in the Middle East or in … Greece and Italy, where they go when they first arrive in the EU', and, third, 'to insist that asylum-seekers stay

Table 2.2 Orthodox analytical paradigms and their characteristics

Paradigm	Analytical focus			Policy focus		
	Scale	Unit of analysis	Identity	Orientation	Destination	Origin
Conservative/ nationalist/ nativist	Biscalar	Individuals, households	Culture, religion, civilization, and race	Pessimist/ growthcentric	Do not come	Border control support
Neoliberals	Biscalar	Individuals, households, firms	Culture, religion, civilisation, and race	Triumphalist/ growthcentric	Integration, temporary migrants	Return migrants and reduce transaction costs
Humanists	Multicalar	Individuals, families	Culture, religion, civilization, gender, and race	Optimists/ growthcentric	Integration (either temporary or permanent)	Return migrants and aid to the sending settlement

Source: author's taxonomy.

put until their applications are processed, rather than jumping on a train to Germany' (for a discussion, see *The Economist*, 2016, p. 9; see also Betts et al., 2017, pp. 1–12, 13–39; Melguizo and Royuela, 2020; Somin, 2020). The conservative state can go all out to criminalize migrants of a certain identity or pass legislation to circumscribe the rights of such migrants (see, for a critical discussion, Collins, 2008; Bryceson, 2019). So, conservatives seek to roll back even minimal rights for migrants.

Neoliberals reach a rather different conclusion. Neoliberalism is highly contested as a political-economic concept (Dunn, 2017). In migration research too, neoliberalism can be vague and problematic, with the possible exception of the broad criteria for what is acceptable migration policy. The neoliberal policy is one of selective acceptance of migration, to the extent that it is 'win–win'. For the destination countries, it is a win because migrants are seen as cheap labour to help in expanding the economy of the destination countries. In this sense, labour itself is commodified and valorized in market terms (Piper et al., 2016). In turn, the emphasis for neoliberals is on importing cheap commodities in terms of how much migrants will hire themselves out or how cheaply they can be disciplined and integrated. The focus is on matching migrants with the needed human capital in the right businesses and firms(Burnazoglu, 2021). Or, as Richard Florida (2003) puts it, attracting the 'creative class' in certain cities, based on which firms will follow this class with the distinctive human capital of innovation (see also Florida and Mellander, 2020). The neoliberal position is, in addition, keeping out migrants with characteristics and identities that are perceived to slow down the wheels of economic fortune in the destination settlement.

For the countries of origin, neoliberals consider migration a win because of migrant remittances (for a more detailed discussion, see Rosewarne, 2010, 2012; Withers, 2019), but also because it is expected that migrants will return with improved human capital and more refined cultures and exposure to help their countries of origin, as shown in Lisa Åkesson and Maria Eriksson Baaz's (2015) book, *Africa's Return Migrants: The New Developers?* So, the emphasis for neoliberals is *temporary* migration, in which there is little social protection for migrants or the promotion of minimal safety nets for migrants, to the extent that those nets will enable them to keep working. It is also common to emphasize reduction in transaction costs to ease the sending and receiving of migrants and their remittances. The governments of countries such as the Philippines, Sri Lanka, and Indonesia have established programmes to promote the international recruitment of migrants, especially women (Rosewarne, 2012; Withers, 2019), while many countries, including Ghana, Senegal, and South Sudan, actively court the return of their nationals in the diaspora, among others through granting dual citizenship, the establishment of ministries in charge of diasporic affairs, and the expansion of national positions which can be occupied by dual citizens (Date-Bah, 2015; Obeng-Odoom, 2016a; Government of Ghana, 2016; African Union (AU) Commission and AU Department of Social Affairs, 2018), even if there remain important fetters on the rights of returnees.

For neoliberals, the solution to the problem of urban labour migrants is neither urban job generation nor the protection/extension of labour rights to migrants because such approaches *increase*, rather than decrease, the impulse to migrate to cities. Indeed, they argue that if more jobs are created in cities, there will be a greater incentive for rural residents to migrate to cities, where they will struggle to find work because of the mismatch between urban jobs and rural skills. So, in the end, more urban jobs will create more unemployment in cities (Todaro 1969; Todaro and Smith 2006, pp. 344–345). This consequentialist approach was famously developed by Garrett Hardin in his work, 'Lifeboat Ethics: The Case against Helping the Poor' (Hardin, 1974). The posited solution is development in the settlements of origin: any attempt to make conditions too good for migrants will only worsen the migration crisis, as—supposedly—more and more people will be attracted to the comfortable conditions.

Aspects of the neoliberal case for migration can be seen in Paul Collier's influential book, *Exodus: How Migration is Changing Our World* (2013). Collier argues that Europe needs migrants, but only a few, and those with certain characteristics. For Collier (2013), which migrants are allowed in depends on their rate and likelihood of 'absorption' into the culture of the hosts (the 'indigenous culture' in Collier's terms). Will migrants assimilate? Will they imbibe the mores of the host nations? Can they be trusted? Do they trust residents? What are the effects of migrants on the trust levels of the indigenous populations of the affluent countries to which they aspire to migrate? What is the effect of migration on the population back in the country of origin?

The answer depends, according to Collier, on which migrants. Black migrants, especially those from Nigeria, are particularly problematic. In Collier's framework, Nigerians are not trustworthy, they do not trust others either, and whether they are professionals or amateur workers, the 'culture' of weak trust and trustworthiness is carried with them. This analysis continues a persistent narrative in books such as *The Bottom Billion* (Collier, 2008) in which blacks, especially Nigerians, are branded as corrupt in their homelands. In *Exodus*, Collier looks at the effect of this attitude in the settlement country and argues that, in fact, more Nigerians in the UK National Health Service will corrupt the system. Next, Collier looks at the effect of the departure of migrants on those who stay behind. Here, too, the outcome is negative. According to Collier (2013), migrants – like all individuals - are selfish and self-interested. They renege on their responsibilities to take care of their families in rural areas and, instead, migrate to Europe to gain better opportunities. So, migration hurts those left behind, as well as the country left behind. This is a new twist to the old story of the brain drain, but the emphasis is not on the destination settlement trying to entice new brains, but rather on individuals acting in their own selfish interest, migrating to be better off and neglecting all other obligations and bonds.

Finally, Collier (2013) examines the effect of migrants on trust in the destination areas. Here, he argues that too many migrants, and especially certain migrants in an area with a different culture, leads to a reduction in trust levels. People in host communities become less trusting of other 'indigenous' hosts. They retreat and stay in their rooms to watch TV and hang out with their families. Collier (2013) suggests that racism is rational and justifiable on account of the incompatibility of cultures, the clash of cultures, and the unwillingness of migrant cultures to meld into the host culture.

This argument is a rehash, indeed a reincarnation of the thesis presented and defended by Samuel Huntington in his book, *The Clash of Civilizations and the Remaking of World Order* (Huntington, 1996). Huntington's book sought to go beyond Francis Fukuyama's *The End of History and the Last Man* (1992), which had claimed that capitalism has triumphed and, hence, debates between economic systems were no longer valid. Huntington's solution is to claim that we can put aside economic issues now because capitalism has triumphed and, instead, focus entirely on the incommensurability of cultures, to wit, the clash of cultures. According to this view, certain cultural values are acceptable, others are not. Huntington argues, for instance, that 'South Koreans valued thrift, investment, hard work, education, organisation, and discipline. Ghanaians had different values. In short, cultures count' (cited in Chang, 2015, p. 33). As culture is, in this view, destiny and unchangeable, immigrants from certain cultures are not welcome.

Much like neoliberals, humanists take a more positive view of migration, to the point of optimism. Their arguments are cast more in terms of human rights and the need for destination settlements to help migrants. Joseph Nevins's arguments for regarding 'migration as reparations' or as a payment for a climate debt to migrant-sending countries such as Honduras, El Salvador, and Guatemala because the US has contributed to the climate disasters that drive migrants from their homes in these areas can be regarded as a case in point (see Nevins, 2019). Humanists argue not only in terms of human rights or ecological debts, however. Their arguments can also be couched in economic terms.

One example is the case for more migration on the grounds that, like free trade, migration drives development in the Global South (Gollerkeri and Chhabra, 2016). Another example is the claim that migrants can support destination settlements, especially if they are integrated well or are helped to learn the new ways of the destination population. Or, simply, the measurement of success for migration is how well integrated the migrants are. Doug Saunders's book, *Arrival City* (2012) is a good example of this approach. In this book, Doug Saunders tries to see things both as an urbanist and as a migrationist. As an urbanist, he explains the processes of rural–urban migration and how cities across the world are expanding because of the drift of urban dwellers to the countryside. As a migrationist, he describes how migration to some of the world's biggest cities such as Nairobi, London, Toronto, Amsterdam, and Istanbul is changing the environment of these cities. From both perspectives, cities are important.

The concept of 'arrival cities' refers to various realities. The arrival city is that part of the village which has become urbanized. The arrival city is also that part of the already established city where migrants first settle when they move away from their village. It is the part of Paris and Chicago, among other cities of the world, where transnational migrants settle when they arrive in the host country for the first time. These parts of the city serve as a springboard for migrants to jump to the more affluent neighbourhoods. Although the arrival city may be regarded as the 'margins' (Saunders, 2012, p. 57), it is 'neither rural nor urban' (Saunders, 2012, p. 16). It is the peri-urban. The arrival city performs many functions, but, according to Saunders, its most important function is to provide opportunities for social mobility. Synonyms such as the 'gateway city' (Saunders, 2012, p. 82) clearly emphasize this function. Others, such as 'outskirts' (Saunders, 2012, p. 71), 'slum' (Saunders, 2012, p. 11), 'informal settlement' (Saunders, 2012, p. 13), and 'informal economy' (Saunders, 2012, p. 41), are commonly used in reference to the lack of such opportunities, but they also connote or constitute 'arrival cities'.

Saunders contends that arrival cities should be encouraged, defended, and extended. For example, Saunders argues that human capital development through education, language teaching, and stronger property rights and entrepreneurship development will address the problems of migrants and fix any problems about the incompatibility of cultures (Saunders, 2012, p. 270). Here, proof that some residents in the 'arrival city' are becoming real property owners marks the beginning of the arrival city (Saunders, 2012). In the humanist case for migration, social protection is demanded, but *temporariness* is hardly questioned (for a critique, see Rosewarne, 2010, 2012) and the cultural superiority of the host tacitly extolled by an uncritical acceptance of policies for integration. It is further contended that such 'superior' cultures can be learnt, hence the emphasis is on assimilation and integration and the return one day to the country of origin to enlighten those left behind.

In this sense, humanists do not emphasize 'brain drain', but rather 'brain circulation' from the poor to the rich countries and back to the poor, sending countries. It is this argument that is made in Lant Pritchett's work, *Let Their People Come* (2006). What makes Pritchett's analysis interesting is that, instead of the tendency of neoliberals to emphasize recruitment of the best brains, enabling them to accumulate some income, sending remittances while migrants, and subsequently returning home, Pritchett prefers that unskilled workers are enabled to migrate, remit while still migrants, and, in due course, return. Prichett's argument is that if the really poor and unskilled are allowed to benefit from migration, the poor countries will benefit from the process.

The orthodox framing of migration has the added advantage that it is more likely to assuage the fears of citizens in the receiving countries who are concerned that migration institutionalizes a process in which only a few of the best brains come from the sending country. The last words on the humanist approach must be given to Pritchett (2006, p. 11):

> There are obvious benefits to 'brain circulation' that might offset the traditional fears of 'brain drain', but it is almost certainly the case that if rich countries choose exclusively those migrants of higher productivity and grant them permanent status, this pattern of the 'three Rs' (recruitment, remittance, and return) is less favorable for the migrant-sending countries than policies emphasizing remittances and return.

Challenging the Orthodoxy

Challenging this orthodox framework implies questioning the 'push–pull' paradigm. As I have argued elsewhere (Obeng-Odoom, 2017a), this approach can be useful for analysis, but it is inherently problematic. Centred largely on 'exit', it neglects 'voice' and 'loyalty', to use the typologies of Albert Hirschman (Hirschman, 1970), and how they arise and are used both endogenously (see Hirschman, 1970, p. 15) and exogenously. Even when faced with difficulties, many groups stay (see, for example, Olarinde, 2021, pp. 4-5), while voicing their concerns initially through petitioning those who cause or can address the problem, protest (e.g., for change of one leader, for regime change, regime transformation, or new regime developed internally based on democratic processes, or for a complete change in political-economic system) subsequently, and then either scale up the protest or use a combination of voice techniques (e.g., voting), depending on how loyal or attached they are to a place or country (Hirschman, 1970, pp. 81–82). Such loyalty might also help to explain why a country can appeal to its citizens to stay or to move to other places, cities, or countries.

Migration as an exit strategy is hardly the first or initial reaction, in contrast to the assumptions in the push–pull paradigm. Even as an exit strategy, the concept of 'exit'—like that of 'return'—requires rethinking because it is rarely driven by individual cost–benefit analysis alone. Yet, this narrow problematic framing is what, originally, is the economic meaning of exit sometimes equated with 'market', while voice is regarded as a 'non-market', political force (Hirschman, 1970, pp. 15–16, 19). This understanding also explains why economists have tended to focus more on exit, while political scientists tend to specialize in voice, a dualism critiqued by Hirschman (1970), as a springboard for developing a new framework.

Political economists need to focus on both, but even more importantly on the total migration experience, which is greater than the sum of voice, loyalty, and exit. So, it is more effective to consider the decision to migrate (exit)/return as neither entirely economic nor exclusive. Rather, such major decisions are jointly made in consultation with families, sometimes entire settlements and townships. Even if entire settlements do not take part in the decision to move, the decision to return is conditioned by how entire settlements will perceive the migrant, so migration is hardly the product of autonomous individual choice alone (Amantanna, 2012; Tonah, 2021). Rather, it is framed within institutions. Also, as migration can be costly, it is often class-based and shaped by colonial history and new neoliberal and other institutions (Arthur, 2014; Tonah, 2021). Different classes move to different areas, at different times and in different forms or processes.

'Exit' for some may not only connote physically moving away from one city to another or one country to another. Where people go, how they go, and when are usually class-based and moulded by institutions. For some, exit means moving from one part of the city with disadvantages to another; for others, it means directly moving to other cities in a country or outside of it. Most migration in Africa is national, regional, or continental in focus and destination. Of all migrants in the world, African migrants are the ones that keep the most to their region, to wit, 69% of all African migrants move around Africa. And this is not just a case of stepped migration, in which the mobility is from one poor country to the next rich country until they arrive in Europe (Hujo, 2013, 2019; Olarinde, 2021). As the survey of Africans living in Libya by Bob-Milliar and Bob-Milliar (2013) shows, most African migrants in their sample had no intention of moving on: Libya was a destination. So, exit must recognize context and, importantly, the class and nature of migration neoliberal policies (see, e.g., Arthur, 2014; Manby, 2018; Tonah, 2021) and the important roles played by institutions (see, e.g., Amantana, 2012; Bryceson, 2019) in mediating the process.

The various hypotheses that arise from the orthodox framing must also be questioned. The idea that migration must be celebrated because it brings in remittances is questionable. There is a vast literature on how migrants send remittances for a variety of uses: education, family upkeep, health, pleasure, farming, and housing. These flows are conditioned by different forces, including gender, age, destination, and ethnicity (Adaween and Boabang, 2013; Bryceson, 2019), but there are flows regardless and these are from urban to rural and from international to national, but also from local to global, the so-called reverse remittances (Adiku, 2022). Remittances, however, are no panacea, regardless of their size, type, or direction. Research shows that the conditions under which migrants work to earn those remittances can be harsh for both internal and international migrants (Rosewarne, 2012; DeParle, 2019; Withers, 2019; see also Chapter 9 of this book). Regardless of whether they are highly skilled professionals (on professional and society-wide racism against African intellectuals in the US, see Arthur, 2014) or low-skilled emigrés (for a detailed analysis of the harsh work conditions of foreign domestic workers in Hong Kong, see Kwok, 2015), migrants who work in the formal economy face multiple deprivations. Such experiences cast doubt on the humanist case for 'helping' poor countries by admitting their least skilled migrants (see Pritchett, 2006) or of considering migration as reparations (Nevins, 2019).

Many migrants work in informal economies under harsh labour conditions, as detailed research (Bangura and Stavenhagen, 2005; Bangura, 2006; Blaauw et al., 2019) shows. Some deprive themselves of quality housing in the migrant location to live more comfortably later (Kuuire et al., 2016). That future date rarely 'arrives', though, and migrants continue to struggle for years (see Chapter 9), sometimes till they die. While migrants' wages can be depressed by more migrants coming in (as argued by Collier, 2013), the solution to that problem is not erecting borders. Distributing job opportunities and looking at matters of social protection for workers and migrants generally (Hujo, 2013, 2019) could ameliorate 'race to the bottom' tendencies among workers, although ultimately these strategies are also limited.

Is the solution then to provide jobs for all? To give dirty, dangerous and demeaning (3-D) jobs, or jobs that natives do not wish to do, to migrants? Or is it simply to further expand the economy, as a 'rising tide lifts all boats'? These questions have been repeatedly asked, but they have tended to be resolved in favour of more and more growth. This orthodoxy of growth is simple with respect to distribution, but more superficial on the question of ecological sustainability (Boulding, 1964; Jaynes, 2007; Daly, 2019). The idea that the planet can grow forever to solve all problems is driven by a range of military, civil, and even religious interests. It is a central rallying point for existing analyses of migration. The neoliberals welcome the story because it is good for growth: more migrants would help the economy to grow cheaply. Humanists tout the growth potential of welcoming migrants and, even more fundamentally, emphasise how much more sending countries can gain if migrants are sent back to their home countries to contribute to their growth and become like the West.

The idea of returning migrants to help with the development of their countries of origin is also problematic. Lisa Åkesson and Maria Eriksson Baaz's *Africa's Return Migrants: The New Developers?* seeks to problematize the idea that migrants are the new agents of development (2015, pp. 1–3). They argue that this idea is based on wrong assumptions about the transferability of experiences obtained abroad for local home country realities. Even those return migrants who appreciate the different institutions in their home countries must learn that they have to possess different social networks to be able to use their ideas and to apply skills acquired overseas. In fact, it is not always the case that those who stayed behind welcome or work well with professional returnees. Sometimes, too, institutional impediments, 'glocal' policy incoherence, and infrastructural weaknesses can stifle any major transformative initiatives that a well-intentioned returnee may propose or undertake.

It is well known that some migrants have returned to establish successful businesses and, at least in the case of Ghana, to take on many professional roles and policy positions. Returnees have become important politicians in Ghana where the state has been at the forefront of enacting dual citizenship laws to make it manageable for Ghanaians in the diaspora to remain connected to their country of birth (see also Bob-Milliar and Bob-Milliar, 2013; Government of Ghana, 2016). Also, individual Ghanaians in the diaspora have succeeded in getting the Supreme Court of Ghana to interpret the laws in ways that make it much easier to make contributions to national development—a point developed in Justice Samuel Kofi Date-Bah's recent book, *Reflections on the Supreme Court of Ghana* (2015) and *Selected Papers and Lectures on Ghanaian Law* (2021).

In many of such cases, social context and institutions mould outcomes. The point, then, is not that migrants cannot be part of a professional cadre to move a country forward, but that actually doing so is contingent on a number of other factors. These include the type of returnee. Whether skilled returnees worked in their fields of expertise while overseas; their social class in the country of origin, which is likely to have shaped the migration experience in the first place; to what extent the returnee has built links in the country of return while in the diaspora; how well versed the returnees are in the changing political economy of the country of return; local conditions; and how readily local staff are prepared to work with, and share in, the vision of the returnee are all important. A major contradiction, even if all the conditions are met, is that the returnee professionals could develop a dual identity, considering themselves superior to the rest and, hence, potentially re-establishing the inequality and class structures that propelled the migration in the first place (Arthur, 2014).

These contingent forces, however, cannot be reduced to 'culture'. Amartya Sen's book, *Identity and Violence: The Illusion of Destiny* (2006), offers three reasons. First, people are more than just one culture: they have multiple identities. Migrants who are African can also be liberal in their politics and may be middle class. The same migrant may be a political economist and, as such, identify more as a Georgist than a Marxist; they may identify as an institutional economist, a land economist, and an urban economist. The African may also be Methodist or a Catholic, may love photography, singing, sports, and so on. These identities co-exist, even if some are stronger inherently and instrumentally Second, there are varieties within cultures, so even among African cultures there are internal diversities: Ghanaian, Nigerian, Malian, and so on. In fact, even among Ghanaians there are further differences. Third, these diversities have a long history of interactions, based again on multiple identities.

Yet, Sen's critique, while profound, suggests that focusing on identities is the product of confusion or wrong ideas. Denying the *institutional foundations* of identities and opting, instead, for a unique identity by both mainstream and revisionists (who champion programmes to help different cultures to settle in a society which presumably has one grand prevailing identity) is analytically weak. Identities do exist and persist, the question is how to study them (Crenshaw, 1989, 1991; Darity and Mullen, 2020; Darity, 2021). A rational choice approach, its many forms, and varied permutations can be problematic.

The correlation between diversity, trust, and conflict is a case of problematic social science. Such correlation analysis is done as a snapshot. Trend and historical analyses (Pemberton and Philimore, 2018) suggest that if an area is already diverse, additional diversity only increases trust, harmony, and security of minorities, while for communities with dominant races, the recent influx of new races and religions creates tensions. In other words, in an environment where no one race dominates, diversity is no longer a multicultural idea in which different cultures subsist without real mixing, but rather a way of life. From this perspective, the solution to tension is not less, but more, diversity.

Consequently, the argument by some humanists that too much migration leads to a lack of cohesion, conflicts, and racism, which in turn leads to the election of far right and conservative governments (see Collins, 2008), is similarly remiss. Racism and trust are stirred and sustained by more complex factors, such as the downturn in the economy, the historical treatment of certain races, and the stereotyping of races as 'good' or 'bad', rather than migration per se. Racism does not arise autonomously: historical and contemporary institutions—including the market, the state, and the media—drive and can alter it (Hamilton, 2018; Darity and Mullen, 2020; Darity, 2021). For instance, racism in Young, a community with a large number of Afghan migrants in Sydney, was driven largely by leaflets circulated by the Australia First Party, in which nationalists claimed, without proof, that Afghans were gang-raping Australian women, doing drugs, and shooting police officers (Stilwell, 2003, p. 236). Other media houses have attempted to construct more positive images of Sudanese migrants in Australia (Wickramaararchchi and Burns, 2017), but that is precisely the point: racism is social and institutionally constructed.

More fundamentally, much of the mainstream analysis of migration overlooks capitalism as an economic system that periodically drives mass migration. Bringing the economic system back into the analysis of social change has been strongly advocated as a corrective (Chen, 2019). In particular, the question of private property in land, along with its role as the motor for hunger, disease, and war, have not been carefully analysed (Obeng-Odoom, 2017b). Land, and land rent especially, tends to be neglected in the analysis of the institutional exit factors that tip the scales against voice and loyalty to stay (Hirschman, 1970). The host countries may have some policies to paper over the cracks in their own system and mask the poverty and social unrest, but benign conditions in the host countries are mostly enjoyed by a minority, notably landlords. These landlords include those who derive their position primarily from extracting rents and those whose position is cemented by both rent and profit from wealth. The privileges of landownership increase with migration, especially if migrants are subjected to the workings of the market mechanism in land. In addition the rise of, new landlords might compound the problem.

Political economists have tried to address these analytical and practical problems. They contend that an individual and household-based analysis is highly suspect and limited in its ability to explain migration, whether it is internal (e.g., rural–urban), external (international), or a combination of both. Existing orthodoxy ignores the class and institutional aspects of migration and how they change over time. A much stronger explanatory framework, according to this critique, is the historical-structural framework. According to Alexandre Abreu (2012, p. 61):

> a number of features common to the various theoretical accounts within this perspective can be identified that make it possible to characterize this approach as a whole: i) its structural emphasis and lack of (even concern for) a theory of individual migrant agency; ii) the fact that migration, both internal and international, is regarded as part and parcel of broader processes of structural change (i.e. development), rather than as a 'discreet element of social reality that can be subjected to separate investigation' ... iii) its typical recourse to an inductive and/or dialectical—in a word, historical—methodology, in contrast to neoclassical theory's hypothetical-deductivism; and iv) its rejection of 'equilibrium' as a structuring principle.

Global labour market segmentation is a key focus of this historical structural methodology. The drawing of one cohort of migrant workers into 3-D jobs and

the institutionalization of this process through restrictions on employment or residence are important points of emphasis, along with the problematic targeting
of certain cohorts of workers, based on ethnocentrism, racism, and sexism, to
underpin the characterisation of migrant workers stereotyped to fill particular occupations through recruitment processes organized to vet professional or skilled
workers.

For structural analysts, there are positively reinforcing structural biases, which
are not entirely distinct from the new institutionalist economics focus on rules,
which is seeping into neoclassical development economics (see, e.g., Betts et al.,
2016; Clausing, 2019a, 2019b), which is increasingly reflective of libertarian arguments for migration without limit on a 'win–win' basis (see, e.g., Somin, 2020).
Yet, for the Marxian structuralist working in this field (see, e.g., Rosewarne, 2010,
2012, 2020a, 2020b), global uneven development is key: state-sponsoring labour as
an export-earning efficiency in the global allocation of labour resources, increasing
employment levels, and local processes designed to attract migrant workers to
particular areas to fill systemic labour shortages all complement the picture.

Perhaps, where there is practical divergence between institutionalists focusing
on rules is that the structuralist is strongly critical of qualified liberalization of international mobility, which tends to be praised by the new institutionalists, or even
neoclassical analysts. For Marxists (e.g., Rosewarne, 2010, 2012, 2020a, 2020b),
such segmentation opens up borders to a range of different migration categories
that are also socially differentiated. Among these categories are permanent
residents with employment rights and defined resident and work rights with respect to occupation and, or, location rights. There are also the temporary residents
whose rights are much more inferior and overstayers with the least secure rights,
who are forced to work under challenging conditions. Underneath this pyramid
are illegal or irregular migrants.

In practice, the use of this approach has strongly focused on class and work
(Rosewarne, 2020a, 2020b), even when *land,* property rights, and other institutions strongly mould the nature of those who work the land. Additional theorizing
is needed to nuance these insights further. It is striking that the and international
migration crisis comes at the heels of land grabbing on a global scale and global systemic racism and nationalism. There is already research compiled in Fred Pearce's
2012 book: *The Land Grabbers: The New Fight Over Who Owns the Earth*, showing
that land grabbing has triggered internal and international migration crisis when
people whose land has been taken away from them seek new lives and livelihoods
without roots in the soil as waged labourers.

Conclusion

Migration is complex. It has become increasingly more complicated, too. The dominant, orthodox approach has also become more diversified. Yet, as this chapter has shown, even in its variety, the existing approaches to studying migration are fundamentally problematic. The present alternatives are necessary, but they are not sufficient to embrace the complexities, complicates, and cosmopolitanism engendered by the current waves of global migration (see also Appiah, 2019; Champlin and Knoeder, 2020). By definition, practice, and experience, immigration policy deals with the race question, questions about identities, and their interdependence (Champlin and Knoeder, 2020). Clearly, individualism as a methodological orientation cannot serve as a foundation for holistic analysis.

Structuralism is a much firmer pathway, but it has typically struggled with questions about minorities other than workers, and typically stumbled when faced with how to further theorize the links between land, property rights, race, class, ethnicity, gender, nationalism, and the migration crisis on the global scale, a crisis which throws up complex questions about institutions (see also Leonard, 2016; Singerman, 2016; Hamilton, 2018; Obeng-Odoom, 2020b; Bromley, 2016, 2019 Obeng-Odoom, 2020b; Darity and Mullen, 2020; Darity, 2021).

Both the prevailing orthodoxy and heterodoxy are highly problematic paradigms for investigating the complexities of twenty-first-century migration. Deontological methodologies, typically utilised by philosophers (see, e.g., Wellman and Cole, 2011; Carens, 2013; Bertram, 2018), advocate socially detached analyses. However, as Thomas Nagel, a philosopher himself, has carefully demonstrated (Nagel, 1986, p. 3), such approaches create a false sense of objectivity, philosophical errors, and the denial of reality. They are inappropriate for dealing with political-economic realities. So, it is necessary to develop a new framework. If it is to be relevant and credible as a theoretical compass, however, such a framework must take land, institutions, and identities such as race, gender, and class seriously.

3

Towards a New Framework

Humanity faces multiple challenges, including economic uncertainty, health crises, inequality, systemic racism, segmentation, and stratification, together with the stresses of global migration. As Chapters 1 and 2 have shown, mainstream ecology and economics are incapable of addressing these complex, long-term problems. Orthodox economics theories are out of kilter with reality. Economic models, built on assumptions of stability and certainty, are in disarray. Political economy has historically sought a way out of the fog, but some of its alternatives are also problematic. To extend the relevance of political economy as a formidable alternative, however, it needs to draw on other currents of thought that have long been marginalized, of which one is Georgist political economy (GPE). Originating from the writing and teaching of Henry George in the late nineteenth century, GPE provides both a critique of and an alternative to classical and neoclassical ways of interpreting economic issues (George, 1883/1966, 1885, 1898/1992). The practitioners of 'occult science', as George called the orthodoxy (George, 1898/1992, p. 205), did not welcome this alternative and have deliberately marginalized its study ever since (Gaffney, 1994; Harrison, 2016, 2020). However, contemporary concerns with growing concentration of economic wealth and power, enclosure of the commons, and socio-spatial injustice (Stilwell, 2019; Obeng-Odoom, 2020b, 2021) make renewed consideration of Georgist ideas important within modern political economy.

Proponents of the Georgist perspective have made significant progress in developing new explanations, identifying impediments to progress, and offering prescriptive pathways to a more inclusive, safer, and cleaner world (see, e.g., Haila, 2016; Ryan-Collins et al., 2017; Ryan-Collins, 2021). Yet, GPE still receives relatively little attention. As shown by Michael Hudson's (2008) extensive survey of the existing criticisms of this school of thought, the continuing obscurity is due to GPE's presumed singular focus on land, assumed exclusive emphasis on policy ('land value taxation'), and the uninspiring nature of its reformism.

To counter these caricatures, it is pertinent to set out the character and continuing relevance of GPE, showing how its methodology can be applied to current political-economic and socio-ecological problems and how it may be developed further as a major school of political economy, drawing on both institutional economics (I) and stratification economics (S). This chapter addresses these issues and develops the *GIS* alternative methodology—an amalgam of Georgist political economy (G), institutional economics (I), and stratification economics (S)—in four sections. The first ('Political Economy') clarifies the canons of GPE. The second ('Liberty') shows how the insights arising from GPE compare with more orthodox views. The third section ('Progress') assesses the overall status of GPE and its strengths, and weaknesses, paving the way for the final section ('Institutions'), which develops a comprehensive framework of GIS as an alternative to both mainstream economics and its current alternatives.

Political Economy

Many schools of thought existed during GPE's apogee, the Gilded Age. The prevailing ideas were diverse, but George thought that none sufficiently systematically probed the political economy of land. It took courage to offend the landed aristocracy, so most of those who theorized about rent did so apolitically, emphasizing the natural aspects of soil fertility and location. David Ricardo, for example, focused on the effects of differential soil fertility and location (Ricardo [1817] 2001). Other political economists, failing to distinguish adequately between land and capital, accorded little or no attention to landed property: the dominant focus on the relationship between capital and labour subsumed land under capital. The French physiocrats took a detour from this main road, but they only ended up on the farm, searching for answers to agrarian questions. So, in general, key concepts in political economy (e.g., 'value in use' and 'value in exchange') were discussed without systematic reference to land (George, 1898/1992, pp. 182–199). Much of political economy was focused on the relationship between capital and labour, subsuming land under capital. When land was explicitly analysed, its study was usually restricted to its quality and location within rural areas, not to its wider political-economic significance.

GPE emerged to confront and correct this neglect. As the universities were largely complicit in protecting landed interests (Jorgensen, 1925), GPE had no place in such scholarly environments. In contrast to the older 'scholastic political economy' and mainstream 'occult science', George set out to develop what he claimed to be a true science of the people. George had no formal higher education. He related to his subject personally, driven by his own poor economic circumstances and the poverty of other people he observed. Mass poverty in an already wealthy America taught him that it was not the behaviour of individuals that caused poverty. Moreover, migration and the struggle of migrants showed him that many posited 'solutions' to poverty could worsen the problem.

George's historical reflections on the effects of privation, progress and plunder in ancient Egypt also revealed to him that poverty was not just a feature of so-called 'backward' societies (George, 1884). Egypt had been the beacon of global civilisation, but it was also the cathedral of oppression and structural inequality. Because these problems predated the capitalist economic system, they could not all be attributed to capitalism. George argued that socialism could not be relied on to redress these serious problems either (George, [1883] 1966, pp.176–178, 191; George and Hyndman, [1885] 1914). Rather, the key was to be found in an analysis of land in relation to both labour and capital; and the remedy for ongoing poverty among plenty would need to address the land question in a specifically Georgist way. Henry George's broad aim was to explain *structural* inequality and its corrosive effects, including global *systemic* poverty. Seen in this light, land is both a problem and a solution in GPE. Processes of land transition and transformation interact with labour and capital, shaping the forms that poverty and inequality take. Analysis of these processes is infused with particular principles, of which three are cardinal: first, 'That all men have equal rights to the use and enjoyment of the elements provided by Nature [Second,] That each man has an exclusive right to the use and enjoyment of what is produced by his own labor' (George, 1886/1991, p. 280), and third, that wealth arises from the exertion of labour on matter used for the satisfaction of human need. Therefore, increase in wealth does not entirely come from capital, but also from labour and wider public as well as social interactions (George, 1892/1981, 1883/1981). Thus, it is the private appropriation of socially created increasing rent by landed interests that is the means by which wealth becomes more concentrated.

With these diagnoses, Georgists typically propose three solutions: first, untaxing labour incomes to ensure that workers get a fuller reward for their produce, while promoting a labour-based, anti-monopoly system of production; second, keeping land as a commons or, if land is already privatized, taxing away the rents generated by technological change, speculation, population growth, public as well as social investments in infrastructure that increase land values; and third, investing the resulting revenues in comprehensive social and public policies.

The building blocks of GPE can be found in *Progress and Poverty* (George, 1897/1935), which is George's best-known work, but particularly in *The Science of Political Economy* (1898/1992), which was his last book before his death. Interpretations of his contribution, however, vary. Phillip Bryson (2011, pp. 1–24), for example, seeks to show that, although George was not as lettered as his contemporaries, he was familiar with their theories and largely used the same tools as other economists at that time, namely induction, deduction, and experimentation. Others (e.g., Stilwell, 2011) recognize George's standing, pointing to key concepts in his approach such as value, wealth, distribution, and growth. Here are echoes of the wider classical political economy of which George is a part, but against which he was a dissident critic.

While George used the *same names* for the principal concepts in classical political economy, he gave them *distinctive meanings*. Consider value, for example

(George, 1898/1992, Chapters 10–14). George appreciated the classical and Marxist labour theories of value but, for him, labour was the source of *some, but* not
all, value. Land value, for example, does not solely arise from labour: speculation,
population growth, social, and public investment are important drivers, too. Even
without the application of labour to improve it, land can still gain in value.

Another example concerns the notions of 'use value' and 'exchange value', commonly used in political economy and by Marxists in particular. George regarded
the distinction between the two as forced (because each contains elements of
the other) and considered the sequence of how they are related by Marxists to
exchange to be problematic (George, 1898/1992, Chapter 10). For George, ex-
changeability follows value; value does not follow exchange. George preferred that
the analysis of value be restricted to exchange only, although recognizing that at
the heart of this exchange value was use value. It is from this line of analysis that
George's distinctive preference for land value taxation arises. No tax can fall on
land with only use value, as would be the case for land set aside from market
relations, such as areas reserved for use by indigenous peoples or as national parks.

Although working primarily with the (sometimes modified) tools of classical
political economy, George did introduce a few *new* concepts, such as *value in production* and *value in obligation* (George, 1898/1992, Chapter 20). The former refers
to the contribution of labour, to which George argued that no tax should apply. The
latter refers to value increases arising from imposed exertion, indebtedness, slavery, and bondage, these being oppressive extractions that make no contribution to
production *per se* and to which tax should be applied.

Wealth is the subject of distinctive analysis, too. The standard political-
economic approach is to distinguish wealth, which is a stock, from income, which
is a flow. Land, therefore, is usually considered to be 'wealth'. In GPE, however,
wealth is anything produced by labour. The focus on wealth is not so much on how
it is distinct from income but, rather, on how its generation, purpose, and distribution are distinct from land (George, 1898/1992, Chapters 15–20). Some wealth is
capital, which is produced by labour. The rest is *improved* land. Therefore, capital
is clearly distinct from land, as is labour, and their particular production processes
are different.

Their roles and their respective rewards are also different. Whether public or
private, common or concentrated, wealth must satisfy *desires*, an idea introduced
by George to collapse the artificial distinction between 'needs' and 'wants' (George,
1898/1992, Chapter 11), widely used in mainstream economics inspired by Lionel
Robbins. For these reasons, too, wealth must be widely diffused. But the imposition of a *wealth tax*—often canvased in other schools of political economy—is
regarded as the wrong way to try to redistribute wealth. Instead, a more appropriate policy would be the reconstruction of land and landed relations (George,
1892/1981).

For all these reasons, land—its features, forms and functions—is the most crucial and distinctive factor in GPE. In *A Perplexed Philosopher* (George, 1892/1981), George provided a particularly wide-ranging description of land. In his own words:

> Land—to us the one solid, natural element; our all-producing, all-supporting mother, from whose bosom our very frames are drawn, and to which they return again; our standing-place; our workshop; our granary; our reservoir and substratum and nexus of media and forces; the element from which all we can produce must be drawn; without which we cannot breathe the air or enjoy the light; the element prerequisite to all human life and action.
>
> (George, 1892/1981, p. 140)

Indeed, land is special in many ways. Not only is it distinct from capital, but it is also governed by special rules.

The principle of equal rights is key. To quote George again:

> When men [sic] have equal rights to a thing, as for instance, to the rooms and appurtenances of a club of which they are members, each has a right to use all or any part of the thing that no other one of them is using.... . But where men have joint rights to a thing, as for instance, to a sum of money held to their joint credit, then the consent of all the others is required for the use of the thing or of any part of it, by any one of them. Now, the rights of men to the use of land are not joint rights; they are equal rights.
>
> (George, 1892/1981, pp. 30–31)

These principles also apply to indigenous land.

As George said:

> Although within generally vague territorial limits each tribe may claim the right to exclude other tribes, yet the idea is not that of property in the land, but of that sort of separation which took place between Lot and Abraham, and the relation of the members to the land is not that of joint ownership but of equal right to use such regulations as in the earlier stages become necessary, being merely those which secure this equality in use.
>
> (George, 1892/1981, fn. 21)

The significance of this principle is that of sharing the earth. Consent is needed when land is reduced in supply, but at every point, land value is the preserve of the entire community.

Land rent, then, requires special attention. As George wrote: 'The term rent, in its economic sense - that is, when used, as I am using it, to distinguish that part of the produce which accrues to the owners of land or other natural capabilities by virtue of their ownership - differs in meaning from the word rent as commonly used' (George, [1897] 1935, p.165). Conferred by the privilege to control land used in the creation of wealth, rent is determined not so much by fertility or even location, but by monopoly power. George again: 'Rent, in short, is the share in the wealth produced which the exclusive right to the use of natural capabilities gives to the owner. Wherever land has an exchange value there is rent in the economic meaning of the term. Wherever land having a value is used, either by owner or hirer, there is rent actual; wherever it is not used, but still has a value, there is rent potential. It is this capacity of yielding rent which gives value to land. Until its ownership will confer some advantage, land has no value' (George, [1897] 1935, p.166). Rent can be enhanced by location, by productivity, or by exertion. More fundamentally, rent is conditioned by general progress within society.

Rent has been widely discussed in political economy, including an authoritative review by Nicholas Kaldor (see Kaldor, 1956), but to understand rent in Georgist terms it is crucial to take account of the importance of 'marginal land'. 'George makes it quite clear that marginal land is not unproductive land, but merely the least productive land available at a particular time and place' (Cleveland, 2020, p.564). This marginal land, or 'extensive margin', is the floor below which neither rent nor wage can be set. The extensive margin is important in GPE because it sets the conditions for the determination of wages and rents, both of which are tied to land. However, even more fundamental is the privilege of individual control that creates and sustains land rent. Without private appropriation of land, there is no rent. According to George: 'Rent, in short, is the price of monopoly, arising from the reduction to individual ownership of natural elements which human exertion can neither produce nor increase' (George, [1897] 1935, p.167). This price for the individual power to control land when capitalised or aggregated becomes land value. It can be actual or residual: so, rent also arises when landlords hoard land, use it solely for their own needs, or purport to develop land banking for social purposes (Yau and Cheung, 2021). Because socially created rent tends to increase with wealth, its private appropriation usually constitutes a brake on the rewards of both labour and capital.

In Marxist political economy, questions of (land) rent, rentierism and 'rent-based capitalism' are considered. Yet, land is not a primary concern in such analysis. Land is not given a special explanatory place in the 'circuit of capital', either. Indeed, in this circuit, land is subsumed in the concept of capital, consistent with the typical Marxist emphasis on capital and labour. Land is of

secondary importance, usually considered separately in programmes of (land) na-
tionalisation. In the George-Hyndman debate (see George and Hyndman, [1885]
1914), Henry George made these distinctions clear, emphasising the fundamental
differences between Marxist-socialists and Georgists with respect to 'socialism and
rent-appropriation'. For Georgists, the analysis of rent (see also Harrison, 2021) is
conceptualised differently from Marxist thinking and is primarily focused on land.
Georgists seek to socialise land rent, whereas Marxists wish to remove rent. For
Georgists, the inequalities of incomes and wealth are themselves caused by how
land is treated, particularly through individual private property rights.

Indeed, while in Marxian thought rent is a subset of surplus value, for Georgists, surplus value is a subset of rent. The limited quantitative evidence on the
relative size of these two—rent and surplus value—shows that rent is much bigger
than surplus value (Giles, 2019, p. 29). Landlords, then, can be—and often are—
even more powerful than capitalists. Unlike capitalists, however, landlords make
no direct contribution to the process of wealth creation. Rather, they absorb and
privately retain the fruits of progress, while they externalize poverty to the masses.
No matter what policy is implemented, the owners of land capture its gains. It
is this dynamic that explains the coexistence of progress and privation and why
greater prosperity increases poverty.

Land value and economic rent are, therefore, fundamental to the analytical
foundations of GPE. George himself was at pains to distinguish economic rent
(the focus of GPE) from rent used in general conversation. One distinction is that,
while 'rent' used in common conversation does not refer to 'latent or potential'
rent, economic rent also refers to residual value. The essence of his distinction is
that economic rent arises not so much from individual human exertion or from
the effort of landlords. Other uses of the term refer to the products of human exertion such as buildings (e.g., rent paid because of ongoing services provided by a
house builder). In cities, however, these two notions of rent can be interlocking,
as apartment rent strongly reflects factors unrelated to apartment owners' efforts
(George, 1897/1935, pp. 165–172).

What is called 'economic rent' in GPE should really be called 'net product'. According to George, 'Net product is really a better terminology than rent,
as not being so liable to confusion with a word in constant use in another
sense' (George, 1898/1992, p. 150). More fundamentally, greater prosperity increases rent, variously referred to by George (1898/1992) as land power, *pro-
duit net*, net product, unearned increment, or economic rent that accrues to
landlords. This dynamic also makes the economic system prone to structural
inequality.

These were the breakthrough propositions and arguments in Henry George's
Progress and Poverty (George, 1897/1935) and *The Science of Political Economy* (George, 1898/1992). These books were complemented by two other more
methodological texts: *A Perplexed Philosopher* (1892/1981) and *Moses* (George,

1884), the former providing the scaffold for *The Science of Political Economy* (George, 1898/1992), while the latter provided the springboard for *Progress and Poverty* (George, 1897/1935). Other more recent Georgist texts (e.g., Bryson, 2011; Pullen, 2014; O'Donnell, 2015; Haila, 2016; Ryan-Collins et al., 2017; Giles, 2019; Harrison, 2021) can be used to supplement the exposition of GPE.

Overall, George's argument is that socio-ecological problems arise from the unequal access to land, the private appropriation of socially created rent, and the deprivation of the rights of labour through taking away or reducing what is due to labour. While other factors might be named as 'causes', they are, in fact, derived from these fundamental contradictions and, hence, are symptoms of deeper causal influences (George, 1883/1981). It is a position that is analytical, not dogmatic, as shown by the way in which George described his approach in *The Science of Political Economy*:

> [...] if political economy can be called science at all, it must as a science, that is to say from the moment the laws of nature on which it depends are discovered, follow the deductive method of examination, using induction only to test the conclusions thus obtained (p.98) [...] Thus, in the main, the science of political economy resorts to the deductive method, using induction for its tests.
>
> (George, 1898/1992, p. 100)

Beyond deductive and inductive reasoning, George called for 'imaginative experiment', seeking to 'separate, combine or eliminate conditions in our own imaginations, and thus test the working of known principles' (George, 1898/1992, p. 100). George and many contemporary political economists influenced by Georgism have applied this approach to various social problems: housing (Stilwell and Jordan, 2004a); poverty and inequality (Stilwell, 2011, 2019; Obeng-Odoom, 2020b); sustainability (Stilwell and Jordan, 2004b; Obeng-Odoom, 2016a, 2021); and trade (Obeng-Odoom, 2018a, 2020a). Developing a GPE approach to global migration is important, but it must be done in the context of other approaches and considerably broadened. For these purposes, it is useful to examine the economics of liberty.

Liberty

The nature of liberalism warrants careful consideration. Many critics claim that GPE is 'liberal' or a reflection of 'liberalism'. However, that claim is misleading. GPE is centrally about sharing the commons (Obeng-Odoom, 2021), whereas liberalism is about enclosing it. Examining how this enclosure shapes migration

throws further light on GPE because it extends the literature from a mere application of GPE to migration (Beck, 2012; Obeng-Odoom, 2017b) to challenging the
contention that GPE is merely about land and liberty.

To probe these issues more deeply, it is necessary to clarify the meaning of
liberalism. According to *The Economist*:

> [l]iberalism—the Enlightenment philosophy, not the American left—
> starts with the assertion that all human beings have equal moral worth.
> From that stem equal rights for all. Libertarians see those principles as
> paramount. For left-leaning liberals, equal moral worth also brings an
> entitlement to the resources necessary for an individual to flourish.
>
> (*The Economist*, 2020n, p. 48)

This context can help to clarify the usual refrain that promoting free movement is a
liberal project. The ideological commitment to the free circulation of commodities,
people, and finance as a way of addressing social problems further illustrates the
point. Globalization, the liberal argument goes, guarantees liberty and prosperity.
Foreign Affairs, the leading American foreign policy journal, recently published
Kimberly Clausing's essay that vigorously makes these claims (Clausing, 2019b).
Clausing's book from the same year, is, notably titled *Open: The Progressive Case for
Free Trade, Immigration, and Global Capital* (Clausing, 2019a). Beyond the work
of one economist, influential though she is, we need to analyse wider institutions
of liberalism.

The Economist newspaper is, perhaps, peerless in this regard. It has promoted
free movement of capital and labour since its inception. 'Barriers to movement
make the world poorer', *The Economist* (2019d, p. 15) recently diagnosed. It has also
supplied the antidote: 'Unlock that door' (*The Economist*, 2019d). 'Open borders
ease the flow of exports as well as individuals', the paper argued, contending further
that '[e]very year people make €1.3 billion crossings of the EU's internal borders
along with 57m trucks carrying 2.8 trillion ($3.7 trillion) of goods' (*The Economist*,
2016, p. 20), so I stick to migration in this chapter.

Read by nearly 1.5 million people around the world, *The Economist* is the most
powerful exponent of economic liberalism (Zevin, 2019, p. 1). No single work by
an academic economist has achieved its growing coverage. The advocacy of liberalism in this newspaper is largely based on a distillation of economic theory.
Many economists have their work discussed in *The Economist*. Among them are
Edward Glaeser, Paul Collier, and David Cutler (*The Economist*, 2019d, 2019e).
Economic concepts are used in the newspaper, too. 'Voting with your feet', a phrase
coined by Charles Tiebout and extensively used in mainstream neoclassical urban economics (Obeng-Odoom, 2013, pp. 20–21), is frequently mentioned (*The
Economist*, 2019d, 2020p, p. 41).

The Economist is usually read by the most influential economists, politicians, and world leaders. Not all its readers are mainstream, though. A study by the Pew Research Center shows that, in the US at least, 59% of the newspaper's readers are typically progressive (Gottlieb, 2019, p. 78). Notable regular readers in the past were Karl Marx and Hugo Chávez. Others are Barack Obama and Angela Merkel (Zevin, 2019, pp. 1–40). Ever since 1843, when it was formed, the mandate of *The Economist* has been to 'support the higher circles of the landed and monied interests' (Zevin, 2019, p. 30). Promoting free trade is integral to that mandate (Zevin, 2019, pp. 21–70). So is defending migration as a spatial solution to social problems. I have analysed free trade elsewhere (Obeng-Odoom, 2020c).

According to *The Economist* (2020p, p. 7), migration is 'a powerful tool that can lift up the poor, rejuvenate rich countries and spread new ideas around the world'. These claims permeate the newspaper. Lead stories on migration are quite common in the paper, as are special reports on migration. 'A Plan for Europe's Refugees: How to Manage the Migrant Crisis and Keep Europe from Tearing Itself Apart' (*The Economist*, 2016, pp. 9–10, 19–22) is one such article. 'Locked Out: When and How to Let Migrants Move Again' (*The Economist*, 2020p) is another. Between January and June 2020, during which time COVID-19 was declared a pandemic, *The Economist* has undergone three phases. During the first, the newspaper continuously emphasized the benefits of markets over the state. 'Markets can fail, but the state is more prone to failure' is a commonly argued position in the newspaper.

Like mainstream economists, in fact, that is the official position of the newspaper (Gottlieb, 2019). 'The Horrible Housing Blunder', a lead story in January 2020, excoriated the visible hand of the state in housing provision (*The Economist*, 2020a). This was followed by 'Big Tech's $2trn Bull Run' (*The Economist*, 2020b), extolling the beneficence of market regulation for technology, finance, and urban development. In the second phase, *The Economist* signalled a possible pandemic. 'It's Going Global' (*The Economist*, 2020c) is how the newspaper announced it. Economic questions were next raised, leading to a vigorous discussion about 'The Right Medicine for the World Economy' (*The Economist*, 2020d), 'The Politics of Pandemics' (*The Economist*, 2020e), and the economic consequences of closure under the caption, 'Closed' (*The Economist*, 2020f). As soon as *The Economist* declared 'The Next Calamity' (*The Economist*, 2020g), it also started focusing more strongly on the poorer nations. I have reviewed the newspaper's coverage of Africa elsewhere (Obeng-Odoom, 2020a), but not phase three of *The Economist's* coverage on migration, which highlights the conditions of internal and international migrants from the Global South.

In this third phase, too, migrants continue to be discussed, but mainly as part of a broad range of topics: 'The Business of Survival: How COVID-19 Will Shape Global Commerce' (*The Economist*, 2020i); 'The 90% Economy' (*The Economist*, 2020k); 'A Grim Calculus' (*The Economist*, 2020h, pp. 39–40); 'Seize the Moment' (*The Economist*, 2020l, pp. 25–26); 'Your Country Needs Me: A Pandemic of Power Grabs' (*The Economist*, 2020j, pp. 25–26); 'Locked Out: When and How to Let Migrants Move Again' (*The Economist*, 2020p). These stories are suffused with orthodox economic analyses. They dominate the 'Europe' and 'Asia' sections, as well as the columns on 'Middle East and Africa' in the newspaper.

The Economist's views on the causes and effects of migration are cast in economic theory. Migration arises from individual choices, from a 'tragedy of the commons' (Hardin, 1968, 1974, 1993) in which a rational, self-interested, or optimizing motive-driven individual or household migrates for either real or perceived opportunities (Todaro, 1969; Todaro and Smith, 2006) that are greater than those prevailing at the source of migration. The process is, therefore, cast within an individual-centred calculus of 'push and pull factors' (Ravenstein, 1885, 1889) that combine to address the 'tragedy of the commons' (Hardin, 1968). The emigration process is selective, competitive, and expensive. However, for-profit traffickers, vloggers, and migration consultants provide information and advice that reduce the transaction costs (Williamson, 2009; *The Economist*, 2020o, p. 29, 2020p, pp. 41–42). The emigrants can be legal or illegal, voluntary or involuntary, but either way, migration is a journey from a place of poverty to a place of plenty.

Economic growth in this land of opportunity is limitless. As noted by *The Economist*, '[t]he idea that more migrants means fewer jobs for locals in the long run is an example of the fallacy that the economy has a fixed "lump of labour" … Migrants bring a greater diversity of skills to the workforce, allowing the labour market as a whole to operate more efficiently' (*The Economist*, 2020p, p. 7). This win–win 'land of opportunity' is devoid of structural long-term discrimination. Like Gary Becker's human capital theory, nations which discriminate against migrants, much like employers in Becker's theory (Becker, 1962), will eventually diminish in the global market of nations because it will be too costly for them to be competitive without accepting cheap migrant labour.

Not only would such nations or employers deprive themselves of cheaper workers, but they also would irrationally set themselves up to pay for more expensive local workers. If there is any lingering discrimination, it must come from the workers in the receiving countries (for a detailed critical discussion of human capital theory, see Darity and Mason, 1998; Stilwell, 2019, Chapter 6; Obeng-Odoom, 2020b, Chapter 4). While temporary society-wide discrimination is acknowledged, *The Economist* contends, like Milton Gordon, the eminent assimilation theorist (see Gordon, 1964), that this discrimination is trivial, or, to use Gordon's exact term, 'extrinsic' (Gordon, 1964, pp. 78–79). If unemployment exists or persists for migrants, it must be because of either information asymmetry in the job search process or a function of migrants' lack of human capital. Therefore, migrant unemployment is both frivolous and frictional (Burnazoglu, 2021). It arises from ignorance of other cultures, lack of opportunities to interact, and the lack of assimilation through intermarriage (Gordon, 1964, pp. 80–81). Extrinsic dis-crimination systematically declines when one's accent, for example, becomes more similar to the dominant accent in the host country. Where there has been evidence of migrant success, *The Economist* (2019d, p. 9) attributes this achievement to in-creasing human capital, including the growing ability of migrants to speak English 'very well'.

Like Gordon's theory of assimilation, *The Economist* prioritizes migrant con-formity. According to *The Economist* (2016, p. 10), 'so long as they are allowed to work, refugees assimilate and more than pay for themselves'. In contrast to 'melting pot' arguments that 'migrants' ways of life need to be encouraged to interpenetrate those of residents', this exclusive penetration thesis holds that migrants need to integrate or assimilate to be accepted. A relic of the eugenics movement, this the-ory is not overtly racist, but it covertly suggests that certain races need to *improve* to be included. As with Gordon's assimilation theory, migrants go through stages of assimilation (Gordon, 1964, pp. 70–71). The '[c]hange of cultural patterns to those of [the] host society' is a fundamental first step in Gordon's theory. This acculturation must lead to a second step: the '[l]arge-scale entrance into cliques, clubs, and institutions of [the] host society, on [the] primary group level'. Stage three is amalgamation or '[l]arge-scale intermarriage'. Identificational assimilation is stage four. Here, there is '[d]evelopment of [a] sense of people-hood based ex-clusively on [the] host society'. Stage five is a thorough process of embracing the new society. Gordon states it simply as an '[a]bsence of prejudice. Attitude recep-tional assimilation.' The final two stages point to total assimilation in the form of behavioural assimilation and surrender to civic assimilation. There should be no discrimination beyond this point.

This 'liberal theory of race', as *The Economist* (2020n) recently called it, is individualistic, atomistic, and idealistic. The theory 'asserts the dignity of the in-dividual and the legal, civil and moral equality of all people, whatever the colour of their skin. It believes in progress through argument and debate, in which rea-son and empathy lift truthful ideas and marginalize bigotry and falsehood' (*The Economist*, 2020n, p. 7). This liberalism explicitly questions more materialist con-ceptions of racism as power. Rather, it conceives of the root of racism as ignorance, so its redress is education and wider human capital development. 'Liberalism thrives on a marketplace of ideas, so diversity has a vital role … Liberalism does not fight power with power … Instead it uses facts and evidence, tested in debate, to help the weak take on the strong' (*The Economist*, 2020n, p. 7). Steeped in the ideology that it is equality of opportunity alone that matters, this liberal view of race is explicitly against affirmative action.

What the liberal view advocates is 'economic policies that improve opportu-nity. You do not need to build a state based on identity. Nor do you need tools like reparations' (*The Economist*, 2020n, p. 7). Within this liberalism, the past is history; it is dead and gone. Reference to it is all 'discourse' within 'the new ideology of race' (*The Economist*, 2020n, p. 7). What is needed, instead, is to deal with the here and now through more growth. 'Economic policies that are race-neutral, which people qualify for because of poverty, not the colour of their skin, can make a big difference' (*The Economist*, 2020n, p. 7). Integration must be based on more marketization. Preferable steps, as *The Economist* (2020n, pp. 8 and 15) sees them, include using rent-assistance vouchers to ensure inclusion in housing markets, offering financial advice to the poor to teach them to manage their resources, and putting the poor in schools where they are taught the geometry of growth and the arithmetic of opportunity. The goal is to help migrants and minorities. The strategy is to break through the race wall that blocks out the potential of migrants.

Within this framework of causes, effects, and integration, migration policy must obey *The Economist's* four golden rules (*The Economist*, 2019d, pp. 15–16). First, walls are needed. They enable nations to bargain with migrants. Second, migrants are temporary workers. They are not citizens, so make 'it easy for them to work and hard … to claim welfare benefits' (*The Economist*, 2019d, p. 15). Third, only useful migrants, such as those who have the ability to assimilate, those who can pay for auctioned visas, and those who can be indentured through 'surtaxes to their wages for a period, and transfer the money to citizens', must be allowed to immigrate. Fourth, migrants must trickle, not flood in.

These rules are liberal, not nativist. *The Economist* might share aspects of the 'tragedy of the commons' diagnosis of the migration crisis proposed by Garrett Hardin (1968), but not Hardin's specious eugenics. According to this spurious science, the diversity migration introduced into society undermines national unity and can incentivize greater breeding among inferior races (Hardin, 1968, 1974, 1991, 1993). Such concerns contrast with *The Economist's* more liberal position, which can be summarized in its rules of migration and many other articles published in the newspaper (see, e.g., *The Economist*, 2020h, pp. 39–40, 2020j, pp. 9–10, 15, 18–19, 25–26, 2020l, pp. 25–26). *The Economist* presents migration as a solution to the long-term crisis of capital. Widely articulated, this migration paradigm constitutes a major orthodoxy, reflecting the confluence of conservative, humanist, and progressive thinking, infused with traces of libertarianism (see, e.g., Somin, 2020).

Consider, for example, the ultimate libertarian body of thought: the highly influential school of public choice economics pioneered by James Buchanan. This field reserves for migrants, blacks in particular, the position of 'untouchables' (Wilkerson, 2020). They can be seen, but never as equals. Founded in large part to challenge the US Supreme Court decision in *Brown v. Board of Education* (1954) to allow the integration of black people into public schools, public choice analysis promotes assimilation or segregation, not multiculturalism and certainly not cosmopolitanism. By supporting private education (because private providers cannot be compelled to admit black people and migrants), public choice analysis is also supportive of landlords (MacLean, 2017). As servants of the landlord class, migrants, especially blacks, must at all times be allowed to work.

To obtain landed property, however, markets must be allowed to decide through market exchange. If that happens, property becomes a guarantee for the individual liberty of migrants (Buchanan, 1993), but the process cannot be forced. This 'calculus of consent' (Buchanan and Tullock, 1962) is a win–win situation, clearly blurring the distinction between liberalism and libertarianism (see, e.g., Somin, 2020). In essence, the two philosophies are on a spectrum: from right wing to new right, from wet to dry right (Stilwell, 2006, pp. 71–72), but they share the same umbilical cord. These analyses also raise questions about the progressive case. Humanists support migration for more humane reasons, but so do liberals. Either way, migration is seen as a response to opportunities. Whereas *The Economist* (2019a, p. 10), a liberal institution, writes, '[t]o get richer, leave your village', humanists, or even progressives, might well say 'to progress, migrate'.

Progress

Critical of their dominant migration paradigm, GPE sees the purported progress in the 'land of opportunity' thesis of liberals as lands of contradictions. Henry George based his original theory of migration on the Irish migration experience (George, 1883/1966, Chapter IX). So did *The Economist* (Zevin, 2019, pp. 44–49). The Irish case study must be taken seriously for this reason. My previous analysis (Obeng-Odoom, 2017b) must also be updated. George first looked at the structural reasons for the forced migration of the Irish. He went beyond describing the Irish famine, being keener to examine its social and political-economic foundations. Next, he examined the conditions in the host country (the US), to where many Irish moved. Then he offered his major recommendation about land and liberation. People should be free to move. There is one earth for all. However, true liberation comes when private property in land, both in the origin and at the destination of migrants, is abolished, while property in the products of labour is guaranteed.

For GPE, widespread migration is partly driven, and particularly sustained by land concentration and the enslavement of labour. As George pointed out in *Social Problems* (George, 1883/1966, Chapter IX), the monopolization of land in Ireland was at the root of the Irish problem. A few people had captured Irish land. Not only were they extracting rent from tenants, they were also hoarding land from the Irish. Galloping rents kept swallowing wages. Workers were left both frustrated and impoverished. The reward for work—the wage—itself was the target of so much taxation that, coupled with the growing rent, workers became more indebted. Most had to migrate from richer to poorer areas, from safer to more hazardous locations. The British Establishment was adamant that the visible hand of the state could not be used to support the struggling Irish population. *The Economist* was critical of any attempt to mitigate the problem through intervention. For the newspaper and its politically well-connected editors, the principle was to let the market decide (Zevin, 2019, pp.44–49). Facing death and deprivation, with voice silenced, the Irish had only one option: insurrection.

The British colonizers colluded with the landed elite to prepare a response and the two-fold strategy was to ensure that the interest of the landed elite was protected. The first strategy was to invest in the army to hold down protest. For *The Economist,* 'laissez-faire may best be furthered through the barrel of the gun' (Zevin, 2019, p. 51). The second strategy was 'to effect large scale emigration out of Ireland' (Zevin, 2019, p. 51). To support this plan, *The Economist* and its editor were key in disseminating it, by playing the role of central outlet, preparing the mind and consciousness of the public on the plan, explaining the plan when it was eventually publicized, and attacking its critics (Zevin, 2019, pp. 46–47). The British state considered giving some little 'aid' to the poor, but *The Economist* kept up the pressure to maintain principle over practice. Free trade was enough. 'No forgiveness was to be shown to small tenants unable to pay rent, or who faced starvation if they did' (Zevin, 2019, p. 45). What support was given aided the two-pronged plan, namely to impose martial law if the poor resisted and to ensure that those who could bear the hardship no longer emigrated to America (Zevin, 2019, pp. 44–48). The prospect of 'greener pastures' in the US looked good for both the migrants and the authorities. However, the social dynamics that gave rise to the Irish problems also plagued the US.

For George, therefore, the Irish had become 'human garbage' (George, 1883/1966). He gave two reasons to illustrate the point. First, population increase from migration would force land rent to escalate. This does not mean that migration worsens rent; rather, private property in land creates the condition for rising rents. Second, the Irish problem would enable some Irish landlords to benefit twice over. Rents from Ireland constituted one aspect; economic rent from the US another. Without doing anything about private property in land or improving the long-term conditions of labour, the migrants would be worse off either way.

GPE is distinct in that its policy focus is the granting of permanent migrant status. Guaranteeing full migrant rights at work is another policy and extending social protection to migrants is a third. GPE turns the attention to structural contradictions about rent, value, and wealth. The destination for migrants is, indeed, a land of contradictions. Only their redress can guarantee true liberty for migrants; not seeking to focus on assimilation processes, for example.

Like all schools of political economy, GPE has its critics. Michael Hudson (2008) has documented the twelve most common criticisms, ranging from GPE's apparently unconditional support for free trade to its history of popularity on the streets, rather than in academic circles. GPE is typically regarded as narrow and its emphasis on land is usually seen to be marginal. Georgist political economists tend to respond by diagnosing the source of the critique and probing whether it arises from ignorance, vested interests, or institutional bias. They offer either clarification, criticism, or a counter-punch. However, whether this strategy is effective is a moot point.

Many of the biases against GPE are indeed partisan or born from ignorance, yet, GPE requires reconstruction in many respects. Even with migration, it is striking that GPE tends to neglect many pressing serious concerns. Overlooking race, oversimplifying the changing role of the state, and overstating the promise of migrant entrepreneurship are some examples (Beck, 2012; Pullen, 2014; Obeng-Odoom, 2017b). Initially, George's analysis was explicitly racist (George, 1935/2006; O'Donnell, 2015; England, 2015). He moved away from this approach, subsequently coming to consider it unscientific. Human beings are 99.9% the same genetically, regardless of race (Bangura and Stavenhagen, 2005, p. 4). Also, race-based analysis undermined George's rent-based theorizing.

Yet, dealing with race by de-emphasizing it and proposing a so-called race-neutral economic policy is also problematic. Overlooking the *colour* of rent is a fundamental weakness of GPE. Race shapes economic processes. Race filters economic outcomes and forms the basis of much economic theorizing (MaClean, 2017; Obeng-Odoom, 2020b, 2021; Darity and Mullen, 2020; Darity, 2021). Whether by James Buchanan or John Locke, theories of property were carefully crafted to privilege a predominantly white landed elite. They were also intended to keep racial minorities, especially black people, in their place. The global history of slavery, Jim Crow, and modern capitalism illustrates the point (Hamilton, 2018; Darity and Mullen, 2020). They also shape migration processes.

This systemic process of social stratification applies not just to land, but also to labour and capital. In the interest of maintaining profit, the leisure of the '1%' and the comfort of the middle-class, minority racial groups who seek decent work are sidelined. The typical argument of employers is cultural, usually suggesting that particular minorities (e.g., African-Americans and indigenous people) do not desire to work 'hard' enough compared to others (e.g., recent African migrants). This comparison is flawed, however: the typical African who migrates is not comparable to the African-American who does not. S/he is more similar to African-Americans who move internally or internationally (Hamilton, 2018). Moreover, particular highly selective programmes take Africans to America and elsewhere. These migrants tend to have substantially different experiences, which cannot be compared to features in the generalized host residents. Indeed, migrants who are employed might accept the advertised conditions because some work is better than no work.

However, their children have to contend with ever-lowering floors because newer migrants are induced to offer their labour more cheaply. With this process, too, migrants have much less protection against abuse. This process reflects class differentiation among migrant labour, but it goes beyond Marxist constructions (Rosewarne, 2020a, 2020b). Rather, it reflects a racialized class structure whose institutionalization has created a *racialized* and *intergenerational* migrant. The racial composition of this class of migrants shifts over space and time. According to Gerald Jaynes:

> Southern African Americans outperformed northern-born Blacks; when southern rural migration dried up in 1970, Blacks began losing jobs to Puerto Ricans from the Islands, who later passed the baton to South East Asians, who in turn were losing to Mexican and Central American migrants as the twentieth century neared its end.
>
> (Jaynes, 2007, p. 14)

That is the position in the US and the Americas, but the process can be found in Europe and Australia, too. If claiming to be relevant, GPE can neither neglect nor relegate these matters.

Much is required of the state in GPE, but its state theorizing is undeveloped. If states are to be the vehicle for radical reform by introducing comprehensive land taxation, perhaps even replacing other taxes on incomes going to labour and capital to create the well-known Georgist single tax, it asks a lot of states, both in the Global North and the Global South to engage in comprehensive fiscal reform. Do they have the requisite will and capacity? Even if a state has both, it is unclear in what ways it would be possible to confront the kinds of resistance the class of landlords are likely to put up. Can all these be addressed by the Georgist theory of the state (Petrella, 1984)?

The current state theorizing within GPE is limited. It is pertinent to note that the modern state is typically an avenue where *institutional racism* can be transmitted through the assessment and execution of land value tax, as well as the provision of public services (Bangura and Stavenhagen, 2005; Bangura, 2006). This implies a different structure to GPE's *assumed* social state. Institutions, such as colonial programmes, that shape where migrants settle are also overlooked or over-simplified in GPE and nor does GPE consider the hierarchy of states in the global order (England, 2015, pp. 134–135). Giving so little attention to this hierarchy is a significant weakness.

The political economy of small businesses has usually received much more attention in GPE (see, e.g., George, 1898/1992, Chapter 6). Yet, little can be found on migrant business, migrant entrepreneurship, and innovation in the process of economic development, although these themes are central to the study of migrant economic strategy to counter structural barriers (Collins et al., 1995; Collins, 2016). The theme is also at the heart of methodological debates about how to explain the outcomes of migrant businesses (Wang and Warn, 2018). Neglecting the political economy of migrant businesses, including their creation and operation, is therefore questionable, so is downplaying the importance of innovation among migrants and creativity within migrant communities.

Also, critics (see, for example, Chandra, 2021) of GPE typically represent it as too narrowly focused because of its central concern with the land question. Henry George himself was confronted with this charge. He developed a systematic response in many publications, including *Protection or Free Trade* (George, ([1886] 1991). However, in 'The Crime of Poverty', he illustrated his position with an anecdote, based on a conversation between two people, one of whom considered the 'money question' more fundamental, saying:

> The money question is a very important question; it is a more important question than the land question. You give me all the money, and you can take all the land… [Responding to this, his] friend said: Well, suppose you had all the money in the world and I had all the land in the world. What would you do if I were to give you notice to quit (George, 1885)?

Modern Georgists tend to respond to criticisms of their focus on land by diagnosing the source of the critique, and probing whether it arises from ignorance, vested interest or institutional bias. In response, they typically offer clarification or a counter punch. However, whether such responses have been effective is an open question. Generally, GPE requires more work on its analysis of institutions, structural racism, and global economic development.

Institutions

Georgist political economy (GPE) can be reconstructed as institutional economics. Doing so is analytically feasible. Henry George's *Moses* (George, 1884) addressed itself to institutions. As George himself noted, '[i[t is true that institutions make men, but it is also true that in the beginnings men make institutions' (George, 1884, p. 3). Perhaps, GPE has become overly focused on Henry George who, like Moses, advocated certain institutions. Those Georgists who focused, instead, on institutions more widely founded a larger field of liberation, namely institutional economics. These economists engaged GPE, but they also criticized aspects of it, and ultimately transcended it and, through careful engagement, they built a much more comprehensive approach. J.R. Commons, for one, a towering figure in institutional economics, owed a clear debt to GPE. As Chasse points out, 'In 1883 John R. Commons … started reading Henry George … It would influence [him]' (Chasse, 2017, p. 1). Not only did GPE influence him, but 'he became an annoying true believer' (Chasse, 2017, p. 27), so much so that he and others 'organized a Henry George club' (Chasse, 2017, p. 27).

Even though Commons was later to broaden the examination of 'the problem' from the singular focus on land and, hence, to consider a range of other institutions and their redesign as possible solutions, Commons always attributed his decision to side with workers to Henry George (Chasse, 2017, p. 1). Therein lies an intriguing aspect of GPE: its biggest political base in George's days was among workers, including migrant labour. Indeed, it was the study of migration that became the foundation of J.R. Commons's institutional economics (for a review of this history, see Obeng-Odoom, 2018c). R.T. Ely was also a critical admirer of GPE (Obeng-Odoom, 2016b, p. 176). Ely (1914, pp. 14–16) contended that the tendency by Georgist political economists to attribute to labour all its wage could overlook the debt of labour to others, including women who create the conditions of social provisioning for workers. Many contemporary institutional economists, such as Frank Stilwell (see, e.g., Stilwell, 2016, 2019), also suggest other ways of developing GPE.

Institutional economics itself needs broadening out. Liberty and liberation entail more than what institutional economics was founded to support. Research in border studies and planning (see, e.g., Anderson, 2013; Mezzadra, 2013; Jones, 2016; de Genova, 2017; Green, 2018; Vickers, 2019) provides avenues for fruitful engagement and departure. As Table 3.1 shows, this body of work on migration has much in common with institutional economics. Border and planning scholars have much to teach economists, too.

Research in border studies (e.g., Anderson, 2013; Mezzadra, 2013; Jones, 2016; de Genova, 2017; Green, 2018; Vickers, 2019; see, for a discussion, Oliveri, 2014; Fabini, 2015; Sager, 2016; Simonneau, 2017; Lemberg-Pedersen, 2018), focusing on multiple identities, is an obvious point of similarity, as is its challenge of current mainstream analyses and policies of migration. Its insights on borders, meanings, and implications are valuable, both for citizens and non-citizens, and so is its creative and penetrating critique of humanistic approaches to migration centred on 'communities of values' (Anderson, 2013). Such 'communities', however, are premised on the erroneous view that merely becoming a citizen assures inclusion in society without carefully considering continuing legal and political-economic barriers faced by dual citizens (Aleinikoff and Klusmeyer, 2000; *Asare vs Attorney General*, 2012). The theoretical floodlights border studies provide on identities, the multiple meanings of walls and borders, and the stronger and sustained links between borders, walls, colonialism, neo-colonialism, racism, and territorialization can strengthen institutional economics generally because institutional economics can, classically formulated, be quite complicit in eugenics.

Accepting these insights, then, is a strength of institutional economics that can be developed. Institutional economics has its own distinctive features, as Table 3.1 shows. Consider, for example, its unit and scale of analysis, its concept of the state and the public, and its vision. The 'trans-action' or, generally, interactions constitute the bedrock of the old institutional economics approach to analysis. This dialectical engagement cuts within and across scales. In this sense, a critical view of the state is similar to that which is utilized in border studies. However, not only

Table 3.1 Other migration studies vs institutional economics

Analytical paradigms	Border studies	Planning	Institutional economics
Unit and scale of analysis	Borders and walls, usually at the transnational scale	Planning processes, usually at the local scale	Multi-scalar transactions
Outlook on current migration/migration policy, and vision for the future	Critical outlook on current mainstream migration policies because they are violent, territorializing, and supportive of capital; positive vision of a borderless, nationless world	Critical outlook on current migration and migration policies because migrants create 'communities of value' (Anderson, 2013, quite similar to humanistic concerns); not necessarily more migration but, if there is, it must add to the 'communities of value'	Critical outlook on current migration/migration policies because they diverge from their expressed vision, they exacerbate social problems, divert attention from their key driver, and, hence, extend and recreate structural problems in the world economy. Its vision for an alternative world is inclusivity, much like the border studies approach. There are, though, significant differences, including (a) the role of the state; (b) the place of land, and the nature of capital and labour; and (c) the evolution of the 'public' into the 'public-commons' milieu.
Identity	Multiple identities	Multiple identities	Multiple identities
The state	Largely a critique of government, the legislature, and the media, with many advocating the demise of the nation-state, sometimes close to anarchy	Largely a positive view of the Weberian state, particularly the government and the legislature	An evolutionary and historical critique of the state (legislature, executive, media, judiciary) that recognizes that the state could simultaneously be a source of danger and potential, depending on the balance of interests that constitutes it and the actions and inactions of the other institutions that constitute 'collective action'. This concerted action is also shaped by the nature of the individuals who make up the states. However, such individuals are not selfish, 'free agents', who are simply rent-seeking, as claimed by public choice theorists, but instead they demonstrate the diversity of the 'institutionalized mind'.

Continued

Table 3.1 *Continued*

Analytical paradigms	Border studies	Planning	Institutional economics
Public	Pursuit of inclusive multiple identities	Pursuit of 'communities of value'	Pursuit of inclusive multiple identities and an evolving symbiosis between the 'public' and the 'commons'
Relationship to postcolonialism	Adoption of current trends in postcolonialism which focus on the politics of colonialism, not the much older tradition of political economy	Little or limited engagement	Adapts institutional economics to postcolonialism such that the institutional political economy becomes postcolonial. In the tradition of the earlier work of political economists such as Walter Rodney (1972/2011), but with a focus on wider questions about institutions.

Source: author's summary vis-à-vis the proposed reconstruction of GPE as institutional economics.

does the institutionalism canvassed here problematizes the idea of the state used, especially in border studies, but also a much wider, and more coherent view of the state is proposed. In GPE, the state is considered a potential source of 'trouble', but it could also be a vehicle for progress. Granted that the state is the site of much trouble, why do a few states support, not reject, migration? The institutional economics proposed in this book considers that the trouble with many states arises not from the state itself (or not always with the state itself), but as a result of the control of the state by dominant interests, locally, globally or both, which rewrite the 'working rules' of the state.

These rules are not harmoniously produced, however. They arise from particular evolving contexts and processes of contests from within the state apparatus (government, legislature, media, and judiciary) but also outside of it internally and internationally . They are the product of 'collective action', which includes 'politics' but also the economy and many other concerns. Frank Stilwell, Australia's leading institutional political economist, once wrote, 'An intermediate construction recognises the need to keep the focus on the whole, but also to emphasise tensions between the parts' (Stilwell, 2006, p. 237). In this analysis, institutional economics probes differentiation but also intersectionalities across the democratic, socialist, capitalist, and bureaucratic aspects of the state at various times. It also investigates the evolution of these intersectionalities (Stilwell, 2006, p. 237). It is from such an analysis, and from relating the state to the world economic system, that the complex nature of the state is established in institutional economics.

Border studies, on the other hand, would usually consider politics, but, as systematic reviews of its key books (e.g., Anderson, 2013; Mezzadra, 2013; Jones, 2016; de Genova, 2017; Vickers, 2019; see, e.g., Oliveri, 2014; Fabini, 2015; Sager, 2016; Simonneau, 2017; Lemberg-Pedersen, 2018), have shown, they tend to neglect economic analyses and the influences of other important institutions. Indeed, its intriguing new 'theory of control tuning' (Niemi, 2018) is centred almost exclusively on the state and its relationship with autonomous individuals. Even in the study of 'sovereignty', greater weight is given to the 'state'. In *Institutional Economics* (1934b/2009), J.R. Commons raised an early institutional economics objection to this approach:

> The meaning of the word 'politics' has usually been limited to the activities designed to get control of what was deemed to be the dominant concern, the State. But with the modern emergence of innumerable forms of economic and moral concerted action, it is found that the similar complexity of personalities, principles, and organizations is found in all concerns. The fact that the sovereign concern uses the sanction of physical force has seemed to give dominance to it, as indicated by the word, 'sovereign'. But this is illusory, since, as we have seen, sovereignty has been the gradual, but incomplete, extraction of violence from private transactions, and other concerns dominate the state.
>
> (Commons, 1934b/2009, p. 751)

The idea in border studies that the current reaction to migration trends is 'capitalist' is also quite incoherent. The current state of the nation-state across the world is far more plural and represents a field of contest of competing interests, rather than simple pro- or anti-capitalism. No doubt there is quite a general problematic gaze of the state on migration, but the problem is not just about profit-based capitalism, which is the key emphasis of border studies. Even within capitalism, growing profits, while worthy of attention, could soar even more, should the vision of migration as a kind of compensation for colonialism (championed by some border scholars such as Joseph Nevins, e.g., Nevins, 2019) be realized. So, the approach to the state in border studies is not always coherent.

In contrast, the approach to the state that I propose is much wider, far more coherent, and far more nuanced. I propose to include other institutions such as the market, the church, and the university along with *their web of relationships*. Within the notion of the state, I am also interested in probing other sub-institutions, such as the army and property rights. My focus, even within the (nation-) state, is not only centred on capital and labour, but also on land, labour, and capital and their internal relationships such that not only profit and wages are important concepts but also land rent and how it is shaped by diverse state rules and rules established and implemented elsewhere, both locally and globally.

Unlike border and planning studies, with their undeveloped theories of the relationship between the state, other institutions, and individuals, original institutionalists have carefully considered this mosaic of relations by recognizing that individuals who constitute the actors in the state are neither without blemish (the position often taken in planning studies), nor always rent seeking (as is usually argued in public choice theory), nor insignificant (which is the implication of border studies, some of which can be quite inflexible and structuralist in their claims). Rather, in my proposed alternative, both the individuals and their combinations matter for the operation of the state—but not just as free-standing, selfish individuals. Rather, these individuals reflect and create what J.R. Commons (1924) called 'the institutionalized mind', which was his way of calling attention to individuals as *social* and evolutionary beings, whose so-called 'free' choices shape and are shaped by other social forces and institutions. This crucial idea throws light on the institutional economics position on *agency* and, hence, requires a full quotation:

> If it be considered that, after all, it is the individual who is important, then the individual with whom we are dealing is the Institutionalized Mind. Individuals begin as babies. They learn the custom of language, of cooperation with other individuals, of working towards common ends, of negotiations to eliminate conflicts of interest, of subordination to the working rules of the many concerns of which they are members. They meet each other, not as physiological bodies moved by glands, nor as 'globules of desire' moved by pain and pleasure, similar to the forces of physical and animal nature, but as prepared more or less by habit, artificial transactions created by the collective human will. They are not found in physics, or biology, or subjective psychology, or in the German Gestalt psychology, but are found where conflict, interdependence, and order among human beings are preliminary to getting a living. Instead of individuals the participants are forces of a going concern. Instead of forces of nature they are forces of human nature. Instead of isolated individuals in a state of nature they are always participants in transactions, members of a concern in which they come and go, citizens of an institution that lived before them and will live after them.
>
> (Commons, 1934a/2009, pp. 73–74)

These nuances suggest that, while the institutional economics approach to migration recognizes agency and the potential of using state action positively, this optimism is conditional and contingent. J.R. Commons and many other institutionalists, including R.T. Ely, Thorstein Veblen, Gunnar Myrdal, and K.W. Kapp, acknowledge that individual action can be constrained and even manipulated, and the state can be problematic. J.K. Galbraith, for instance, provided a sustained critique and wide demonstration of these possibilities, while maintaining that the state is in no way perpetually held hostage by them. Instead, he held that, based on reworking institutional configurations, the state could transform or be transformed (see, e.g., Galbraith, 1956, 1958/1998, 1973, 1977, 1979; for commentaries on Galbraith and the common themes in the wider original institutional economics approach to the state, see Stilwell, 2006, pp. 207–244, 355–363; Berry, 2013; Klimina, 2018). Framed as part of the question of power, this approach to questioning the state is far more dynamic, recognizing that there are usually contending and contrasting multi-scalar forces within and around the state that shape and are shaped by it.

Analytically, this complex 'collective action', or 'concerted action', as J.R. Commons called it (Commons, 1934b/2009, p. 753), is more nuanced. It implies that change and continuity comes not just from the state (the planning studies view), nor just from anarchy (the border studies view), class (the Marxist, structuralist view), or from individual actions and market forces (the neoclassical economics views), but from a diversity of sources and their collision or cooperation. Nevertheless, the strength of a nuanced and multifaceted approach can also pose a difficulty for systematic investigation because analysing complexity can appear messy. Still, institutional economics provides one way of doing precisely so, an approach which Commons characterized as 'the method of analysis, genesis, and insight'. At the general level, Commons argued:

> The method of analysis consists in breaking up the complexity into all the supposed similarities of behavior, and then giving to each similarity a name which designates it as a proposed scientific principle to be tested by investigation. The method of genesis consists in the discovery of changes which have occurred in the past as explanations of why the present situation exists as it is. The method of insight consists in understanding the ways of leadership and followship.
>
> (Commons, 1934b/2009, p. 753)

Within this broad framework, specific methods for particular questions can be developed.

There are, however, a few cross-cutting themes. Consider gender and race. Much has been written about 'the feminization of migration'. The modest contribution this book makes to this approach in this respect is partly to further illustrate this trend (see Chapter 4), stressing its multiple characteristics, partly to attempt to show how it intersects with race, ethnicity, class, rent, and wage employment, as well as how it simultaneously coincides with and diverges from discrimination against men, discrimination against white women, men and women combined, and migrant women of diverse races. Kimberlé Crenshaw has long established the value of this analysis (Crenshaw, 1989, 1991). More particularly, this book tries to point out the institutional roots of the feminization of migration. By this intersectional approach, institutions too are, therefore, a recurrent point of conceptual reference, as is the range of approaches in economics that has become the defining ways of analysing migration.

The economy is a second cross-cutting issue. Neoclassical economists typically consider the economy to be a separate sphere of exchange and organization, different and distinct from the environment and society. In this view, firms are competitive, profit-maximizing units that are mere price takers. They are not discriminatory because discrimination is too costly. Entrepreneurship and innovation arise from individual initiatives without any systematic institutional and social provisioning. Incentives are purely based on the individual who seeks to maximize utility and the firm that seeks profit. Profit is upheld because it drives growth, which, in turn, drives wider social, even beneficial, environmental outcomes. Hence, following these views, limitless (green) growth is advocated. There is no place to address systematic institutional reprogramming to address discrimination and racism.

Institutional economics is more evolutionary, more comprehensive, and more ecological in its conception of the economy. As I have argued elsewhere (Obeng-Odoom, 2016b, 2020b, 2021), the emphasis is on wider economy–ecology–society linkages, whether these are through mechanisms advocated by Karl Polanyi, Joseph Schumpeter, Henry George, Herman Daly, or K.W. Kapp. Enterprises and entrepreneurship need not be for profit. Some may make profit, but they are not for profit. Social enterprises can flourish without being capitalist or transnational, with residual social programmes being called 'local content' or 'corporate social responsibility'. There is also a clear acceptance that there are 'limits to growth', 'limits to inequality', and limits to 'the right to work', a historically used tactic for continuing growth ad infinitum.[1] The redistribution of work, equal work, quality, and

---

[1] This alternative conception of entrepeneurship, either of mini capitalists or big corporations, is common in neoclassical versions of institutional economics called 'new institutional economics'. Its central contention is that private property rights or clear property rights that can be exchanged at low (or no) transaction costs are crucial for businesses to flourish, for innovation to thrive, and for individual freedom to prosper. In this field, work in the informal economy is primarily business for profit, so small entrepreneurs are, or should be, seeking profit. Growth ad infinitum continues to be its core concern. Private property is the path for clean green growth. The advocates are Hernando de Soto, Oliver Williamson, Ronald Coase, Terry Anderson, Gary Libecap, Armen Alchian, and Harold Demsetz. *The Economist* is also a trenchant advocate. The reference to institutional economics in this book is to the so-called 'old institutionalists', who should properly be called the 'original institutionalists', such as R.T. Ely, J.R. Commons, Gunnar Myrdal, Joseph Schumpeter, K.W. Kapp, and J.K. Galbraith. We can also include J.M. Keynes and Henry George, both of whom founded their own schools of economics.

socially useful work are some of the key demands in the institutional economics approach.

There is a need to analyse 'the ideology of unwanted jobs', too. As Gerald Jaynes (2007, p. 6) has argued, doing so could entail asking two critical questions. First, what is the racial identity of the most marginalized migrants? How has their race, interlinked with other identities, contributed to their marginalization? In what ways is there a 'race to the bottom'? These questions ought to be addressed within the context of the many similarities between global slavery and global migration, which creates a race to the bottom. 'Each new migrant cohort which finds the wages and working conditions of the host nation preferable to the conditions they left behind displaces the children of previous cohorts' (Jaynes, 2007, p. 13). This process hurts migrants as a whole because, even in the short-run, the implications of this race to the bottom are corrosive. Migrants cannot obtain effective legal protections from exploitation and they cannot directly benefit from policies, either.

Clearly, then, insights from border and planning studies, together with postcolonial and feminist studies, percolate the approach of this book. They do not, however, define the book's own transdisciplinary political-economic methodological and ontological orientation situated in institutional economics. Existing books develop more anthropological, planning, or geographical, but not economic analyses of migration, as many reviewers have pointed out (see, e.g., Oliveri, 2014; Fabini, 2015; Sager, 2016; Simonneau, 2017; Lemberg-Pedersen, 2018).

The analyses developed in these books are precious for the social economics of migration, but their marginalization of political economy raises important tensions. Consider the vision of a borderless world championed in border studies (see, e.g., Anderson, 2013; Mezzadra, 2013; Jones, 2016; de Genova, 2017; Vickers, 2019). The focus on the rights of migrants is crucial for an inclusive society but, as a few writers in border studies point out, border scholars need not romanticize what the extension of citizenship to migrants can do because many subjects are the victims of much discrimination. Such analysis could help to strengthen the proposed approach, but the contradictions of 'communities of value' (Anderson, 2013) do not end at the borders of discrimination; they transcend and undermine them.

Some examples can illustrate the point further. Even if all migrants were included with full and equal rights accorded to citizens of value, would the contradictions end? Border studies suggest so; the rest of the book suggests not. Materialist growthism could generate further contradictions that non-economic analyses find difficult to appreciate. There are many books that provide such economic analyses, but the particular economic analysis to be developed in the proposed framework constitutes the third important cross-cutting distinction.

Instead of *sudden change*, this framework relies on the concept of *cumulative change*. It is an idea which is common to the work of institutional economists such as J.R. Commons, Thorstein Veblen, and Gunnar Myrdal, developed, respectively, in *Myself* (Commons, 1934c/1964), *Absentee Ownership* (Veblen, 1923/2009), and *An American Dilemma* (Myrdal, 1944).

Yet, as stratification economists and analysts (e.g., Cox, 1945; Darity, 1982, 1995; Hamilton, 2018; Darity and Mullen, 2020) have noted, institutionalism has either no general theory of race with respect to global migration or, when it provides one, it is usually problematic. Consider Gunnar Myrdal's celebrated book on the subject (Myrdal, 1944). While widely acclaimed, the book struggles with developing a robust theory of race, along with many other problems. Four are particularly serious. First is looking at race without its intersections with class, gender, ethnicity, colour, and caste. Second is reducing racism to beliefs and attitudes, suggesting racial consciousness elevates racial minorities in the class hierarchy. Third is considering economic interests (in those cases when such material interests are the focus of some attention) as secondary or subordinate to so-called 'culture'. A final critique is that institutionalism reduces race to binary, black and white categories. Stratification analysts (Cox, 1945; Darity, 1982, 1995; Darity and Mullen, 2020) try to address these problems in three ways. First, they emphasise that identities are omnipresent and diverse and are continuously produced, reproduced, and transformed in the process of migration. Second, they focus on the centrality of economic interests to stratification by, among others, race, colour, caste and other identities, including how they are interlinked. Third, they study major institutional changes about race and the creation of new institutional forms to address problems of identities, including reparation regimes.

Thus, my proposed approach is far more sensitive to social context than the work that privileges free-standing autonomous individuals (neoclassical economics), households (the new economics of labour migration (NELM)), or only class (Marxist economics). If the rules that shape markets and class relations are considered institutions, then this book expands the analyses of existing work and, hence, could at some points be regarded as 'Marxist'. Yet, the new framework does not encourage the typical single story of the Marxist political economy, nor is it that of neoclassical economics, or NELM, even if these are taken seriously. Emphasizing property rights, land, and rents in relation to capital and labour, for example, is not typical of the Marxist analytical approach, which tends to privilege capital because the significance of land is alleged to diminish as capital becomes more advanced, whereas in this book, this Marxist idea is reversed because, as the book tries to demonstrate, land becomes even more significant as societies become more complex. As an *evolutionary* approach, this GIS political-economic orientation of the book is also quite distinct from the Marxist *revolutionary* approach to social change.

Fieldwork data at the micro level are important for my approach, but these data are complemented with macro, meso, and meta data. Unlike existing frameworks, therefore, this proposed reconstruction is methodologically different and much wider in its coverage, investigating the causes, effects, and policies of migration at diverse geographical scales. In terms of scope, too, my approach tries to develop a multi-scalar, multidimensional, and intersectional analysis of migration.

Based on this approach, theorizing is pivotal, but it needs to be complemented by concrete study. In this respect, framing must be matched with empirical, bottom-up attempts to reconstruct the state, understand agency, and address questions about the public, postcolonialism, and migration more widely. In this respect, GPE can expand its framework from land and liberty to land and liberation. Even more widely, questions about new ways in which social change evolves and the state is financed, reframed, and reconstructed can be considered. Doing so signals an expansion of the established frameworks of migration to wider concerns about institutions and beyond, to stratification economics.

Conclusion

This chapter has clarified the nature and methodology of GPE. It has also shown how GPE can be applied and expanded. Fundamentally different from both mainstream and most heterodox economics approaches, GPE offers a novel and radical approach to understanding and transcending global migration crises. The centrality of land to the approach is unmatched in any other school of political economy. However, it should be acknowledged that GPE also has important limitations. The inability to probe *structural* racism is one of them. Limited theorizing of the state is another. More theme-specific limitations abound. With respect to migration, the neglect of entrepreneurship, innovation, and migrant businesses in the process of economic development is glaring.

These weaknesses do not undermine GPE as a school of political economy, but they are serious enough to warrant taking concrete steps with and beyond it. The first step is to forge stronger relations between GPE and other schools of political economy. Original institutional economics is one obvious possibility, as is Marxist political economy (MPE). Neither is particularly strong on postcolonial economic analysis, as I have more systematically discussed elsewhere (Obeng-Odoom, 2018c, 2020b). So, engaging stratification economics, a new and flourishing subfield of political economy at the centre of which is the study of race, can be a second step to reconstruction. A third must lead to even more empirical analysis.

4

Internal Migration

Introduction

Internal migration is substantial, but it is either ignored or considered insignificant in migration studies. When considered, its explanation is caricatured. In Africa, research about internal migration depicts it as simple, not subtle. So, in richer countries such as South Africa, internal migration is deemed rational and the norm (Mulcahy and Kollamparambil, 2016), while in the poorer nations in Africa, internal migration is typically regarded as 'abnormal', especially in terms of rural–urban migration of the youth (for a review, see Obeng-Odoom, 2010a; for an example, see Government of Ghana, 2016, p.6). Yet, as a continent with a relatively youthful population, researching the nuanced experiences of young people and groups should be a priority, at least along with investigating other institutionalised experiences that are caricatured.

What research exists does not typically probe the ecology, economics, and political economy of their migration (see, e.g., Gough and Langevang, 2016; Afutu-Kotey et al., 2017; Amankwaa et al., 2020), however. There is research on street children (see, e.g., UN-HABITAT, 2000; Amankwaa et al., 2020), but these studies specifically focus on children and youth as gangsters involved in pickpocketing and other social vices such as drug use, either because the urban social economies in which the children find themselves provide no means of employment, because of improper upbringing, or because of a breakdown of the children's families. Others provide excellent analysis of the everyday economic activities of the youth, but their focus is not on the intersection of their migrant status, gender, class, and socio-ecological contexts that shape their experiences.

The more theoretical literature can be divided into three themes. Economists strongly favour internal migration as a spatial fix for individual problems of migrants. Charles Tiebout (1956) strongly argued that individual migrants are much better off migrating than remaining when they find their conditions of life worsened by state intervention in economic processes. Many of such economists (e.g., Mulcahy and Kollamparambil, 2016) recognize that there could be some urban problems as a result of internal migration, but such challenges are temporary in their analyses. For example, problems such as short-term separation from family and friends, and behavioural 'problems' induced by false expectations are trivial and transient compared to the benefits of migration.

Primarily because the state is deemed problematic by mainstream economists, their research (Todaro, 1969; Todaro and Smith, 2006, pp. 344–345) contends that the solution to the problem of urban labour migrants is neither urban job generation, nor other forms of state intervention because such uses of state power would *increase* rather than *decrease* the impulse to migrate to cities. Many mainstream economists argue that if more jobs are created in cities, there will be a greater incentive for rural residents to migrate to cities, where they will struggle to find work because of the mismatch between urban jobs and rural skills. So, in the end, more urban jobs will create more urban unemployment. From this perspective, migrants and markets need to be left alone. If there is going to be some support for migrants, mainstream economists contend (see, e.g., Somin, 2020; Book, 2021) that the specific economic interventions must support free markets which, over time, can address any migrant problems through the process of growth and wealth accumulation itself.

In this way, migration is depicted as 'win–win', at least in the long run and within the cost–benefit calculus. Border studies scholars, activists, humanists, and many international non-governmental organizations (NGOs) propose policies which differ from specific economic policies favoured by mainstream economists. However, this win–win trope is ever present in much of the progressive literature, too (see, e.g., Walia, 2021). Apart from putting the case for opening borders whether internal or international, national or global, these transdisciplinary groups of scholars, activists, and practitioners also put the argument for supporting migration as a way of escaping problems, a path for 'helping others', and a sure growth-building process.

Ecologists (Hardin, 1993), ecological economists (Daly, 2019), and some Marxist political economists (e.g., Songsore, 2011), on the other hand, admit that rural–urban migration—like all migration—creates growth, which for Marxists arises from capitalist exploitative relations. But precisely because of this drive for, and actual endless growth, (internal) migration also drives environmental and moral hazard. As trenchantly argued by Hardin (Hardin, 1993) and strongly implied in Kenneth Boulding's (1964) work, more of such migration encourages rural residents to increase breeding, and to perpetuate both growthism and urban giantism. This trend is likely to make cities grow beyond the limits that the earth can comfortably carry. Rural development or 'integrated rural development' is, therefore, a much better policy.

One way to ascertain these contradictory claims is to subject them to empirical investigation. Internal migration in Ghana provides a useful case study for that purpose. The country has long developed a raft of policies, including *National Migration Policy for Ghana* (Government of Ghana, 2016) and what was then a draft *National Urban Policy* (Government of Ghana, 2010a). Other institutions such as the *National Youth Policy* (Government of Ghana, 2010b) and the *National Urban Policy Framework* (Government of Ghana, 2012) exist as a response to substantial internal migration related to ecology, economics, and political economy.

Existing research (Owoo et al., 2020) shows that unemployment and underemployment remain serious national challenges in the country. At the same time, the existing studies on these ecology–economics–political economy phenomena (e.g., Baah-Boateng et al., 2019; Yeboah, 2020) are quite simple. Subtle concepts and theories are not their focus (see, e.g., Tipple and Speak, 2006, 2009; Owusu et al., 2008; Owusu, 2010; Anyidoho and Steel, 2016). Two important publications have sought to address these gaps. These are John Arthur's *Class Formations and Inequality Structures in Contemporary African Migration* (2014) and Vivian Amantana's *A Sociological Study of Street Children in Ghana: Victims of Kinship Breakdown and Rural–Urban Migration* (2012). Arthur introduces class elements, but lacks nuanced empirical content (see Obeng-Odoom, 2016a), while Amantana's research provides detailed empirical insights, but lacks strong class and institutional analyses (see Obeng-Odoom, 2015a). Neither takes institutional economics seriously, nor consistently engages land and stratification economics, although these additional perspectives are crucial to analysing the nature, causes, and effects of internal migration.

This chapter combines the insights from these two major studies and draws on additional sources of existing data within the broad methodology of this book, as described and defended in Chapter 3. The evidence questions all the prevailing positions on migration research.

Neither the decision to migrate, to stay, nor to return is based on individual calculations alone. Socio-ecological reasons loom large in the range of reasons for migration such that migrants are not only simply driving growth and environmental crises, but they are also the product of such crises. Also, it is too simple to attribute migration to capitalist exploitation alone. Similarly, rural poverty does not provide sufficient explanation for rural–urban migration. Instead, 'circular and cumulative processes', shaped by institutional and structural rather than individual and household-based motives, mould internal migration processes. Land and property rights are central in this transformation which raises questions about the claim that urban migration is a panacea for unemployment; much like the categorical contention that urban, migrant-led farming provides the triple win of food security, food sovereignty, and food sustainability.

The experiences of migrants on urban farms and on the streets in urban centres are evidently diverse, but most of them are underemployed. Most intend to return to their origins, but whether they do so, when, and how, is conditioned by the class, ethnicity, gender, and other identities of the migrants (such as whether they are married or single) and changing social institutions, such as land and property rights, which pertain in rural, peri-urban, and urban contexts. For these reasons, policies framed around the assumptions in mainstream analysis of labour migration, such as removing urban bias and enhancing rural development, have merely reinforced the process of uneven and stratified urban and regional development.

The rest of this chapter is divided into four sections. 'Socio-Ecological Migration and the Feminization of Migration' discusses the broad context of internal migration. The sections on 'Urban Farmers' and 'Street Workers' provide exposition of two particular types of internal migration. Finally, 'Explaining Internal Migration: From Individuals, Households, and Structures to Institutions' shifts the discussion from exposition to explanation.

Socio-Ecological Migration and the Feminization of Migration

Many people migrate for socio-ecological reasons. Of these people, farmers from the northern parts of Ghana stand out. They can be called socio-ecological migrants in another respect: many previously worked in environmentally degrading mining activities. As they were made redundant or were laid off, they returned to farming (Abdul-Korah, 2006; Obour et al., 2017), usually a much greener economic activity. Many migrate to farming areas in southern parts of Ghana. Others move into farming in other parts of northern Ghana (Abdul-Korah, 2006; Obour et al., 2017). Generally, the experiences of socio-ecological migrants have been the theoretical battleground for Malthusian and Marxist theories (Abdul-Korah, 2006). The Malthusians have typically claimed or suggested that Northern Ghana is simply overpopulated and migration is a natural response. From this perspective, migration can only worsen the Northern Ghana problem because it sets up negative incentives for the problem to reproduce itself both in the north and in the south. Globally, this dynamic would undermine the carrying capacity of the earth. Population control, from this standpoint, is a much more effective solution (Hardin, 1993). How this control of population or prevention of more population/migration is to be done varies widely, from monetising the right to have children (Boulding, 1964), blocking the right to migration entirely (Hardin, 1993), or giving development aid to prevent people from migrating (Daly, 2019). All these are expected to put 'limits to growth' (Meadows et al., 1972; 2004). Marxists (e.g., Songsore, 2011) have insisted that it is, rather, capitalist colonial economic policies that created the north–south drift. The typical Marxian solution is rather to improve labour conditions, and conditioning, along with curtailing the capitalism inherent in which is the labour question.

Both approaches shed light on the migration question, but they can be nuanced. While the household sizes in the three northern regions of Ghana (Northern, Upper East, and Upper West) are among the highest in Ghana, their rates of decline have been among the fastest in the country, as Table 4.1 shows.

In most cases, the rate of change in the northern regions is more than twice what pertains in the Greater Accra region, a major migrant destination. So, the

Table 4.1 Households in Ghana by region,* 2010–2017

Region	Household size, 2010	Household size, 2016–2017	Rate of change, 2010–2017 (%)	Direction of change
Ghana	4.4	3.8	13.6	–
Western	4.2	3.8	9.5	–
Central	4.0	3.9	2.5	–
Greater Accra	3.8	3.4	10.5	–
Volta	4.2	4.4	4.8	+
Eastern	4.1	3.5	14.6	–
Ashanti	4.1	3.2	22.0	–
Brong Ahafo	4.6	3.9	15.2	–
Northern	7.7	5.8	24.7	–
Upper East	5.8	5.2	10.3	–
Upper West	6.2	4.8	22.6	–

Source: adapted from Ghana Statistical Service (GSS), 2018, p. 6 (Ghana Living Standards Survey, Round 7). * Additional regions have been created in Ghana since the Ghana Living Standards Survey (Round 7) was conducted.

Malthusian prediction is not borne out by the evidence. Like the rest of Ghana and Africa, many residents of the northern regions were also migrants before formal colonial policy making, so the Marxist analysis can also be problematized.

Both approaches oversimplify the experiences of women. Even when analysts explicitly embrace the experience of the 'feminization of migration' in which they consider 'women' migrants, both the Malthusian and Marxian approaches tend to overlook how gender intersects with ethnicity, migrant status or type, and class over time and space (Crenshaw, 1989, 1991; Nyantakyi-Frimpong, 2020). Women are increasingly becoming the face of migration. Between 1960 and 2019, the difference between the share of migrants who were male and those who were female reduced from 0.3 to 0.1. In addition, more women now migrate independently (Roose et al., 2020, p. 5; Koido, 2021). Yet, women have other identities. Some are mothers. Their children have also swelled the ranks of migrants. This growing presence of women and children in migration can be called 'the feminization of migration'. Living on the streets complicates these identities.

Street children and urban streetism in Ghana and the feminization of migration have become an increasing focus of research.[1] Part of the reason is the sheer number of such children: some 168 million children worldwide, aged between 5 and 17 years (Bermudez et al., 2020, p. 148) and the growing number of women on the streets of cities in Ghana. However, their experiences and those of children need

[1] According to the Children's Act, 1998, a child is a person below the age of eighteen years (Government of Ghana, 1998, p. 1).

to be set within the context of the wider intersecting forces of ethnicity, class, and migrant status mediated by particular institutions in the country.

Globally, research on children has had a long history, dating back to the 1950s and 1960s, when criminologists, sociologists, and psychologists typically studied children and youth gangsterism. More recently, geographers and anthropologists have become interested in the 'geographies of children and youth' and have focused mainly on the transition to adulthood and social experiences of children and young people (Gough, 2008; Amankwaa et al., 2020). A third reason is the sheer number of children on the streets, which makes them look like the only street people.

So, in this chapter, my analysis focuses instead on historical landmarks (precolonial migration, colonial migration, and post-colonial migration), within which the intersectionality of gender, class, ethnicity, and migrant status need to be considered (Crenshaw, 1989, 1991; Nyantakyi-Frimpong, 2020). Pre-colonial migration in Ghana is distinguished by seasonal changes in weather conditions being almost its sole driver (Abdul-Korah, 2006). In less favourable weather, northern farmers would usually migrate to southern Ghana in search of favourable arable land. They would usually go alone because they had every intention of returning, and they usually did. The journey was to work seasonally and they would obtain land as stranger farmers. Land tenure arrangements would be such that they would share the produce with the landlords. Depending on the landlords' contributions, the migrant farmers could have half or one-third of the produce.

This practice continued into the colonial period. What changed, however, was the introduction of commercial farms, with cocoa becoming a major crop. The colonial government vigorously supported cocoa production and actively forced labourers from northern parts of Ghana to work on such farms. Over a period of time, a pattern was clearly established and, although forced labour was abolished by 1936, some farmers from the northern parts of Ghana began to go to southern cocoa farms to work as labourers, rather than as sharecroppers (Abdul-Korah, 2006). Still, the arrangement was quite temporary, even when there was mass migration arising from economic depression (Abdul-Korah, 2006). Farmers still migrated alone. Some still went to places like the Brong Ahafo region, but many more went to the Ashanti region to become labourers on cocoa farmers.

The independence era left these practices in place, with state farms recruiting more farmers for such purposes. So, from an era when migration was largely driven by environmental factors, the migration of farmers was increasingly instigated by social structures and social institutions. All these forms of farming persist to this day, with the economic structure largely unchanged, except in a few cases such as the abandonment of the state farms.

Another significant change is that climatic conditions seem to have become more uncertain. Accordingly, northern migrants have become more permanent migrants. Surveys of Dagaaba farmers in the Brong Ahafo region, for example

(Abdul-Korah, 2006; Obour et al., 2017), show that they are now becoming permanent migrants. Not only are husbands migrating with their wives and children, but wives are also migrating with their families, while some women migrate alone. Additional surveys (focused on wives) to determine the nature of migration patterns corroborate this pattern. Unlike previously, now wives are migrating with their husbands. They are part of the feminization of farming in Southern Ghana in a transformation in which 'seasonal migrants have become settler migrants' (Obour et al., 2017, p. 154). Women and children are also part of workers on the streets of cities.

I have analysed some of the experiences of migrants elsewhere, for example, in oil cities such as Sekondi-Takoradi and Abidjan (Obeng-Odoom 2014, 2021). In these cities, migrants, particularly women and children, are involved in sex work and the recycling of urban waste, occasioned by the increasing commodification of water and labour. There is also a substantial amount of research on migrants in mining towns in Africa (see, e.g., Bryceson and MacKinnon, 2012; Marais et al., 2021). What I seek to do in the rest of this chapter is rather different, focusing instead on the experiences of urban farmers, traders, and head porters in Ghana and elsewhere in Africa in order to provide a firmer canvas for developing new explanations of internal migration.

Urban Farmers

Urban food production requires attention because it plays a substantial role in providing food for residents in cities, regions, and city-regions across the world (Karg, 2016; Cabbanes and Marocchino, 2018). Urban agriculture is central in this sense. Migrants are not just involved in urban agriculture; they tend to dominate it (Obosu-Mensah, 1999, 2002). Like rural agriculture, urban agriculture is dominated by men, but the involvement of women is well known and widely documented (see, e.g., Nyantekyi-Frimpong et al., 2016; Afriyie et al., 2020). Also, much like rural migrants in southern regions, urban farmers refer to ecological reasons for migrating. Again, migrants involved in urban agriculture might occupy rent-free, but they increasingly pay for the land they obtain—much like rural migrants—in one of three ways.

The first is *abunu*, a share tenancy in which the produce of the migrant farmer is split into two between the landowner and the farmer. The second is *abusa*, a share tenancy in which the farmer surrenders two-thirds of their produce to the landowners. The third is caring, in which the farmers, in exchange for tilling the land, do not surrender a proportion of their food produced, but take care of the land for the urban landlord (Obosu-Mensah, 1999, 2002; Nyantekyi-Frimpong et al., 2016; Afriyie et al., 2020). These practices make urban agriculture quite similar to rural agriculture, although there are important differences between them. Most fundamentally, the land question distinquishes urban agriculture from rural agriculture. As empirical research (Fuseini, 2016; Nyantekyi-Frimpong et al., 2016; Afriyie et al., 2020) shows, the nature and future of urban agriculture is constrained by the increasing commodification of urban land and the dynamics of urban land rent in ways that are different from the nature of rural land with little or no *location* rent.

These similarities and differences are historically informed. Urban agriculture has a long history in Africa. For instance, the colonial officers in Ghana farmed urban land (1873–1956); next, post-colonial government bureaucrats (1957–1972) did so, too, and then urban agriculture became a national policy in 1973 when the then Kutu Acheampong government declared Operation Feed Yourself,[2] a programme to attain national food sufficiency (Obosu-Mensah 1999, 2002). Urban agriculture was practised in Kenya in 1899 and in Zambia in the 1920s and 1930s and has persisted to this day (Hampwaye 2008). The 1980s saw a dramatic rise in interest in urban agriculture as a survival strategy for those who lost their jobs due to the austerity measures implemented during the structural adjustment era of the 1980s and early 1990s. Similarly, in cities such as Freetown, Sierra Leone, where war led to substantial rural–urban migration and, hence, reduced the population in rural areas involved in farming, urban agriculture has remained a key livelihood strategy (Dubbeling et al. 2010; Lynch et al. 2013). Nevertheless, agricultural research and policymaking continued to focus on rural areas (Prain and Lee-Smith, 2010; Lynch et al., 2013; Cabannes and Marocchino, 2018; Bryceson and Jamal, 2019) neglecting urban agriculture.

La Vía Campesina, formed in 1993 as a peasant-based movement to demand food sovereignty, primarily focused on rural and peri-urban areas and not as much on the urban food question (Desmarais 2007; Riddell 2009; Cabannes and Marocchino, 2018). The first time large-scale, formal research was conducted on urban agriculture was in the 1990s, when Jac Smit, often called the father of urban agriculture, led a team of experts to undertake and write a formal document entitled, *Urban Agriculture: Food, Jobs and Sustainable Cities*, a revised edition of which was published in 2001 (Smit et al., 2001). Researchers interested in Africa had previously studied urban agriculture (e.g., Maxwell et al., 1998; Levin et al., 1999; Maxwell, 1999; Maxwell et al., 2000), but they had done so on a small scale. The work by Smit et al. (2001) and the Harare Declaration, made in 2003, gave urban agriculture a major international and formal stamp of approval.

The Harare Declaration was made by five East African and Southern African countries to promote urban agriculture and give it a broad appeal. It called for the acceptance and promotion of urban agriculture as essential to the life of cities in Africa. Since the making of that Declaration, the United Nations Human Settlement Programme (UN-HABITAT, 2008, 2010) has supported the campaign for urban agriculture in its two reports on the state of cities in Africa by recognizing the potential of urban agriculture, although not in any detailed form. In addition, the work on urban agriculture tended to neglect urban land, informality, climate change, and urban food sovereignty (Cabannes and Marocchino, 2018). Thus, it is essential to address questions about jobs, incomes, security of land tenure and the experiences of urban migrants generally.

Many migrants work on urban farms. Usually, they do so alone, but they have also formed associations which provide the space for them to discuss how they can enhance their personal conditions and transform circumstances in their place of destination. They have, for example, formed *nnoboa* groups, or communal labour groups, which put their collective labour power into the clearing and preparation of individual members' farms. Such groups discuss wider conditions at the place of migrant origin, too (Obour et al., 2017; Baada et al., 2019). Remitting is one way, but there are many other ways in which migrants make contributions through urban agriculture to host settlements, livelihoods, economy, and society generally.

Take food production. It is estimated that 90% of the vegetables consumed in Accra and Kumasi are produced in those cities. Numerical evidence of the share of urban agriculture in total agricultural production is hard to find, but one estimate put it at 15% in 1998 (Zezza and Tasciotti 2010). In Burkina Faso, Kinane et al. (2008) have noted that 'since the 1960s the number of sites on which exotic vegetables are grown has increased in the city of Ouagadougou alone from just a few to more than 50, representing about 2500 hectares' (Kinane et al., 2008, p.25). A study, involvingy 100 people in Bameda, Cameroon (Ojong 2011), shows that as much as 42.1% of the respondents depend on urban agriculture for a living.

In Freetown, the first large-scale survey of people involved in urban agriculture (Lynch et al. 2013) shows that for about 65% of the participants, urban agriculture is the main source of livelihood. According to Ludovic and Lebailly (2011), in 2008, urban agriculture contributed some 18,848 tons of vegetables in Niamey, Niger. Also, some 14% of the rice needs of Antananarivo, Madagascar, are produced by urban agriculture (Aubry et al., 2012). Another way to gauge the contribution of urban agriculture to food supply is by looking at the share of the urban population involved in urban agriculture. According to Prain et al. (2010), on average, some 35% of people in cities in Africa report that they are involved in urban agriculture. Lusaka, Zambia (49%), Maputo, Mozambique (40%), and Addis Ababa, Ethiopia (50%), to name just a few, all have a substantial share of their urban population involved in urban agriculture.

In a handful of cities, only a small share of the population engage in urban agriculture. In Accra, for example, according to the analysis of Prain et al. (2010), only 15% of the population and 3.4% of households are involved in urban agriculture. However, in urban Ghana as a whole, at least 28% of households are estimated to be engaged in urban agriculture (Ghana Statistical Service 1995, 2008). Thus, although there is no quantitative figure of exactly how much urban agriculture contributes to total food supply in Africa (Prain et al. 2010), the estimates for people involved in urban agriculture and how much it contributes to the total food supply in urban areas in individual countries suggest a substantial contribution to the food supply in African cities.

Urban agriculture makes an important contribution to the incomes of farmers, too. While most urban agriculture is informal (Cabannes, 2012; Cabannes and Marocchino, 2018) and, hence, data on incomes can be hard to find, national estimates give some indication of the contribution of urban agriculture to incomes. In Yaoundé, Cameroon, Prain et al. (2010) identified that urban farmers typically have earnings that are 50% in excess of the minimum wage, while heads of households involved in urban agriculture in Kampala, Uganda, earn 70% more than the per capita income in the country. In Accra, urban agriculture contributes about 15% of the incomes of those households that are financially stressed (Armar-Klemesu and Maxwell 1999; Nyantakyi-Frimpong et al., 2016). There is also some evidence that urban agriculture makes substantial contribution to poverty reduction in both the city and the country (Ghana Statistical Service 1995, 2008; Obeng-Odoom, 2020b). In Niamey, Niger, Ludovic and Lebailly (2011) found that urban farmers can obtain from about $1,200/acre/year to slightly over $4,000/acre/year, depending on the produce grown.

While in most cases earnings from urban agriculture seem to be higher than per capita incomes, caution is needed in interpreting the evidence for various reasons. First, the figures must be treated as estimates because of the difficulty in delinking various sources of income from urban agriculture—a challenge, which, in turn, is linked to issues of record keeping. Second, although a range is used in most of the figures, it is not clear to what extent the range is flexible enough to capture the variety of earnings that accrue to farmers, depending on what crops and varieties are grown and whether the incomes are derived from a variety of sources. Third, the figures are not directly comparable because they have not been adjusted for purchasing power parity and do not show any temporal characteristics. In spite of these challenges with data availability, collection, and interpretation, the numerical evidence complements the qualitative evidence, further suggesting that urban agriculture contributes substantially to incomes in cities in Africa (see also Larson et al., 2012; Battersby and Watson, 2018).

Urban agriculture is sometimes promoted as a categorical panacea whose only challenge is administrative neglect in the planning process (Cabannes and Marocchino, 2018). Framed that way, much could be said in support of urban agriculture. Apart from contributing significantly to food supply and incomes, urban agriculture avoids speculative financialization and is not accompanied by large-scale dispossessions. Research by Cabannes (2012) and Cabannes and Marocchino (2018) show that most urban farmers use informal, small-scale, communal credit systems called *osusu* (in Ibadan, Nigeria), *susu* (in Accra), and *tontines* (in Porto Novo, Benin). Urban farmers in Africa exhibit little or no tendency to take loans from formal financial institutions. In turn, they do not provide the conditions conducive for the growth of speculative finance (Cabannes, 2012; Cabannes and Marocchino, 2018; Battersby and Watson, 2018). Further, by definition, expropriation is rare, as urban agriculture in Africa takes place in backyards, beside drainage systems, around factories, on street corners, and on rooftops (Dubbeling et al., 2010; Battersby and Watson, 2018).

In Accra (in Ghana) and Freetown (in Sierra Leone), for example, most urban agriculture is done on land under 1 acre (Armar-Klemesu and Maxwell, 1999; Obosu-Mensah, 1999; Lynch et al., 2013; Nyantekyi et al., 2016) and, on average, farmers till about 0.21 ha of land in Kinshasa (Lebailly and Muteba, 2011). Indeed, most urban agriculture is done by poor people, not elites who are typically involved in the process of land grabbing (The RUAF Foundation, 2008, 2011; Afriyie et al., 2020). The poor are able to start urban agriculture with little or no support, as urban agriculture has low barriers to entry and exit (Dubbeling et al., 2010; Bellwood-Howard et al., 2018). Thus, for all its merits, urban agriculture does not have the social cost that accompanies mechanized, large-scale farming.

Yet, the experiences of farming migrants have been very difficult both in rural and urban contexts. Kwaku Obosu-Mensah (1999, pp. 94–96, 121–152) has documented the privileges of male farmers, especially those from the south in terms of access to land and other farming resources. These southern farmers are more affluent. Farming is more of a hobby and they have a much stronger security of land tenure. They do not live with the uncertainties of migrants from northern parts of Ghana. These southerners may be migrants, but are usually employed by the state or in comfortable formal private employment with stable income and status. They farm for pleasure and for home consumption and rarely sell their produce. Migrant farmers from the northern parts of Ghana are different. They till on squatted land. This land can be beside street gutters and roads, or under transmission lines and in other hazardous areas. Women migrants from the north are discriminated against and women farmers from the northern parts of Ghana have experienced widespread difficulties. A strong explanation is the relationship between the home region, land ownership, and the type of cultivation. Migrants are worse off in this tripartite calculus. As strangers, their relationship to land is both insecure and uncertain. They are most predominantly involved in open-space agriculture, with women migrants being particularly worse off.

A recent study (Baada et al., 2019) based on careful interviews with forty-five women farmers from the northern parts of Ghana working in the Brong Ahafo region finds that they experience widespread discrimination. If married, they constantly have to negotiate access to and control of farm land and farm produce. If single, they usually get the worst types of land from male landlords who, in addition, impose far more stringent terms of land use on them. Women are typically given smaller plots of land and must surrender more of their produce than men. Sometimes, in addition to share tenancy practices, women also have to pay regular land rent. Widowed women fare even worse. Their security of tenure evaporates as soon as their husbands die. Many are thrown off the land. Others have to face new land tenure rules. If a woman has sons, the situation can be mitigated. If she has only daughters, the situation remains difficult. In general, women who do not obtain land, but have to sell their labour, are paid much less than men.

All migrant farmers face problems and are in a less strong position than their hosts (Abdul-Korah, 2006; Obour et al., 2017; Afriyie et al., 2020). They lose their farm produce to pilfering. They lack sufficient income to invest in their farms. They lack adequate land and security of tenure. In the process of urban sprawl, migrants tend to be the first to lose their land. With dwindling wages and asset, they must paradoxically pay more of their wages in rent, as urban property prices continue to increase with the commodification of land (Afriyie et al., 2020). Other farmers from Southern Ghana do much better than northerners, who tend to farm land with insecure tenure (Obosu-Mensah, 1999; Fuseini, 2016; Bellwood-Howard et al., 2018). In urban settings, there is the additional problem of unsupportive officialdom which sometimes perceives urban agriculture to be an inefficient use of land that is much more difficult and more expensive to access in urban settings (Obosu-Mensah, 1999, 2002; Nyantekyi et al., 2016; Bellwood-Howard et al., 2018). Migrant farmers have also started to experience far more climatic uncertainty in their destination regions compared to what they faced previously.

It is, however, Northern Ghanaian women who bear a disproportionate amount of these challenges and suffer additional challenges (Baada et al., 2019). They bear the brunt of migrants in general, but being migrant women, and in particular migrant women from the northern parts of Ghana, their situation is even worse. They are in fact the least favoured in the land distribution hierarchy. These discriminatory practices do not just apply to the rural Brong Ahafo region. They are more widespread in Ghana (Hall et al., 2017; Obeng-Odoom, 2014, 2020a).

Technical planning continues to be advocated as a way to address these problems. Formalization is particularly popular, although it is given the makeover of an inclusive process (Bellwood-Howard et al., 2018). In this posited solution, urban agriculture would need to be recognized by official planning channels. Zoning for urban agriculture complements the process. Finally, urban land can be rented to urban farmers, local engineers and geologists can be retained to provide professional advice, and local lawyers can draft the required legal instruments to address the land problems faced by migrant urban farmers. Other than formal recognition of such schemes in initiatives such as the Accra Working Group on Urban and Peri-Urban Agriculture (AWGUPA), Issahaka Fuseini's (2016) research shows that such technical solutions face significant problems. Not much progress has been made from such technocratic solutions.

Taking Tamale as one case study area, Fuseini (2016) shows that the city has not experienced the posited triple win of food security, food sovereignty, and food sustainability, nor any other posited benign outcomes. The reasons for these problems include the lack of participation, low-level participation in planning preparation and implementation, the lack of transparency to structural imbalances in power relations, and a tendency towards centralization without complementary grassroots decentralisation.

To address these problems, urban farmers resort to one or more strategies in the face of growing urban land problems (Afriyie et al., 2020). They might intensify their use of land by diversifying the range of crops they grow, while relying more on chemicals and pesticides to improve yield. Other farmers resort to land extensification in which they bring into production more marginal land. A third strategy is to find non-farm work.

So, although previous attempts to analyse such problems and resulting strategies emphasise regional and global food chains, participatory urban planning, and urban governance to enhance food security, food sovereignty, and food sustainability within and across cities, regions, and nations (Kang et al., 2016), urban land rent (not simply urban land tenure problems or population growth) compels migrants to adopt problematic practices. For example, increasing intensification potentially increases toxification from agrochemicals, which weaken the natural fertility of the soil, potentially contaminate the resulting food produced, and potentially undermine the health of urban farmers, particularly female urban migrant farmers (Nyantekyi-Frimpong et al., 2016; Afriyie et al., 2020). Increasing diversification raises the spectre of food imports from other cities within but also across nations and regions within which cities are embedded. In Ghana, such imports could be from Southern to Northern Ghana or from Burkina Faso or Brazil to Ghana (Kang et al., 2016). In turn, the posited benefit of local food sustainability, food security, or food sovereignty can be questioned.

In any case, the success of these strategies is contingent on class, gender, ethnicity, and other identities. Migrants—migrant women from the north in particular, and women in general—typically lack the power and resources often possessed - in general - by those in the southern parts of Ghana. Original or further migration becomes another strategy combined with seeking non-farm work. These women also migrated in part due to ecological pressures either because their parents' farms were not doing well, because as farmers in their own right their farms were not doing well, or because they had experienced a combination of these setbacks. Either way, they left their farms or farm work to migrate to southern parts of Ghana, but they did not work as farmers there. In more recent times, too, feminists have strongly put the case for a feminist analysis of migration from Northern Ghana concerning non-farming activities (Abdul-Korah, 2006; Obour et al., 2017).

This call is clearly justified, given the growing number of female migrants from northern parts to the southern parts of Ghana (Amantana, 2012). There is, however, a significant tension within this literature (Hodzic, 2017; Darkwah, 2019). Not only does it reflect a Western saviour mentality, but it also tends to portray local black scholars as inferior, as it sets the agenda for the black activists to follow. A more insidious aspect, too, is that local activists, much like global feminists, seem to strive to show their own importance, rather than to carefully reflect on local conditions. Surveys and systematic interviews could, perhaps, help to throw more light on the feminization of migration, a confluence of both economic and ecological forces of migration crystallized within social and political-economic forces.

Street Workers

The number of children in Ghana is on the rise. Consider Accra. Street children in the city in 1990 were about 4,000. Six years later, the number of street children increased to approximately 10,400. In 2003, the figure shot up further to 15,300, by 2009 it was 30,000, and by 2011, 50, 000 (Catholic Action for Street Children (2010). In the Greater Accra Region as a whole, there were 60,495 street children in 2011, projected to have increased to 80,000 in 2016. Most of these children, specifically 66 per cent of them, are born to migrants (Djaba, 2017). Other migrant children work elsewhere, including an estimated 43% of children in Ghana who work in other places, such as on cocoa farms (International Labour Organization, 2010). For these reasons, the problem of street children has historically been the focus of both media (e.g., IRIN [The Integrated Regional Information Networks now called The New Humanitarian], 2007) and scholarly (e.g., Speak, 2005, 2019) focus.

The United Nations International Children's Emergency Fund (UNICEF) notes that there are three types of street children. First, there are abandoned children, who are without families because of death or simple abandonment. Second, there are street children who have homes and may go to sleep at home after work. Third, there are street children who do have homes but only go home occasionally, such as during Christmas. In Ghana, street children typically congregate at major road junctions. Children in all three groups can be found in Ghana (Kansangbata, 2008). Street children are involved in many economic activities on the streets, such as emptying rubbish bins for a fee and shoe repairing, cleaning, and polishing. Some also run errands for traders or wash dishes at restaurants, while others sell sachets of cold water, toffee, oranges, and dog leashes. Their mode of selling, such as running after moving cars which slow down when the traffic lights turn red, can be risky and they are frequently subject to verbal abuse (Obeng-Odoom, 2009). There are other street workers, too.

Table 4.2 Kayayei in Accra and Kumasi, 2019

Theme	Number of women	Percentage
Age group		
10–14	37	7.4
15–19	466	92.6
Marital status		
Married	79	15.8
Single	415	82.8
Divorced/widowed	2	0.4
Cohabitation	5	1.0
Livelihoods		
Kayayo business only	471	93.6
Multiple livelihoods	32	6.4
Residency		
Accra	253	50.3
Kumasi	250	49.7
Ability to remit money		
Yes	181	36
No	322	64

Source: Alatinga, 2019, pp. 1,727–1,728.

Most scholars focus on women porters, typically called *kayayei* (or *kayayo* in the singular). There are male porters who may be called 'truck pushers', but the feminization of migration literature prioritizes women. Most porters migrated from Northern Ghana. Most of them are women, and the majority of them are only transient in their job. As with street children, estimating the number of porters is difficult. Estimates from the Catholic Action for Street Children (2010), however, suggest that, in 2006, there were over 7,000 *kayayei* in Accra and its neighbouring areas. Kumasi has many *kayayei*, too.

Alatinga's (2019) recent survey of 503 female porters offers a helpful overview. All of the women are from the northern parts of Ghana and all of them live on the streets. As Table 4.2 shows, most of them are single and most of them work only as *kayayei*.

The mean daily income of the majority who work only as *kayayei* was 13 GhC (US$2.41), while those who do much more moonlighting earn 42 GhC (US$7.89) daily, on average (Alatinga, 2019). Compared with incomes reported in a similar survey in 2005 by the Regional Institute for Population Studies (RIPS) and the Institute of Statistical, Social, and Economic Research (ISSER) in which, of the 641 migrants surveyed, only 2.2% earned between 11 and 30 GhC and 94.5% earned less than 11 GhC (Adaawen and Owusu, 2013, p. 43), it seems that the incomes of *kayayei* have increased substantially. Although most *kayayei* would want to, they are generally unable to remit money. Those who are able do so have to work for several months before they can save up some money.

Migrant savings require some commentary, too. Banking institutions have proliferated in urban Ghana, but they remain largely inaccessible to such migrants. The required minimum payment is one reason. The lengthy amount of time needed to queue in order to withdraw money from the banks is another. *Susu*, a more indigenous, cooperative way of saving, avoids these problems. In addition, it affords the opportunity for street workers to borrow money when needed. Hence, surveys of *kayayei* show that *susu* is their most common way of saving. Others keep their money at home. In the RIPS/ISSER survey, for example, 59.3% of all *kayayei* interviewed participated in *susu*, 10% kept their money at home and some 9% saved their money with someone else. Only 2.1% kept their money in a bank (Adaawen and Owusu, 2013, p. 44). Usually, savings are eventually remitted.

At the household level in the migrants' regions of origin, the money is spent on food, daily family upkeep, or taking care of migrant children or siblings. In the RIPS/ISSER survey (Adaawen and Owusu, 2013, p. 51), as much as 66.9% of all remittances went on this use, along with personal uses such as buying personal needs (4.0%) and preparation for marriage (1.1%). Other uses had much wider social ramifications, such as trading (10.5%), investment in building (4.3%), and farming (1.1%). Unlike the few females from southern parts of Ghana who seek to live on the streets permanently (Amantana, 2012), *kayayei* from the northern parts of Ghana tend to aspire to return. Those who are married into polygamous families usually return to perform their conjugal obligations, then return to the streets, while the other wives carry out theirs (Yeboah, 2010). Some aspire to a definite return, and some actually do return home and eventually marry (Yeboah, 2010; Amantana, 2012).

Urban research in Ghana grossly overlooks the contribution of *kayayei* to the country's urban economy. None of the major books on Accra contains even an entry or substantial commentary, on *kayayei*, including Richard Grant's *Globalizing City: The Urban and Economic Transformation of Accra, Ghana* (2009); Ato Quayson's *Oxford Street, Accra: City Life and the Itineraries of Transnationalism* (2014); and Naaborko Sackeyfio-Lenoch's *The Politics of Chieftaincy: Authority and Property in Colonial Ghana, 1920–1950* (2014). Other books show the important historical contribution of Nigerian immigrants to the formation of Accra. John Parker's *Making the Town: Ga State and Society in Early Colonial Accra* (2000) is one example. Deborah Pellow's *Landlords and Lodgers: Socio-Spatial Organizaton in an Accra Community* (2002) is not just another example, but an exemplar. Yet, none of these books systematically acknowledges the major contributions of *kayayei* to the transformation of the city's urban economy.

'Informal Income Opportunities and Urban Employment in Ghana' (1973), Keith Hart's classic study of Accra, attempted an input–output analysis, but it concentrated on the substantial interactions between the informal and the formal economy. A logical next step is to recognize that the globalizing dynamics of Accra described by Richard Grant (2009) and Ato Quayson (2014) are strongly subsidized by *kayayei*. Monetary transactions in Accra's congested urban markets are facilitated by *kayayei*, who serve as human means of transport, reducing transport and transaction costs more generally. *Kayayei* enable transactions to take place. Without *kayayei*, Accra's urban economy would contract, on account of the slowing down of trade, the increase in trade expenses, and the leakage of resources out of Accra, to other cities such as Kumasi and Cape Coast. *Kayayei* make direct payment to city authorities, too. In one study (Agyei et al., 2016, p. 306), *kayayei* were paying a market toll of GhC 0.50 (US$0.16) on a daily basis. So, *kayayei* also serve as income generators for city authorities.

In Accra, where it is estimated that there are 15,000 *kayayei* (Agyei et al., 2016, p. 298), the city authorities could gain up to US$876,000 in daily market tolls from *kayayei* alone. In Kumasi, where the estimated number of *kayayei* is a much larger 23,000 people (Agyei et al., 2016, p. 298), the figure is much bigger: US$1,343,200. We do not have corroborative evidence, but the precise magnitude is not the focus. It is the importance of such fees for city authorities that truly matters. At least in Kumasi, the evidence suggests that between 2006 and 2008, the share of fees in total internally generated funds doubled (Obeng-Odoom, 2010b). The contribution of *kayayei* to these fortunes is substantial. Together with their wider influence on the urban economies of Ghana, female head porters can be regarded as engines of export for cities and import substitution for urban economies in Ghana. They are part of the country's urban economic base.

The actions of these migrants are heroic, but the tasks required to undertake such work are arduous. Women use simple equipment, such as pans and baskets (Agarwal et al., 1997). It is usual for women to carry the loads on their heads, while the practice for men is to push the load on trucks or to carry their wares in bags. Both women and men tend to work from dawn to dusk and walk for several hours a day (Hutchinson, 2003; Yeboah and Appiah-Yeboah, 2009; Yeboah, 2010). Transporting goods by means of porters is a cheaper medium than using vehicles (Grieco et al., 1995; Turner and Kwakye, 1996), but while the male porters can work in markets and streets in different parts of urban society, female porters are restricted by norms to only certain parts (Awumbila and Ardayfio-Schandorf, 2008). In turn, men carry more, heavier loads with machines, while women use their human strength. Finally, men possess a stronger bargaining power and earn higher incomes (about 50% more) than women (Awumbila and Ardayfio-Schandorf, 2008, p. 177; Agarwal et al., 1997; Yeboah, 2010; Anyidoho and Steel, 2016).

In general, porters miss out on education. In Alatinga's (2019) survey of 503 female *kayayei*, nine out of ten of the female head porters had not completed their schooling and 36.4% had no formal education. The rest had primary (24.1%) or secondary (40%) education. Many (29%) are on the streets to generate some money to continue or start education but, as Alatinga's survey shows, most of these girls seem to be spending a greater part of their school years working on the streets, with money only trickling in. Even their health and well-being are compromised. They spend significant amounts of time sleeping on the streets in places such as pavements, in front of kiosks, and in shops and shacks, all structures or locations where essential municipal services, such as water, are lacking (Alatinga, 2019). Landlords in Ghana are generally abusive of tenants (Owusu-Ansah et al., 2018), but *kayayei* must also endure discrimination.

Many will not be allowed to rent a home at all because they are considered social deviants, whose only deserving place in society is the worst leftover spaces. Even for this poor rental space, rent is vigorously demanded, but with no tenant facilities or rights (Gyami, 2019, pp. 52–54). This poor accommodation feeds into poor health. Many sustain long-term injuries from carrying loads, others are exploited and sexually abused, harassed, and violated (Amantana, 2012; Bermudez et al., 2020). Almost all these women have 'homes' and families and may visit them on special days, such as during the Christmas period (Hutchinson, 2003; Alatinga, 2019), but they live in the harsh street environment of Accra and Kumasi for most of their time as migrants, during which time they sometimes go without food or eat poorly.

Head porters use several strategies in order to cope with and adapt to the fast and harsh work environment. Sometimes they may take up offers by NGOs that offer temporary shelter (Amantana, 2012). To avoid the problem of sexual abuse and street fights, *kayayei* normally do things together, consciously avoid confrontation and quarrels, and form intimate relationships with men who offer them physical protection (Awumbila and Ardayfio-Schandorf, 2008). Where they decide to cohabit with male porters, systematic research (Adomako and Baffour, 2019) shows that many struggle with intimate partner violence (IPV). This violence, in the form of physical and verbal abuse, has three corrosive effects. First, IPV impairs the physical health of the female porters. Second, it distorts the social networks of the porters who, after internalizing persistent beatings, become aggressive to their fellow porters. Many lose friends in the networks as a result. A third cumulative effect is the loss of income. Beaten and broken, many have to spend days at home to recover before they can return to work. So, cohabitation and marriage, while offering some protection and the opportunity to save a little on rent, also have their own dangers and difficulties.

The feminization of migration, entailing the structural problems women and children face as migrants, then, brings with it many social pressures, as well as psychosocial and economic challenges. Apart from the difficulty in finding jobs, Amantana's *A Sociological Study of Street Children in Ghana: Victims of Kinship Breakdown and Rural–Urban Migration* (2012) shows that street children are exploited both internally and externally. Internally, older street children bully the younger ones, physically stronger ones bully weaker ones, and children who have stayed on the street longer bully newcomers. This internal exploitation takes various forms, including extorting money from weaker ones, renting out street spaces to weaker individuals, and taking other items away from weaker street children. Externally, some customers pay less than is due street children, refuse to pay them altogether, or abscond with money owed to street children.

Ghanaian street children are recurrently exposed to hardship and danger. According to Amantana's (2012) book, the Ghana Police Service is not really effective in protecting the children because it typically takes a passive posture towards street children exploitation. Typically, the Police Service neither aggravates nor attenuates the multiple exploitation that street children face. Left to survive on their own, much like the discards in the streets of Tamale and Accra, left as prey for flies and the vagaries of the weather, the children adopt several coping strategies to remain alive. First, they might seek assistance from NGOs, some of which offer temporary accommodation. Alternatively, they may save up their money with trusted traders (although this trust is sometimes broken and the children lose their money). Third, when one of them is ill, the others may contribute some money to send the person to hospital or back to the person's home region. As the food supply to these children is insecure, they eat whatever they can find, sometimes from the streets or the dump.

Occasionally, the children beg the public to give them food or money. In doing so, some feign physical disability, such as blindness, to court public sympathy. Some of the children—when nothing else works—will pick pockets or steal some food to survive, or turn to prostitution for quick money. While most of the time, a 'survival of the fittest' mindset is imposed by the hardships, there is some solidarity; for example, when a children is sick.

Other coping strategies used by street children demand additional analysis because they are quite serious. Eating less, or less often, in order to save and remit some money is commonly practised as one coping strategy. Its ramifications for well-being are widespread (Yeboah, 2010). Another mode of survival relates to ways of making a living. Some, albeit very few, female migrants are engaged in multiple modes of livelihoods, much like the situation elsewhere in Africa (Ojong, 2011, 2020). According to Amantana (2012), such female migrants are typically from Southern Ghana. Although Alatinga's (2019) study shows that this is a small group, it is important to reflect on their activities.

Consider street hawkers. As with street children, it is hard to know the size of this group. Brown et al. (2010) report that one association of street vendors in Accra has about 6,000 members. This number is conservative because there are numerous vendors who remain unrecorded or who operate outside associations. In Accra, street workers can be found almost everywhere, even though they tend to be concentrated in commercial enclaves, such as Kwame Nkrumah Circle, Kaneshie, Makola, and OSu, particularly 'Oxford Street' (Asiedu and Agyei-Mensah, 2008;

Quayson, 2014). Hawkers on urban streets are a multicultural group. They come from all ethnic groups in Ghana. There is no strong evidence that hawking is dominated by women, although the commodities that are sold are divided along gender lines. Women typically sell food, such as roasted plantain and bread, often carried on the head, while men usually use other methods (for a more detailed description, see Overa, 2007). On average, hawkers obtain about US$2 a day as profit (Asiedu and Agyei-Mensah, 2008; Anyidoho and Steel, 2016). Hawkers differ in how they sell their wares.

In the literature, three modes of selling have been identified; namely, itinerant, stationary, and semi-itinerant vendors (Asiedu and Agyei-Mensah, 2008; Adaawen and Jørgensen, 2012; Asante and Helbrecht, 2020). Itinerant vendors are always on the move, while the stationary vendors sit at fixed places. Semi-itinerant workers have features of both stationary and itinerant vendors in the sense that they sometimes work from fixed locations and move away either to avoid police harassment or to find a better location for their wares. Generally, because of the nature of their work, hawkers have a love–hate relationship with operators of more 'formal' shops and consumers alike. At times, the relationship is cordial, and some hawkers retail the products of shop owners for a small fee. But sometimes shop owners do not approve of the activities of hawkers. This is evidently the case when hawkers are perceived as competitors or when hawkers are thought to be selling poor-quality goods (Asiedu and Agyei-Mensah, 2008). Consumers find the street vendors easy to deal with because they are more accessible, more flexible, and more dynamic. Hawkers, moreover, offer variety and diversity of products because they are numerous and can be found everywhere. On the other hand, some consumers feel that hawkers worsen human congestion in urban society (Asiedu and Agyei-Mensah, 2008). The real risks, however, are borne by the hawkers themselves, many of them women. Weaving their way in between moving cars to sell to both drivers and pedestrians, the risk of injury and actual injury are recurrent concerns.

Explaining Internal Migration: From Individuals, Households, and Structures to Institutions

The rational choice model of the causes of streetism in Ghana is a useful starting point, but the existing situation in the country is far more complex, often confounding the dominant explanations that are centred on individuals, households, and structures. Table 4.3 shows that, in general, the level of poverty in the migrant-sending areas (the Northern, Upper West, and Upper East regions of Ghana and rural areas generally) is much higher than the migrant-receiving areas. A straightforward rational model would conclude that this poverty is the sole driver of migration.

Table 4.3 Regional poverty profile of Ghana, 2005–2017 (in percentages)

Region	2016–2017		2012–2013		2005–2006	
	Poverty incidence	Poverty gap	Poverty incidence	Poverty gap	Poverty incidence	Poverty gap
Western	21.1	4.9	20.9	5.7	22.9	5.4
Central	13.8	3.6	18.8	5.6	23.4	5.6
Greater Accra	2.5	0.5	5.6	1.6	13.5	3.7
Volta	37.3	13.0	33.8	9.8	37.3	9.2
Eastern	12.6	3.1	21.7	5.8	17.8	4.2
Ashanti	11.6	2.7	14.8	3.5	24.0	6.4
Brong Ahafo	26.8	8.8	27.9	7.4	34.0	9.5
Northern	61.1	26.7	50.4	19.3	55.7	23.0
Upper East	54.8	23.8	44.4	17.2	72.9	35.3
Upper West	70.9	37.6	70.7	33.2	89.1	50.7
All Ghana	23.4	8.4	24.2	7.8	31.9	11.0
Urban	7.8	1.8	10.6	2.5	12.4	3.7
Rural	39.5	15.1	37.9	13.1	43.7	15.4

Source: adapted from Ghana Statistical Service (GSS), 2018, pp. 13 and 19.

This push and pull theory would seem consistent with recent surveys, which ascribe the phenomenon of migration entirely to poverty. Alatinga's (2019) survey, for instance, shows that more than 60% of those surveyed in Accra and Kumasi migrated because of the lack of economic opportunities in the areas of origin. The RIPS/ISSER survey, discussed in the previous section, also came to similar conclusions (Adaawen and Owusu, 2015). The Ghana Statistical Service surveys have arrived at similar conclusions, namely that a lack of sufficient economic opportunities at the source of migration. In Accra, for example, a GSS survey in the early 2000s (Ghana Statistical Service, 2008) showed that 41% of migrants claim they migrated to the city because they lacked opportunities in their 'home regions'.

However, migration kept increasing, even when rural poverty declined between 2005/06 and 2012/13 (Obeng-Odoom and Jang, 2016). Migration from the northern parts of Ghana was persistent even in pre-colonial times, when the north was relatively prosperous (Dickson, 1966, 1968). So, the poverty-migration nexus is not entirely compelling. Neither can ecological factors alone explain north–south migration in Ghana. Climatic conditions in the northern parts of Ghana have always been relatively unfavourable compared to the south.

No one reason can account for this historical trend of north-south migration. Besides, this line of analysis hides the changing nature of migration. For instance, in the past, Dagaaba farmers migrated on a temporary basis to the Brong Ahafo region as stranger farmers (Abdul-Korah, 2006). With the changing climate, they have continued to migrate, but they have become more permanent migrants. Practices such as female genital mutilation were previously cited as drivers of migration, but such norms are on the decline (Hodzic, 2017; Darkwa, 2019). Wars have always ebbed and flowed.

Therefore, it is more useful to view the analysis of causes in terms of cumulative and interdependent political-economic and socio-ecological forces. Within these broad drivers, explanations need to recognize the intersections of gender, class, and ethnicity within changing historical contexts. Colonialism officially made northern regions the labour reserve for the country's transformation. Hence, migrants from the northern parts of Ghana were induced to move to the south. Such migrants have not necessarily made rational, individual calculations. Ethnographic research (Amantana, 2012) points to institutional forces, such as the breakdown of kinship fosterage; social expectations of both sons taking care of the family in the absence of the father; daughters providing homemaking items such as cooking utensils; the breakdown of the family through death, divorce, or abandonment; and their combination with persistent weak rural economies as being among the more important drivers of migration. Research (e.g., Lentz, 2013; Kwoyiga, 2019) shows that residents in the north typically find new ways of organising their communities in the face of substantial institutional transformation. However, eventually, with the breakdown of voice mechanisms for decision making, nationwide institutional programmes that sustain north–south migration, and global transnational agricultural programmes that lead to the expulsion of rural farmers, families, and communities from their land, exit becomes almost inevitable.

Perhaps, it is these reasons that provide the strongest case yet for considering voice, exit, and loyalty (Hirschman, 1970) seriously. In any case, migration appears to be part of social change. It is not simply that people are leaving agriculture, as for a review, see Yaro, 2006; Bryceson and Jamal, 2020). Rather, synergies between urban and rural areas are being continuously forged (Bryceson and Mbara, 2003), making it increasingly common for rural products to be sold in urban areas and urban activities to benefit rural economies. This evidence collapses the dualism between urban and rural areas and the emphases perpetuated by most mainstream urban economists, who claim that urbanization starts from deagrarianization (O'Sullivan, 2012) or that agrarianization starts from cities (Jacobs 1969), where advances in agriculture 'trickle down' to rural economies.

Viewed through the gaze of the public, all street life is the same, entailing outdoor cooking for the family or for sale. However, the social conditions underpinning the processes of how people come to live on the streets differ. Some people end up on the streets because of a breakdown in the family as an institution. Family reasons and social practices, such as arranged marriages to shrines, widowhood rites, and betrothal marriage, might drive people, especially those from the northern region, to exit where they live for cities in Southern Ghana. That is usually the case when voice mechanisms for redress are brittle or broken and social pressures are compounded by conflicts, such as the one between the Konkombas and the Nanumbas in Northern Ghana. According to the Ghana Statistical Service (2008), 22 out of every 100 migrants in Accra cite these factors as reasons for migrating. Amantana's (2012) study shows that street children mostly regard the streets as temporary, although a few—notably from Southern Ghana—would like to remain permanently on the streets. In terms of causes, Amantana uses the push–pull discursive framework, but the factors discussed are beyond the usual 'economic' or 'rational choice' models in economics.

Another important reason for exiting instead of voice or loyalty without exit (Hirschman, 1970) is death, especially of a father. For women and children, social practices and systems of inheritance which prevent them from inheriting the estate of a father and a husband may worsen their plight at home, and, in turn, drive them onto the streets. Sometimes, the widow may remarry in order to become economically stable, albeit dependent on her new husband. Moreover, her children from the earlier marriage may not be accepted in the new marriage. At other times, the children may be accepted, but abused and, in a situation where women have the weaker position in a marriage, a woman may not be able to stand up for her children. In turn, the children may be forced out onto the streets, a process that is hastened if the child is orphaned (Speak, 2005; Awumbila and Ardayfio-Schandorf, 2008), setting in motion what can be called 'crisis streetism' (Speak, 2004, pp. 476–478; see also (IRIN [The Integrated Regional Information Networks now called The New Humanitarian], 2007; Arthur, 2014).

The contradictions in land tenure at the source of migration provide a helpful prism for explanation. Most migrants tilled the land for food production, which was used by the household, and only a little of the harvest was reserved for exchange. How much land was tilled depended on the size of one's family. However, the arrival of Europeans and the commencement of colonialism significantly altered the system. The demand for cocoa by Europeans led to the commercialization of land. Families that could till more land were able to get more cash from the sale of cocoa. In turn, such families expanded their farms by using the services of hired labour (Hill, 1963; Caldwell, 1969; Peil, 1972; Sandbrook and Arn, 1977; Austin, 2007).

The effect of the new 'cash economy' was widespread. After its corrupting influence on traditional authorities, who started selling land to 'strangers' and 'natives' alike, people with more money could get more land and, hence, accumulate even more wealth. In turn, the practice of credit became more popular. The growing indigenous power groups lent money at high interest rates, setting in motion tendencies for mortgagors who defaulted to be driven off their land or to abandon their land and migrate to the cities. Not all migrants were originally engaged in cocoa farming. Migrants from the Northern Volta, and Upper regions were more typically engaged in subsistence farming, focusing on food production. But they too suffered from similar pressures. The state offered more support to the production of cash crops (for the purpose of exporting them) and the industries that were set up mainly required cash crops as raw materials. These tendencies led to a rise in the demand for land for cash crop farming and a fall in the demand for land for traditional food crop production. Subsequently, 'peasants' were forced to migrate to cities (Sandbrook and Arn, 1977,13–21; Howard, 1978, 1980; Firmin-Sellers, 1996; Austin, 2005, 2007).

Cities in Africa are not 'abnormal'. They, too, create opportunities, not simply perceptions of urban economic prosperity. Institutional processes shape these conditions, too. Caldwell's (1969) pioneering study showed that people in rural areas perceive life in cities to be more attractive than in the country. This perception has been strengthened by the disproportionate investment in cities over time. Economic liberalization has made it possible for investment to be poured into already 'developed' parts of cities such as Accra (Yeboah, 2000, 2003; Benjamin 2007; Grant, 2009; Stacey et al., 2021). In 2004, for example, Greater Accra alone was home to 78.7% of the 1,282 investment projects registered by the Ghana Investment Promotion Centre (CHF International, 2004). This disproportionate investment reflects an historical pattern. A capital city, Accra is the centre for both political and economic power. It is also the seat of Ghana's first 'World Trade Centre', a growing hub of financial activities in the city (Yeboah et al., 2021). As I have explained elsewhere (Obeng-Odoom, 2020d), a number of real estate development rules, banking practices, and foreign investment norms combine to give Accra its institutional power as a location of real and speculative capital. As many studies and surveys (Boakye-Boaten, 2008; GSS, 2008) show, the combination of rural institutions and urban institutions within the global system of growth and change, therefore, continue to shape internal migration.

But beyond rural–urban migration, people already living in urban centres are also enticed by conditions on the street and their supporting institutions. That is, there is a perception that sometimes the streets bear more promise than the home. Such attraction is particularly strong for children in broken homes who have suffered abuse (Boakye-Boaten, 2008). Other children may work on the streets in order to support their family (Kangsangbata, 2008). Institutional factors that contribute to urbanization are very strong. In the case of Accra or the Greater Accra Metropolitan Area (GAMA), for example, economic considerations underlie 41% of migration (GSS, 2008). Such economic activities and institutions may be formal in the sense that employment-creation systems, including a registered corporate entity such as Airtel and Glo telecommunication businesses, may contract individuals and households to sell their phone cards. Or households and individuals may decide to sell the product of their labour, such as brooms.

There are institutional factors, not merely expectational pull factors, as is typically argued in neoclassical urban economics (e.g., Khan, 2021). Rather, the decision to migrate is based on actual evidence of others returning to the rural areas as mostly better off than they were when they lived in the country. Also, actual interviews show that street children assess their conditions as improved (in the sense that at least they have some work to do and are often able to save up) and much better than what they were in their place of origin. But even when such improvement does not occur, children would, unless they were ill, generally stay on the streets not due to expectations of success, but because returning to the country is socially constructed as a failure, not only by the migrant children themselves, but also by their families.

Exit factors are also important. People who suffer from war, from some social practices, and from lack of opportunities at home are typically forced onto the streets, especially when, even if they are loyal, they lack voice (see Hirschman 1970). Researchers sometimes suggest that 'push and pull' factors are the only causes of urban streetism (see, e.g., Speak, 2005, p. 479; Speak, 2019), but this view may need to be modified because some street people are born on the streets. Indeed, Hart (1973, p. 88) famously remarked that 'we need not think all of those who enter informal occupation do so as a result of failure to obtain a wage-job'.

Natural increase through birth can also cause streetism. From an historical perspective, there is some evidence, mainly from the work of the Marxist geographer Drakakis-Smith (1987), that after independence, there was a surge of local Africans to cities to occupy the positions of the hitherto colonialisers, even though such positions were inadequate in number. In turn, some of such migrants ended up on the streets. It can be postulated that some of them may have had children while living on the streets. Evidently, as with people elsewhere, people on the street give birth to children who grow up and work on the streets.

There are also contemporary cases of natural increase. Through consensual intimate affairs or rape, many women on the streets end up becoming pregnant and will have to raise their children on the streets (see, e.g., Boakye-Boaten, 2008). Hawking increases the chance of becoming pregnant. There is an organic link between the economic stability of street women and street children and the likelihood of being used as sexual objects (Speak, 2005, 2019). The link can be shown in different ways. For example, hawkers' economic insecurity makes them vulnerable to giving in to sexual advances by some men who offer material inducements or lure unsuspecting women into illicit affairs (see, e.g., Keller et al., 1999, p. 76 for the story of two teenage hawkers). Streetism, then, brings with it many social pressures, as well as psychosocial and economic challenges.

The neoclassical and new economics of labour migration (NELM) accounts propose three types of policy considerations to 'address' internal migration: curtailing urban bias, reducing the urban incentives for migration, and rural development. In the words of M.P. Todaro and S.C. Smith (2006, p. 345):

> ... programs of integrated rural development should be encouraged. Policies that operate only on the demand side of the urban employment picture, such as wage subsidies, direct government hiring, elimination of factor–price distortions, and employer tax incentives, are probably far less effective in the long run in alleviating the unemployment problem than policies designed directly to regulate the supply of labor to urban areas. Clearly, however, some combination of both kinds of policies is most desirable.

In Ghana too, such policies were directly recommended by the country's experts. For instance, according to K.T. de Graft-Johnson (1974, p. 485):

> The answer to the dual problem of rural–urban migration and unemployment seems to lie in an integrated rural development policy, where attempts to raise rural incomes are accompanied by steps to provide essential amenities and all necessary infrastructure in the rural areas, supported by rational planning in the urban areas. A clear-cut government policy of encouraging and providing the necessary incentives for the establishment of industries, large as well as small, in the rural areas will go a long way to curbing the excessive drift to the urban centres.

Such policies, together with others intended to reduce the 'urban bias' in urban Ghana (e.g., structural adjustment programmes), were staunchly implemented by successive governments in Ghana. Budgets for rural electrification and agriculture, among other things, were increased. However, as one review of these policies show (Obeng-Odoom, 2013, pp. 27–33), they did not succeed in stemming the flow of rural–urban migration. Instead, they led to the development of smaller urban centres and a wider network of urban systems. Consequently, the Government of Ghana began to emphasize urban development from 2000 onwards in response to the global interest in cities as the engines of growth.

Successive governments have supported skills for work programmes in rural areas, the goal of which is to enhance the skills of rural residents in finding work in rural informal economies (see Robert Palmer, 2007). Of these programmes, informal apprenticeship has been favoured by the Government of Ghana, concentrating on areas such as micro and small-farm agricultural activities, service, retail, and manufacturing activities. There has also been some donor support of vocational skills training for informal activities in rural areas, especially the World Bank's Vocational Skills and Informal Sector Support Project and the International Fund for Agricultural Development Rural Enterprise Project. In general, these programmes are often in the form of short-term training delivered by local formal training institutes, either to upgrade skills or prepare for informal economy employment (Palmer, 2007). Aside from this more formal support of the rural economy, traditional informal apprenticeships are conducted under more experienced people and other elders in the rural societies for all job types.

The Ghanaian state has sought to address the issue from the perspective of institutions, but its policies are contradictory. On the one hand, the state has put in place several measures to improve the status of children and women. The steps taken include the creation of the Ghana National Commission of Children (GNCC), various ministries of gender, children, social protection as well as the Women and Juvenile Unit of the Ghana Police Service, the Department of Social Welfare, and the Child Labour Unit of the defunct Ministry of Manpower Development and Employment. These state institutions work collaboratively with an estimated 150 local and international NGOs and international bodies, such as UNICEF and the ILO, to advance the course of the marginalized. There are also many legislative frameworks that have been enacted to back public policy that is germane to improving the conditions of street people. Notable among them is the Children's Act of 1998, the Criminal Code (Amendment) Act of 1998, and the Human Trafficking Act of 2005 (see ECPAT International, 2008 and Kangsangbata, 2008 for a more detailed discussion). All these legislations and institutions provide a glimmer of hope for urban citizens who live and work on the streets.

On the other hand, however, there are several policy practices which reverse the gains. One notorious practice of successive urban governments in Ghana has been the forced eviction of people who live in 'inadequate', 'not acceptable', and 'not up to standard' structures (Tipple and Speak, 2006, p. 58). Similarly, there is a perennial attack on the livelihood of people who live in these structures, including street people. In turn, homeless, informal, and street people are mostly 'on the run'

(Asiedu and Agyei-Mensah, 2008), except at night, when they sleep on pavements, in front of kiosks, or at street corners. It would seem, therefore, that the government is implicitly encouraging people to sleep on the streets: it chases them off the hawking base, away from the slums, but not off the streets, where they live. These tensions require more effective policy responses.

Conclusion

Internal migration is substantial and dynamic. Over time, it has also become complex. These forms and features of international migration also raise several questions. How can we describe internal migration? Why do people move? What are the effects of internal migrants on society, economy, and environment? Studying internal migration provides theoretical and empirical insights not only to ascertain the migration-environment nexus but also to understand the granular and the grand in global migration research. Yet, internal migration is usually neglected in 'global' migration analysis. This chapter highlights key features of internal migration in general, showing how they differ and are differentiated over both space and time and across groups. While socio-ecological and political-economic factors are, in general, important to explain circular and cumulating drivers of internal migration, their explanatory power is contingent on the particular group of migrants being studied and the institutions that mediate their experiences.

In this sense, the emphasis on natural causes (Malthusianism), natural choices (neoclassical economics), or social structures (Marxian analysis) that characterize most of the existing research on internal migration is limiting. So are the win–win or win–lose representations of internal migration. Migrants send remittances back home, they appear to 'escape' some problems when they migrate, and they contribute to feeding residents in the destination settlements. Indeed, migrants make substantial contributions to sustainable food systems and provide a pathway for food sovereignty.

Yet, the humanist argument sometimes supported by some progressive economists, including Lauchlin Currie (1976) who famously made that point in the 1970s, that migration, particularly rural-urban migration, should be promoted as 'a spatial fix' for underdevelopment is rather optimistic. In fairness, this position typically points to scale economies that are, indeed, found in cities, but calling urban problems merely as 'diseconomies of scale' trivialise the seriousness and complexity of the challenges faced by rural-urban migrants. As this chapter has shown, internal migrants face multiple institutionalized social problems, most importantly related to land. Substantial and widespread, these problems are also persistent and malignant, not simply attributed to 'size' nor are they linked to simply 'class'.

They are formidable challenges which differ in terms of migrant status, age, gender, class, and other social identities. These problems are also mediated by institutions such as land and property rights. These complexities are often overlooked in existing migration policies. Based on simple characterizations steeped in mainstream migration frameworks, such policies and programmes have been unsuccessful in seeking to address the migration question. In the context of the recent and recurrent economic crises on a world scale, the limitations of both analytical and policy frames have become even more serious.

5

Economic Crises and Global Migration

Understanding Crises: Separatism, Structuralism, and Institutionalism

Explaining internal migration is relatively straightforward compared to the exposition and explanation of global transnational migration, which is far more exacting. Apart from its much bigger scale, global transnational migration occurs alongside global economic crises. Whether these crises are separate or interlinked and, if so, in what ways are important questions, often asked in a variety of ways (see, e.g., Showers, 2014, pp. 310–311). On the one hand, migrationists focus on the nature of the current transnational migration 'crisis',[1] as suggested by the United Nations High Commissioner for Refugees (UNHCR) (UNHCR, 2017b), while economists analyse economic crises without necessarily investigating the migration crises. That was evidently the case with the 2008 economic crisis, the recent global economic crisis.

The body of scholarship on these crises is vast in scope, but narrow in analytical range. The paradox in which more research creates less understanding (Cobb, 2021) is particularly applicable to global migration crisis. The many special issues on the transnational migration crises (see, e.g., the volume 54 May issue of *New Perspectives on Turkey* in 2016 and the volume 12(2) issue of *Postcolonial Text* in 2017) have sought to address some of these problems. However, the tendency of these existing 'migration studies' has been to consider the transnational migration crisis not as part of, but apart from, economic and environmental crises. These separatist analytical approaches, in turn, have created unsatisfactory claims about the causal relationship between 'civil' war and the transnational migration crisis, as well as problematic contentions that emphasize how irrational financial greed in the US was the causal mechanism for the 2008 economic crisis.

The approach used in this book, combining Georgist political economy (GPE), institutional economics, and stratification economics (for a discussion, see Commons, 1924; Veblen, 1920; Galbraith, 1958/1998; Stilwell, 2003; Stilwell et al.,

---

[1] The idea of a transnational migration crisis is put in quotation marks not because it is denied, but because the expression itself is used with caution and critical reflection. It is, indeed, telling that in public debates both in the West and the seemingly neutral United Nations agencies, this register of words started to be used more often only when significant numbers of refugees crossed borders of the Western countries, mainly in the European Union. Previously, the presence of refugees in the Global South had not been considered a 'global crisis'. This dynamic itself signals the different and differential values placed on problems in the various parts of the world system and the continuing burdens of 'imperialism and unequal development' that Samir Amin (1977), a leading Global South thinker, carefully demonstrated.

2008; Hamilton, 2018; Yagi, 2020), maintains that, while creating its own institutions, the Global South is interdependent. Capitalism, for example, interacts with non-capitalist institutions, some of which facilitate or constrain its material needs. In this approach, therefore, concepts such as growthmania (Mishan, 1967) and 'social costs' (Kapp, 1950/1971) are not mere ideas, but constructs linked to certain material interests (Harvey, 1973). In using this approach to address the two questions stated at the outset of the chapter, I seek to analyse crises holistically and, hence, to recognize that crises are not independent of the economic system in which they occur and recur. In this sense, private property and how it evolves in the wider context of the global system, is, therefore, of particular importance in the analysis of crises. I draw on publicly available data published, among others, by the UNHCR, the 9/11 Commission, Middle Eastern and African scholars (El-Gamal and Jaffe, 2010; Gitau, 2018) to address the following questions: what are the interconnections between economic crises and migration crises? How are the ramifications of such crises experienced by diverse groups? Why are existing policy solutions so ineffective?

I question various analytical approaches that consider crises separately and problematize structuralist positions that see crises as interconnected, but grounded entirely in contradictions of capital. Instead, I argue that, much like the 2008 financial crisis or the global crises of the 1980s (Harrison, 1983), the transnational migration crisis, of which the refugee crisis is only one part, is rooted in the dominant economic system and its interactions with other economic systems. So, separatist analyses are mistaken. However, these crises arise not just from contradictions of capital, as the structuralist schools claim. Privatizing land, privately appropriating socially created rents, and pursuing imperial monopolistic accumulation strategies that rob labour of its wages are critical drivers of the prevailing crises of the twenty-first century. Not only do these two crises share a common origin, but they are also mutually reinforcing.

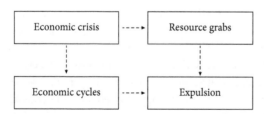

Fig. 5.1 Analytic framework
Source: Author's depiction.

As suggested in Figure 5.1, *economic cycles* are strongly influenced by the political economy of the Middle East and North Africa (MENA). The root of the tensions and contradictions in MENA is not just 'all about oil' (Klare, 2003), as is often popularly conceived (Harvey, 2003). It is not even just a case of 'militarized neoliberalism' in specific countries (Doran, 2007), or the neoliberalization of the entire region, which is a dynamic often called the vision for a 'New Middle East' (Klein, 2007).

Rather, at the heart of the MENA phenomenon is the relentless pursuit of profit-led and rent-based growth championed by Washington. Under capitalism, 'growthmania' (Mishan, 1967) is inherent because capitalism is an expansionary system in which financial and landed speculation, wars, colonialism, neocolonialism, and modern imperialism structurally generate cycles of boom and bust. Not only did these cycles trigger dispossession and displacement in the MENA region, but they also sparked wider *economic crises* for the world. Paradoxically, *resource grabs,* or the attempt to salvage the situation by shifting investment into common land, seemingly a more durable vehicle, led to additional levels of dispossession and displacement. *Expulsion* and transnational migration (including the refugee problem) are cross-cutting effects, which arise both in economic cycles and during economic crises and can simultaneously trigger economic cycles and economic crises.

This drama of land, labour, and capital is played out at different scales, but particularly in capitalist cities, which provide a concrete canvas to bind financial capital and transnational migration crises together. As spaces of capital, such cities provide the financial capital to fund resource grabs (in a process that is quickly transforming rural and peri-urban land). The interest in such resources is mainly restricted to their landed exchange value (to adapt the Marxian concepts, see Harvey, 1973, 1978). It is the rate of investor returns that is the central logic for the flow of funds into rural, peri-urban, and urban land in peripheral cities in a process of uneven, albeit combined, global urban economic development (Obeng-Odoom, 2016b; Bertini and Zouache, 2021). In 'The Urban Process under Capitalism' (Harvey, 1978), cities, especially those whose functions strongly include providing finance and credit, switch financial capital from financial centres to peripheral cities through the rapid transformation of rural and peri-urban land into gated estates and corporate investment sites (Obeng-Odoom, 2014, 2016a, 2021a; Haila, 2020).

Indeed, not only are these cities revolving doors for privately appropriating socially created rent and switching financial capital from one sector to another, or from one city to a peripheral city, they also provide the conditions to concentrate power, and institute the engines of the 'growth machine' (Molotch, 1976) to produce and consume petroleum amidst many spatial inequalities and social stratification (Obeng-Odoom, 2020b). Consequently, existing transnational migration policies, based on the theory that refugees, for example, are fleeing from (internal) civil war caused by a clash between greedy dictators and freedom fighters, are mistaken. Similarly, migration policies, based on the idea that the refugee problem is a function of population, are also mistaken.

Destination policies, such as building walls and creating detention centres, are misconceived. Simply declaring 'sanctuary cities' to help refugees fleeing from civil war, even if well-intended, is misinformed. Revisionist attempts by new institutional economists, notably Alexander Betts and colleagues (2017), requires careful attention. These alternatives seek to go beyond the encampment of refugees who appear to be 'burdens' for host nations. To address the encampment problem, they consider refugees as rational agents who need to be empowered to engage in transactions, among other things, with capitalist businesses (Betts et al., 2017, pp. 186–199). The European Union (EU) appears to support this position through the implementation of its Refugee Skills Profile Tool. As shown by Merve Burnazoglu (2021), although the tool is supposed to ensure a flexible way of matching the skills of refugees to relevant employment avenues, inbuilt within the tool are assumptions about able-bodied rational individuals who must be willing to assimilate to be useful in a society rebuilt along the visions of aid donors seeking to exchange money for the right to exit. Although under this framework refugees recurrently fail to find work, advocates of this framing are oblivious to the systemic discrimination against refugees (Burnazoglu, 2021). Instead, they blame the refugees for their lack of human capital or blame their poor searching and matching skills. Either way, such stratification leads to the creation of hierarchal and segmented labour markets.

This sorting process, therefore, is one of standardization. Not only does this new institutional economics alternative fail to draw attention to root causes and institutions that generate and maintain conflict and 'brand' refugees as 'others', but the solutions proposed by new institutional economics also sanction the status quo of inherent cycles and crises. Thus, under the present economic order, economic cycles, economic crises, resource grabs, and the expulsion of refugees are yoked and braided together. Posited solutions within this global system merely reinforce the process.

To flesh out these arguments, the rest of the chapter is divided into four sections. They offer analysis of economic cycles, economic crises, resource grabs, and expulsions.

Economic Cycles

Both in the media and in neoclassical research economics more generally, the role of war in economic cycles is misunderstood. It is common for the media to represent the refugee crisis as a product of 'internal strife, war, the dictates of authoritarian regimes, and the collapse of governments in the Global South' (Chowdhury, 2017, p. 1). Mainstream economics represents war even more simplistically. At one extreme, it is denied that war plays a significant role in the capitalist economic system (Sherman, 2006, p. 520). At the other extreme, mainstream economics offers a caricature of the place of war in economic matters. One view, following Garrett

Hardin's 'tragedy of the commons' theory, strongly developed in new institutional economics, sees refugees as a function of overpopulation (see Hardin, 1974, 1993) or a lack of market-oriented institutions (Betts et al., 2017). Blaming the victims of war themselves and absolving rentiers of complicity, this view follows the much earlier 'economic science' of Reverend Thomas Malthus to deny that war is a function of economic cycles based on a system of rents (Remoff, 2016). Another approach—common in neoclassical economics—is merely to consider war a reflection of greed or grievance by local actors who destroy the local economy and make everyone worse off (Collier, 2009a, 2009b). In this depiction, neoclassical economists consider the deployment of the army simply as a 'public good' (for a critical discussion, see Gaffney, 2018). The emphasis in the neoclassical story is simply for the army, or any other institution, to clear the paths for refugees, as rational agents, to do business as usual in order to enhance migrant livelihoods. This process, according to the neoclassical theory, impacts on the growth of the local economy where the refugees are located (for a detailed defence review of this literature, see Betts et al., 2017, pp. 1–39).

The reality, however, is far more complex. Under the prevailing economic order, war is at the heart of economic cycles. Indeed, the centrality of war to the thriving of capitalist economies is the essence of Kondratieff long waves, a well-known model, developed by Nikolai Kondratieff, that suggests that war-based macroeconomic cycles can be sustained for about fifty years (Stilwell et al., 2008, p. 268; Beasley, 2019). So, war, conflicts, and 'defence' are 'normal' ingredients of economic cycles. Wars are not only sparked by economic interests, but they can also create business opportunities for transnational corporations, not only from the countries of the aggressors, but also from the nations of the aggressors' allies (Stilwell et al., 2008; Chung, 2019). To foster business, sometimes wars must be fought, expanded, or sustained.

Sometimes too, these wars are fought to seemingly prevent business interests or economies in the North from falling into financial difficulties/economic decline. Often, they are fought to keep the economy of the aggressor stable. Systematic research (Stilwell et al., 2008; Chung, 2019) shows that wars cast well-known effects on the macro-economy, driving economic growth (e.g., through technological innovations, jobs created through military-industry complexes, and sheer profiteering). The notion of 'military-industrial complex', coined by President Dwight Eisenhover, was developed conceptually by J.K. Galbraith (1967, 2004) who saw the symbiotic relationship between war economy, industry, and military. According to him, 'the stability of production depends on a large volume of military expenditures, quite a few of them for weapons ... Additionally, the weapons culture ... underlies the macroeconomic stabilization of the economy' (Galbraith, 1958/1998, p. 257). In this cycle, wars reflect another face of fossil-based, rent-induced, and profit-led production.

War tends to help to prop up and expand the capitalist economy, but it also creates contractionary forces—as the leading economist, H.J. Sherman, himself a former soldier, has consistently shown (Sherman, 2006, 2011; O'Hara and Sherman, 2004). This type of production is primarily for profit; not for human need.

Thus, the production of cars, guns, and luxury goods feature prominently in the war economy. Its expansion, however, is often at the cost of public provision for human services. Shifting public resources from public-spirited causes and social needs into destructive processes tends to reduce effective demand over time. In turn, not only does the economy contract because of the lack of demand, but also because of the lack of the Keynesian multiplier, which helps economies to expand when there is direct state intervention on the demand side. Peacetime follows with expansion too, but the nature of the expansion is rather different. In this 'peacetime growth', economic expansion arises from investment in a stable, healthy, and safer society, which usually generates more inclusive social change.

Private interests and transnational corporations seek more aggressive accumulation, however. Often, these expansionary activities extend overseas investments and pressurize nation states to open up their economies for transnational capital. This 'arms race' takes particular forms in the Global South. There, the military-industrial complex *creates* the need for war, for armament, and for the Western supply of weaponry. Even when arms are given as 'gifts', their maintenance and spare parts need to be bought from the transnational corporations in the Global North, further stirring the northern incentive to create or maintain this dependency by producing the *need* for a 'foreign enemy' or 'internal insecurity' (Robinson, 1979/2009, p. 122).

In this process, private property is needed to reduce transaction costs and to secure individual investment (Griethuysen, 2012). As an institution that facilitates capitalist 'growthmania' (Mishan, 1967) or, 'the growth machine' in the urban context (Molotch, 1976), private property has to be created, defended, and extended. This capitalist dynamic of *continuing* growth, depending on the audience, could be justified as profit making (often told to share-holders), job creating (strategic communication to convince the general population), creating environmental sustainability (the gloss strategy for being seen by officialdom both locally and globally to be doing something for the environment), and creating peace by attacking the 'enemy' (an oft-used strategy to justify war to electorates in the Global North).

Private property-based 'growthmania', then, is a major underpinning logic of war which, in turn, is used to establish new regimes of privatizing the commons on a global scale. In this process, creating private control (through transnational corporations) over commonly or publicly held oil resources, developing fictitious commodities such as private land, expanding precarious labour, and creating more money debt are key stepping stones (Polanyi, 1944/2001). These privatizations also occur through economic warfare in the form of World Bank/International Monetary Fund (IMF)-imposed programmes that coerce indebted nations to privatize their oil commons.

Thus, when it is said that wars are the forces driving the global refugee problem, it must be recognized that these wars are not merely *endogenous* and refugees are not merely running away from internal wars. There are external 'investments' in such wars for access to resources or for the wars themselves to generate economic opportunities for business interests (Klein, 2007; Beasley, 2019). Wars may not be 'all about oil' (Harvey, 2003), but oil is usually part of the story. The US army, for instance, is recurrently deployed to fight in such wars or to maintain business and to nourish the US army, which is itself quite dependent on oil (Gaffney, 2018).

Whether this is what *resource wars* (Klare, 2001a) is all about requires further analysis. According to the best-known interpretation, developed by Michael Klare, resource wars are not simply the result of ethnic, sectarian, and internal civil strife. They tend, instead, to be driven by the relentless desire for oil, depleting resources, increasing population size (e.g., through forced migration), and creating internal democratic deficits (see also Klare, 2001a, 2001b). Thus, this interpretation is quite Malthusian (Michael, 2003). Indeed, by overlooking colonialism, neo-colonial imperialism, and the broader political economy of war (that is, capitalist 'growthmania', and the spread of private property), this existing interpretation of resource wars is limited.

Consider the recent war in Syria. The standard narrative is that Asad is a dictator who kills his own people. The majority of Syrians rose up to depose him because of his dictatorship. The Syrian government brutally put down the popular protests. So, the US-led West must intervene and seek a regime change (for a review of this standard narrative, see Anderson, 2015, 2016). For political economists (see, e.g., Harvey, 2003; Doran, 2007; Stilwell et al., 2008; Obi, 2009, 2019), however, wars in the MENA—the zones where there are most resource wars and most refugees—cannot be understood without an appreciation of the commitment of the US to a New Middle East that creates conducive conditions for US firms, provides a base for the US military, and guarantees access to Middle Eastern oil resources.

It is important to study Syria–US relations and how they have evolved. The leading accounts of these complex relations (Seale, 1965, 1988; Ismael, 1989; Brown, 1989) show that Syria and the US have not always been at loggerheads. According to Patrick Seale and Linda Butler:

> until 1996, their relations with the United States had, by their lights, been reasonably good. At Asad's two meetings with Clinton … the American president had, to Asad's satisfaction, reaffirmed his commitment to the search for a comprehensive settlement on the basis of land for peace; and … the United States had shown a sustained interest in the Syrian–Israeli negotiations.
>
> (Seale and Butler, 1996, p. 29)

Although Syria continued to be on the list of countries supposed to be supporting terrorism, Patrick Seale and his colleague found that in Syria, it 'was seen as due to

Israeli influence in Washington rather than to any deep-rooted American hostility'. Indeed, there was even a Syrian–US alliance at one stage (Seale and Butler, 1996, p. 33), notably when Syria supported the US-led Iraqi intervention.

What changed was that Asad's Syria resisted Washington's attempts to control the Middle East or to exclude other competing power groups from such control, both being attempts to ultimately strengthen Israel. Specifically, the historic move by former US Secretary of State Warren Christopher to secure Syria's agreement to curb the activities of Hizballah forces failed, as Asad would not accept the US vision for the Middle East. According to Patrick Seale and Linda Butler (1996, p. 30), 'Upon leaving Damascus, Christopher remarked bitterly that his relationship with Asad would "never be the same again".'

It is within this context that the uprising of 2011 ought to be understood. In this methodology (Anderson, 2015), it is also important to pay attention to the identity of those who were initially involved in the uprising, investigate how their place was later taken by others and in what ways, over time, the initial freedom fighters, their insignia, and the characteristics of the alternative leadership they sought became replaced with a vision of changed leaders and regimes. Beyond Western-dominated media accounts, it is useful to study detailed political economic and ethnographic research that is sensitive to the complexities of the Middle East. The characteristics of US leadership are important, too. President Obama sought to carve an identity or a legacy as a non-interventionist leader; but President Trump's approach was rather different (Yahya, 2019). Regardless of differences, however, as Joshua Landis (2012) and Maha Yahya (2019) have suggested, it is important to seek answers to questions about what would happen in Washington if there was an initial, locally based protest against a regime that is not at present pro-Israel or pro-American.

This political-economic approach to the analysis of the uprising and war in Syria has been developed by the political economist, Tim Anderson (2015). Using this approach, he shows that the 2011 uprising was neither armed, nor directed towards regime change. Indeed, the rapid infiltration of the uprising by armed extremists quickly forced those seeking genuine reform to abandon the movement, leaving in their wake an armed extremist group supported by the US. As is well known, the US could opportunistically infiltrate any local opposition in order to bring down the regime of its opponents, who are branded in extremely negative ways so as to produce global consensus on intervention. This strategy is well documented (Klare, 2003; Coll, 2004; 9/11 Commission, 2004) and, as shown by Christopher Doran (2007), in the Middle East, the approach was successfully implemented in Iraq and Afghanistan, the latter having the highest number of refugees in the Middle East after Syria, and probably being the springboard for more refugees after the 2021 victory by the Taliban.

The war tactics utilized in Afghanistan by the US are now better understood (Brisard et al., 2001). The Afghan War was not only about terrorism, but also about the control of oil in the Middle East, and Afghanistan more specifically. Indeed, the second reason was so strong that it often impeded the first, as state-backed transnational corporations (TNCs) preferred a US-backed Afghan 'united' government to a genuine, but unpredictable, Afghan leader. Such an arrangement would also help the American state, which wanted to balance the oil power concentrated in the hands of Russia by expanding its own access to oil and guaranteeing its existing hold over current oil contracts and strategic location. Indeed, the American state itself often acts like an oil company (Brisard et al., 2001; Beasley, 2019). Secretary of Defense Donald Rumsfeld worked with, indeed assisted, Vice-President Dick Cheney as chairman of Halliburton, a company that provides services to the oil industry, while a one-time US National Security Advisor, Condoleezza Rice, was manager for Chevron. Indeed, former Secretaries of Commerce and Energy Donald Evans and Stanley Abraham worked for Tom Brown, a major oil company (Foreign Affairs, 2001). Afghanistan was not only useful because of oil, though; it also provided other strategic benefits. As a country, Afghanistan provided a pathway to accessing other fossil-rich former Soviet or Soviet-controlled areas (e.g., the operations of Unocal to siphon oil from Turkmenistan via pipelines through Afghanistan to Pakistan) without going through Iran, which was hostile to US interests. The World Bank would be interested in this approach and it would finance the oil projects because of the belief that it would bring jobs and development to Afghanistan (Coll, 2004, pp. 301–313). This strategy is now commonly used.

Such was evidently the case in the Sudanese war (Ayers, 2010). On face value, that war was simply the product of internal conflicts between intolerant 'tribes' complicated by the distinct religious intolerance of the north against the south. In practice, while such tensions exist, they are part of a much wider system. It is not a coincidence that 'Of the 58 Chapter VII-mandated United Nations peacekeeping operations since 1990, 32 have been in Africa' (Herro et al., 2009, p. 49). Internal factors contribute to the conflict in Darfur and the wider Sudan–South Sudan wars, but there are also wider global forces that sustain the wars (Herro et al., 2009, p. 59). The framing of Sudanese states as 'fragile' or 'failed' might differ qualitatively from framing Middle Eastern states as 'terrorist', but both framings prepare the grounds for Western intervention (Lambourne and Herro, 2008, p. 276). The history of such Western tactics of creating divisions and turning around to provide 'stability' is revealing.

The British colonial policy of indirect rule is a case in point. This approach to governing the ex-colonies consistently created a divided society in which North Sudan was empowered over South Sudan by privileging the north and northern ways of life by giving more powerful colonial positions to northerners, as well as privileging their systems of ideas. British colonial rule, therefore, officially pursued a policy of uneven development. These 'legal foundations of capitalism', as J.R. Commons (1924) called such rules, helped to cement the domination of North Sudan over South Sudan.

War paves the way for, and is also the result of, capitalist accumulation. Through the so-called 'war on terror', obstacles to accumulation were removed. Sudan's fate then, is not only a struggle over resources between the Muslim-dominated north and the non-Muslim south, it is also a struggle in which world powers such as the US and its deputy Israel staunchly support South Sudan against North Sudan and its allies such as Libya (Young, 2012; Chigudu, 2019; Yahya, 2019). In turn, South Sudan too supports the establishment of an embassy in Jerusalem, much like Donald Trump's US. The Sudanese war itself has been about oil and the role of oil TNCs.

There are local conflicts over land, aggravated by land degradation and environmental pillage. But much of these conflicts arise from oil exploration as well. Oil exploration has despoiled the land in such a way that there is growing tension between farmers and herders (Pantuliano, 2010). As several studies (Pantuliano, 2010; Nour, 2011; Young, 2012; Chigudu, 2019) have shown, the process of producing the wonders of an oil economy has also created significant challenges. Water has become toxic because of oil extraction, oil drilling has damaged drainage systems, and oil extraction has led to both dispossession and displacement.

Thus, studies of Sudanese oil extraction strongly suggest that the simple stories of war must be problematized. At the root of such wars is a complex story of colonialism, imperialism, and unequal access to land and resources, especially oil. Such wars are a function of more complex forces, namely the need to guarantee US internal oil supplies, including the need for the US army to be continuously fed with oil for its needs. Second is the need for the US to disempower its competitors by denying them access to vital energy sources. Finally, America's morbid fear of the Middle East, either because it has the power to unsettle the US by denying it crucial oil supplies or by empowering US competitors against the US, is a recurrent reason for US wars in MENA, as it is for US allies. This much is clear, but the role of oil and the political economy of MENA in the last economic crisis is not well understood.

Economic Crises

The Middle East must be taken seriously in analysing the causes of the crises. A major location of global oil production, studying MENA alongside the US must be part of a wider methodology of analysing economic crises (El-Gamal and Jaffe, 2010; Yahya, 2019). According to El-Gamal and Jaffe (2010), as oil supply falls, the global oil price rises, which, in turn, forces consumers to use less oil. So, there are systemic reasons to show why oil will continue to be with us—beyond new discoveries. The Middle Eastern strategy of keeping oil in the ground, they note, is a market or profit-driven approach to artificially create oil shortage in order to enhance the price of oil (El-Gamal and Jaffe, 2010, p.136).

It could be argued that the three interrelated factors of financial markets, energy markets, and the geopolitics of the Middle East combined to cause a global imbalance which, in turn, generates cycles of boom and bust. Each of these three factors had its own cycles, too (El-Gamal and Jaffe, 2010). For instance, one cycle can begin in the oil market when oil supplies fall, triggering increases in the global oil price which, in turn, drives producers to increase supply, following which prices fall and supplies subsequently fall for the cycle to begin again. While the Organization of the Petroleum Exporting Countries (OPEC) tries to mediate to attenuate the inherent cycle, only in a few cases has it been able to substantially change the pattern and, even then, for only a short time (El-Gamal and Jaffe, 2010). In this sense, the Middle East crisis relates to internally and externally imposed conflicts, how such conflicts affect the supply and price of oil, and the various ways in which the region serves as a plant for recycling petrodollars in the form of arms trade.

Colonial, neocolonial, and imperial machinations occur in regions outside of the Middle East. The work of the US and the UK to try to access and control both oil and forces of resistance to counter imperialism in favour of local autonomy are crucial parts of the puzzle. In this sense, much of the 'terrorism' of the Middle East is 'oiled' (El-Gamal and Jaffe, 2010, pp. 66–67). Price, supply, demand, and scarcity, then, tend to be socially and politically constructed. This emphasis on the interrelationships between energy markets, financial markets, and the geopolitics of the Middle East is useful in another respect. The oil market is, in particular, prone to instability as the activities of local producers lead to booms and busts, driven by the interaction of supply and demand (El-Gamal and Jaffe, 2010). The ramifications of these dynamics tend to be global.

Through both property development and urban transportation, cities played an important role in the lead-up to the 2008 crisis and the effects of the crisis were also particularly adverse for cities. Mason Gaffney, a well-known Georgist economist, for example, has shown how speculative urban property development and real estate investment, especially in the US and China, were stepping stones to the crisis (see, e.g., Gaffney, 2015), while Jago Dodson and Neil Sipe (2010) have shown how the crisis resulted from excessive reliance on oil-based automobility. Partly driven by speculation-inspired suburban development, partly by speculation-driven increasing property prices in the city centre, and particularly by the roads lobby, including oil transnational companies, suburban living intensifies reliance on the automobile. In turn, the rise in oil prices had a major effect on urban and suburban residents, whose wages were swallowed by the price increase. These analyses, however, must be further extended because how this speculation embroils and is, in turn, embroiled in the political economy of MENA and the world economy ought to be investigated.

The link between oil and debt is a useful point of departure. With the growing reliance on oil vis-à-vis its supplies, the price of oil increased. This was not just a case of 'peak oil theories', as developed by M. King Hubbert (1974), which suggest that physical scarcity is what drives oil price hikes. Rather, a combination of policies such as oil subsidies, hoarding, and speculation drove the increases in the price of oil which, in turn, excited rentiers to speculate even more about oil (El-Gamal and Jaffe, 2010). As the US, in particular, became more dependent on oil in a process of rising oil prices, its debt increased beyond what its rising dollars and growing economies could sustain. These unsustainable levels of debt and of accumulation also increased the pressure to go to war or to seek to control the Middle East (Michael, 2003; El-Gamal and Jaffe, 2010).

Financialized real estate played a major role in this process. The rising price of oil induced property-fuelled speculation by investors, both inside and outside of the Middle Eastern region, who bought shares floated in the property industry. The realization that the property prices were inflated caused panic and investors withdrew their money, taking it, instead, to Europe and elsewhere to invest in hedge funds, whose managers, paradoxically, invested the money in oil futures. Such speculation, in turn, created conditions for the bubble to trigger further increases in oil prices, resulting in excitement and even more speculation in the Middle East and elsewhere until there was a sudden burst in 2008.

What we had, then, was a bubble-and-burst story with origins in the Middle East, intensified by systemic problems in the rest of the world (El-Gamal and Jaffe, 2010, pp. 144–147). In this sense, the centre of action was not in the US, but, rather, in the Middle East. However, as Kate Showers (2014) has recently shown, with the tensions in the Middle East, the realization that the region cannot solve the West's energy crisis, and the pressure on the West to refocus its search for energy on 'sustainable' energy for a cleaner environment, the age-old Trans-Atlantic Slavery strategy has been invoked. Under this strategy, Continental Africa is the key location for 'renewable energy', whether in the form of slave labour, vacant land, or both. Either way, the affluent classes in the West drained Africa's resources for their own pleasures which, as described by Thorstein Veblen (1899/1979) and J.K. Galbraith (1958/1998), are quite wasteful. This vast amount of waste was shocking when it was first described, but, as Mike Berry (2013), in his reassessment in more recent times, has shown, the issues of resource depletion arising from elite consumerism and waste have probably become worse. This background brings the ongoing resource grabs in Africa into sharp perspective.

Resource Grabs

According to Fred Pearce (2012), at the height of the crisis in 2008, investors moved en masse to Sudan to buy up the resources of the country. US firms (Jarch Capital, Nile Trading and Development, and its affiliate, Kinyeti Development) in particular, obtained long leases of parcels of land, some of which were 170 times the size of Manhattan (Pearce, 2012, p. 42).

Resource grabs are not limited to MENA. The network of this regime of accumulation can be found around the world: in Europe, South America, the US, and in the Middle East. Particular spaces, such as the New York Stock Exchange (NYSE) and the cities where power and wealth are concentrated, have played a major role in these resource grabs (Liberti, 2013; Ouma, 2020). Indeed, Joshua Leon wrote, in *Third World Quarterly*, that:

> Leading global cities like New York, London, Hong Kong, Chicago and Singapore are not merely impressive collections of factor endowments. They are also sites of concentrated power with coercive influences beyond municipal boundaries .... Juxtaposing data on global connectivity with the location strategies of private firms, we learn that the world's most successful global cities are also sources of exploitative accumulations of land.
>
> (Leon, 2015, p. 257)

In these cities, it is the rentier class that drives the financing of resource grabs. Incidentally, it is also those whose needs are most met by this international division of labour. Unlike Karl Polanyi (1944/2001), who considered land a '*fictitious commodity*', for this class of urban investors, land is a *real* commodity. For the urban elites, resident in capital cities such as Khartoum, Juba, and Addis Ababa, 'development' is often their posited reason for encouraging resource grabs. However, it is the need for foreign exchange—or what one state official called 'money in strong currency' (Liberti, 2013, p. 16)—that is a major driving reason for land grabbing. In turn, much of the sale is done in strong, rather than local, currencies. Even more fundamentally, many host nations are facilitating land grabbing for their own survival; that is, they survive because they serve the needs of powerful nations which need African land and they, in turn, offer protection to the land grabbing-endorsing regimes. The competition to get this strong currency, however, leads to some ridiculously low land prices. For example, research shows that in Mozambique, the price for 1 hectare of land is $1; in Ethiopia it is 50–70 cents, and, in the Central African Republic, land is free for the first investors who arrive (Liberti, 2013).

This model of land pricing is strongly encouraged by the world development agencies, including the World Bank and the Food and Agriculture Organization (FAO). Ideology is not their only reason for offering this support. Rather, these development organizations are materially invested in the system of land pricing. The World Bank's International Finance Corporation (IFC) is itself a land investor (Liberti, 2013, p. 101; Voeten, 2021, p. 5). So, when these organizations—especially the World Bank—turn around to devise the so-called *Principles for Responsible Agricultural Investment* jointly developed by FAO, the International Fund for Agricultural Development (FAD), the United Nations Conference on Trade and Development (UNCTAD) and the World Bank Group without grassroots input, what they are doing, in fact, is creating a market for themselves.

This self-interest or conflict of interest is rarely declared, except, perhaps, in the investment community, in which the World Bank is seen as a big investor. In turn, the Bank's investment practices signal what other investors could do (Liberti, 2013; Voete, 2021). In this sense, the *World Development Reports* are, essentially, investment prospectuses for the world of investors. Smaller reports, such as *Rising Global Interest in Farmland* (World Bank, 2011), may be designed to interpret markets, but they also manipulate them. Thus, when World Bank researchers claim—in their contribution to *The World Bank Economic Review* (Arezki et al., 2015)—that it is not speculation that is driving the hikes in land prices, the researchers are making a self-interested statement couched in 'scientific' econometrics.

Empirical research, involving direct observations and interviews with investors (Liberti, 2013; Ouma, 2020), has established that land grabbing is largely speculative. A business for TNCs, these land supermarkets have displaced many small-scale farmers in Brazil, Ethiopia, and Tanzania, indeed in much of Africa. However, resource grabbing does not begin and end in Africa. Indeed, land grabbing, whether as ideology, process, or social practice, has roots and branches all over the world, although only a few TNCs and powerful nations control the vast expanses of land (see Liberti, 2013, pp. 147–148; see also Ouma, 2020). So, the persistence of modern day *latifundia* is real. Its effect has been 'The eviction of millions of small farmers in poor countries owing to the 220 million hectares of land, or over 540 million acres, acquired by foreign investors and governments since 2006' (Sassen, 2014, p. 3). These expulsions require further analysis.

Expulsions

Saskia Sassen's research paves the way. In her book, *Expulsions* (Sassen, 2014, see also Sassen, 2020), Sassen documents how financialization and carbon trading, in particular, expel a broad range of people. The book highlights 'the countless displaced people warehoused in formal and informal refugee camps' (Sassen, 2014, p. 3). This process of dispossession, displacement, and expulsion lies behind transnational migration in general. Sassen's research calls into question so-called 'voluntary' economic migration, driven, to a large extent, by the contradictions of Lockean capitalism in a global geopolitical context. This wider process has been theorized elsewhere (see, e.g., Obeng-Odoom, 2017a) and demonstrated by writers such as Stephen Castles and his team (e.g., Castles, 2017; Castles et al., 2012; Castles et al., 2014; Castles and Miller, 2011) and more recently by Stefan Ouma (see Ouma, 2020). Where more emphasis is needed is the *journey* from displacement to seeking *refuge*.

Refugees typically contract smugglers to help them escape to the new country of their choice. While the experience is smooth in some cases and, hence, such smugglers are considered 'saviours', in most cases, refugees are duped, raped, or even killed in a journey characterized by uncertainty along the way (Tinti and

Reitano, 2017). If refugees are victims, they are also sometimes compelled by life-threatening circumstances to use whatever means possible to survive (Tinti and Reitano, 2016). This focus on the agents of migration (the human traffickers), their profit-making activities made possible because of the pressure to run, the obstacles to overcome, and the possible perceived prize ahead, helps to stress the urgent need for holistic policies for refugees (Emser, 2017; Perdigao, 2017). They must prevent deaths and reproduction of refugees. 'Death' because many refugees die trying to leave harm's way. Between 2020 and 2021, at least 3, 773 people from Africa died trying to reach the Canary Islands. Of these, 1,851 died in 2020, so more people have died in 2021 (Jones, 2021, p. 12). As Table 5.1 shows, expulsion has become worse since the commencement of the 2008 crisis. Between that time and 2018, the number of official refugees doubled from about 10.5 million to 22.5 million people.

According to UNHCR (2018), 55% of the world's refugees come from MENA. Specifically, most refugees come from Syria (5.5 million), Afghanistan (2.5 million), and South Sudan (1.4 million). The experiences of refugees have been detailed in several publications (e.g., Netto, 2011; Oka, 2011; Betts et al., 2017; Gitau, 2018), so only a brief account is needed here. Aside from deaths, these experiences are dire and worsening, so refugee policy has become an increasingly important theme in migration research (see, e.g., Castles et al., 2012; Eder and Özkul, 2016; Tinti and Reitano, 2017).

Yet, in the light of the reinterpretation of the refugee problem in this chapter, we need to revisit refugee policy. In particular, policies at the destination sites (such as confinement in detention centres, refugee camps, sanctuary cities, and the continuum of economic solutions from livelihoods and impacts to refugee economies which stress that '[r]efugees represent opportunities for business and entrepreneurship', Betts et al., 2017, p. 7) and the sites of origin (such as regime change) need to be reconsidered.

Detention Centres and Refugee Camps

A major policy position in migration studies is to build detention centres and refugee camps. The humanitarian orientation in this approach is supported by United Nations institutions, international donor organizations, and the state. These institutions intend that detention centres and refugee camps contain refugees in isolated areas so that they do not influence the ways of life of the host communities. In this policy position, refugees are expected to be detained for a while, sent back when the source of danger is removed, or processed further for other destinations in Australia, the Americas, or some European countries.

The more economic approach is to emphasize migrant livelihoods, impacts, and, at a much wider institutional scale, develop entire refugee economies. The first two approaches, as Alexander Betts and others have shown (2017), are neoclassical

Table 5.1 Refugees and other displaced people since the 2008 crisis

Year	Refugees	Asylum-seekers (pending cases)	Returned refugees	IDPs (internally displaced persons) protected or assisted by UNHCR	Returned IDPs	Persons under UNHCR's statelessness mandate	Others of concern	Total
2008	10,489,800	825,800	603,800	14,442,200	1,361,400	6,572,200	166,900	34,462,100
2009	10,396,500	983,900	251,500	15,628,100	2,229,500	6,559,600	411,700	36,460,800
2010	10,549,700	837,500	197,700	14,697,900	2,923,300	3,463,000	1,255,600	33,924,700
2011	10,404,800	895,300	531,900	15,473,400	3,245,800	3,477,100	1,411,800	35,440,100
2012	10,498,000	942,800	525,900	17,670,400	1,545,400	3,335,800	1,329,700	35,848,000
2013	11,699,300	1,164,400	414,600	23,925,500	1,356,200	3,469,200	836,100	42,865,300
2014	14,380,100	1,796,200	126,900	32,274,600	1,822,700	3,492,100	1,052,800	54,945,400
2015	16,111,300	3,225,000	201,400	37,494,200	2,317,300	3,687,800	870,700	63,907,700
2016	17,185,300	2,837,100	552,200	36,627,100	6,511,100	3,242,000	803,100	67,758,100
2017–2018	25,400,000	–	–	–	–	–	–	–

Sources: UNHCR (2017a, p. 13; 2017b, p. 208; 2018).

in origin. They are part of the mainstream argument that refugees are rational individuals whose actions should be analysed like other economic agents. The microeconomics of cost–benefit analysis, therefore, is what should guide refugee policy. If the net advantage of considering refugee labour is positive, then the question of refugees becoming burdens no longer arises. However, new institutional economists contend that the emphasis on impacts shifts attention away from the refugees themselves to their social contexts and livelihoods, emphasizing only the process of earning a living and not the entire market experience.

On the basis of these criticisms, new institutional economists posit refugee economies as a solution. The best-known work on the subject sees 'refugee economies' as 'resource allocation systems relating to the lives of refugees' (Betts et al., 2016, pp. 40–63). The assumption of a rational individual is retained, but it is recognized that the individual's activities are shaped by institutions so they are not as free-standing as in mainstream neoclassical economics. As Betts and his collaborators note:

> [we] will argue that refugees are in a distinctive economic position because of their positioning between three different sets of institutions. First, they lie between state and international governance. They are partly under the authority of the state and partly under the authority of international organizations. Second, they lie between the formal and informal sectors. They usually have some legitimate access to the formal economy but also frequently face regulatory restrictions compared to citizens. Third, they lie between national and transnational economies.
>
> (Betts et al., 2016, p. 9)

The role of transaction costs is strongly encouraged in this approach, so the promotion of property rights is common, as is the encouragement of transnational businesses, along with other social enterprises to work with migrants (see, e.g., Betts et al., 2016, pp. 186–199). This new institutional economics framework is often justified as ensuring a triple win for the state because its burden of care is broken, for refugees themselves because they become workers and for the international community because its aid to refugees become sustainable.

Yet, the approach by new institutionalists is marketization. The advocacy of more markets in urban centres and elsewhere extols the virtues of capitalist exchange. While recognizing their limits, solutions such as the extension of private property rights in land is recommended. Apparently, refugees are not being allowed to trade enough. By marketizing land, for example, the advocates of this approach claim that they can ensure security of tenure, better incentivize refugees, and better ensure that refugees know 'the rules of the game' (Betts et al., 2016, pp. 130–132). The use of digital technology is also promoted to ensure that information asymmetries are addressed. So is human capital development. According to this line of analysis, refugees need to acquire more education to enhance not only their income but also their choices of where to live and life choices generally, including choice of networks (Betts et al., 2016, pp. 205–209). In short, the new institutional economics approach builds, uses, maintains, and facilitates markets as solutions:

> Today, there are new opportunities to adopt more market-based approaches. Recognizing and understanding the economic lives of refugees themselves, and the ways in which they interact with markets as consumers, producers, buyers, sellers, borrowers, lenders, employers, employees, and entrepreneurs.
>
> (Betts et al., 2016, p. 211)

This approach is institutionalized by the EU through its Skills Profile Tool for Third Country Nationals (Burnazoglu, 2020). The approach does not break away from orthodoxy. Rather, advocates consider that the approach seeks 'to build on what exists' in a process in which '[s]upporting refugees' capacities rather than just their vulnerabilities offers an opportunity to rethink assistance in ways that are more sustainable for refugees, host states, and donors' (Betts et al., 2016, p. 211). Refugee economies must, therefore, be taken seriously.

Yet, like the neoclassical emphasis on 'impact' and 'livelihoods', refugee economies, as a new institutional economics alternative, can be seriously limiting. Emphasizing market-based interventions, private-sector solutions, enabling the environment through, for example, institutionalizing property rights, along with research to promote marketization (Betts et al., 2016, pp. 212–213), the approach has no regard for the social economy. The approach also neglects the embeddedness of the economy in wider social relations. The silence concerning the lives and struggles of the people and the emphasis on economic integration at various scales (Betts et al., 2016, pp. 211–222), although there are clear documented policies and experiences of socio-cultural, religious, and political integration (e.g., Manatscal et al., 2020; Zuber, 2020; Paquet and Xhardez, 2020) raises fundamental questions.

Consider education, for example. International students are thought of as refugees in Australia. As Chapter 8 shows, these students face significant barriers in Australian society, including inadequate access to adequate housing, funding, and wider social support. International students face pervasive discrimination in employment but also elsewhere in Australian society, such as in the realm of housing. A recent study (Hartley et al., 2019) of international students of refugee status further nuances the claims I make in Chapter 8. According to the study (Hartley et al., 2019), not only do international students lack language support, they also have to pay high fees which, in turn, forces them to take more courses so that they can finish studying in the shortest possible time. However, an increased workload brings its own stress and mental health problems, for which these students have little or no social support. Uncertainty about their status as refugees compounds their struggles and stresses in an environment where they have limited social protection and, even worse, face systemic inequalities and barriers. These matters are of only marginal concern to the new institutional economist (see Betts et al., 2016), for whom markets are asocial.

Yet, actually existing markets in real life are socially embedded (Polanyi, 1944/2001, 1957). One of the refugee students interviewed by Lisa Hartley's team (Hartley et al., 2019) stated that education is more than human capital. It is certainly not just about returns on human investment. As the student puts it, '[m]y study is the purpose of continuing my life. If that is taken away from me, I am nothing' (cited in Hartley et al., 2019, p. 7). So, in the light of the original institutional and stratification economics perspective developed in this book, the actual experiences of the people in the camp are, perhaps, what is most interesting to consider. In this sense, the case of Kakuma Refugee Camp (KRC) in Kenya is worth exploring further. Well known around the world as a major refugee camp in terms of its sheer size and longevity, it was built in 1991 by UNHCR and the World Food Programme. It has been a 'home' for refugees who come from countries such as Uganda, Rwanda, Congo, Ethiopia, Somalia, and Sudan. As one of the world's most important refugee centres (alongside Dadaab, also in Kenya), the experiences of KRC are worth examining.

One of the most recent pieces of empirical research on the subject has been published by Lydia Wanju Gitau (2018). According to her study, the South Sudanese who have fled from war are one of the most traumatized refugee groups in KRC. Their trauma, formed after living in a war zone, is complicated by their struggle to flee from there. The escape from war is a journey that is both risky and arduous, as is life in the refugee camp itself. National peace treaties, however, merely focus on bringing peace. Part of the reason for this narrow focus is the view that all that refugees need is to be taken away from danger or to be helped to meet their daily needs. In fact, the situation is far more complex.

Gitau's study—entailing ethnographic research in the Kakuma refugee camp— shows that the trauma is gendered. Women are afraid of being raped, as they were in the war zone, while men feel helpless, as they cannot play their traditional roles of providers and protectors. The camp is important, and many refugees express gratitude. However, it does not necessarily help; indeed it often hinders, in the management of trauma. For instance, men, not used to getting the same portions of food as women, suddenly have to cope with this situation in the camp. This is hardly a case of the triumph of feminism, however. Women are not given equal educational opportunities in the camp. Even the claim to peace in the camp is, itself, questionable because the peace KRC offers is in an island, while parts of the refugees are on the mainland and, hence, cannot find peace.

Yet, these refugees are not simply passively fading day by day. They are resilient in the sense that they try to think positively about the future. Other strategies refugees have devised include developing a faith in God, supporting one another, developing inner strength, taking personal responsibility, and creating a vision for their lives. Some have indeed started social enterprises which bring in just enough to enable them to take their children, including daughters, to schools outside the camps (Gitau, 2018, pp. 79–94).

From this perspective, giving refugees peace is not enough. It is not even enough to help refugees to settle or hire themselves out to the business world, as new institutional economists advocate. Unless 'peace is seen as everything', a phrase which refugees in the camp themselves use quite often (Gitau, 2018, pp. 109–110), the pursuit for peace is a narrow vision. Peace is not just the absence of war, but entails the development of social relations with others and living within a flourishing community. Peace is strengthening, not mutilating, identity through integration, or learning to behave like others. Peace is tolerating others, not seeking to become like others. Assimilation or integration can be paradoxical because, at least in the case of the South Sudanese in Kakuma Camp, they were not only fleeing from war, but they were also fleeing from a war whose underpinnings included a specific form of militant Arabization or Islamization (Gitau, 2018, p. 2).

Peace is meeting one's material needs, including the recurrent problem of 'scarcity' in the camp (Gitau, 2018, pp. 49–50, 54–55), sometimes described as *homo sacer* (the accursed man), a life without citizenship or rights, a fleeting and empty life which 'begs filling' (Gitau, 2018, p. 55). It involves the political needs of addressing the destruction of relatives, friends, and families left behind, as well as social needs. Peace is everything. The material basis of peace is crucial. For instance, refugees in the camp wear the UN ration card, which is used to claim food, around their necks to show that their very lives hang on it (Gitau, 2018, p. 75). Those whose work in refugee camps is to offer psychological support and health support recurrently report that the refugees ask them for material support (Gitau, 2018, pp. 75–77). Material needs, however, are not independent but interdependent. Citizenship is a strong claim because it helps to unlock rights to health care and other things (2018, p. 76), but although it can unite many needs, it is not sufficient in itself. Also insufficient is the typical UN response of seeking to prevent the risk of statelessness in South Sudan or other country of origin (2018, p. 76) instead of pursuing citizenship in the new country of settlement.

Generally, refugees respond to their conditions by voicing, improvising, and exiting (Oka, 2011). They voice their criticisms in various ways. For instance, one refugee said: 'There are many problems with the food they give. When we came, it was with my mother and six children, my husband died in Somalia. We were given a house but no mattresses, no blankets' (cited in Oka, 2011, p. 247). Another said, 'They think just because we are refugees in Africa and all Africans have to be the same and eat the same that we will all eat sorghum and maize. We are not Ethiopian or Bantu, we are Somali' (cited in Oka, 2011, p. 252). In turn, many refugees have improvised by developing informal economies within the refugee centres to trade what they receive for other goods and services that others within the camp, or elsewhere bring to them. Others receive remittances from relatives and friends who live outside the camp. A few improvise by working in low-tier work within the camps, as members of the UN groups who earn paltry pay, although in this way they obtain greater access to supplies within the camp.

Could better urban governance be a solution? Border towns, in particular, make this a difficult question to answer. These towns are neither rural nor urban. They have their own identity. Current forms of urban governance, focused mostly on facilitating urban economic activities and offering services such as waste management for refugees, do not realize that much of the dynamics of the 'urban face' of refugee life is in fact peri-urban (Carpi and Boano, 2018). But these problems cannot be improved by simply looking at them as rural either. Indeed, the experiences of border towns in the Middle East, such as Halba (Lebanon), Killis (Turkey), and Ar-Ramtha (Jordan), teach us that what is important is to balance the three: to focus intersectionally on cities, on rural areas, and on peri-urban areas. These issues cannot be left to the market, as the effects of implementing neoliberal urban policy now show, and if only market forces are considered, this leads to awkward outcomes (Carpi and Boano, 2018). Long-range planning is useful and in order to be truly helpful must acknowledge that some migrants have a rural orientation on account of their upbringing. The policies adopted must outlast the humanitarian assistance programmes now in place because the forces that impel the 'refugee crises' are far more complex.

Sanctuary Cities

If refugee cities are limited in what they can do, are sanctuary cities better for refugees? The defiance of sanctuary cities creates tensions within the state, although whether these tensions are revolutionary or reformist depends on the strategies utilized by these sanctuary cities. In sanctuary cities in the US and Canada, for example, there is a more explicit attempt to protect illegal migrants and refugees and, hence, to openly defy the federal authorities. 'Don't Ask, Don't Tell' (DADT) policies constitute one proactive approach. Such policies prohibit city authorities from asking questions about the migration status of refugees and illegal migrants and refrain from basing the supply of their municipal services on whether residents have legitimate papers. DADT policies also mean non-cooperation with federal migration authorities, unless federal laws obligate cooperation (Bauder, 2017, p. 176). In the UK, support for refugees in sanctuary cities is more overt. Usually, the support takes the form of gestures by diverse social groups within certain cities without overtly challenging the state. The interest, appears to be more about changing the discourses of hostility to welcoming discourses (Bauder, 2017). Generally, however, the arguments on which they are based—that sanctuary cities do not breed crime and that, instead, they enhance the contribution of refugees and migrants—have been found to be compelling. In one study (Gonzalez et al., 2017), it was shown that sanctuary cities do not have more crime than elsewhere. Indeed, it has even been shown that, as they lead to more cooperation with the authorities, sanctuary cities enhance inclusiveness and safety in cities.

Sanctuary cities, however, can only be considered part of a wider solution. They do not really come with additional rights for refugees or additional economic support for them. They also do nothing for the rentier and capitalist problems that refugees face in their new destinations, although we know that refugees experience substantial discrimination in cities. Assimilation programmes might mean and, perhaps, even do well. They have, for example, helped refugees to gain new skills. They sometimes produce tangible outcomes, too, including enabling some migrants to obtain particular jobs. However, they have their limitations. As Gitau's (2018) study shows, refugees suffer psychological problems that are often ignored in the processes and policies of 'integration' and 'assimilation' (see, e.g., Manatscal et al., 2020; Zuber, 2020; Paquet and Xhardez, 2020).

These policies and programmes do not say anything about business cycles, about the crises of land, nor about the political economy of war. These sanctuary cities, in fact, do not help in improving source conditions. Such policies and programmes adopted so far do not say anything about property conditions in the sanctuary cities. They do not assist the work conditions of migrants, and they do not usually support migrant education improvement. The policies are, therefore, humanist but not radical. The attempt to link sanctuary cities to basic urban economic and political rights has been quite unsatisfactory. Indeed, in Los Angeles, a major sanctuary city (Gonzalez et al., 2017, p. 31), migrant women have continued to get work but, as Morales and Ong (1991) and Storper et al. (2015) have shown, they have been chronically underpaid, contributing to increasing inequality in the urban economy.

Similar concerns have been recorded in Jordan. There, Katharina Lenner and Lewis Turner (2019) have shown that under the 'Jordan Compact', refugees from Syria are not confined to camps. They are instead actively integrated into the Jordanian economy, underpinned by the idea that these refugees are individual profit-maximizing entrepreneurs. At its inception, the policy aimed to extend some 200,000 work permits to refugees from Syria to energize the Jordanian economy. Hailed as a radical shift in the refugee crisis, what happened, in fact, was a radical rightward shift to neoliberal framings of the refugee issue, in considering labour as a commodity or a lever for 'development' in a humanitarian framework. While employment has increased, so has underemployment, discrimination, and rental hikes. The Jordan economy is based on an aggressive, export-led growth model, which weaves low-paid labour into this model in a wheel of fortune in which migrants are caught. This neoliberal transformation has merely worsened the experiences of migrants.

Regime Change

Perhaps, the migrants would not have exited, had regimes changed. This is quite a common US solution. Yet, the attempt to address the problem through regime change in the source country is equally unsatisfactory. The case of refugees in Syria and the inadequacies of regime change as a policy have been analysed by Tim Anderson (2017), so only highlights of the thesis and anti-thesis are presented here. Critics of existing regimes claim that such regimes have lost credibility and, hence, there is widespread discontent with those regimes.

Buoyed by Western presses, the images are graphic and compelling. In this context, the seeming critique of the critics becomes difficult to swallow, even when the evidence collected for exaggeration and misrepresentation is strong (Anderson, 2015, 2017). Both sides are unlikely to make much progress, however. One reason is the proxy war that, until recently, was ongoing between the US and Russia. A second reason is that the ethnographic evidence is not so clear-cut concerning pure hate or pure love for the regimes. It is known that those seen in the street protesting are against, but, at the same time, their material needs are provided by the regimes (Carpi and Glioti, 2018). In turn, the protests could only be said to be expressions of displeasure, not pressures for regime change. In any case, regime change could only be a temporary solution. As the experience of Afghanistan shows, after instituting a new regime, the US could not maintain its preferred system of government ad *infinitum*. The forces of the Taliban in Afghanistan have eventually taken back the power which they lost.

In short, none of the policy positions offered provides compelling alternatives. They are based on the principle of neutrality or the idea that internal forces alone led to the problem of refugees, which is highly contentious. More fundamentally, these policies do not acknowledge the place of the political economy of war, resource grabs, wider accumulation, and economic cycles. They must, accordingly, be fundamentally questioned.

Conclusion: Towards Resistance and Reconstruction

Migrants exercise agency in the form of resistance. They also signal ways for possible reconstruction. Often cast in Marxian revolutionary terms, resistance has been documented by Obeng (2019), who described how African migrants in China revolted against racism on the streets of Guangzhou. Yet, there are other forms of resistance that are non-Marxian (Robinson, 1983). One such theory is how the reproduction of the built environment that conditions and shapes migrant experiences generates resistance and revolution. Resistance centred only on how borders exclude migrants can divert attention from resistance within borders. 'Insider' experiences can help to better understand actual migration experience, which often diverges from prototypical depictions.

The built environment is a major point of departure. Benedict Anderson's latest work, *The City in Transgression* (2020), discusses how migrants use the built form as resistance. Like university life, the book's opening statement goes, the process and the experience of migration can be quite depressing. But many of the students, many of the migrants, will also go on to something greater that will make the analyst, the teacher, proud. This analogy brings into sharp focus the tensions and contradictions that characterize migration and mobility, the optimism and pessimism in the process of movement.

Andersen's book does not only 'transgress' these matters, it also transcends resistance, which is typically seen as organized mobilizations against capital in the form of uprisings. Behind the cameras and the curtain of publicity, along with the glitz of media razzmatazz, many migrants are involved in covert resistance, a silent revolution. This art of resistance is inscribed on the canvas of the built environment. What the built environment means for Anderson is important because that conception must shape his analysis. Accordingly, his book's only reference to the nature of the built environment must be stated in full. 'A constructed stage for the collective ideal,' writes Anderson, 'the built environment is a coordinated system of connections and disconnections, ruptures and repetitions in variations of movement. Routes between home and work are parceled in states of consciousness and partial numbness' (Anderson, 2020, p. 38).

Underlying this idea of the built environment seems to be a Lefebvrean conception of the built environment as 'production of space' (see Lefebvre, 1974/1991), a social system in which production, exchange, and consumption are represented in built form. Yet, Anderson (2020) is a bit more concrete and far more contrarian than Lefebvre. If Lefebvre was looking for the logic of production and projection of form over substance, Anderson is investigating disorder and the substance of form in the activities of migrants. For Anderson, therefore, the built environment is, just as importantly, characterized by making homes out of public spaces, creating slums, loitering, spraying graffiti messages and trading in open spaces, in short, drilling spaces in built form, a transgression that often eludes planners. What makes this emphasis on the built environment new is not only that the spaces have been created, but also that they have, over time, been transformed into spaces of reticence, residence, and resistance (Lefebvre, 1974/1991, p. 4). Such space become platforms of transcendence, too. This is evidently the case where a built form used as a symbol of control is sprayed with graffiti to symbolize steps toward liberation.

Civil society groups seeking to help migrants to assimilate also miss this emphasis on the built environment. We do, however, need to pay attention to these socio-spatial forms of resistance, as the Australian geographer, Kurt Iveson, suggests in his book, *Publics and the City* (2007) and more recently argues in his co-authored book *Everyday Equalities: Making Multicultures in Settler Colonial Cities* (Fincher et al., 2019). Studying the built environment and its many characterizations and (mis)appropriations provides rare insights into the sociology of migration and the political economy of mobility. Both migration policy and mobility planning stand to gain from these lessons.

The scope of Anderson's book is broad. Cities in both the Global North and the Global South are engaged. Complexity is dissolved in engaging personalized and picturesque analyses. Visual ethnography brings the subject matter closer still. Case by case, transgression after transgression, a kaleidoscope of human mobility and resistance in the twenty-first century leaps from the pages of the book. Anderson wants these transgressions to be applauded, not merely apprehended. His argument is that these are acts of human ingenuity. Unlike John Turner's *Housing by People: Towards Autonomy in Building Environments* (1976/1977), which saw such acts as the first point of call, Anderson's call for recognition, rather than criminalization, seems conditional. It must come only when public and social policy have failed to provide public and social housing. The subtext, then, appears to be that migrants, both individually and collectively, have shown that they can address market and policy failures.

For economists, this analysis might bring to mind a reincarnation of Richard Musgrave's concept of merit goods. Planners can learn new lessons in participatory planning. Activists that subscribe to Julius Sello Malema's principles of economic freedom can see them articulated in a new space, within a new body of conversation. But whether they recognize and affirm them or continue to overlook them, the silent revolution cannot be stopped. As Anderson (2020, p. 21) notes, '[w]hile their innovations have not been applauded and instead have become the site of projected fears and targeted bodies, their persistence will nevertheless create new spaces from which the civil in civic society can emerge'. In short, these insights seep into, and significantly strengthen, what has been called 'reconstructed urban economics' (see Obeng-Odoom, 2016b).

These arguments unfold as various forms of resistance: 'Movement'; 'Urban Mobility'; 'Indeterminant Occupation'; 'Ousted Vagrancy'; 'Collective Anarchy'; 'City in Transgression'; and 'Unbounded Mobility'. These captions are rather general, but their contents are acute. The 'Introduction' sets the scene. 'Movement' contextualizes the scale and complexity of the problem. 'Urban Mobility' shows the many ways in which migrants experience the built environment, produced and maintained by a strict code of spatial control. 'Indeterminant Occupation' charts the troubles and tribulations that migrants go through, reflecting systemic failings of planning and migration policy.

'Ousted Vagrancy' documents individual acts of migrant agency and ingenuity (such as roaming, loitering, and homelessness) to resist their manipulation.

'Collective Anarchy' is an analysis of organized migrant resistance (e.g., rogue sites and slums that adapt urban space for migrant use) to orthodoxy. 'City in Transgression' shows how cities transform, or need to transform in the face of long-term crisis and failure, to embrace the centrality of mobility to humanity. 'Unbounded Mobility' closes the book by defending its treatise with even greater verve. Open walls can bring freedom to all. Behind closed walls, migrants show how to attain this freedom through resistance.

In analysing resistance of migrants, Anderson's book can be located in a long tradition of radical scholarship. It is particularly suffused with the spirit of the development geographer, David Drakakis-Smith, who makes similar arguments in *The Third World City* (2000). In more recent times, such arguments can be found in the work of the Iranian scholar, Asef Bayat's. *Life as Politics How Ordinary People Change the Middle East* (Bayat, 2009) is, perhaps, the closest to *The City in Transgression*. Yet, Anderson's book is novel in three important respects. First, it analyses the actual experiences of migrants. Second, it focuses on both the Global North and the Global South. Third, its methodology is an intriguing use of case studies. Several pertinent books serve as the bricks that make up this grand structure. Rarely are books so diverse engaged in such pluralist and historical ways to show migrant resistance.

Yet, there are some issues that need to be raised. In general, it is not clear how comparable are the books that are so carefully knit together to tell the stories of resistance. Written at different times and for diverse audiences, methodological formalists might well be right to question the basis for Anderson's enthusiastic mixing. If the point is not about comparison, but rather to present mobility as a historical project, this concern could be described as merely academic. Still, the comparability of events could be questioned. Is the '2010 Arab Spring' (Chapter 5) the same as the '2019 Hong Kong protests'? More fundamentally, were the protestors in Hong Kong, Egypt, or Tunisia all—or even mostly—migrants? It may also be argued that theories of migration per se are not central to the book, but engaging some of such theories could have helped to extend them and enrich the book. Perhaps, a more compelling concern is the lack of reference to reviews of the books that are used as case studies. How did peers receive the books at the time they were written?

However, the absence of such verification or questions of comparability do not essentially undermine the book's central arguments. Anderson's record of nearly three decades of excellent, meticulous scholarship, including two previous major books, should inspire confidence in both his data and their analyses.

Although Anderson sets out to write 'a succinct account of human mobility and resistance in the 21st century' (Anderson, 2020, p. 1), he ends up doing much more. Not only does he unveil a new way of studying cities and mobility, but he has also offered much-needed answers on how cities might be reconfigured to better support migrants, their families, and friends. *The City in Transgression* is a breakthrough in how to study the city and make urban policy for people, not for profit. Here is a welcome transgression from orthodoxy.

A similar welcome transgression is Yafa El Masri's 'The Complexity and Contradictions of Humanitarian Neutrality: Observing the Challenges of UNRWA and Palestinian Refugees in Lebanon' (2019). Its context is the response of refugees to the neutrality doctrine adopted by international organizations. According to this doctrine, not only international organizations but also its staff and beneficiaries should refrain from expressing their sentiments, even if they have life experience of certain relevant issues that can be substantiated. A strict application of this doctrine means that even Palestinian refugees who regularly experience oppression cannot express their outrage. In this context, as Yafa El Masri's study shows (Masri, 2019), such refugees use graffiti on the walls of international organizations but also elsewhere to denounce both oppression and the neutrality principle of international organizations. While this reproduction of the built environment expressed at night is erased by staff of international organizations in the day time, over a longer period this resistance has contributed to a reinterpretation of the neutrality principle to enable beneficiaries to express themselves and to make staff speak out about what they have seen. Yafa El Masri hails this victory as freedom, arguing that it is confirmation of Amartya Sen's theory of development as freedom. In this alternative, Masri (2019) seems to claim that no neutrality, as a framework, is a sufficient analytical and political canvas for freedom.

Yet, like Anderson's study (Anderson, 2020), Yafa El Masri's (2019) line of analysis has its own limitations. Sen exaggerates the emancipatory power of 'human capital', often suggesting that education is not only necessary but also sufficient for liberation. Sen's work and its individualistic foundations have been carefully unpacked and critiqued by Charles Gore (1997) and I have discussed the limitations of the human capital theory in neoclassical economics and Sen's own idea of human capital elsewhere (Obeng-Odoom, 2020b, pp. 18–155). Hence, repeating a detailed analysis here is unnecessary. Suffice it to note that for Masri to situate resistance within a human capital framework is to run into similar impediments as with Sen's individualistic and instrumentalist conceptions of freedom.

In general, migrant resistance is all too often situated *within* particular spaces, and within the conditions against which migrants resist. This hyper agency overlooks or underplays global structures. Questions of land and territory receive much less attention, but they are central to migration. Certainly, they sit at the interstices of what is usually called 'the migrant town'.

6

The Migrant Town

Liberty Plains

The migrant town is a major source of insight and instruction. Migrant experiences shine through such towns. Answers to questions as to how such towns are formed, what ways migrants influence their local spaces, how they shape the host economy and its society, and how migrants, including their children, experience social stratification. Although much of the research that seeks to address these questions is typically focused on migrants from white-majority countries (e.g., Manatscal et al. 2020; Zuber, 2020) or on white migrants who migrate to rural, peri-urban, and urban spaces (see survey findings in Krivokapic-Skoko and Collins, 2014), there has been substantial research on minority migrants, too (see, e.g., Collins et al., 2020).

There is, however, the need to revisit these claims because of significant recent changes in the racial, ethnic, class, religious, and gendered composition of migrants and immigrant (Collins et al., 2020) and much sounder evidence is now available to address the research questions (Coles, 1971, 2003; Markaki and Longhi, 2013; Çaglar and Schiller, 2018). Mainstream and dominant representations cannot be dismissed in this process because they provide the narrow framework - yet dominant - migration research. Evidence from years of systematic study shows that when migrants are deemed to exert pressure on the facilities of the host communities, are unemployed, and make little or no contribution to the host economy and society (and they often are so deemed), negative attitudes towards migrants are considerably heightened, sometimes reaching feverish conditions. The current 'migration crisis' in Europe, the Americas, and elsewhere in the world exemplifies this view. Migrants are generally perceived as unwanted.

Stereotypically, immigrants and migrants are portrayed in both proper science and popular scenes as parasites. So, they are not deserving of any more benefits than their wages. The neoclassical public choice economist, William A. Niskanen, for example claimed that even if nations do not need to wall out migrants, they need to wall in the welfare state: 'Build a wall around the welfare state, not around the country' (cited in *The Economist*, 2019d, p. 8). This is because migrants do not contribute to the welfare state. Niskanen argues: 'The simplest way to make sure that migrants do not abuse any given benefit is to make them ineligible for it, for five or ten years or permanently' (cited in *The Economist*, 2019d, p. 8). In this account, the troubles and tribulations of migrants are hardly considered. Humanists and liberals, on the other hand, provide win–win tropes. Not only do migrants make an overwhelming contribution to economic growth, but they also help themselves and introduce touristic new 'cultures'. Migrants can have challenges, the humanist argument goes, but they can be addressed by assimilation, integration, and education.

Evident in the discourse of 'compassion' used by those few countries that are taking steps to welcome migrants is testament that migrants are perceived to be parasitic or, in other words, drawers of socio-economic benefits and hewers of security and political tranquillity. Their perceived ecological footprint complements the picture (Boulding, 1965; Daly, 2019). These negative sentiments are particularly acute in cities where pressure on amenities is concentrated and more visible. In turn, migrant towns around the world are commonly described as spaces for criminals, illegal, and dishonest activities, poor housing, blighted conditions, crime, grime, and insecurity (for a discussion of multiple representation of migrants, see Collins, 2008, 2013; Çaglar and Schiller, 2018). The evidence from a relatively small collection of studies (e.g., Stilwell, 2003; Saunders, 2012; Davidson and Gleeson, 2013; Çaglar and Schiller, 2018; DeParle, 2019; Collins et al., 2020), however, problematizes this perception. In all these studies, perceptions, attitudes, and ideology are the primary focus. Economic interests are secondary. In extending the state of the literature, the prevailing hierarchy of forces of inertia and change need to be subjected to careful empirical scrutiny.

So, the remaining questions are the following: how do such towns form? In what ways do migrants transform urban space? How do migrants experience social stratification? The empirical referent of the study is Lidcombe, a migrant town in Sydney, Australia. Lidcombe:

> in Auburn municipality and on the traditional lands of the Dharug people, centres upon the railway station and a small shopping centre. It extends north to Parramatta Road and east to Rookwood Cemetery. On the western and southern boundaries it merges into Auburn and Berala. The land is fairly flat, but generally slopes down towards the Parramatta River.
>
> (Kass, 2008, n.p.)

This focus is important in three ways. First, the study context, Australia, is significant because it has an explicit multicultural—even cosmopolitan—policy (Collins et al., 2020). Australia is, therefore, appropriate to test Gordon's assimilation theory and such like. In addition, focusing on Australia breaks the traditional emphasis of migration research on the UK, Europe, and the US (Riley and Weale, 2006; Betts et al., 2017; Burnazoglu, 2021). Migration research in Australia abounds, too. Yet, this chapter contrasts with the focus of research in Australian migration studies, which have tended to be centred mainly on migrant businesses (e.g., Collins et al., 2011; Collins, 2021), labour conditions of temporary and permanent migrants (e.g., Hugo, 2008; McGrath-Champ et al., 2011; Rosewarne 2020a, 2020b), and the political economy of remittances from migrants in their home countries (see Chapter 9), not migrant contributions to the transformation of towns in Australia—except for a few respectable exceptions (see, e.g., Stilwell, 2003; Collins et al., 2020).

Second, this chapter is the first, after an earlier effort (Obeng-Odoom and Jang, 2016), to provide a scholarly study of Lidcombe as a migrant town, a major migrant hub in the heart of the southern hemisphere's largest necropolis (Emerson, 2001, p. 24). The *Sydney Journal* has documented the experiences of other nearby suburbs, such as Berala (Gordon, 2008) and Croyden (Johnson, 2009), but even these studies do not primarily examine migration and do not focus on the highly important town of Lidcombe. Even the famous, *Liberty Plains: A History of Auburn, NSW* was criticized for overlooking Lidcombe in the 1983 and 1986 editions, prompting a revised edition, prepared in 1992 (see Hedges, 1992). That revision, however, does not address the migration question.

Finally, and more broadly, this chapter draws attention to land, property rights, and other institutions, including class, race, and religion, and how such institutions, in turn, mould the transformation of both the built environment and the urban economic structure of Lidcombe. These emphases are often missing or, when available, centred on mainstream theory in the bourgeoning literature on cities and migration (e.g., Glaeser, 2011; Saunders, 2012; DeParle, 2019). So, this chapter responds to several calls for more nuanced research on migrant towns (see, e.g., Serra 2012; Davidson and Gleeson, 2013; Obeng-Odoom, 2013; Department of Infrastructure and Transport, 2013; Collins et al., 2020).

The data informing my analysis are derived from multiple sources, seven of which need emphasizing because they provided particularly helpful insights: (1) repeated unstructured interviews with people who have lived in the town over the past ten to thirty years, including railway workers, library staff, shopkeepers and migrant entrepreneurs, residents, and post office workers; (2) historical material from the Lidcombe and Auburn libraries where I searched and examined past issues of *Auburn Review*, which is the community newspaper for the area; (3) enquiries at real estate agencies in Lidcombe and nearby suburbs; (4) transect walks in the Rookwood Cemetery, the wider case study area, interspersed with visual ethnography to capture photographic information extracted from plaques on historical or historic buildings and gravestones; (5) church sermons; (6) statistical information taken from the Australian Bureau of Statistics bulletins; and (7) various publications by the Auburn Council (now called the Cumberland Council), the local authority of the town. These methods have usually been neglected in the study of migrant towns, but they are justified, particularly in the case of Rookwood Necropolis, now Lidcombe. 'The cemetery's memorials form a visual social document of the origins of our community and the multicultural influence of immigration' (Murray, 2016, p. 117), as recently noted by Lisa Murray, a public historian and Australia's leading scholar on Sydney cemeteries.

Like the rest of the book, this chapter draws on a methodology centred on the combination of Georgist political economy, institutional economics, and stratification economics (GIS). Contrasting with the neoclassical economics emphasis on individual rational factors as drivers of migration within an ahistorical profit-maximizing narrative, the GIS approach emphasizes migratory processes as part of structural change in society where, apart from class, other identities are treated as secondary and institutions are often perfunctory to the analysis. The approach I utilise in this chapter, instead, considers individual reasons for migration, but mainly as a dialectical relationship with group motives for movement, internally and externally, and is oriented towards inductive reasoning (Abreu, 2012). A version of this approach was successfully used by Frank Stilwell (2003), when studying the migration of Afghan refugees and their ramifications for local and regional economic development in the town of Young in Sydney. Since then, more than forty other studies have followed with equal success or drawn on this work.[1] While this approach does not result in definite models with quantitative and categorical answers and, for these reasons, some economists oriented to econometric or equilibrium analysis may regard it as weak (see, e.g., Molho, 2013; Tanis, 2020), the approach has important strengths, including the stratification economic analysis of race.

Thus, unlike mainstream economics models, which simply assume that discrimination cannot exist in a competitive market, this approach considers structural racism carefully. In Australia, a country where 'three out of four [people] ... have a "racial bias"' (*The Economist*, 2020m, p. 44) and a history of brutal assimilation and land seizures (Grieves, 2003, 2009; Foley, 2011; Foley et al., 2014), this approach is clearly more appropriate. Also, the approach is more transparent and amenable to public scrutiny, more 'real-world' based, as it embraces diversity, uncertainty, and a complexity of factors often overlooked in restrictive neoclassical economics models based on contentious assumptions of *homo economicus,* win–win equilibrating conditions, and perfect information (Stilwell, 2003)—all of which are inapplicable to the present chapter.

The chapter argues that life in Lidcombe is substantially different from the stereotypical view about migrants, immigrants, and their towns. Lidcombe is located within, over, or across the largest necropolis in the southern hemisphere (Emerson, 2001, p. 24), with over 600,000 burials and some 200,000 cremations in the cemetery, has been transformed by migrants. Twenty-first-century migration,

---

[1] Data from *Google Scholar* search (key words used 'Frank Stilwell, Afghans'), as of 18 November 2020.

composed largely of what has been called 'immigrant minorities' (Collins et al., 2020, p. 2), has transformed this town.

Unlike in 1904, when the town's population of 4,500 people were either white Australians or white people from the UK and elsewhere (Hedges, 1992), today the town has over 15,000 people from over thirty different countries. Major changes can also be seen in the class and religious composition of the local population, which was previously largely white, working-class Christians. Those who lived in Lidcombe in the 'olden days' could hardly recognize it now: a diverse, middle-class and multi-faith town.

The built environment has evolved to give it the appearance of a cosmopolitan suburb. Physical changes can be seen in terms of Chinese architecture on display in religious sites, the presence of a wider range of churches and denominations, the unmistakable presence of the Auburn-Gallipoli Mosque, and various inscriptions that point to non-Anglo influence.

These changes are consistent with the findings of recent work (Collins et al., 2020) in other migrant towns in Australia, but Lidcombe also shows some other forms of transformation not previously highlighted in the literature on the changes in the built environment of migrant towns. Crucially, family houses are increasingly being replaced with apartments and resident landlords are becoming absentee owners. As land and property values undergo major upward changes, so do class and racial configurations take on more complex forms. Even the process of producing the built environment has transformed in ways that differ significantly from the past, when the labour structure was relatively homogenous in its class and racial composition.

The local economy has, accordingly, changed substantially. Previously regarded mainly as burial grounds for locals, Lidcombe has grown into a vibrant and diversified local economy made up of not only import-substituting industries but also export-promotion ones. So, the transformation of Lidcombe has released economic energy into the wider, Sydney metropolitan and Australian economy. Here is a story of an overall positive socio-economic transformation driven by minority migrants. Lidcombe is now seen as the 'home of the 2000 Olympics', the 'headquarters of Korean churches', and a 'home away from home'. Cemetery-related industries persist, but they no longer constitute the mainstay of the local economy, which is currently highly diversified. Economic activities such as food, retail, hairdressing, pharmaceuticals, real estate, and entertainment activities adorn the streets, highlighting a story of growth and change.

However, this transformation has simultaneously brought the town's Achilles' heel into sharp perspective: the forces of gentrification triggered by private interest in land have created soaring property prices which, in turn, make Lidcombe no longer the affordable neighbourhood that welcomed migrants and assisted them in achieving their 'Australian dream' a decade earlier. Indeed, many of the migrants who have transformed Lidcombe are also victims of exploitative work relations. Not only are they poorly paid and work long hours without special protections, as temporary residents on working holiday visas, but they are also excluded from Australian social protection systems and their usually limited command of the English language means that their access to the wider private market is restricted. Immigrant employers, themselves victims of discrimination and exploitation, which forced them to establish their own businesses, have also become conveyer belts of similar social forces. These complexities and contradictions play out in migrant schools, built on the land of disposed indigenous people of Australia. These forces of inter-group and intra-group stratification and historical marginalization and inequality once again stress that migration itself is neither panacea nor pariah. Attitude about the migrants in Lidcombe might have changed, but they have not challenged economic interests and forces that keep the migrants in the periphery of Australian society.

The rest of this chapter is divided into four sections. The next section, 'Necropolis', is a socio-economic history of Lidcombe, focusing on its structural fragility and instability before the coming of migrants. 'Metropolis', the second section, examines the socio-spatial transformation of Lidcombe during its second wave of migration and its attendant growth and change. 'Grave Injustice' analyses the tensions and contradictions inherent in this great transformation in the third section. Finally, 'Children of Crisis' probes the pitfalls and possibilities for inclusive transformation based on the nature of Lidcombe's urban economic structure.

Necropolis

Lidcombe is a migrant town located in the Western part of Australia's global city, Sydney. The town initially gained national and international prominence as a necropolis. 'Now covering some 283 hectares, Rookwood Necropolis is Australia's largest cemetery, and is believed to be one of the largest Victorian-era burial grounds in the world' (Murray, 2016, p. 117). The original land around which the town formed was close to a creek, named after its proprietor, Samuel Haslam in 1804. Haslam's Creek, as the area initially came to be called, was mainly inhabited by white immigrants from the UK. Like the wider New South Wales region, these settlers were '[m]ainly poor Irish [who] formed about a third of the total population of the colony' (Mitchell, 2008, p. 308). That was evidently the situation in Sydney, where demographic analysis focused on whether people were Irish or non-Irish. The Irish population dominated Lidcombe so much that, according to Terry Kass's (2008, n.p.) entry in the *Dictionary of Sydney*, 'Lidcombe ... was in some ways an Irish centre.' Residents of Lidcombe used the creek for both domestic purposes and relaxation (Hedges, 1992). In this sense, at least, Samuel Haslam had a significant effect on Lidcombe.

Haslam was not alone, though. Between the early 1820s and early 1830s, there were many other land owners whose actions were also influential. Sir Thomas Brisbane, George Tuckwell, and George Sunderland were among them. However, as the account of John Mitchell (2008) shows, Father John Joseph Therry was the landowner whose activities would change the course of Lidcombe. An Irish man and one of two Catholic priests appointed to do pastoral work in New South Wales during the colonial days, he was one of the first to purchase lots in the area now called Lidcombe. He did so to extend his pastoral work, but also to extract rents. As he had fallen out of favour with the Church and was no longer paid his £100 annual salary, he speculated in land for a living. His business strategy was to buy low and sell high. So, he paid only £15 to Patrick Kirk for a 60-acre lot and only £40 for a 160-acre lot from George Sunderland in 1831 and 1834, respectively to sell at higher prices later. As the account of Terry Kass (2008) shows, both Kirk and Sunderland were part of a long list of early settlers (whether freemen or ex-convicts) who obtained land in Lidcombe almost for free.

This burgeoning land market became a growing feature of white settler colonialism. Louise Johnson (2015) has attributed this transformation to the prevalence of stolen and, hence, cheap land and the discovery of gold in Australia in the 1850s. Within the context of global history, we can extend Johnson's analysis to what was happening in Ireland, too. The Irish famine of 1845–1849, itself driven by land grabbing from the Dharug Indigenous Australians (Kass, 2008; see also Chapter 3), combined to bring more Irish to Australia. Together, these ricocheting factors sustained a vibrant land market in Lidcombe. A further investment 'opportunity' struck when lawyers for the Sydney–Parramatta Railway Company offered to buy ten acres of land from Father Therry. The company sought to use the land for the construction of the then proposed Parramatta to Sydney railway line in 1855. Father Therry took the offer and was paid £100, instantly making a windfall of £97.5 or a 3,900% rent gain. This was not the beginning of rentierism, however. Therry's rent gain only reflected the rent gap arising from the extraction of rent from land stolen from the Indigenous people of Australia. Until the 1990s, when the High Court of Australia finally accepted that Indigenous people had prior rights to land, which became known as the Mabo Case, white Australia regarded black land as *terra nullius* (*Mabo vs Queensland (No 2)*, 1992; Johnson, 2015). This was evidently the case at Lidcombe. As noted earlier, those from whom Therry bought his land would make windfalls, too.

Other landowners or speculators seeking to become landowners in the area, determining that a railway station at Haslam's Creek would revive the local economy and drive up land values, persuaded Father Therry to give further support to investment in the area. Father Therry was in favour of the idea and so was the railway authority, but the proposers had to bear the £700 cost of founding a train station. Therry contributed the very £100 he had obtained from selling his land to make the establishment of the station possible (Mitchell, 2008). So, Father Therry was not only someone who sold land for railway transport to start in Lidcombe, he also invested in the development of the township. The station, Haslam's Creek Station, was eventually opened in 1859 (Pollen, 1988), providing a strong economic foundation for Lidcombe.

According to the account of Stanley Hedges (1992, n.p.), 'completion of the railway radically changed the status of the district'. Roads to make this district an independent suburb were constructed, the first being John Street on Lidcombe North, named after Father Therry, in 1862. Another road was built and a subdivision, the 'Town of St. Joseph', announced to commence the journey of settlement expansion (Hedges, 1992). The railway station was a major driver in propelling the urban development of Lidcombe.

In 1862, the New South Wales Government purchased 200 acres of land to establish what has been labelled the 'largest cemetery in the Southern Hemisphere' (Emerson, 2001, p. 24). Father Therry died in 1864 (Mitchell, 2008), his will clearly stating that his land be auctioned upon his death with the substantial proceeds going to the Church at St. Ann, Lidcombe. This provision also made it possible for many stonemasons to buy land in Lidcombe, next to the cemetery (Kass, 2008), which was completed in 1867 and was named, Haslam's Creek Cemetery. To serve its purpose of being the final resting place for everyone in Sydney, the cemetery had to be accessible. The construction of mortuary stations was quickly commenced to provide the connecting points for trains to convey funeral corteges, mourners, and visitors to the cemetery. Lisa Murray's (2016, pp. 108–120) authoritative guide to the study of Sydney cemeteries shows that the first, a Mortuary Station on Regent Street, was completed in 1871. Others were built at strategic points. What was striking about the mortuary stations was their picturesque architecture. Rave reviews were published in leading news outlets, such as *The Illustrated London News, The Town and Country Journal, The Sydney Mail,* and the *The Illustrated Sydney News.*

However, residents of Lidcombe opposed the developments. While there was no recorded evidence of NIMBYism in Lidcombe at the time, residents of the area fiercely protested the connection between the name of their town and that of the burial grounds. The stigma was real. Representative comments included: 'All you have to do "is to walk over and drop in" ...', and 'The majority of people say, "it will be time enough to go to that suburb when life is over"' (1904 observations about Lidcombe, quoted in Hedges, 1992, p. 232). There was concern that the town was run by 'tombstone men and gravediggers' (1904 observations about Lidcombe, quoted in Hedges, 1992, p. 233). Real estate agents were concerned, too. So, it was quite common for them to offer land for sale in the 'Town of St. Joseph surrounding Haslam's Creek Railway Station' (Hedges, 1992, p. 224) without making any reference to the cemetery. The authorities responded to the protests by changing the name of the suburb to Rookwood in 1878. Some say that the choice was a reflection of the title of a book by William Harrison published around 1838 (Pollen, 1988;

Emerson, 2001), but one newspaper account suggested that the name was chosen to reflect the abundance of rooks (a crow look-alike[2]), which could commonly be found in the area. If so, Rookwood sounded more appropriate than Fitzroy and Norwood (Hedges, 1992), which were some of the other suggested names.

The municipality of Rookwood was incorporated in 1891, several years after the change of name. Seven further years after incorporation, residents began another wave of protests for the same reason: the link between the name of the cemetery (Rookwood Cemetery) and the suburb, the municipality of Rookwood. There were other negative markers that drew the displeasure of the protesters. For instance, in 1879, 1,340 acres of land were obtained in Lidcombe for a planned home for delinquent boys. The 'Boys Reformatory Cottage Homes', as it became known officially, was deemed a white elephant because it was never used as a reformatory, although its architecture was, like the mortuary stations, the focus of much praise (Mealing, 1988, entry 1). According to a plaque provided by the Australian Bicentennial Authority and affixed at the entrance of the present-day gate house in 1893, the facility was converted into the Rookwood Asylum for Men. The purpose was to house the poor, elderly, and weak whose conditions had been caused or aggravated by worsening economic problems that created a depression at the time. It seems the major concern for the protesters was the name association of Rookwood to the cemetery.

However, the protests need to be seen in a wider context. The federation of British colonies in Australia, which formed one grand settler colony in 1901, also birthed the infamous 'White Australian Policy'. In this official position, only white people would be tolerated, indeed actively encouraged, to immigrate to Australia. 'Their' land, under the Real Property Act of 1900, would be guaranteed. This Torrens system, arguably a move by White Australia to use constitutional law to protect its stolen land, helped to give security of tenure to whites. White Australia Policy (officially, the Immigration Restriction Act of 1901) was a further attempt to increase white solidarity and 'mateship' against all others. Many white people responded favourably and migrated to Australia (Johnson, 2015). The population of Lidcombe was, therefore, not marginal.

As Table 6.1 shows, the number of people in Lidcombe was increasing rapidly. For the three periods (1891, 1901, and 1911) for which data are available, the average change of the population was more than 800%. Lidcombe was also becoming the home of much white wealth in terms of buildings. So, whether numerically, demographically, or economically, the demands of Lidcombe residents had to be taken seriously. This complemented the prevailing ideology of Australian settlement. According to Louise Johnson (2015, p. 116), this meant 'A high tariff wall

---

[2] Newspapers also said there are no rooks but there are crows. However, since both crow or caw, the word rook is quite acceptable (extract Hedges, 1992, on p. 234).

Table 6.1 Population growth in Lidcombe, 1881–1911

	People	Percentage change	Buildings
1881	247	–	424
1891	2,084	743.72	–
1901	4,496	115.74	502
1911	5,418	20.51	722

Source: adapted from Kass, 2008.

to support the development of domestic industry; centralized wage fixing and dispute resolution to keep unemployment low, strikes minimal, and wages high; and a migration policy that explicitly favoured "whites".

Accordingly, in 1914, the town was renamed Lidcombe, an amalgamation of the names of two former mayors, Mr. Lidbury and Mr. Larcombe (Pollen, 1988; Emerson, 2001). This name has remained to date. The name, Rookwood Asylum for Men, was also changed to the Lidcombe State Hospital (Mealing, 1988, entry 1). These changes reflected the complexities of functions that the facility had to perform. An armament depot site, the functions perhaps also reflected the growing medical needs in the light of casualties from the First World War (1914–1918), signs of which can be seen in the many monuments of veterans erected in Lidcombe. Life after 1918, when the war ended, was not easy, as shown by ANZAC Day events to recollect the role of Australian and New Zealand forces fighting alongside Britain and the Allied Forces. Veterans who returned to Lidcombe bore those marks. Others had to endure them, too. The drive towards a life of comfort to these returnees and to rebuild broken economies led to a growing surge in construction. Kass writes: 'The war Service Homes Commission provided single cottages or small groups of cottages in Lidcombe. In November 1919, it bought a series of allotments in the Marne Park Estate to build cottages in group schemes' (2008, n.p.). Building needs remained. To meet them, the building boom had to continue, but that brought the need for overseas labour into sharp focus. Across Australia, the prevailing view was, consistent with White Policy, to bring in white refugees from Europe alone (Johnson, 2015). When that supply was deemed inadequate, other racial groups were enticed.

Diversity among the Australian population grew. Combined with growth-based protectionism, manufacturing strengthened the economy. This trend pertained in Australia generally, but Lidcombe was a major part of the story. Represented there were industries producing electrical goods, motor cars, steel, and other construction materials (Kass, 2008). Coloured migrants would make monumental contributions to the manufacturing boom in the post-war years (1919–1929).

The Great Depression of the 1930s brought this boom to a halt and matters worsened over time. Depression wrought substantial ramifications for Lidcombe. Mayor Hedges (1992) captured these corrosive consequences under the caption, 'Depression Years'. For the large number of poor people in Lidcombe in the middle-to-late 1920s, the notion of a 'depression' might have been strange, as they had always been dependent on state support (notably the dole but also non-monetary supplies, such as blankets and military clothing) and the help of the Lidcombe Benevolent Society. Yet, the depression brought distinctive challenges. The Lidcombe local council embarked on massive retrenchment. The wages of the remaining staff were reduced and the local economy became particularly weak. Terry Kass (2008) shows that some 23% of the residents of Lidcombe were out of work during the Depression. Lidcombe Council was forced to accept the government's 'dole for work' programme. People got the dole as payment for the work they did. Even then, so many people remained unemployed and a 'camp for the unemployed' had to be maintained between 1931 and 1932. So limited were employment opportunities that, at one point, the council had to use 'draws' to allocate the few jobs available. The Lidcombe Unemployed Workers' Union (Hedges, 1992) was responsible for the remaining poor and, as noted by Kass (2008), soup kitchens were organized for children and those out of work.

Lidcombe served as the heart of the war industries in Australia. Terry Kass's (2008) account is revealing. Bomber engines were manufactured in Lidcombe. High-quality steel was also manufactured in Lidcombe by the Australian Forge and Engineering Pty Ltd. Plants in Lidcombe were also producing Rolls Royce Merlin engines that helped power Mustang fighters. Keynes once noted that stabilizing the economy could be done even with useless and destructive activities, if there was no political will to use the powers of the state to provide human need (Stilwell, 2012, p. 270). In Lidcombe, this admonition was taken literally. Both useful (supporting the unemployed) and useless (providing ammunition to kill others) activities in Lidcombe changed its face from just a necropolis to a suburban metropolis.

Metropolis

So, it would appear that these Keynesian dicta paid off. As with the wider Australian and global economy, the 1940s ushered in another era of prosperity. Industrialization was a major engine of growth and change, as was urbanization. Not only did cities become important, but 'metropolitan dominance' also became the spatial expression of a long boom which stretched through the 1950s, '60s, and '70s. Sydney alone contained 59% of the population of New South Wales in 1971 (Stilwell, 1980, pp. 5–7). This process of clustering generated significant agglomeration economies. In the words of one long-term resident, Lidcombe was 'a bustling enterprising suburb, that had it's [sic] own council and a close-knit community spirit' (Auburn Review, 1988, n.p.). A cooperative was established to kick-start a massive housing programme, making it possible for many residents to become homeowners (Hedges, 1992). With a vibrant Australian-wide national economy and a booming local Lidcombe economy, the employment rate in the town increased, too.

The town had its own bakeries and dairy farms, deliveries, and an aircraft engine factory. The town council had an ambitious programme to improve the quality and quantity of housing, as well as the local infrastructure (Hedges, 1992, p. 285). According to local accounts, at one point there were six banks in the town. Fruit, food, and fashion shops blossomed. There were as many as five bakehouses in Lidcombe alone. These local businesses employed many residents, but others worked in the railways, the hospital, and the town's cemetery business. The rest worked elsewhere, including in a major abattoir in the current Olympic Park. The state abattoir generated employment for 1,600 people, including substantial numbers from Lidcombe (Hedges, 1992). Others were employed in major industries and business units either in or around Lidcombe. Examples of such companies were Ford, Australian Forge, De Havilland, Janson's, Bradford Insulation, and Australian Electrical Industries. Other employers were Dairy Farmers, Barbcock and Wilcox, the Egg Board, Tooyer's Brewery, and Coats Printing. Socially, the population was small, but cohesive and enjoyed a sense of camaraderie.

The economic expansion in Lidcombe also stirred a significant interest in entertainment and leisure activities. Dance clubs were formed. Sporting activities were also organized. At home and at work, the trilogy, 'respect, responsibility, and discipline' was strictly taught and upheld by both the young and the old, a point emphasized by two long-term residents whom I interviewed. At the town governance level, a decision was taken to enhance efficient management by merging Lidcombe with Auburn in 1949 to form the Auburn municipality (Emerson, 2001). It was a controversial decision because some residents, and even councillors, considered the merger unwise because, among other reasons, Lidcombe would have to shoulder debts it had not incurred (Hedges, 1992). Nevertheless, the merger went on and, at the time, did not seem to constitute a break in progress—either at home, at work, or at the level of town administration.

Lidcombe's era of prosperity was organically linked to the boom that the Australian economy as a whole was enjoying during this period. The post-Second World War boom (1945–1975) was not linked to imperial Britain's economic architecture, although Britain, the colonial landlord of Australia, had founded the Australia settler colony and had supplied it with labour and capital from 1788 to the 1890s. Between 1946 and 1948 and 1966 and 1968, there was a 65% decline in the share of Australia's export to the UK and a 56% fall in imports from the UK (Broomhill, 2008). Australia increasingly looked to the US, the new global power, and to Asia, its neighbour, for trade, and even cultural exchange. Increasingly, foreign companies opened branches in Australia to partake in the boom but also to contribute to it (Broomhill, 2008). Consistent with the prevailing view at the time, the Australian government embraced Keynesianism and expanded the arm of the public sector in providing housing and health, education, and food subsidies to Australians (Broomhill, 2008). The economic structure of the economy diversified.

Although the primary sector was still substantial, indeed ascendant with respect to mining towns (Stilwell, 1980, p. 7), manufacturing industries increased their share of employment and revenue generation. The boom created the need for migrant labour. Rural–urban migration was necessary, but not sufficient. So, after 1947, the Australian government embarked on an active policy of recruiting settler migrants. Immigration then accounted for roughly half of the population growth in Australia. It would seem that Europeans, particularly British, and Oceanians, especially New Zealanders, were the most visible in the stream of migrants that responded to this policy initiative (Collins, 2008). The first non-English-speaking migrants to Lidcombe were Russians, Croations, Ukrainians, and Poles (Ashton, 2008). Italians, too, were among the first to arrive, soon establishing a meat factory on Joseph Street. There were enough Ukrainians to warrant the establishment of a huge Ukrainian Church on Church Street in 1958 and a Youth Centre and a High School on Church Street and Joseph Street, respectively.

The first major wave of migrants in Sydney as a whole was in the 1960s, following the long post-Second World War boom in the Australian economy (Ashton, 2008). They were actively recruited and legitimized through the well-known declaration of Australia as a multicultural country in the 1970s (Castles, 1987). Multiculturalism meant that migrants 'were to be permitted a large measure of cultural autonomy, while at the same time special institutions and measures were introduced to ensure access and equity and participation for all Australians irrespective of their origins' (Castles, 1987, p. 1). These migrants worked across sectors, but primarily in the secondary and tertiary sectors. As shown in Table 6.2, the share of employment in the various industrial sectors changed dramatically.

In the primary sector, the share of employment dropped by more than 70%. The booming secondary and tertiary sectors, however, largely absorbed these losses. Unemployment rates declined, too, as Table 6.3 shows.

Table 6.2 Sectoral shares of employment in Australia, 1901–1971 (%)

Sector	Years				Sectoral change	
	1901	1931	1954	1971	Difference	% difference
Primary	33.9	24.4	15.2	9.2	−24.7	72.9
Secondary	16.2	19.0	28.3	24.2	+8	49.4
Tertiary	50.9	56.6	56.5	66.6	+15.7	30.84
All sectors	100	100	100	100	–	–

Source: adapted from Stilwell, 1974, p. 39.

Table 6.3 Unemployment rate in Australia, 1961–1972 (%)

	1961	1962	1963	1964	1965	1966	1967	1968	1969	1970	1971	1972
Australia	2.3	2.2	1.8	1.1	1.0	1.4	1.4	1.3	1.1	1.1	1.4	1.9
Sydney	2.3	1.8	1.4	0.8	0.7	1.0	1.0	0.9	0.7	0.6	0.9	1.4
Non-metropolitan* (Sydney)	2.2	2.8	2.6	1.7	1.5	1.5	1.6	1.6	1.4	1.5	1.7	2.5
NSW**	2.2	2.2	1.9	1.1	0.9	1.2	1.2	1.1	1.0	0.9	1.2	1.8

Source: Stilwell, 1974, p. 50.
* Includes Australian capital territory; ** includes both other urban and rural areas in Sydney.

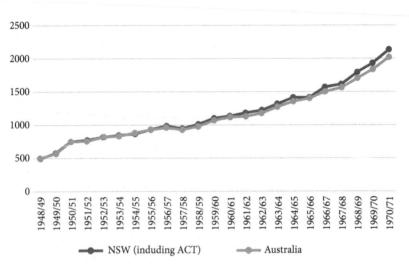

Fig. 6.1 Per capita personal income (AUD), 1948–1971

The data in the table are only indicative. They understate the magnitude of unemployment and say nothing about underemployment. Coupling together rural
and other urban areas in 'non metropolitan (Sydney) areas' can be misleading
about trends. At the same time, labour is quite mobile. Specific residency might
not be the best way to ascertain unemployment levels. Yet, the key point, namely
that the boom was accompanied by job creation and a reduction of unemployment,
seems sound. Evidence from per capita income surveys corroborates the point. In
general, the economic climate was good. Wages for labour were, broadly, increasing in Australia, but particularly in New South Wales (NSW). There, as Figure 6.1
shows, per capita personal income was slightly higher than that which pertained
in Australia more widely.

Table 6.4 Manufacturing employment in the subregions, 1972–1976

Subregion	1972	1976	Change in manufacturing employment	Percentage change in manufacturing employment
Central Sydney	139,420	106,174	−33,246	−23.8
Inner Western	26,751	21,318	−5,433	−20.3
Southern	90,858	83,936	−6,922	−7.6
South-Western	10,622	12,222	+1,600	+15.1
Western	87,364	83,956	−3,408	−3.9
Northern	40,591	36,360	−4,231	−10.4
Gosford-Wyong	2,983	3,748	+765	+25.7
Newcastle	43,122	38,670	−4,452	−10.3
Wollongong	34,018	32,325	−2,693	−7.9
Total	475,729	418,709	−58,020	−19.8

Source: Stilwell, 1980, p. 102.

Represented by the dark line overlying the grey line, per capita income levels in NSW were generally higher for most of the long boom. Conditions in Lidcombe were generally booming, too. Indeed, by the end of the boom and the commencement of Australia's second cycle of decline, which one informed political economist (Broomhill, 2008, p. 21) calls 'the crisis of the 1970s and 1980s', Lidcombe, located in the South Western subregion of Sydney (Table 6.4), was one of only a few places where the boom continued.

By the 1980s, however, it appears that the recession had caught up with Lidcombe, too. The wider Australian economy had become stagflationary. Not only did growth slow down, but inflation also increased. Neither Keynesianism on a global scale nor the Keynesianism of the Australian Labour Party could address the problems of stagflation. Unemployment and structural changes subdivided the working classes. Migrants were far more affected, and so were migrant areas (Stilwell, 1980, pp. 8–10). Lidcombe was one of them.

The *Auburn Review* of 1988 carried a story captioned, 'Let Lidcombe live again!' (exclamation mark in the original), which captured the mood of that era. The person interviewed for the story was Publicity Officer of the Lidcombe Community Improvement Association and former alderman, Keith Huteau. He talked of the death of the Lidcombe Chamber of Commerce and his desire to see its revival. His diagnosis of the problem is even more telling. According to the paper, 'He said the death knoll of Lidcombe was the introduction of the new expressway, which he said had taken the main stream of customers away from Lidcombe shopping centre.' Two long-term local residents with whom Mr Huteau's diagnosis was discussed for this chapter, agreed with this, but offered a further explanation. The expressway had been responsible for the demolition of businesses and some houses and, hence, took away not only business but also some of the social 'good old days' feeling from the town. The rise of automobility also moulded residents' desires to drive out of Lidcombe and the suburb more widely. They could access bigger and cheaper supermarkets elsewhere, too. As argued by Louise Johnson (2015), across suburbs in Australia, this development led to a decline in the prosperity of small- and medium-scale shopping centres in Lidcombe.

The tertiary sector was down, too, although its decline has been explained differently. Some residents suggest that the removal of the centre of administration from Lidcombe also took away some of the shine from the suburb. It definitely led to the demise of town hall activities, but as this happened in 1949, its effects may have taken time to be felt. At the more national and global levels, factories that had hitherto employed Lidcombe residents were folding up or deterritorializing to save costs, including trade union demands for better and higher wages. Internationally, oil price hikes and advances in techniques of production, respectively increased the cost of production and diminished the size of purchases from Australia, whose exports had substantial amounts of primary agricultural or raw materials (Stilwell, 1998; Broomhill, 2008). Of the business units mentioned earlier, only Tooyer's Brewery and Coats Printing still remain today. Others, such as the Royal Australian Airforce, continue to have posts in Lidcombe, but they are dormant, if not extinct. Regardless of the precise cause, by 1988 and through the 1990s, socio-economic activities in Lidcombe were down. The banks left; jobs plummeted; the roads were bad.

Many of these problems reflect the contradictions in growth-led, rentier capitalism. The Australian Labour Party, for one thing, failed to arrest the growing contradictions of growth. Instead, its policies strengthened both capital and landlords, who significantly benefitted from rising rents from state investment in infrastructure (Stilwell, 1980, pp. 7–8). Creeping austerity programmes rolled out by the Australian Labour Party did not help. It lost power. Notwithstanding, the succeeding government continued this monetarist turn. For example, it disestablished the Department of Urban and Regional Development. Public houses in the vicinity of George's Avenue were also sold off. This 'economic rationalist' paradigm (Stilwell, 1979, 1998), as neoliberalism came to be called in Australia, worsened the recession.

The political interest in globalization produced contradictory outcomes. Wealth concentration increased in the hands of the mighty, and so did marginalization. The rest were poor. This pattern had a spatial expression, too. The suburbs, especially those in the Western part of Sydney (including Lidcombe), were not prospering and, in fact, seemed to be bearing the brunt of the forces of globalization beginning to gain prominence in modern Australia. At the same time, business entities favoured the 'importation' of migrant workers to fill shortages for much lower wages (Stilwell, 1998).

However, the turn of the millennium marked a boom in migration to Australia (Collins, 2008) and, according to local accounts, to Lidcombe as well. Local Australian factors, especially the Olympics, were powerful magnets, but there were strong exit factors, too. The 1997–99 Asian crisis, for instance, led to notable emigration from Asia (Castles, 2008). Overall, the year 2000 was a watershed in the life of Lidcombe. The 2000 Sydney Olympics changed the face of Sydney and its suburbs. One researcher described the mood after the announcement that Sydney would be the site for the 2000 Olympics as 'jubilant' (Handmer, 1995, p. 355). The Olympics propelled the then Auburn municipality as a whole, leaving in its wake urban projects that would generate income for the city authorities. Of the four hotels currently in Lidcombe, at least two were built in the lead-up to the Olympics, making 'the Olympics' an insignia of the town.

Houses were constructed and an Olympics platform (an additional railway line), lifts, and a major highway (Olympic Drive) were developed to welcome visitors and entice some of them, at least, to consider taking up residence in the town. Sales of tickets went up, visitors rented places in Lidcombe, and, importantly, Lidcombe received considerable attention, both locally and nationally. The Olympic railway line was opened and traffic in Lidcombe increased. Being a junction station, Lidcombe was gradually showcased to the world and to other migrants in Sydney who had not previously lived in Lidcombe as a prosperous town connected to other parts of Sydney. A modern railway system, the Lidcombe Railways, has continued to be an important aspect of life in Lidcombe post 2000.

Of particular significance was the construction of the Olympic Village in Lidcombe. Glearne Searle's account (Searle, 2012) is particularly insightful. It shows that the village was built on a vast tract of land that cost the state government of New South Wales 70 million Australian dollars. Not only was it meant to house 15,000 officials and athletes, the village also had to be sustainable, both during and after its construction. Hence, the private sector that led the development of 665 houses was also tasked to install solar panels, provide remediation of the land, and build the village using sustainable construction practices. Together with the actual construction of the village, substantial labour would be needed.

This opened the way for another wave of migration to Lidcombe. A few non-UK migrants had lived in Lidcombe before 2000, but the twenty-first-century wave of migration to Lidcombe was distinct in terms of numbers and diversity. From the early 2000s up to 2013, people born in countries where English is not the first language constituted 59% of the population (Auburn City Council, 2013b) of Lidcombe. Lidcombe is part of a broader, Auburn municipality made up of other suburbs, prominent among which are Auburn, Berala, Homebush Bay, Regents Park, and Silverwater (Auburn City Council, 2013b). More recently, much of the population of Lidcombe migrated from non-English-speaking countries, too. Although a substantial share of the migrant population is Asian, migrants come from more than thirty countries (Obeng-Odoom and Jang, 2016;

Auburn City Council, 2015a). Hence, the migrant influence in contemporary Lidcombe is different from the typical UK- and New Zealand-dominated migration flow (Collins, 2013) and distinct from the previous waves of migration to Australia.

We know from local accounts and systematic urban research (Stilwell, 1974, 1980, 1998) that the population growth in Sydney and its suburbs is largely driven by immigration. The first wave of white population in Lidcombe is in decline both numerically and proportionally. A common reason for the increase in migrant population in Lidcombe, according to the accounts of some migrants with whom I discussed the subject, is relatively cheap housing and easy access to other parts of Sydney, on account of the rail links. Another reason is that increase in the population of particular groups begets further increases, as others are attracted to the location for a variety of reasons, such as the provision of enticing information, and community and other social support. The increase in housing prices elsewhere, notably in Strathfield, a nearby suburb to Lidcombe, also led to some migrants coming to Lidcombe (Han and Han, 2010). Migrants have favoured the town, among others, because housing in Lidcombe is more affordable than in other Sydney suburbs.

Many other reasons explain the attraction of Lidcombe. It is accessible to the central business district (CBD) and other locations where migrants work, shop, and socialize. Lidcombe is also a migrant town. While this specific reason may sound tautological, migrants have tended to gravitate towards areas known to offer social, religious, and economic support, contrary to neoclassical economic theories about how migration is an individual, rational affair (Molho, 2013). These reasons were commonly given by real estate agents, shop managers, and railway and post office workers whom I interviewed. A pastor at a Korean church predominantly attended by Koreans and in whom church members confide, preached a sermon on 12 January 2014 on the topic. He confirmed the three reasons but added a fourth, namely that God had brought the migrants to Lidcombe for the town's transformation.

There is a wide variation in exit factors applicable to countries of origins. Different, and sometimes similar, conditions apply to the over thirty nationalities that live in Lidcombe today (see, e.g., Han and Han, 2010 for Korean migration to Sydney; and Moustafine, 2011 for Russian migration to Sydney). Taking the Korean case as an example, the ban on migration was lifted in the late 1990s, paving the way for greater emigration.

Migrants have typically moved in as families, although many single individuals have come in, too. According to the community profile on household size (Auburn City Council, 2013b), currently only 15% of households have a single member. The rest are two persons (26%), three persons (21%), four persons (21%), five persons (9%), or six persons (7%). Broadly, these are similar for Lidcombe, too. Such group migration challenges the individual-based explanations and their dominance and domino effects or versions in neoclassical economics (Molho,

Table 6.5 Employment and unemployment in Lidcombe, 2016

Employment	Lidcombe	%	NSW	%	Australia	%
Worked full-time	5,543	55.7	2,134,521	59.2	6,623,065	57.7
Worked part-time	3,070	30.8	1,071,151	29.7	3,491,503	30.4
Away from work	503	5.1	174,654	4.8	569,276	5.0
Unemployed	842	8.5	225,546	6.3	787,452	6.9

Source: Australian Bureau of Statistics (ABS), 2016a.

Table 6.6 Employment structure in Lindcome, 2016

Employment	Lidcombe	%	NSW	%	Australia	%
Professionals	1,985	21.8	798,126	23.6	2,370,966	22.2
Technicians and trades workers	1,439	15.8	429,239	12.7	1,447,414	13.5
Labourers	1,201	13.2	297,887	8.8	1,011,520	9.5
Clerical and administrative workers	1,123	12.3	467,977	13.8	1,449,681	13.6
Community and personal service workers	852	9.3	350,261	10.4	1,157,003	10.8
Managers	824	9.0	456,084	13.5	1,390,047	13.0
Sales workers	821	9.0	311,414	9.2	1,000,955	9.4
Machinery operators and drivers	559	6.1	206,839	6.1	670,106	6.3

Source: ABS, 2016a.

2013) and Australian migration policy (Collins, 2013). According to Australian Bureau of Statistics (ABS) data in Table 6.5, some 91% of these new people are employed.

The unemployed are actively looking for work. The evidence that one recruitment company, Max Employment, has registered 1,400 job seekers (Auburn Review, 2014) suggests that migrants are not merely waiting for the dole to be handed out to them. Their contribution to local, municipal, and urban economic development has been substantial, contrary to claims that they are a drain to the Australian economy. This can be seen in the data on the occupation structure in Table 6.6.

ABS data can further throw light on migrant contribution. According to the economic base theory in urban economics, cities can develop their urban economies by expanding their basic industries (those industries in the urban economy that generate exports) and at least by keeping their non-basic or non-exporting industries. Although these do not bring in export revenues, non-exporting industries act as import substitution and, hence, save the incomes in the urban economy from leaking (Markusen, 2006; Engelen et al., 2017). With these points in mind, we can look at the economic activities in Lidcombe today. They are mainly clustered on two streets, which collectively form the commercial centre: John Street and Joseph Street. There, the icons of non-Anglo influence mark the cityscapes. Shops depict images and writings of Asian and Middle-Eastern influence, which changes the colour of the urban economic structure.

Table 6.7 follows the International Standard Industrial Classification of All Economic Activities Revision 4. The table provides details of typical economic

Table 6.7 Survey of economic activities in Lidcombe, 2018

Industry	Head count (minimum)	Activities
Mining and quarrying	10	Crushing of stones, production of tombs, making graveyards
Manufacturing	1	Meat production
Construction	3	Small-scale construction industries, involving a few people, often families or closely linked groups; they include construction work, wall repairs, and the maintenance of buildings
Professional, scientific, and technical services	2	Schools and training centres
Transportation and storage	5	Moving companies and several taxi drivers
Human work and social work	18	Health: dentistry, optometrists, pharmacists, massage, hospitals
Accommodation and food services/Activities	35	Hospitality activities, including the provision of hotels, pubs, and guest house facilities. Eateries, cafes, and restaurants, including local entities such as Dooleys and transnational chains such as Subway and MacDonald's.
Real estate activities	7	Buying, renting, selling of properties, property management, and the development of properties
Financial and insurance activities	2	The Commonwealth Bank and Kaparty Credit Union
Wholesale and retail activities	12	Grocery shops and bakeries
Education	5	Schools and private-tuition services
Other services	7	Bakeries, salons, dry cleaning, funeral services such as funeral planning

Source: author's field survey, 2018.

activities. I collected the data by a headcount, an accepted research practice in urban economics (Stilwell, 2003) when no such raw data can be found. They are minimums, rather than maximums. These industries generate jobs for Lidcombe residents and others who work in the township. Migrant businesses in particular have made a significant contribution in employing migrants.

Economists have tended to classify these as 'ethnic economies' (for a critical review of this literature, see Wang and Warn, 2018). Their features, according to these economists, range from the enterprising ethnic individual, 'homo culturalis', to economic enclaves. Where they have faced severe barriers in Australia (Collins and Norman, 2018), according to this cultural view of ethnic economies, it is because their black culture is problematic. Conversely, the boom in ethnic businesses must be a reflection on Chinese and Korean cultures. These cultures, according to this view, are enterprising and promote hardwork.

In a modified form, Aboriginals would be patronized under the claim that Australian colonialism has driven out any interest in enterprising behaviour, or that indigenous cultures and networks impede progress. Broadly, these views sit within the human capital and 'social capital' literatures, which posit that these immigrant or migrant ethnic entrepreneurs have a wide range of ethnic social capital, stretching from loyal co-ethnic customers to co-ethnic workers and co-ethnic relatives that help them out (Wang and Warn, 2018; Çaglar and Schiller, 2018). This cultural explanation of local economies of migrants is at the heart of new economics of labour migration and new institutionalism. Shading into this cultural economics is Austrian economics, with its strong focus on individual rational behaviour.

This cultural interpretation is highly problematic, however. Surveys of Chinese, Vietnamese, and Korean so-called ethnic entrepreneurs (see, e.g., Collins et al., 1995; Collins and Shin, 2012; Wang and Warn, 2018) show that many of them are in intermarriage arrangements. Many of them have workers from diverse cultural groups. Many have customers from a diversity of cultural groups, too. More fundamentally, their class positions matter, so does their gender. More widely, it is of significance how these migrants came to Australia, whether as voluntary or involuntary migrants, during which years they arrived, and what conditions prevailed during their time of arrival. For these reasons, too, it is more useful to consider the so-called ethnic economies as embedded in a wider society and economy, as Karl Polanyi (1944/2001, 1957) famously argued.

However, beyond simple embeddedness, it is useful to stress that the economy reflects a wide range of institutions. In Australia, specific immigration programmes shape outcomes about entrepreneurship. It matters whether entrepreneurs arrived under the Business Migration Programme, Business Skills Migration, or Humanitarian Immigration (Wang and Warn, 2018). Migrants with particular experiences and a certain minimum experience and skills are selected into Australia under these programmes (Wang and Warn, 2018). In addition, as experiences elsewhere show (Hamilton, 2018), such migrants have unobservable skills, such as risk tolerance, ambition, and adventure that are much higher than the average in their region of origin. Their health is much better, too (Hamilton, 2018). Further, it matters that upon arrival, migrants have benefitted from the Ignite Small Business Start-Ups programme (Collins and Norman, 2018). These processes of high selectivity and special attention upon arrival have important implications.

Analytically, the institutions of migration matter greatly. They are mediated by race, gender, and class, which, in turn, are moulded by where migrants come from and what prior experiences they have had. Culture is not a good explanation. The intersectionality of gender, race, and class is moulded by wider micro, meso, and macro contexts in Australia but also globally (Wang and Warn, 2018). This inter-sectionality should inform our analysis of ethnic, class, and gendered experiences, too (Crenshaw, 1989). This investigation must feed into a wider reflection on the local economy of Lidcombe within the wider Sydney and Australian economies.

Not all employed people work in Lidcombe, a feature of the suburb which has been systematically determined by the city authorities in its community profile (Auburn City Council, 2013b). The evidence can be complemented by looking at the large flow of people who leave the town and entrain for other destinations during the rush hours at Lidcombe Station. Similarly, the sudden influx of people from outside Lidcombe around 6–7 p.m. on a weekday is an indication that not all who live in Lidcombe work in the city. But the combined effect of the movement in and out of Lidcombe suggests that some migrant expenditure (e.g., on shopping and eating at work) impacts on other local economies outside of Lidcombe, including the bigger Auburn City municipality and elsewhere.

A record of the quantitative contribution of Lidcombe is not readily available, as the Australian Bureau of Statistics, from which the City Council collates much of its data, does not seem to offer this finer disaggregation. Qualitatively, however, we know that Lidcombe itself has a variety of occupations, sales being the most conspicuous and most visibly active in serving the local population and people elsewhere, so migrant expenditure impacts on the local economy more directly. As suggested in Table 6.7, Joseph Street, a commercial hub of the town, is lined with shops selling groceries, a bakery, hairdressers, restaurants, bars, and a pharmacy. Joseph Street can also boast business entities such as a medical practice, a tax agency, legal services, and bars. Also available is the multinational fast food provider, McDonald's. Victoria Street East holds a small industrial base, a modest business park, and a couple of small-scale industries, such as a removal company. In the Northern part, there is also a long and busy commercial street interspersed with the long-established industry of Tooheys Brewery, hotels, and bars. This is John Street.

Until the COVID-19 pandemic, the trend of business was upwards judging by the rate at which new commercial activities are springing up. Over the past couple of years, three more Korean restaurants had been added. This is conspicuous on

Joseph Street, but also in other places. Apart from being a visible business, real estate agencies are springing up in the town, I counted at least three new ones in 2018, all located in the commercial precinct of Joseph Street. One of these was an 'add on' to a hitherto small jewellery and groceries shop, while the others were new agencies. We do not have accurate data of their profitability, as this information is not readily available. However, we know that Lidcombe is a middle-class town, no longer a working-class suburb, as it used to be.

While my interactions with residents over the past few years show that much of the working population lives in Lidcombe, admittedly not all the workers live in this migrant town. The key point, however, is that even areas in the town closest to the cemetery now enjoy substantial economic vibrancy. The funeral and burial industry remains active, to be sure, and there is an industry for engraving and monument making that employs local stonemasons. One is operated by the trust that manages the cemetery, but there are at least two more that are privately owned.

The Guardian Funeral Home is also active in planning for and preparing funerals on contract. This death-related industry actively advertises its activities, including in *Auburn Review*, a municipality newspaper, but visits to the premises of some of these entities also confirm that they are active. However, the local economy is now more diversified. There is much to commend about migrant enterprises in Lidcombe, but a lot can also be done to improve them. As leading Australian migration scholars (e.g., Collins et al., 1995; Collins and Shin, 2014) have shown, without such enterprises, migrants might find it difficult to flourish. Not only do they improve the economic well-being of the entrepreneurs, but they also contribute to revitalizing the local economy by providing a source of income and a rallying point for socialization and reducing unemployment.

In terms of business growth, the evidence appeared positive, at least prior to the outbreak of COVID-19. By asking shopkeepers, restaurant operators, and customers about where clients came from, I was able to conclude that the export base of Lidcombe is expanding. In one case, at a restaurant when I posed the question to the owner, a family seated at a table nearby responded that they were not from Lidcombe, but they liked to eat in Lidcombe.

In their book, *Immigrant-Food Nexus*, Julian Agyeman and Sydney Giacalone (2020) note that immigrants are increasingly feeding cities and nations. So not only can we not discuss migration without food, we can also not discuss food without discussing immigrants, their recipes, foods, tastes, and their entire sociology of food. This focus must necessarily expand the discussion from what Australian political economists call 'migrant workers in Australian agriculture' centred on rural questions, labour, and globalization (for an overview, see Rosewarne, 2020a, pp. 5–12) to considering the place of food in cities. Doing so shows that, in Lidcombe, the food industry serves the additional role of driving urban economic change, as well as powering local food sufficiency. In this sense at least, migrants add to sustainable urbanization.

Table 6.8 Median weekly incomes in Lidcombe, 2016

Median weekly incomes	Lidcombe	%	NSW	%	Australia	%
Personal	524	–	664	–	662	–
Family	1,495	–	1,780	–	1,734	–
Household	1,571	–	1,486	–	1,438	–

Source: ABS, 2016a.

Prior to the era of substantial wave of non-white migration, the mining and quarrying industry was a well-known basic industry in Lidcombe. That has changed. The suburb subsequently became better known for its funeral activities. In more recent times, the wholesale and retail activities industry also serve as 'exports'. People come to Lidcombe for its Korean delicacies. This has been facilitated by the train lines converging on the township, so people can easily get on and off when doing their shopping. So, in Lidcombe, typical non-basic activities do not really exist, except perhaps salons and local pubs. Food in Lidcombe is widely sought after by outsiders. In turn, the food industry brings in income to Lidcombe, while the availability of other services, such as health salons, and real estate agents, operate to prevent leakages from the system. Considered together, the urban economy could be said to be booming in the midst of vibrant food sovereignty (through local food production and use). However, the fruits are concentrated in the hands of a few winners (who only consider Lidcombe as an investment machine) and many losers (who consider Lidcombe to be their home), in a process in which the former displace the latter. This is a grave injustice.

Grave Injustice

Median incomes are much lower in Lidcombe than elsewhere in Australia. As shown in Table 6.8, this situation is particularly stark. Given that over 70% of residents in Lidcombe are renters, the effective income of residents must be even lower.

Table 6.9 shows that renters in Lidcombe pay rent to individual landlords (rented) or to banks and financial institutions (mortgage). Table 6.10 provides evidence that rents and mortgage payments in Lidcombe are much higher than similar outgoings in NSW and Australia more broadly.

Using the 30% affordability measure, it is clear that there is a significant affordability problem in Lidcombe. Only 81% of the renters pay less than 30% of their income as rent, compared with 87% in NSW and 89% of renters in Australian society more broadly. A similar spatial disadvantage applies to monthly median mortgage payments, too. So, taking Lidcombe as one case of migrant conurbation, in spite of the grit of hard work, they are worse off.

Table 6.9 Types of housing tenure in Lidcombe, 2016

Tenure types	Lidcombe	%	NSW	%	Australia	%
Owned outright	1,452	25.2	839,665	32.2	2,565,695	31.0
Owned with a mortgage	1,771	30.7	840,004	32.3	2,855,222	34.5
Rented	2,277	39.5	826,922	31.8	2,561,302	30.9
Other tenure type	37	0.6	23,968	0.9	78,994	1.0
Tenure type not stated	223	3.9	73,763	2.8	224,869	2.7

Source: ABS, 2016a.

Table 6.10 Rents and mortgage payments in Lidcombe, 2016*

Rent/mortgage payments	Lidcombe	%	NSW	%	Australia	%
Median rent (median monthly mortgage) repayments	470 (2,100)	–	380 (1,986)	–	335 (1,755)	–
Households where rent payments (monthly mortgage payments) are less than 30% of household income	–	81.0 (90.5)	–	87.1 (92.6)	–	88.5 (92.8)
Households with rent payments (monthly mortgage payments) greater than or equal to 30% of household income	–	19.0 (9.5)	–	12.9 (7.4)	–	11.5 (7.2)

Source: adapted from ABS, 2016a.
* Mortgage figures are in brackets.

Many poor but hardworking migrants have exited Lidcombe, mainly as a result of rising rental value induced by land speculation. What is at issue is the enclosure of land and the rules that encourage the commodification of land. These rules also support the privatization of publicly generated rents. In turn, prices of real estate started soaring faster than many of those living in Lidcombe could afford, but slower than what was happening in other parts of Sydney, for example Auburn. This process commenced in the mid-to-late 1990s, with the announcement, plans for, and execution of massive development related to the 2000 Sydney Olympics (Randolph et al., 2005). It has since continued, creating grave injustice.

Workers who contributed to developing Lidcombe can no longer afford to live there. These included Irish expelled from Ireland for reasons of poverty. They were poor. Kathy Mealing (1988, introduction) describes the spatial expression of this poverty in their housing situation: "Auburn boasts few grand houses, as the main inhabitants were ordinary working men and women, and the following stories often show that these houses were more than just a 'roof over our heads'". In modern times, however, workers who continue to support the economic base of the suburb, and, hence, to create its continuing land values, cannot live in Lidcombe. They have, in essence, been digging their own graves, as their work has contributed to increasing the land values. They have removed the land from under their feet. Capitalists exploit migrants by overworking and underpaying them. Many landlords, on the other hand, live overseas. They do not work, yet they reap the windfalls from Lidcombe. These same landlords deprive the public of what it contributes to growing land values, together with widespread socio-spatial racism covered by a veneer of multiculturalism.

Of these injustices, gentrification (e.g., Kotze, 2013; Monare et al., 2014; Tsenkova, 2014) is particularly important. In the literature on spatial segregation, this process seems to be subordinated to the behaviour of migrants and locals, or to the failure of the state in creating moral hazard or seeking to do good by providing public housing, which tends to sort migrants into ethnic spaces (Andersen, 2020, pp. 1–33). The process of gentrification is far more complex.

As the experience in Lidcombe shows, land is central to the creation of grave injustice. Gentrification in Lidcombe is similar to the transformation of urban and suburban development in Sydney more generally in the sense that it forced out poorer people into areas adjoining the Olympics site and drew in richer people (Stilwell, 1998). However, it is peculiar in the sense that money and migrants co-mingled to produce a distinct urban form not only to drive out its own population, but also to transform the population and property markets in neighbouring suburbs.

The data in Table 6.11 illustrate these trends. The median rental prices for houses and units in Lidcombe are much higher than Auburn, indeed than anywhere else in Australia. Yet, both the house auction clearance rate and the rate of change of the population in Lidcombe show that a substantial number of people are moving to Lidcombe. Many of these people are richer than the usual migrant.

This process is further complicated by the renting practices of owners, who are now slowly moving out and renting out their properties to renters. Consequently, absentee ownership—that is, renter-occupied housing—is on the rise in Lidcombe, although, apart from Berala, other migrant areas are experiencing a decline in absentee ownership. The relatively high vacancy rate in Lidcombe (second in comparison with Auburn, Berala, and Regents Parks) but, indeed, in all the migrant areas, signals that speculation is an important part of the process of change in the property market.

The process of migrant gentrification cannot explain the peculiar case of Lebanese and Turkish migrants. For them, research (Burnley, 2006; Mourad,

Table 6.11 Property values in Lidcombe and its neighbouring suburbs, 2018

	Lidcombe	Auburn	Berala	Regents Park
Physical size	6km^2	9km^2	2km^2	2km^2
Population change (2006–2011)	22.2% (+)	13.8% (+)	22.2% (+)	19.6% (−)
Total property sales	289	460	57	80
House auction clearance rate	60%	47.60%	68.80%	55.60%
Median rent				
House	A$580	A$500	A$500	A$475
Unit	A$520	A$450	A$380	A$410
Median sales price				
House	A$1,300,000	A$950,000	A$950,000	A$923,000
Unit	A$720,000	A$550,000	A$475,000	A$480, 000
Absentee ownership	37.9% (+)	46.4% (−)	40.6 (+)	43.5 (−)
Vacancy rate	1.81%	2.43%	1.27%	1.66%

Source: adapted from Ray White Lidcombe, 2018.

2009) suggests that the completion of the Auburn–Gallipoli Mosque in 1999 drew Turkish migrants, including some of those in Lidcombe, to move to Auburn. The mosque, which is a major religious meeting ground for Muslims in the area be they from Lebanon, Turkey, or elsewhere, was substantially financed by the Government of Turkey, with support from local Muslim migrants. It attracted some of the Turkish and Lebanese migrants in Lidcombe to move to Auburn not only because some could find accommodation in residential facilities also owned by the mosque administration, but also because a larger population of Muslims, Lebanese, and Turkish live in Auburn, creating a 'home away from home' and setting in motion a powerful magnet for more Muslim migrants from Turkey, Lebanon, and elsewhere to congregate.

The 'religious factor', however, is a poor explanation for the decline of the Croatian population in Lidcombe between 2001 and 2008. As research by Val Colić-Peisker (2004) and Walter Lalich (2004), published in the authoritative *Croatian Studies Review*, together with a local account and the analysis by Ilija Šutalo (2004), in his book *Croatians in Australia: Pioneers, Settlers and Their Descendants*, show, the changing nature of migrants from Croatia is a better explanation. Unlike the earlier Croatian migrants, who were mainly working class and found the suburb and its cheap housing with gardens comforting, and, hence, stayed in the suburbs for a longer time, the younger and newer groups of migrants, with better English language skills, better professional qualifications, and better potential to increase their incomes, stayed in the suburbs for only a short time and then moved to better localities. Working-class migrants continued to migrate to Australia, but Lidcombe was no longer attractive, given its growing numbers of apartment housing, which the Croatians did not find ideal for family life. Besides, Croatians in Sydney had themselves invested heavily in providing community facilities outside of Lidcombe, entailing religious, educational, and entertainment facilities, all of which contributed to making Lidcombe a less ideal place.

A modified version of the 'push out' hypothesis can be offered to explain the substantial decline in the share of migrants from the UK who reside in Lidcombe. While substantial numbers of white Australians in Lidcombe moved out during this process, they were not just forced out by richer migrants. Indeed, for some migrants, the white residents moved out because they were not willing to mix with the incoming migrant groups. Others contend that the shops for white Australians were not doing well with the coming of migrants, who typically shopped from migrant outlets, rather than Australian stores, and so Australian shopkeepers relocated, shops and all. A perception that Lidcombe is for migrants may be another reason dissuading white populations. Attrition is certainly part of the panoply of reasons, as old-time residents passed away and their children moved out. The subsequent lack of interest in a suburb predominantly filled by, and regarded as being for, migrants is yet one more reason. Lidcombe had always had a stigma of being a necropolis, so it has never really been a location of choice for white and wealthy Australians. White people who moved in during the formative years of the city worked primarily in the cemetery (Hedges, 1992), or for the railways (Mitchell, 2008), or the abattoirs, or the factories then abutting or existing within Lidcombe. Also, some of them left because they sold their property to migrants.

Others may have moved out to enable their children to attend better schools, or no longer having any children to attend local schools, a few may have chosen to live elsewhere. So, a combination of reasons, rather than one overarching driver, explains the decline of white population in Lidcombe. However, as suggested by Burnley (2006), the concentration of high-class, all-white neighbourhoods in Sydney has always given strong support to the view that race and class interact to structure settlement patterns in the city.

Although still diverse, Lidcombe has increasingly become a 'Korean Town'. A major reason for this shift is that the price of real estate in Strathfield, a neighbouring town, whose population is dominated by Koreans, has become increasingly less affordable. Lidcombe, then, has offered an escape route from the heating property market in Strathfield. The increasing Koreanization of Lidcombe is itself drawing in other Koreans. That said, the population and social culture in Lidcombe are diverse, including the co-existence of different types of church. One physical location where diversity is literally on display is the Lidcombe Remembrance Park, where peoples from all nationalities meet for social activities, relaxation, and light exercise.

Children of Crisis

Gini coefficients do not exist for Lidcombe. Even if they were estimated, however, they would only tell us about differences in income, not about racial exclusion more broadly. For that, Gordon's theory of assimilation (Gordon, 1961, 1964) suggests that by merely declaring integration, racism ceases. That position is questionable. Research (Collins and Reid, 2012) on the experiences of migrant teachers supposedly integrated in New South Wales, where Lidcombe is located, shows widespread exclusion. Migrant teachers experience name-calling and stereotyping. Their accent is mocked. Their experience is devalued and their prospects for professional and personal advancement are limited. Widespread casualisation is the more common experience of immigrant teachers. It is, indeed, rare, for migrant teachers to obtain permanent jobs in Sydney schools. For all these reasons, a new approach is needed.

Robert Coles pioneered such an approach in *Children of Crisis* (Coles, 2003). Coles' book was written in the wake of the 1954 *Brown vs Board of Education* ruling. This ruling, inspired by Gunnar Myrdal's study, published as the *American Dilemma* (Myrdal, 1944), made it illegal to segregate black and white children. Coles sought to understand the ramifications of integration on the psychological stress of the children, their teachers, and parents. Coles, the psychologist of Ruby Bridges, the first black six-year-old who was taken to an integrated school as a result of the desegregation rules, occupies a major place in the political economy analysis of discrimination. But, in addition to becoming Bridges' personal psychologist, in *Children of Crisis*, Coles offered key lessons on studying race.

Five of those lessons are particularly important for our analysis. The racist problem is not idealist. It is materialist, in the sense that it has a clear material logic to maintain privilege and power. Coles's second insight is that mere rules for integration or punishment against segregation do not address deep-seated structural problems of racism and stratification. In fact, such laws could lead to backlash at job places, shops, schools (involving both teachers and students), and housing. Third, children notice, internalize, and project what is going on around them. Studying their drawings, talking to them, and observing them illustrate these points. Fourth, blacks and migrants behave well, or at least in the same way as whites, who are often assumed to be the superior race. Finally, only social change, including comprehensive social protection, can address the problem of racism.

Examining the experiences of children provides one way of determining how inclusive Lidcombe is. Lidcombe Public School is the best place to look. Its current number of enrolled students—813—is not only quite substantial, but also represents an increase in size, as shown in Table 6.12.

The school is multicultural and integrated. Languages spoken at home by the students are broad-ranging. At the last count in 2019, the authorities identified

Table 6.12 Enrolment in Lidcombe Public School, 2016–2019

Year	2016	2017	2018	2019	% change in enrolment, 2016–2019
Girls	312	369	392	385	23.40
Boys	363	393	415	428	17.91
Total	675	762	807	813	20.44

Source: adapted from NSW Government, 2020, p. 16.

forty-five languages. The most common ones were Chinese, spoken by 26% of the students. Others were Korean (19%) and Turkish (12%). Arabic (12%), English (6%), and Vietnamese (2%) constituted the remaining languages spoken by the students. A popular Lidcombe Public School song captures the mood of positive multiculturalism:

> We are from Lidcombe School (clap! clap! clap!) …
> Learning in harmony is what we do best!
> Our students come from many different lands.
> United on Australian soil is where we choose to stand.
> Respecting one another and everyone we meet.
> Learning in harmony makes our lives complete.

As students in Australia can only attend public schools in their local government area, the words in this song complement the statistical information about diversity. Compared with the sparse population of the past, Lidcombe is now bustling with human activity and vibrant with population growth.

But should these be taken as proof of inclusion? Tell Them From Me surveys, regularly carried out among students and teachers in New South Wales (NSW), provide one way of analysing the issue. Lidcombe Public School regularly publishes key aspects of the surveys in its annual reports. In 2020, the school did not take part in the survey because of restrictions linked to the global COVID-19 pandemic (New South Wales Government, 2021, p. 28), but it did so before then. Stretching from 2016 and 2017 to 2018 and 2019, the following statement has always appeared in the reports:

> Lidcombe Public School celebrates Harmony Day every day of the school year. Multicultural education is embedded in all school pro-grammes, policies and procedures, as evidenced in the Tell Them From Me survey results, outlined in this annual report. The school has an

anti-racism contact officer elected each year and very few (if any) complaints are received in relation to racism. Student issues concerning
racism are appropriately managed using the school's Discipline Code.

(NSW Government, 2020, p. 33)

All this is encouraging. However, teachers are not as diverse as the student body.
Although not discussed in the school's annual reports, census data show that more
than 81 per cent of teachers in NSW are born in Australia (Collins and Reid, 2012,
p. 42). Indeed, even the few 'overseas' born teachers are predominately from the
UK, the US, Canada and or New Zealand, which contribute 54.19 per cent of the
overseas born teachers (Soong, 2018). This skewed distribution for a school system
that is increasingly non-white risks making the school itself a major transmit-
ter of inequalities and social stratification. Sociological research in Japan (Koido,
2021) where Japanese teachers dominate the school system makes the point. There,
a two-tiered school-intake system in which going to school is compulsory for
Japanese children, but not so much for immigrant children, teaching methods that
prioritise the needs of Japanese children, and a social system in which immigrant
parents are employed under precarious conditions all combine to create privilege for Japanese children and discrimination or social stratification for immigrant
children.

Australia is a different country, but these reasons provide additional grounds
to be interested in what the few complaints are usually about and just how 'few'
they actually are. Some responses can be found in the 'Findings from the 2017
Speak Out Against Racism (SOAR) Student and Staff Surveys' (Priest et al., 2019).
According to these surveys:

More than half (60%) of the participants reported seeing other students being racially discriminated against by their peers. This included
being left out, teased, or treated with less respect by other students.
Students from South Asian backgrounds (74%) and African backgrounds (68%) reported witnessing the highest levels of racial discrimination being directed towards students by other students. Nearly half
(43%) of students reported seeing incidents of racial discrimination
directed towards other students by teachers.

(Priest et al., 2019, p. 4)

Following Robert Coles (2003), this racism reflects the wider racism in Lidcombe.
As noted by Coles:

Any discussion of what a given child (or one of his drawings) has to
say about racial matters, school problems, or mob scenes must take

pains to put the child's social observations, his prejudices and partiali-
ties, into the context of his home life. By that I mean to insist upon the
young child's strong inclination to reflect his parents' views; but even
more, transfer to the neighborhood his personal tensions and struggles, so that other children, not to mention teachers or policemen, take
on a meaning to him quite dependent upon how he manages with his
parents, brothers, and sisters.

(Coles, 2003, p. 19)

This racism also intersects with class. Racial minorities of a higher class can abuse
people from the same race who have a lower status, class, and power. The widely
known, representative story of Mr Kim, as carefully analysed in *Sydney's Construction Union Strategy and Immigrant Worker Issues: A Roman Catholic-Marxist
Perspective* by Jenny Kwai-Sim Leung and Kieran James (2017, pp. 78–98), is a
case in point. Although not a child, the case is illustrative of the intersectionality
across race, class, and migrant status. A South Korean national, Mr Kim, was employed from 2004 to 2006 by a Korean-owned company located in Lidcombe. He
worked seven days a week for an average of sixteen hours a day for three years.
The company paid him no superannuation, benefits, travel allowance, or overtime
payments, nor was he insured. His only reward was AUD 10/hour, cash-in-hand.
In 2005, Kim was involved in a grave work-based accident, instantly losing four
fingers. After paying initial medical bills of AUD 3,600, the company abandoned
him. Nobody would help him to pay AUD 100,000+ of medical expenses. Worse,
the company reported him to the authorities, intending that Mr Kim be de-
ported to Korea. Kim became stranded, homeless, and jobless. Kim's experience
has come to symbolize exploitation in Lidcombe, but it is not unique, nor is it
peripheral.

Exploitation and expulsion are planted deep in the history of Lidcombe, as
earlier shown. This history is not only limited to Lidcombe, however. As Louise
Johnson (2015) has carefully shown, it is a history of suburban Australia. The land
on which Lidcombe stands was stolen from Indigenous people. The British colonial authorities claimed that land in Lidcombe, like the rest of Australia, was *terra
nullius*. This 'no man's land' was granted or sold cheaply. The ensuing land market
became global. Speculators bought their share. Land was for investment purposes.
They did not have to live in Lidcombe or in Australia for that matter, but they
controlled the heart of Lidcombe from afar.

Together with landowners in Australia, they reaped the benefit from public investment and from the work of labour. Capitalists who financialized the suburbs by
investing in mortgage facilities helped to drive this land speculation by financing it.
The Australian state, both regional and federal, also disproportionately supported
landowners because of its actions and inactions. Landlords sought to undermine

taxation arrangements by avoiding them. They evaded them by also buying more land in areas outside the taxation regime. They lobbied against the imposition of more taxes. In the end, revenues from Britain, including rents extracted from its many colonies in Africa, were used to develop an infrastructure which, in turn, increased land values in suburban Australia. In Lidcombe, this process has effectively kept Indigenous people away, first, by force; next by the market; then by a combination of these forces. Poorer migrants for whom Lidcombe was originally a home have had to flee to more marginal areas. Others can no longer come in. If this grave injustice is to be resolved, the city's current urban economy would need to be radically restructured.

Conclusion

Migrant towns have become a major feature of global migration, but their form and nature, ramifications for society, economy, and environment as well as for racial realities continue to be caricatured. The dominant view holds that a migrant footprint is most emphatically negative. Even where they are the focus of more careful attention, migrant towns are simply reduced to transient spaces, 'arrival cities' (Saunders, 2012) where *individual* migrants first settle and then move away when they are successful. Questions about how such towns form, in what ways migrants transform such urban spaces, and how migrants experience issues such as social stratification are, therefore, pertinent questions for the analysis of contemporary global migration analysis. This chapter questions the stereotypes. Strongly associated with death and the dead, Lidcombe, a major migrant town in Australia, is bustling with economic activity and renewal. Not only has the southern part, formerly mainly a settlement of the dead, been revamped with lively migrants actively working within and without the local economy, but also the northern part has continued to be vibrant and well settled.

The makings of life have not only impacted Australia, the host country, positively through an expansion in its economic activities via multiple channels, such as building, banking, and billing, but also through the variety of its social and moral economies. Significant changes in the built environment can easily be seen. Chinese architecture is palpable, as is the conspicuous presence of a wider range of churches and denominations of churches, along with the visible presence of the Auburn-Gallipoli Mosque. The many non-Anglo iconographies provide a visible reminder of the widespread effect of migrants on the built environment in Lidcombe.

Clearly, these changes are consistent with the findings of Jock Collins and his team of political economists, who have recently studied other migrant towns (see Collins et al., 2020). Yet, my own methodology led me to other findings about Lidcombe. Property relations are rapidly changing in this town. Where single-storey family houses dominated, now high-rise apartments are becoming the norm. Previously, landlords were resident in Lidcombe; now they are absent. Increasingly a rentier space, the process in which land and property values surge has been a vital part of transforming the class and racial make-up of Lidcombe. As this chapter has shown, in addition to the more visible changes, the political-economic process for producing the built environment has also been undergoing clear transformation, as can be seen in the racial composition of construction labourers, for example.

Throughout the change and continuity of Lidcombe, there is no sustained evidence that migrants are exerting untold and undeserving demands on the Australian public. As contributors to Australia's common wealth, and as active workers, migrants should be entitled to their own share of the national cake. This is especially true as there is no proof that migrants have been a drain on public resources through the maintenance of peace and safety, as the crime rate has fallen drastically over the years (Auburn City Council, 2013a). Not only have migrants brought life to Australia, but they have also revived Australian lives. Migrants have transformed a dead city. The funeral industry still exists, but Lidcombe's local economy is more diversified today and looks poised to achieve further socio-economic progress.

These findings significantly extend the existing literature on migrants, which assumes that they are in the diaspora, but the 'attachment to their homeland' suggests that they do not invest in their host countries (Min and Park, 2014). In the case of Lidcombe, there is attachment to 'home' in the sense of bringing 'home culture' to Australia (e.g., eating out on a scale never before seen in the area), but the migrants have also transformed an old and dying township.

Far from just one ethnic enclave in the town, as other research suggests happens (Kim, 2014), or one regional and racial group of migrants investing in the investment property market, as my earlier study of African migrants in Sydney (Obeng-Odoom, 2012) shows, the town is populated and transformed by migrants from different races, ethnicities, and regions. In this sense, the study also extends the literature on migrant transformation of towns that has previously concentrated on refugees and single nationalities or ethnic enclaves (e.g., Stilwell, 2003). The wealthy white Australians have largely moved out, but they have hardly been 'pushed out' to occupy less ideal places. So, unlike the situation when the white population in Australia forced out black and indigenous groups in Australia to live in worse and isolated places (Jang, 2015), the white population who used to live in Lidcombe have moved to 'better places' and have economically benefitted from their departure. In turn, the story of Lidcombe is not merely a case of displacing the white population or simply a story about individual migrants becoming successful, as some research (e.g., Saunders, 2012) in the literature suggests.

There are important problems, such as increasing property and persistent racism. Even if the public perception of Lidcombe residents has improved, such changes in beliefs, attitudes, and ideologies have not radically altered the economic position of migrants in Lidcombe. Admittedly, these problems are generally symptomatic of migration in Australia. Besides, the lack of cohesion leads to possibilities for policy intervention, linked with opportunities to foster greater inclusion. Wider awareness, through research publications disseminated in the community newspaper, *Auburn Review*, together with multiple communication through written, visual, and audio means, can all be used to inform and sensitize. A study of migrants in the US conducted by Jerry Park (2013) also shows that religious groupings are often vectors of insularity and ethnicity. However, they can also be avenues for change, perhaps even becoming the avant-garde in the process of cosmopolitanism, if they set out to make changes to their own organizations which, in turn, might provide the grounds for inclusion. This latter possibility is documented in more recent research (e.g., Manatscal et al., 2020; Zuber, 2020; Paquet and Xhardez, 2020), too. However, merely improving inclusion without changing institutions do not go far enough.

Free and quality public education, including multicultural and cosmopolitan English language speaking and writing courses, could be offered by the council and the Australian authorities more widely to residents. New institutions that deliberately create and sustain education inclusion could also be created. Again, such a strategy would be limited. Much of the existing stratification is tied to the ownership and control of land in Lidcombe and the crippling charges on labour. Real estate pricing and prices that are often pushed up through speculation are particularly problematic because they may result in bubbles and, hence, deepen problems of affordability and stratification in the local economy. Such problems force labour to hire out under conditions that are inimical to itself. Workers endure much exploitation, in part due to pressure on them to house themselves by paying rising rents. So, not much change can take place without altering existing urban land tenure. Implementing a Georgist single taxation programme to 'cool down' the urge to speculate in a booming local economy could be considered. In addition, public and social housing could be expanded, with particular and special affirmative support for indigenous Australians, who were the first groups of people to be dispossessed of their land in Lidcombe. In these respects, too, designing and implementing a carefully considered comprehensive reparations programme would need to be part of the alternatives to the orthodoxy.

Starting such reforms for housing for migrants could be controversial, but the city authorities could push these measures through if they chose to, especially now, when the council has a strong migrant base. For the same reason, there could be greater mobilization to oppose taxes on income, while promoting quality self-employment and decent employment both within the private and public sectors. However, an analysis of the precise nature of the politics of change and the political economy of how different interest groups could resist change or be roped in to support change will have to wait for another time.

For now, it suffices to stress that migrants have brought life to Australia's dead city, life to themselves, and life to their relatives overseas, without exerting undeserved pressures on the Australian national resources.

The story of Lidcombe contrasts with the assumption of individual-based migration. It seems that theories of migration which emphasize how individuals make rational decisions about where to go, how, and when are fundamentally problematic. So are theories of assimilation, which emphasize that inter-racial marriage, for example, and the substantial contribution of migrants to urban economic growth in particular, are rites of passage to avoid racism and ostracism.

7

Working with Hosts

Labour on the Move

So much for migrant towns. Also critical is the political economy of working with hosts because widespread global labour migration is, perhaps, what most generates heated debate. According to neoclassical economists, it arises from real or perceived differences in wages across the world, from differences in returns on human capital between points of origin and destination, and from the general self-interest of migrants (Todaro, 1969; Todaro and Smith, 2006; for a review, see Burnazoglu, 2021). Labour migrants, the argument continues, make rational choices based on expected income. Hence, they move when the actual or perceived prevailing level of income in the intended destination is much higher than their actual current levels of income.

These 'economic migrants', as they are usually called, are 'pushed' or 'pulled' by only material reasons, but they are always supposedly better off after migration (Ravenstein, 1885, 1889). In this process, unemployment is only frictional (see a review by Pishé, 2013; Burnazoglu, 2021), the lack of assimilation temporary, and persistent inequality transient. All these problems merely reflect differences in human capital or information asymmetry, which melt away with time and technological diffusion. Indeed, based on a neoclassical interpretation of W. Arthur Lewis' work called the 'Lewis Turning Point' (for a detailed commentary, see Molero-Simarro, 2017), the typical claim is that migration may cause inequality to rise initially, but, as migrants earn more and more, inequality naturally reduces. Improving the search and match processes expedites the process (Burnazoglu, 2021). Growth is accordingly assured.

So, it is the effect of labour migration on growth and 'catch-up' which are the key criteria for judging success (Clausing, 2019a, 2019b; *The Economist*, 2019a, 2019d, 2019e). In neoclassical labour economics, the effect of immigration on the income of local workers is of interest, too. According to George Borjas (see, e.g., Borjas, 1994, 2002, 2007, 2009), labour immigration tends to reduce the wages of the skilled locals because it increases supply relative to demand. Consistent with the laws of supply and demand, the higher the supply, the lower the price.

Such theories are also advocated by many prominent social scientists (e.g., Gordon, 1961), world leaders, and international organizations. This widespread influence of economic ideas recalls J.M. Keynes's famous statement that:

the ideas of economists ... are more powerful than is commonly understood ... Practical men, who believe themselves to be quite exempt from any intellectual influences, are usually the slaves of some defunct economist. Madmen in authority, who hear voices in the air, are distilling their frenzy from some academic scribbler of a few years back.

(Keynes, 1953/1964, p. 383)

However, these ideas lack consistent empirical verification. In the case of Afro-Chinese labour migration or Afro-Chinese labour migrants,[1] a substantial and dynamic[2] stratum of labour migrants, at least, these issues require investigation. While the global economics literature on migration tends to focus on Europe and North America, there is significant political-economic commentary and research on Afro-Chinese relations. Some of this body of reflections emphasizes the thorny issue of Chinese interest in Africa, probing whether it could be regarded as 'the new scramble for Africa' (*The Economist*, 2019d) or 'China's second continent' (French, 2014). The leading writer on Afro-Chinese relations, Deborah Brautigam (2009), on the other hand, strongly suggests that 'the Dragon's Gift', as she calls her book on the ramifications of China's engagement in Africa (see also Brautigam, 2015, 2019), is likely to achieve far more than years of Western imperialism.

Questions about the two-way Afro-Chinese labour migration has received substantial attention, too, as have issues regarding the Forum on China–Africa Cooperation (FOCAC) and the Belt and Road Initiative (BRI) (see, e.g., Cheru and Obi, 2010; Chen and Duggan, 2016; Lee, 2017; Yu, 2019; Hodzi and Chen, 2020). There is sometimes a tendency to stress a one-directional relationship, even among leading writers (see, e.g., Brautigam, 2009, 2015) in this literature, but many studies (for a recent review, see Achenbach et al., 2020) have been carried out on the two-way or circular Afro-Chinese labour relations. The Chinese in Africa/Africans in

---

[1] Various studies suggest that the size of the Chinese migrant population in Africa increased from 80,000 to over 750,000 between 1980 and 2006 (Ancharaz, 2011; Mohan et al., 2014, pp. 3–6). More recently, these migrants are estimated to be between one and two million people (see, e.g., French, 2014, p. 26; Bodomo and Ma, 2010, p. 286). They work in a wide range of sectors, from mining and small-scale manufacturing to trading. The population of Africans in China is much less, but is substantial nevertheless. Currently, nearly 500,000 Africans (Bodomo and Ma, 2010, pp. 283–284) live in China. These Africans work in various professions, including education, diplomacy, and entertainment. Guangzhou is the single most important place of settlement for African migrants. It is estimated that, alone, Guangzhou hosts 130,000 Africans (Lee, 2014, p. 20). The rest live in cities such as Yiwu (Cissé, 2015, p. 50). Much has also been written about the estimated 150,000 Chinese professionals who were sent to Africa to work in the agricultural, transport, and telecommunications sectors in the 1960s and the beginning of the 1980s (see Mung, 2008, p. 95), but today the range of activities in which Chinese migrants are involved is much wider. For example, it is estimated that there are between 700 and 800 Chinese companies in Africa, operating in 49 out of the 54 countries on the continent. Together, these companies employ about 80,000 Chinese workers (see Mung, 2008, p. 95).

[2] 'Ghana Requires US$650 Billion to Reclaim Environment—Prof. Frimpong Boateng', http://Peacefmonline.com/pages/local/social/201801/341752.php.

China (CA/AC) Research Network, for example, produces excellent studies in this regard.

The focus of this chapter is on the sphere of the economics of labour. First, why do African and Chinese labour migrants move to China and Africa, respectively? Second, what are the socio-economic effects of this Afro-Chinese labour migration? Third, how might migration policy more effectively address these consequences? Although excellent work has been done in this domain, too (see, e.g., Lee, 2014; Mohan et al., 2014; Edwards, 2019), this chapter has a more specific focus on examining the particular claims made in the mainstream economics of labour migration literature and, hence, offering another way to appreciate Afro-Chinese relations generally.

To do so, I rely on the existing rich pool of insight and ethnographic detail (e.g., Bodomo, 2012; Freeman, 2017; Özkul and Obeng-Odoom, 2013; Park et al., 2016; Edwards, 2019; Whitaker, 2017) and detailed cases of Chinese or African migration (see Chang, 2008; Ngai, 2016; Tonah et al., 2018; Xu and Chen, 2019) that can help to address the three most intractable questions about labour migration in political economy.

By systematizing existing data, I show that the experiences of African migrants working with Chinese hosts or vice versa is far more complex than what neoclassical economics suggests. Driven, or at least moulded, not so much by the migrant as a rational utility-maximizing individual but by holistic processes of 'circular, combined and cumulation causation' during which migrants tend to create their own opportunities rather than responding to existing ones. African and Chinese migrants working with each other as hosts or even migrants have contributed to economic growth, but at the cost of much socio-spatial displacement and socio-ecological degradation. Added to these social costs is widespread labour precarity. So, the insidious attempts by the state, business enterprise, corporate finance, and capital to consider migration a 'spatial fix' for economic growth are questionable. However, seeking to wall out migrants, embarking on widespread surveillance, pursuing migrant scapegoating, and framing migration as a Malthusian problem are not a panacea.

The social costs of migration, among others, need to be directly redressed by redesigning the institutions that shape the conditions of labour. Doing so would require leaving behind neoclassical economics theories of migration and exposing their vested interests. GIS[3] theorizing, which more comprehensively addresses the labour migration problematic and strongly emphasizes the coupling of migration, economic, and social policy, can usefully be considered an alternative.

To illustrate these arguments, the rest of this chapter is divided into four sections. 'Circular, Combined, and Cumulative Causation' analyses the causes of

---

[3] Georgist political economy (G), institutional economics (I), and stratification economics (S).

labour migration. 'The Social Costs of Growth' probes the growth-inducing effects of migration and its social costs. 'Migration Policy' examines how policy questions relate to these tensions and contradictions, while 'Conclusion: Retheorizing the Economics of Labour Migration' attempts to retheorize labour migration.

Circular, Combined, and Cumulative Causation

Labour migration is driven by forces of circular, combined, and cumulative causation; not just by what mainstream economists call 'opportunities' (World Bank, 2017). Business cycles are important as drivers of migration, as Commons (1907) famously argued. Typically, booms attract migrants, while depressions repel them. However, these business cycles occur within a wider social environment over a long period of time, as the evidence systematized in Figure 7.1a and b illustrates. Consider what Commons (1907, pp. 12–13) described as 'colonial migration'. Such labour migration is not driven by migrants' rational calculations or their interest in business. Instead, some 150,000 Chinese were sent to Africa in the nineteenth and twentieth centuries as indentured labour (Park, 2019). They did not freely choose to move, they were coerced. In Madagascar, the French led the way by using Chinese convicts as conscripts to advance French imperial interests (Tremann, 2013). The Dutch, British, Portuguese, and many others put Chinese labourers to similar uses in the rest of Africa (Park, 2019). Many of those who won their freedom stayed on, so did many of their descendants (*New African Magazine*, 2015; Park, 2019). It seems that the presence of Africans or people of black descent in China can be traced as far back as the Tang Dynasty (618–907 AD), as Obeng's (2019) review of the literature on the history Afro-Chinese relations shows.

These historical reasons provide a context for analysing the causes of labour migration, but they also create path dependencies, as a number of historians (e.g., Akyeampong, 2011; Hobson, 2004) have demonstrated. Figure 7.1a shows three time periods that are particularly important to develop this line of analysis.

The period of Mao Tse-tung's reign (1949–1976) constitutes phase one, the rise of Deng Xiaoping (1978–1992), phase two, and the time thereafter (post 2001), phase three. These three epochs and the interludes between them, parallel the emphasis on internal self-sufficiency, the loosening of internal economic restrictions supplemented with the efflorescence of China as an important global player, and the rise of China as a global force typified, among other things, by China's acceptance of World Trade Organization rules. In Africa, these periods also roughly coincide with three epochs: pre-independence and the colonial period, independence, and post-independence. Pre-independence developments were important. The 1955 Bandung Conference embodied the collective aspirations of the Global South to break the chains of colonialism. African leaders such as Kwame Nkrumah helped to foster South–South cooperation, which often provides the context

(a)   Historical Forces

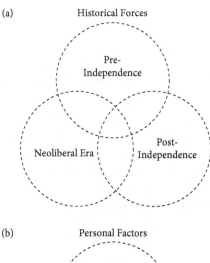

(b)   Personal Factors

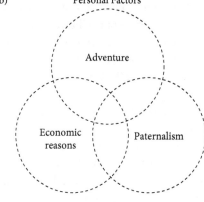

(c)   Combined and Cumulative Causation

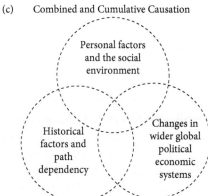

Fig. 7.1 Circular, combined, and cumulative causation

for migration analysis (see Amoah, 2019 for a detailed account of Nkrumahist strategies to promote Ghana–China relations).

The path dependency created by this early history of migration is striking. The migrants who stayed in Africa directed newcomers to various parts of the continent where these new migrants could settle more comfortably. Indeed, early Chinese migrants in Mauritius influenced the decision of many South African-based Chinese migrants (Park, 2019). Also, as many of these early migrants exported local African goods to China (Park, 2019), such trade, together with other factors, shaped the drivers of Chinese migration to Africa. This is not prima facie evidence that Chinese migration to Africa was for opportunity, though many migrants did create their own opportunities. This *creative response*, to use Joseph Schumpeter's phrase (Schumpeter, 1947), challenges the neoclassical labour economics fixation on *adaptive response* to take, rather than to make, opportunities.

The more recent turn to neoliberalism has strongly shaped the discourse on 'opportunities' (Cheru and Obi, 2010; Haifang, 2010), although this rhetoric is at the national level and its theory of entrepreneurship is not as holistic as Schumpeter's theory (Schumpeter, 1947). Most African states court Chinese economic engagement, while China is seeking to consolidate its own economic and political standing in the global community by courting African engagement. Accordingly, Chinese support to Africa is not entirely a matter of solidarity; it is also to promote mutual economic interests. In 2000, Beijing voluntarily waived Africa's $1.2 billion sovereign debt to China. In return, between 2000 and 2005, the value of Africa–China trade increased more than four times.

Crucially, since 2000, every year more Chinese entrepreneurs have moved to Africa. In 2006, the number was ten times higher than in 2003 (Arrighi, 2008, p. 207). More recently, an estimated 800 Chinese businesses have been established in Africa (Mung, 2008, p. 95). Official Chinese statistics show that, in 2008, there were some 140,000 Chinese workers in Africa (Brautigam, 2009, p. 154). In monetary terms, China's foreign direct investment (FDI) in Africa has grown substantially. Between 2011 and 2016, Chinese FDI in Africa grew from $16 to $40 billion (*The Economist*, 2019a, p. 19). Most of these investments influence Chinese labour migration to Africa (McVeigh and Dzradosi, 2019; Ramamurti and Hillemann, 2018, pp. 43–44). Alone, the Chinese state has exported more than 80,000 Chinese labour migrants to work on Beijing-funded FDI projects. Most of these migrants plan to continue living in Africa (Hilson et al., 2014, p. 296). Not only do these state initiatives create opportunities for small-scale Chinese businesses, Chinese businesses (e.g., roads, fishing, or mining) also largely recruit Chinese workers. Together with the small number of Chinese migrants in Africa recruited by African businesses (Park, 2019), the link between business and migration may well seem axiomatic.

Nevertheless, this Chinese path to Africa should be viewed in the context of state restructuring in China. After retrenchments in public-sector jobs led to 60 million job losses in China in the mid-1990s going hand-in-hand with the lowering of the conditions of labour (Bieler and Lee, 2017, p. 4), Chinese workers demonstrated what Karl Polanyi (1944/2001, p. 79) described as a 'double movement'. Specifically, 'the extension of the market organization in respect to genuine commodities was accompanied by its restriction in respect to fictitious ones'. The number of worker strikes increased consistently. The number of strikes in 2005, for example, was eight times higher than in 1993 (Arrighi, 2008, p. 377; for recent data and analyses, see Molero-Simarro, 2017; *The Economist*, 2019f). Migration to Africa appears to have become the other path of the double movement.

The emergence of a new Chinese financial architecture in China facilitates this institutionalized alternative (Cheru and Calais, 2010; Cheru and Obi, 2010; French, 2014; Robertson, 2016; Sanderson and Forsythe, 2013; Sheridan, 2016). Consider the activities of institutions such as the China Development Bank, Exim Bank of China, and the Industrial and Commercial Bank of China. Their lending terms tend to include the employment of Chinese and the creation of conditions that support the further development of the conditions that would support the efflorescence and flourishing of Chinese businesses in Africa. Even when these banks themselves do not impose such conditions, Chinese businesses have tended to hire Chinese labour. These institutions do not necessarily take instructions from the Chinese state. They are private initiatives intent on making China both the world's factory and the world's supplier of cheap labour (Bieler and Lee, 2017).

Thus, in explaining the drivers of migration, it is what J.R. Commons called 'the Institutionalized Mind' that matters. In his words:

If it be considered that, after all, it is the individual who is important, then the individual with whom we are dealing is the Institutionalized Mind. Individuals begin as babies. They learn the custom of language, of cooperation with other individuals, of working towards common ends, of negotiations to eliminate conflicts of interest, of subordination to the working rules of the many concerns of which they are members. They meet each other, not as physiological bodies moved by glands, nor as 'globules of desire' moved by pain and pleasure, similar to the forces of physical and animal nature, but as prepared more or less by habit, artificial transactions created by the collective human will. They are not found in physics, or biology, or subjective psychology, or in the German Gestalt psychology, but are found where conflict, interdependence, and order among human beings are pre-liminary to getting a living. Instead of individuals the participants are forces of a going concern. Instead of forces of nature they are forces of human nature. Instead of isolated individuals in a state of nature they are always participants in transactions, members of a concern in which they come and go, citizens of an institution that lived before them and will live after them.

(Commons, 1934a/2009, pp. 73–74)

While personal factors (Figure 7.1b) and migrant agency can be named as among the drivers of Afro-Chinese migration, they are also shaped by family and other reasons (Castles, 2011, 2012, 2015; Ho, 2012; Mohan et al., 2014; Rosewarne, 2010, 2012, 2014, 2016, 2020a, 2020b). The experience of many Chinese women migrants in Africa is a case in point. Many of these single, divorced, and less educated women consider family pressures to remarry burdensome. Combined with wider social expectations in China, migrating to Africa is institutionally and socially constructed as an alternative pathway (Cissé, 2015; Mohan et al., 2014, pp. 71–72, see also pp. 80–83).

African migration to China confirms this cumulative, circular, and combined causation of migration. The Nigerians, who send an estimated $8 million daily to Guangzhou for business transactions (Lee, 2014, p. 32), are driven by a panoply of factors. The differential cost of production between Nigeria and China is one of them. The prevalence of duty-free regulations that apply to goods exported from China is another (Lee, 2014, p. 34). The limited opportunity for public-sector employment in Nigeria is a third factor. Other African migrants first went to China as students. The Chinese state offers some 5,500 scholarships to African students every year (Obeng, 2019, p. 79). Some of these students become labour migrants during or after their studies for a mosaic of reasons. Moreover, their education in China and intermarriage open new social spaces for them to occupy and shape. These are not necessarily related to business cycles. Their business activities are shaped by other factors (Figure 7.1c) than those that initially motivated them to migrate (Figure 7.1b).

A circular, combined, and cumulative process is at play in all these examples. After the completion of cycles, the next round is not the same. It generates additional forces that drive the migration process. That is how the networks and the social provisioning in the migration process have arisen and are maintained (Tinti and Reitano, 2017). Facilitators of the journey are usually described as 'people smugglers' in English language sources. However, their role is far more complex because they are neither just smugglers nor just saviours. They can be both at different times and neither at other times, especially when they are sometimes migrants themselves. Indeed, they can also be all of these identities at different times (Tinti and Reitano, 2017).

The experiences of internal African migrants in Senegal can further illustrate the point. In an economy with few political-economic options, these migrants hire themselves out at much lower wage rates to Chinese shop owners in Dakar. These desperate Senegalese migrants typically have no work contracts and are quite often fired without due process (Cissé, 2013). Promised a better life, these poor people may migrate for economic as well as for other reasons. This social economics of migration recalls how migrants from elsewhere, such as in Accra, Ghana, straddle the formal and informal economies (Hart, 1973; Ndjio, 2009, 2014; Obeng-Odoom, 2011a). In this process, other complexities arise that become part of the cycle, even if they were absent in earlier drivers of the cycles.

Consider, for example, the Asian financial crisis of 1998. It heralded changes in local but also in wider global political-economic systems. Many Africans from Indonesia and Thailand moved to new areas in Asia for these reasons. Others moved from the Middle East to Asia. Guangzhou was one of their major destinations (Lan, 2015, p. 292; Obeng, 2019). A migrant town, its allure to new migrants signals that migration decisions are shaped by path dependencies. These paths can be broken, however, through the implementation of new laws. The Guangdong provincial government's anti-migration law (Guangdong Act) is a case in point. This law rewards Chinese for reporting Africans who may have overstayed, those who enter China illegally, or Africans who are involved in any illegality.

Simultaneously, the law punishes Chinese who refuse to report such illegal Africans (Lan, 2015). In contrast, in Yiwu, a trading city in the Eastern Province of China, the legal regime is characterized by programmes initiated and maintained by its local leaders to support African migrants. Keen to boost Yiwu's urban economy, these leaders seek to attract migrants by creating an institutional context that makes Yiwu a welcoming city for Africans. Among other things, the city authorities provide municipal services to suit its African community (see, e.g., Bodomo and Ma, 2010; Mathews et al., 2017). Consequently, while Guangzhou has lost many of its African labour migrants, between 2006 and 2009, the number of registered Africans in Yiwu increased from 20,311 to 54,050 (Cissé, 2015, p. 50). Clearly, migration is a socially embedded process, whose drivers act like a relay race. The processes and networks associated with the experience cannot entirely be described as economic or non-economic. As a socio-economic process, various forces drive diverse activities or run their part of the race.

Illustrating that circular, combined, and cumulative causation processes, not utility-maximizing rational choices, shows a lack of congruence between neoclassical economics theory (Todaro, 1969; Todaro and Smith, 2006) and social reality. Although problematizing the mainstream is important in its own right, the analysis, however, shows more than simply distinguishing 'right' from 'wrong'. It also suggests that Afro-Chinese migration has historically been part of wider processes of social change, a new theorising of migration. So, categorizing labour as 'economic migrants' is quite arbitrary. More fundamentally, the drivers of migration are not just about income differences. They are, even more crucially, about wider conditions of work and general prevailing socio-economic environment internally, internationally, and globally. If migration appears quite historical, is widespread, and is a matter of right because we have one earth given to us as a gift, then migration can be facilitated. Doing so for the promotion of capitalist expansionism, to reduce labour and product costs, to encourage recurrent and relentless economic growth, and as a win–win strategy advocated by mainstream economists (Clausing, 2019a, 2019b; *The Economist*, 2019a, 2019d, 2019e), should, however, be questioned. The effects of widening growth on the environment (Daly, 2019) are catastrophic; so are the other social costs of growth.

The Social Costs of Growth

Neoclassical economists (see, e.g., Borjas, 1994, 2002, 2007, 2009) argue that migration creates a zero-sum game during which migrants win because locals lose out on wages. In this view, migrants reduce the wage rate of locals because supply of labour exceeds demand.[4] A new equilibrating process begins to create a win-win scenario, sometimes aided by market-based migration policies. The evidence, in practice, shows a more complex picture of collaboration and complementarities. Consider, for example, the establishment of Chinese enterprises in Africa.

One estimate is that entrepreneurs from China have created some 300,000 jobs for African workers (Mutethya, 2018). The contribution of African labour migrants to urban economic growth in China is similarly substantial. Guangzhou's economy, for example, has evolved. At some stage of the city's history, the Guangzhou economy was regarded as industrial (Akyeampong, 2011; Hobson, 2004), while others (e.g., Mathews et al., 2017) have documented Guangzhou's long history of commerce. Today, the city's economy has been diversified by the economic activities of African migrants. According to Jane Jacobs's (1969) epigenesis theory, activities such as trade transform the local economy. Exports bring in revenue which, in turn, generates further urban economic activities. Growth comes not only from these activities themselves, but also from their clustering, which generates agglomeration economies.

The *agglomeration* of different people also produces advantages. Alfred Marshall described them as knowledge, input, and labour sharing among various firms and economic entities working in the urban economy (Obeng-Odoom, 2016b, pp. 83–106). These advantages spill over to surrounding areas. So, spatial proximity leads to what economists call 'spatial externalities' (Bara et al., 2017). More fundamentally, migrant entrepreneurs themselves innovate by doing new things or old things in new ways, even if these innovations are quite ordinary. As Joseph Schumpeter demonstrated, such entrepreneurship drives substantial economic

---

[4] Original institutionalists and some progressive economists make similar arguments (see, e.g., Jaynes, 2007 and the work of J.R. Commons, discussed in Obeng-Odoom, 2018a), but the cause of wage depression arises from employer manipulation of workers and institutions that sanction such behaviour, from employer monopoly, and from monopolistic competition, not from the autonomous interaction between supply, demand, and price (wage rate).

change (e.g., Schumpeter, 1947). This Schumpeterian theory of interdependent and evolutionary change is reflected in more recent experience.

As one Chinese entrepreneur observed in a study by Lan (2015, p. 297), '[w]e depend on Africans for business. If our government does not allow them to come, we have to close our shops.' More recently, many of the Chinese interviewed in Erica Marcus's research documentary, *Guangzhou Dream Factory* (Marcus, 2017), admitted on camera that they are in business because of African labour migrants (see also Mathews et al., 2017, pp. 72–73). As many Africans cannot operate formal bank accounts by themselves, they rely on new banking forms operated by Chinese residents. Money exchange is another business, usually led by Chinese migrants from Northern China (Lan, 2015). Most Africans in China are quite well educated. Four out of ten Africans in Guangzhou have had tertiary education (Obeng, 2019, p. 76), so Africans bring valuable skills to Chinese cities. Many Africans teach English to the Chinese. They also employ local Chinese people in African businesses (Mohan et al., 2014), including shipping and brokerage (Obeng, 2019). Thus, Afro-Chinese labour migration has added much dynamism to economic growth.

The social costs of this circular, combined, and cumulative economic growth have, however, been devastating. Migrants live a life of uncertainty, a reality which, according to J.K. Galbraith, contrasts with the certainties of economic theory, capitalism, and socialism (Galbraith, 1977, p. 7). Not only do many migrants fail in business, they often live a life of insecurity, sojourning as temporary migrants on yearly residency permits (see Lee, 2014, p. 29, 33). Migrants' bi-racial, Afro-Chinese families and children face widespread racism and ostracism at school and at work (Mathews et al., 2017, pp. 195–213).

They become, as Robert Coles (1971) famously theorized, 'children of crisis'. The local 'growth machine' (Molotch, 1976) that generates economic boom in migrant towns based on iterative and interactive networks and interactions with locals and institutions (Obeng-Odoom, 2016b, pp. 83–106; Saunavaara, 2017; Wang, 2016) also creates major problems. A local property market is called forth by the activities of African migrants, but Chinese landlords extract significant rent by either letting or subletting their shops to Africans. This stream of rental payments enables landlords to live as rentiers, who privately capture rents that are socially created.

Whether Africa is the net beneficiary of this relationship or China is colonising Africa is often the concern, but this dualistic framework is not helpful. The rhetoric of 'urban governance' and, hence, of attracting private initiatives seems to be met by increasing Chinese investment (Obeng-Odoom, 2013). Yet, many Africans have become tenants on their own land. As local land has been leased to Chinese investors to develop shops, many of which recruit Chinese workers, a number of ordinary Africans have faced persistent insecurity of tenure. Sometimes too, African tenants are forced off their land to find alternative shops or housing because they are priced out of new property markets that arise from Chinese property investment. The boom–bust cycles in property markets instantiated by speculative urban development creates uncertainties, while the increases in land prices arising from the construction of expansive road networks generate insecurities from increasing property prices.

This is evidently the experience of Angolans in Luanda. Chinese speculative urban development in Angola and its financing have created spatial and social inequalities. They have also generated widespread uncertainties, especially in Luanda and Kilamba city. One indication of the scale of speculation is that apartment prices, previously pegged at US$120,000, suddenly dropped to US$84,200 for want of what Keynes (1953/1964, pp. 23–34) called 'effective demand'. Even then, locals have been priced out of housing, leading to the concentration of the wealthy in *centralidades* (Cain, 2014; Watson, 2014). Similar comments apply to the experiences of other African countries. While many Africans have been recruited by Chinese businesses in Rwanda, where China Civil Engineering Construction Corporation and New Century Developments has a branch (Lee, 2014, pp. 97–98), many Africans work under difficult labour conditions, much like Chinese workers. This cheap and precarious labour is extracted in a process that has widespread ecological costs.

The import/export analysis that seems to serve as the basis for Brautigam's optimism about the footprint of China in Africa (see, e.g., Brautigam, 2015) is informative. Not only does it put land investments by Chinese in context, but Brautingham's analysis also helps to correct stereotypical views about Africa. Still, it is important to analyse the qualitative experiences of small-scale Chinese miners to illustrate the point. Many of these miners have left the gold mining town of Shanglin in China because of the depletion of its gold reserves (Mohan et al., 2014, pp. 98–99). They have been drawn to Ghana by private labour contractors operating both in China and Ghana, including Shaanxi Mining (Hilson et al., 2014, pp. 300–301). Generally, the operations of these migrant miners in Africa have contributed to major ecological degradation (Beck, 2012; Hilson et al., 2014; Mohan et al., 2014, p. 99; Obeng-Odoom, 2017b). In Ghana, 'a burgeoning illegal Chinese mining population has rerouted rivers and flooded roads used by villagers to access markets, seized farmlands unscrupulously, and bulldozed moats constructed for agriculture' (cited in Hilson et al., 2014, p. 292).

In such a situation, it is tempting to seek arrests of Chinese migrant miners themselves, but such a focus neglects an important dynamic. Most of these migrants collaborate with ordinary and other local Ghanaians or, in other countries, other local Africans who demonstrate their agency in ways that are well documented (see, for example, Mohan and Lampert, 2013; Alden and Large, 2018; Nguepjouo, 2020). In any case, many of the miners are Chinese minorities, including members of Zhuang, a marginalized people in China. As Chinese 'untouchables', their uncertainty is heightened in Africa, where they live a life of insecurity. They feel unsafe and are repeatedly attacked. As easy targets of scapegoating, they are also vulnerable. While they make some money from min-ing, they use much of this income to support their poor and indebted families in impoverished communities in China (Botchwey et al., 2019). Often, these migrants are also exploited and are reliant on networks that capitalize on, and rein-force, systems of inequality. These social conditions cannot excuse their pillaging of the environment, but their actions and inactions should be contextualized to purge them of claims about Chinese peculiarities. The identities of facilitators or 'middlemen', for example, must also be a focus of analysis.

Chinese migrants do not act alone. They are supported by ordinary Africans, politicians, and local leaders alike. This local network facilitates the process of transferring collectively held land into individual migrant ownership. Transna-tional corporations (TNCs) are also involved in this process. Their environmen-tal footprint is colossal. According to the Minister for Environment, Science, Technology and Innovation, it would cost Ghana US$650 billion to reclaim the environment degraded by the combined and cumulative effects of illegal, migrant heavy mining[2] and the activities of TNCs. The 'social costs' (Kapp, 1950/1971) are likely to be much bigger (see, e.g., Le, 2016). The amorphous identities of facili-tators complicate the picture, as Tinti and Reitano (2017) demonstrate in another context.

Still, these networks arise from, and are maintained through, inherent forces of inequality and uncertainty which, in general, have largely been considered to be central to creating, maintaining, and expanding social costs under capitalism (Kapp, 1950/1971; Ramazzotti et al., 2012). Commons (1907) offered one possible explanation of why these networks exist: as reflections of inherent inequality. In contrast to the neoclassical argument that migration always pushes prices down, Commons argued that it can also cause the prices of goods and services to increase. As immigration causes the size of population to grow, blatant or disguised protec-tionism can make population size outstrip the volume of goods and services. As wages are pushed down because more are paid out in rent, migrants are forced to hire themselves out at lower and lower wages to find money to pay rent.

This process siphones social rents into private coffers, concentrating rent in the hands of landlords. The sudden injection of money from migrants could increase land rent, so do the activities of other actors, including the state. This escalation of value is not just from demand, but also from speculation (Botchwey et al., 2019; Obeng-Odoom, 2014). The cost of living rises, further raising rental levels. The switch in the uses of land from agrarian to mining and oil drilling creates similar effects: increasing socially created land values and concentrating their resulting rents in the hands of landlords, as suggested by Henry George (see chapter 3).

Added to these explanations is the problem of dumping. Typically, this is ex-plained in terms of Chinese exports sent to Africa in quantities and prices that paralyse many African textile industries. The effect of flooding local markets with these cheap, mass-produced imitations of local goods, the argument goes, is to reduce the number of employment opportunities for local labour. That line of analysis tends to end up with the advocacy of protectionism. Yet, the problem of dumping is not so much trade, but dumping labour (George, 1883/1981; 1886/1991). Workers imported from China are so devalued that they hire themselves out at much lower labour standards than are locally permitted (Mung, 2008). With the increasing attempt to export Chinese labour (see, e.g., Akorsu, 2010, pp. 206–207; Obeng-Odoom, 2015b) and the systemic private appropriation of social rents, there is a tendency for this practice to force wages down, to keep them there, and to lower labour standards in Africa. Similar practices apply among African employers in China who exploit the lower cost of labour dumped from rural to urban spaces in China. Many African merchants also partake in this 'dumping' (Ho, 2012). In turn, the profit levels of producers and employers as well as the rent levels captured by landlords both in Africa and China have increased substantially, followed by declining work conditions. This evidence (e.g., Aidoo, 2010; Obeng-Odoom, 2017b; Tremann, 2013) bears out early predictions by Commons (1907) that dumping could (a) increase the price of goods and services; (b) reduce wage levels; and (c) raise profit levels, although the mechanisms for doing so more strongly bears out the centrality of rent.

These social costs metastasize into ecological costs. Consider the environmental footprint of Chinese labour migrants who work illegally in fishing and mining towns in Ghana (e.g., Hilson et al., 2014; McVeigh and Dzradosi, 2019). Chinese-dominated illegal trawling has not only created a loss of $65 million to the people of Ghana (McVeigh and Dzradosi, 2019, pp. 26–27), it has also set into motion a process of overfishing. Indeed, through the use of toxic chemicals such as mercury in mining, many water bodies and farm lands have become contaminated and incapable of supporting biodiversity and human livelihoods. Biodiversity has declined, injuries have multiplied, and many human lives have been lost, so the argument goes, as a result of the activities of these migrants (Wilson, 2015, p. 9).

Some of these social and ecological costs also existed *prior* to the involvement of Chinese migrants. However, systematic fieldwork (Hilson et al., 2014; Thornton, 2014; Wilson, 2015) shows that the advent of Chinese involvement in mining in Ghana has substantially *increased* the problems. The more advanced technology utilized by these migrants enriches productivity considerably. Through more substantial production, they also generate worse environmental outcomes. More pits can be dug rapidly, more trees destroyed quickly, a greater number of animals killed more efficiently, and larger doses of mercury dispensed more rapidly. Yet, the widely held view that Chinese migrants are at the forefront of this systematic ecocide and the production of inequality and social problems must be problematized. Indeed, migrants from other parts of Ghana and other countries in Africa are complicit, too.

Among the Chinese, the use of traditional, manual methods of mining (which are less efficient and less brutal in their effects on the environment) might extend the time during which the ecological footprint of this extractivism can be seen, but these old-fashioned methods are still environmentally damaging. Other groups use more mechanized methods. Such is the case with labour migrants from Canada, Portugal, Russia, Spain, India, the UK, and the US, who use more high-tech mining equipment, whose effect on the environment is, no doubt, more damaging (Wilson, 2015, p. 10). Indeed, the many transnational mining corporations with large and generous concessions and benevolent tax breaks that control the mining sector in Ghana are much worse culprits.

This evidence helps to see the limits of recent debates about the role of the state in migration policy. Nationalist sentiments drive the construction of walls. Border studies advocate their removal (Lemberg-Pedersen, 2016; Green, 2018). Humanists prefer the win–win trope of temporary migration, integration, and eventual 'return' (for a discussion, see Obeng-Odoom, 2017b; Manatscal et al., 2020; Zuber, 2020; Paquet and Xhardez, 2020). Yet, as the analysis of Afro-Chinese labour migration in this chapter shows, the role of the state needs to be more carefully analysed.

Migration Policy

If Afro-Chinese labour migration is characterized by uncertainty, inequality, and unsustainability, it is important to analyse the relevance of the two questions typically asked about Afro-Chinese labour migration policy (Amoah, 2016, 2019; Cheru and Obi, 2010; Lee, 2014): Do African states have a clearly designed labour migration policy for China and does the Chinese state have such a policy for Africa?

A survey conducted by the International Centre for Migration Policy Development (ICMPD) and the International Organization for Migration (IOM) shows that bilateral agreements between African countries and China are more common rather than, say, one policy by all African countries with China (ICMPD and IOM, 2015). According to Margaret Lee (2014), not only is there a lack of a coordinated policy, but there is also a lack of cooperation among African states when working with China. For instance, in its dealings with illegal Chinese labour immigrants, the Government of Ghana has been faulted for its failure to collaborate with the Togolese authorities, although doing so is important to better understand how some Chinese pivot from Togo to Ghana (Lee, 2014, p. 99). On its part, however, China is said to have a uniform twin-policy for Africa and African migrants. On the one hand, China's 'go out' policy is the Chinese state's approach to encourage emigration from China but, on the other hand, it seeks, 'complete control' of African migrants within its borders (Graham-Harrison and Garside, 2019). Some of these claims are contentious. The Economic Community for West

African States (ECOWAS) would usually appeal to the *ECOWAS Common Approach on Migration* (ECOWAS Commission, 2008). On a bigger scale, African countries seek to work within the *Migration Policy Framework for Africa and Plan of Action, 2018–2030* (African Union [AU], 2018). Frequently, there are references to both regional and continental-wide policy frameworks. For instance, the Government of Ghana incorporates both ECOWAS and AU policy directions in its own *National Migration Policy for Ghana* (Government of Ghana, 2016).

However characterised, as Ellen Brennan's (1984) work has shown, both Chinese and African authorities seek to restrain migrants in their territory through border controls and labour market regulations about work permits (see, for example, Government of Ghana, 2016, pp. 47–48). Even if the ICMPD and IOM survey showed that some bilateral agreements (e.g., those concluded by Sierra Leone) dispense with the requirement for work permits (ICMPD and IOM, 2015, p. 296), both the Chinese state and the states in Africa tend to institutionalize uncertainty by making Afro-Chinese labour migrants temporary.

Consider the relationship between China and Ghana. Both countries often have designed, instituted, and implemented punitive regulations against employers of irregular migrants and often some reward systems for people who report illegal migrants. Many African states and the Chinese state adopt expulsion and widespread surveillance of migrants. For example, as in China, in Ghana, the state raids markets to confiscate cheap Chinese textiles that are imitations of indigenous Ghanaian prints, using a nationalist discourse to promote a 'Friday wear' of only indigenous textiles and issuing a fiat that all imports of 'African' textiles ought to go through one port to improve the effectiveness of monitoring (Axelsson, 2012). The Government of Ghana also recurrently prosecutes and deports Chinese migrants whose equipment is also confiscated, as shown in Table 7.1. To which must be added at least 45 ongoing cases in the courts of Ghana as of 2nd June, 2021.[5]

Table 7.1 Ghanaian state control of Chinese migrants, 2010–2018

Years	Prosecutions	Deportations	Pieces of equipment confiscated
2010–2013	–	4,500	–
2013–2016	1,405	–	–
2014–2017	–	734	–
2016–2017	701	–	–
2017–2018	–	–	18,593
Total	2,106	5,234	18,593*

Source: adapted from Debrah and Asante, 2019, p. 297.
*Excavators (1,834); water pumps (3,100); vehicles (242); motor bikes (238); Changfa mining machines used for crushing solids (13,179).

[5] see Evan Mensah's One-on-One with Attorney General – PM Express on JoyNews (2-6-21) https://www.youtube.com/watch?v=M2d6qLtsBj4 (accessed 8.09.2021)

Such prosecutions have been greatly facilitated by the judiciary. Not only did the Chief Justice create 7 divisions of the high court of Ghana, but also 7 divisions of the circuit court of Ghana were created to specifically focus on alleged illegalities carried out by (Chinese) immigrants - indeed anyone against whom such allegations are made - in Ghana's mining industry (Kpienbaareh et al., 2021). These dynamics can be found elsewhere in Africa. As noted by Lee (2017, p. 18), the Patriotic Front of Zambia proclaimed 'Zambia for Zambians'.

The effectiveness of these approaches is questionable both in Africa (Hilson et al., 2014) and in China (Lan, 2015), and so are their racist undertones. As fundamentally, the typical responses systematically neglect the economics and political economy of Afro-Chinese labour migration. For instance, the wider question of labour exploitation, the effect of unequal property relations on migration, and the resulting stratification from the social creation but private appropriation of rent are similarly neglected. Focused exclusively on the state, without taking into account the wide range of institutions that condition migration, especially land and its relation to labour and capital, both existing and proposed migration policies are founded on problematic assumptions. The sustained focus on Chinese racism against African labour, often used to justify Chinese exclusive employment practices (Lee, 2014), is understandable because it is widespread (Mathews et al., 2017, pp. 70–79). However, leaving the analysis at this kind of descriptive level is not deep enough, neither is merely instituting Commons' (1907) minimum wage which, paradoxically, seemed to be divisive in advocating one standard for white workers and another, no minimum wage, for blacks (for a discussion, see Leonard, 2016). As argued by Henry George (1891, pp. 64-90) in his open letter to Pepe Leo XIII on 'the condition of labour', even a uniform, universal minimum wage is inadequate because it does not address the labour question which, in effect, is a land question. Without guaranteeing access to land by socialising socially created rent, every migration policy would work to the benefit of landlords. Without access to and control of land, without the socialisation of rent, and without full rights to the rewards of work, labour would be deprived of the opportunity for self-employment, the opportunity for progress, and the opportunity for social protection. Every gain made by labour would have to be paid out to landlords as land rent continues to increase.

A new migration policy is needed. The ingredients of such a policy could include developing race-sensitive and explicitly anti-racist social regulation of current migration processes to facilitate, rather than hinder, Afro-Chinese migration. As theorized elsewhere (Obeng-Odoom, 2017b, 2018a), the reason for supporting migration is largely based on the one planet argument: the idea that all humans have a right to roam the earth freely because it is a free gift of nature. This proposition strongly recognizes the social costs of migration, for which both social and economic policy can be carefully developed. For informal workers outside the realms of documentation, they could self-organize as cooperatives or unions. Doing so could provide social networks that could more easily negotiate and receive diverse institutional support.

The activities of such cooperatives could include (a) community development; (b) ecological development to repair impairments arising from their activities; and (c) helping to provide their members with social protection obtained from various institutions, such as the state and all its geographical and functional arms. Indeed, these co-ops could propose minimum wage regulations in their areas of work and work with other groups to seek not just better conditions of work, but also to work less.

Expansion of the public sector is crucially useful. The point is not to create more work, but to redistribute work such that those who are overworked could be relieved. Permanent residency status could more easily be granted, too. Mutual fears, uncertainties, and insecurities could be allayed by making migrants more permanent, guaranteeing their rights, more socially regulating and supporting those activities which enhance inclusive change and institutionalising ecological sustainability. This social policy and the direct redress of the social costs could be linked to a new migration policy that must guarantee access to and control of land. Labour must be fully entitled to the rewards of work in this sense, that is, also compensating any invisibilised labour performed by those who support workers (e.g., partners who are homemakers). Under this policy alternative, wages are not likely to be paid out in rents. Pressure does not build on labour to work ever more precariously to pay rent, either. When socially created rents are socially collected and put to social purposes, labour conditions could greatly improve. Prosperity in the local economy itself could prevent certain types of migration, encourage other types of migration, and support migrants wherever they are, whether in Alaska, in Singapore (see Haila, 2016; Obeng-Odoom, 2017b), or anywhere else.

Conclusion: Retheorizing the Economics of Labour Migration

Migration research continues to grapple with key questions. Causation is one of them and is closely associated with debates about migrant agency. The migration–economy-society-environment nexus is a second, while a third question relates to labour migration policy. The critical questions are whether migration is driven by the utility-maximizing rational calculations of migrants and in what ways migrants shape the economy. Whether it is through injecting more human capital, driving more trade, or pumping more investment into the economy, the neoclassical theory is that the immigration of skilled labour drives growth. Thus, for mainstream economists, migration creates what political economists call a 'spatial fix'. According to David Harvey (2006, p. 444), '[g]lobal freedom for the movement of capital (in all forms) has allowed instant access to the 'spatial fix' through geographical expansion within a framework of uneven geographical destruction'.

From this perspective, migrating to Africa is a 'spatial fix' for China's internal problems, as is migrating to China a spatial fix for Africa's internal problems. TNCs and micro entrepreneurs across China and Africa must regard migration as a spatial fix too, according to these mainstream accounts. In a sense, a case of a win–win 'migration for opportunity' is put by many mainstream economists, mainstream development institutions, and even humanists. Thus, whether migrants add to or take from the economy, the measure of progress is growth (see Clausing, 2019a, 2019b).

These formulations about the economics of labour migration are unsatisfactory and GIS provides a more holistic view (see also chapters 1 and 3). Georgist political economy demonstrates that the labour question is, indeed, a land question. When private property in land is institutionalised, the tendency is for a worsening of the conditions of labour. Overwork, the destruction of nature, and the disintegration of society in this case accompany migration. Original institutional economics is also an important current. It can help to retheorize the economy. The economy is judged more by its coherence, how it prevents social costs, supports the conditions of labour, and acknowledges ecological limits through the redress of long-term inequalities and social stratification (Abreu, 2012; Bromley, 2019; Bromley and Anderson, 2012; Burnazoglu, 2017; Commons, 1907; Obeng-Odoom, 2018a; 2021a). With Marxist economics, the most visible opponent of neoclassical economics progressively riddled with what Galbraith (1977, p. 7) called 'uncertainty' both in its critique and alternative policy proposals, it is a good time to consider the age-old contention—made by a wide range of institutional economists (e.g., Commons, 1907; Galbraith, 1977; Myrdal, 1944, 1968)—that original institutional economics theories can provide one effective alternative.

This approach, described briefly in Table 7.2 and more extensively and theoretically elsewhere (e.g., Zouache, 2017a, 2017b, 2018, 2020; see chapters 1 and 3), is far more comprehensive. Circular and cumulative causation recognizes that causes are not linear but circular, complex, combined, cumulative, evolutionary, and not necessarily the product of sudden change. This complexity is not merely additive, as in vicious or virtuous circles utilized in mainstream economics, but rather cumulative, such that additional circles can have a much bigger thrust than previous circles. Interventions could change the patterns either upwardly or downwardly at any particular period, but the various cycles are not necessarily the same in force or power. The economy is, as Karl Polanyi (1957) noted, an 'instituted process'. Its formal meaning, centred on idealized living arrangements in which people act like atoms (that is, act alone to make reasoned rational choices for the maximization of their own utility without considering other social relations, society, or ecology), poorly reflects reality. Rather, the substantive meaning of the economy is more useful. Here, the emphasis is on actually existing livelihood arrangements. People depend on one another; they collectively connect to the environment.

The success of the economy, then, is to be judged not so much in terms of growth, but rather in terms of the conditions of labour, the trends in inequality,

Table 7.2 Analytical approach and how it contrasts with the prevailing paradigm

Research questions	Prevailing analytical paradigms	Institutional economics
Causes	Neoclassical economics The free choices of utility-maximizing rational migrants within the individual-centred push–pull framework	Original institutional economics Circular and cumulative causation, involving transactions, institutions, and individuals driven by 'institutionalized minds', not homo economicus assumptions
Effects on the economy	Emphasis is on growth catch-up in an economy that can expand ad infinitum without systematic regard for ecological limits, inequality, or other social costs, and how migration reduces wages of locals through a supply-demand–price framework	Economic coherence, entailing inclusive and socio-ecologically sustainable transformation that is critically conscious of ecological and planetary limits. The economy is dynamic, so one wage gain can support another, not simply undermine it. If migration generates reduction in the local wage rate, the forces of change are cumulative and they relate to monopoly, monopolistic competition, employer exploitation, and institutions that sanction these drivers.
Migration policy	Focused primarily on manipulating the state (typically the government) to ensure market expansion, individual free choices, and growth	Focused on a comprehensive analysis of a wide range of institutions, including the state (government, legislature, judiciary, media), banks, markets, and civil society temporally and spatially

Sources: based on Commons, 1907, 1934a/2009, 1934b/2009; Myrdal, 1944, 1968; Galbraith, 1977; Jaynes, 2007; Bromley and Anderson, 2012; Bromley, 2019.

and the ramifications for a wider society and environment. Attaining these hallmarks of the 'good economy' must be the preoccupation of the state, interacting with other institutions, including landed property rights, markets, and banks, both spatially and temporally. Individual agency is important, but the individual mind is neither free floating nor free standing. It is, according to Commons (1934a/2009, 1934b/2009), 'institutionalized' in that it is transactional, that is, often shaped by its social relations, including conflicts.

The 'colour' of these institutions must be of recurrent interest. As the experience of Afro-Chinese workers shows, much racist scapegoating exists on both sides. So, any retheorizing needs to consider the power of stratification economics (Darity, 2009; Darity and Mullen, 2020; Darity, 2021). The emphasis is not simply that race, colour, gender, class, ethnicity and other identities matter, but how they are theorised is even more fundamental.

Thus, together, GIS helps to more profoundly understand labour migration. In this analysis, the state, too, needs to be retheorized. According to J.R. Common:

> The meaning of the word 'politics' has usually been limited to the activities designed to get control of what was deemed to be the dominant concern, the State. But with the modern emergence of innumerable forms of economic and moral concerted action, it is found that the similar complexity of personalities, principles, and organizations is found in all concerns. The fact that the sovereign concern uses the sanction of physical force has seemed to give dominance to it, as indicated by the word, 'sovereign.' But this is illusory, since, as we have seen, sovereignty has been the gradual, but incomplete, extraction of violence from private transactions, and other concerns dominate the state.
>
> (Commons, 1934b/2009, p. 751)

So, the near-exclusive focus on the Chinese Communist Party when analysing the Chinese state is limiting. So is the neglect of other aspects of the state—including the judiciary—(Zhang and Elsner, 2017), especially as in both China and Africa, judicial decisions increasingly impinge on society, economy, and ecology (Fan and Lee, 2019; Obeng-Odoom and Gyampo, 2017; Zhao, 2019). Dissecting the Chinese state or African states in place, while neglecting their evolution over time, is another limitation of existing research on Afro-Chinese labour migration. An institutional evolutionary and historical critique of the state (legislature, executive, media, judiciary) is needed. This critique would usefully recognize that the state could simultaneously be a source of danger and a potential force for good. Analysts can examine the balance of interests that constitutes the state and probe the actions and inactions of the other institutions that constitute 'collective action' within which the state is moulded.

This concerted action is also shaped by the nature of the individuals who make up the state. Such persons are not necessarily selfish 'free agents' who are simply rent seeking, as claimed by advocates of public choice theory. Rather, so-called 'free choices' usually reflect a diversity of the 'institutionalized mind', partly shaped by local histories and contexts, partly moulded by prevailing global trends, and particularly shaped by interests. In this regard, analysing whether the state in all its spheres (legislature, executive, judiciary, media) has been hijacked by landed interests might be a crucial question for social economists to consider.

Taking these matters into account, analysing the economics of Afro-Chinese labour migration is clearly important. Indeed, this analysis is needed in these current political-economic times, partly for verifying mainstream thinking, partly for contributing to migration policy, and particularly for retheorizing the social economics of labour migration.

8

Education and Experience

Introduction

Most economists regard education as the sure path to flattening the global inequalities curve. Some even contend that education guarantees freedom (Sen, 1999, pp. 293–294; Piketty, 2014, pp. 306–307; World Bank, 2018, pp. 38–48) and almost every economist takes it as axiomatic that education drives innovation and economic growth (Arenas, 2021). Thus, international students are central to what William Kerr (2018) has described as 'the gift of global talent'. International students shape business, economy, and society in the US, but also elsewhere in the world (Kerr, 2018; Nowotny, 2019). Between 1975 and 2012, the number of international students increased about sixfold, from 0.8 million to 4.5 million international students (Arenas, 2021). More recent trend analysis in the *International Migration Outlook 2019* (OECD, 2019, Chapter 3) shows that international students have become a growing and substantial cohort of temporary migrants in the world. That much is well known, as are many aspects of their educational experiences, which tend to be the focus of much higher education research (e.g., Crossman and Clark, 2010; Morrison et al., 2005; Ping, 2010; Russell et al., 2008; Zhou et al., 2008; Wilkins, 2020; Ballerini and Feldblum, 2021).

In economics, more broadly, the higher education pursued by international students is supposed to produce human capital for the students themselves, for the host countries, and for the sending countries (Nour, 2019). A triple win, international student migration is hardly contested. Instead, it is hailed as the elixir that cures cities and regions of their ills.

Urban economists are categorical about these relationships—without examining land and property rights; institutions more generally; social stratification along racial and gendered lines whether in the local labour market, the firm, or within the family (for a more extensive review, see Browne et al., 2003; Obeng-Odoom, 2020b); nor how education itself creates and reproduces social stratification (Bourdieu, 1988). In *Triumph of the City*, Edward Glaeser (2011, p. 27) writes, '[h]uman capital, far more than physical infrastructure, explains which cities succeed ... no other measure does better in explaining recent urban prosperity'. Glaeser's position echoes Garry Becker's (1962, 1974) well-known and highly influential neoclassical theory of human capital. Such is the substantial confidence placed in the human capital theory that even George Bojas, a well-known critic of universal immigration (see, e.g., Borjas, 1994, 2002, 2007, 2009), has recently argued (Borjas et al., 2018) that international student migration is quite special. He points out that it tends to reduce the wages of skilled locals because such students usually remain after their education and, consistent with neoclassical theory of high supply leading to low prices, depress wages. However, so great are their contributions, for example, to the productivity of their local supervisors, that host nations such as the US should not limit international student migration, but should instead seek to direct it to aspects of US society not already served by the skills of local residents.

Similar arguments have been made by other academic economists and professional economists in the media. According to Andreu Arenas (2021), international students outperform local students, whether such international migrants have taken an entrance examination or they have been exempt. Accordingly, Arenas (2021) concludes that human capital is portable. Further, human capital migration should be encouraged by removing barriers to entry such as entrance exams, particularly because the evidence—in terms of courses of study—shows that international students are now crowding out local students. In short, international student migration should be encouraged. *The Economist* (2020q) laments 'the absent student' as a result of the COVID-19 pandemic, but its key concerns relate to the 'wealth of nations' and the growth of cities. So it is with nativists, who rarely question international student migrants, perhaps also because these migrants are, by definition, temporary. However countries are described -capitalist or communist, socialist, or social democratic, -international student migration is strongly supported (Arenas, 2021).

So, not only does the US more readily open its universities and borders to international students, but the World Bank is also willing to offer loans to sending nations to facilitate this process. China offers state-sponsored scholarships, encourages self sponsorships, and drives scientific exchange, while at the same time running a higher education system that valorizes this process (Kajanus, 2015, pp. 46–72). These measures change over time. For instance, while most international Chinese students were sponsored by the state in the 1970s, as of 2018, some 88.9% of Chinese international students were self-funded (Tu and Xie, 2020, p. 69). China, like many other sending countries, considers that international student migration will return to China with the human capital needed to bridge international and global inequalities.

Yet, in all this triumphalism, much less attention has been given to the housing conditions of international students (Ike et al., 2016; Parkinson et al., 2018; Morris et al., 2021). Generally, the social conditions under which such education takes place is considered to be trivial. 'Most of the exhibitors I interviewed were seasoned promoters. They emphasized the importance of understanding what the students and the parents in each country want … In some countries, they were asked about the physical study environment (including student housing ...), but Chinese students and parents rarely showed interest in these' (Kajanus, 2015, p. 49).

It is a major deficit because housing plays a critical role in the process of obtaining quality education (Lubell and Brennan, 2007; Phibbs and Young, 2009; Ike et al., 2016; Parkinson et al., 2018; Morris et al., 2021). The quality of the physical environment and the social relationships developed in student housing have a significant impact on how satisfied students are with their university education (Foubert et al., 1998). Accommodation contributes to the quality of security that students have and the nature of social network that they develop (Paltridge Mayson and Schapper, 2010; Morris et al., 2021). Quality student accommodation drives both the retention and well-being of students, while enabling students to obtain much better grades (Ike et al., 2016; Parkinson et al., 2018). Most fundamentally, a study of housing can help to assess the triple win of international migration.

Therefore, with the increasing globalization of higher education, it is important to (re) consider the 'housing question' (Engels, 1872). As classically posed by Engels, and subsequent Marxists, the housing question pertains entirely to class, notably the working class. International student experiences, questions of migrant status, race, ethnicity, colour, and gender, are usually not of interest. If they are considered as a class, their other identities are typically overlooked, nor is the land question. A reconsideration of the 'housing question', therefore, must take these identities seriously because, by definition, they are crucial to the experience of migrants (see chapters 1 and 3). Researching the housing conditions of international students is clearly one of the most effective ways to understand and potentially change the social stratification that arises from the intersections of race (because the students come from races all over the world), gender, and class, among other identities.

In investigating the housing question this way, this chapter focuses on Australia, surpassed only by the US and the UK in terms of countries with the largest number of international students (OECD, 2019, p. 33). Several studies have been conducted on international higher education in Australia, but they have typically focused on questions of security (e.g., Marginson, 2010a; Paltridge et al., 2010; Hill, 2020), finance (Forbes-Mewet et al., 2011), and 'international students' history of affective encounters with the border', as the subtitle of Maria Elena Indelicato's book, *Australia's New Migrants* (2018), represents it. A few studies have looked at spatial and housing questions in one city or across Australia (see, e.g., Fincher et al., 2009; Fincher and Shaw, 2009, 2011; Ike et al., 2016; Holton and Mouat, 2021; Morris et al., 2021). Many puzzles remain unresolved. This chapter focuses on housing for international students in Sydney, using the University of Sydney as a case study. It answers seven remaining research questions, namely:

1. What are the characteristics of international students in Australia?
2. What is the nature of international students' accommodation?
3. How do international students locate accommodation?
4. How much do they pay for it?
5. How do they find money to pay for it?
6. What problems do they encounter and how do they solve them? and
7. How satisfied are they with their housing experience?

To address these questions, I draw on multiple sources of evidence. These include several surveys and official reports published by student associations, housing authorities, the University of Sydney, and the Australian Department of Education, Employment and Workplace Relations (DEEWR). I incorporate findings from additional surveys conducted by the Australian Centre for Higher Education Research and supplement these quantitative data with personal interviews I conducted with students, student representatives, and officials.

The evidence shows that international students are quite diverse. Some level of stratification already exists among them at the point of becoming students in Australia. Where students come from matters, as does at what level international students study. When they arrive in Australia, these features interact with existing institutions to form unequal relationships, both among them and between international students, on the one hand, and local students, on the other. This stratification is echoed and, arguably, magnified in how international students are housed. The evidence shows that, although on average international students and employers alike are satisfied with higher education in Australia, the university and Australian authorities have not succeeded in providing satisfactory answers to the international student housing questions 2, 3, 4, 5, 6, and 7. Accommodation is one of the major challenges facing international students. They mostly find housing on their own, implying that the housing information provided by the authorities is not particularly helpful.

Both the quantity and the quality of their accommodation are challenging. Apart from the exorbitant cost of accommodation, the discriminatory practices in the search for accommodation, and the exploitation students have to endure at work, international students, along with their families, suffer significant stress and stratification. How these problems are experienced differs among different groups of students, as student surveys show varying degrees of challenging experiences across private rental housing, ordinary student housing, and elite residential colleges.

Contrary to the view that such problems are temporary or frictional because they arise from information asymmetries and ignorance of international students, the housing situation of international students is worsening. In the meanwhile, these students continue to pay increasingly more for their education. They offer reverse remittances to Australians in ways previously overlooked in the reverse remittances literature (for a review, see Adiku, 2022). While the premium for higher education might be said to justify such social costs because most of them obtain employment after their education, human capital through international student migration does not transform structures of social stratification. Class mobility, economic status, and the power of such migrants usually remain marginal or become worse.

Clearly, education can transmit its own social stratification. In Australia, as this chapter shows, student migrants face systemic discrimination at their places of employment. Mental health problems and suicidal tendencies arise as a cumulative result. Female international student migrants have gained greater access to education, as have children of poor parents more generally. However, their social position in the societies from where they departed to study does not change when they return. If anything, the growing cost of higher education and the housing crisis for international students possibly accentuate existing inequalities and social stratification.

Without immediate action to remedy the situation, these structural problems can undermine the quality of higher education in Australia and elsewhere in the Western world where the human capital model of international student migration has been promoted. Although it might be argued that the problem could be resolved by providing more affordable housing, this chapter reveals that doing that alone confuses causes for symptoms and misdiagnoses the root cause of the housing question. Unless the problem is framed in socio-economic terms, central to which is land, as a specific property relation within a wider context of unequal and uneven social relations, the problem is likely to worsen.

The rest of this chapter demonstrates this argument in nine sections. Each one addresses one of the seven research questions. These are tied together in section eight, where policy options are discussed. But first, it is important to reflect on how to research international students and stratification.

Homo Academicus, the Housing Question, and the Social Structures of the Economy

When mainstream economists (e.g., Becker 1962, 1974, Glaeser 2011; Borjas et al., 2018; Arenas, 2021) think about education, they do so using the organizing concept of the rational individual student and her or his, but invariably *his* rational individual teacher. Each seeks to maximize his returns from education. One provides it, the other absorbs it. Both are better off from the production and consumption of human capital. In this process, any discrimination is removed with time through how much human capital a student, for example, accumulates. The test of success is usually the labour market, where successful students are expected to be rewarded for their human capital, comprising of education and experience. For a number of reasons, including increasing cost to producers, human capital is expected to provide protection against discrimination and stratification.

In *Homo Academicus*, however, Pierre Bourdieu (1984) systematically questions these claims using empirical evidence, ranging from the production of education to its distribution and consumption. The evidence clearly shows that several institutions, social networks, and structures constitute 'fields' and 'habitus' that make education itself a key fulcrum for the creation and reproduction of social stratification. Thus, for Bourdieu, the emphasis on the rational individual and how, through education and individual experience, *he* is liberated by maximizing the accumulation of human capital and utilizing it for his self-interest is quite misleading. Instead, as an instrument of power, education can, and often does, institutionalize stratification. It is not that students from poor backgrounds will always be poor or that students from richer families will always be rich. The emphasis, for Bourdieu, is not exactly income, but wealth and power, among others, emanating from the people and networks with whom students study, when, and how.

Housing provides a particularly powerful illustration of these dynamics. As I have discussed elsewhere (Obeng-Odoom, 2016b), mainstream economists attribute its provision to forces of impersonal supply, demand, and price, a framework in which rational individual choices determine how people are housed. If the housing market fails, it must be because land has not been privatized to ensure its free supply. Private developers, therefore, are seen favourably in the mainstream economics framework of housing, as are private landlords and pro-market states. Engels's critique of this housing paradigm (Engels, 1872), downplayed the place of land, highlighting instead how the housing question (that is how to address the quantity and quality of worker housing under capitalism) is a reflection of the exploitation of workers by capitalists. So, both the orthodoxy and its most radical critique downplayed how the private appropriation of socially created land rent drives the housing question, both overlook institutions, and both overlook stratification economics.

I have discussed how Georgists try to address the land question elsewhere (Obeng-Odoom, 2016b, 2021; see also chapter 3), along with how the urban question is approached by stratification economists (Obeng-Odoom, 2020b; see also chapter 3). Briefly, Georgist political economy (GPE) looks for the problems of housing in how rent arises and is distributed, while stratification economics investigates white privilege in housing provision, in contrast to systemic bias and discrimination against blacks and other minorities. I shall revisit both GPE and stratification economics and how they approach the housing question again in Chapter 9.

So it is crucial at this stage to clarify how original institutional economists approach the housing question. Pierre Bourdieu's (2005) approach in *The Social Structures of the Economy* is a useful illustration. In this major work, Bourdieu again takes the human capital approach to task, explicitly challenging Becker about the nature of economic actors. The social economist Asimina Christoforou (2018, p. 280) has particularly highlighted Bourdieu's critique about the conflation of 'economy' (broadly located within social structures) and 'economising' (undertaken by some individuals but, even then, within wider social structures) as relevant to social economists, so is Bourdieu's emphasis on the social construction of supply and demand. Clearly, as Bourdiu (2005) himself argues, housing is a useful illustration because it is often represented by economists to be merely a reflection of individual choices expressed for commodities that are competitively produced in the free markets.

Again, Bourdieu's (2005) empirical study shows much deeper insights, not about liberty, but about stratification institutionalized by various housing laws and state housing policy. The production side of housing, for example, is stratified in the sense that firms involved in housing provision are quite diverse. While giant real estate developers with links to banks and powerful financiers dominate the market in advanced capitalist countries, there are also mid-range developers with much less financial power linked with the giant companies, for example, as subcontractors. Then there are family-based developers with no links to financial power houses.

Either way, these three groups of housing producers use different forms of advertisement and sometimes agents to brand the housing they produce. Working closely with other institutions and building groups, developers directly produce choices. Individual consumers have agency, a point Bourdieu stresses in his relational institutional methodology, but these choices can be overwhelmed or reshaped by deliberate misinformation or information overdose. So, the idea of 'free choice' in the housing market is highly questionable.

So is the homogenizing power of housing. According to Bourdieu, the occupation of the house itself shapes stratification. Houses are bequeathed to children, for example, but also to partners. So, such stratification is an ongoing process of house occupation. Those who inherit this wealth become economically stronger, so do their children and partners, as against those who do not have such wealth. That is because housing-wealthy people do not pay as much rent or do not pay rent at all, but also because they can sublease their housing or use their house to obtain greater wealth from the bank. In this sense, banks, the state, and laws about permits and building all reinforce these processes, which, in turn, interact with demographic changes in the structure of families and the wider economy.

Becker conducted his research in the US, while Bourdieu carried out his studies in France. Mainstream economists have, in more recent times, sought to address Bourdieu's critiques, but they have merely reduced social structures and relational agency in Bourdieu's work to Beckerian cost–benefit analysis (Odabaş and Adaman, 2018). Although these classical contributions and their recent mutations are highly influential, their resulting claims need to be continuously examined across space and time in the light of new empirical material. It is for this reason that Meltem Odabaş and Fikret Adaman (2018) have recently called for the 'Bourdieu–Becker encounter' to be subjected to new processes of empirical verification. Doing so would still be partial, without considering the role of land rent in the hous-ing question, drawing on GPE, and without taking into account stratification economics.

In this chapter, a comprehensive framework would mean examining the interactions between education and housing using international students as a case study of how migrant status, race, land, property rights and other institutions interact and shape the housing question. Verifying these intersections and whether they combine to enhance or constrain stratification have been hinted at—but never satisfactorily addressed—in many surveys (The Sydney University Postgraduate Representative Union, 2010b, pp. 9–11; International Student Sup-port Unit [ISSU], 2010). In one such survey, the records show that 2,652 students visited the online page, but only 1,891 students completed the questionnaire. The response rate was 20%. Most of the respondents (89%) were aged between eighteen and twenty-eight. Of those, 65% were female and 89% were in Australia without their families. For 76% of the respondents, it was their first time in Sydney, 36% were in their first 6 months, 15% in their first year of living in Australia, 16% had lived in Australia for over a year, 9% had lived in Australia for close to two years, and 24% had lived in Australia for more than two years (ISSU, 2010).

To complement the survey results, data from several reports published by the ISSU, the Sydney University Postgraduate Representative Union (SUPRA), the Student Representative Council of the University of Sydney (SRC), and the Ac-commodation Information Service of the University of Sydney (AIS) are also analysed. These additional surveys, notably Ruming and Dowling (2017), Broder-ick and Co. (2017), Parkinson et al. (2018), UNSW Human Rights Clinic (2019), fill in the gaps, are more recent, and shed greater light on the nature of international student migration and international student housing in seven research questions.

What Are the Characteristics of International Students in Australia?

A significant number of international students study in Australia, in spite of the fact that it is geographically quite distant from other countries. In 1983, there were fewer than 20,000 overseas students enrolled at Australian universities; by 1997, their population had risen to about 163,000 (Department of Employment, Educa-tion, Training and Youth Affairs [DEETYA], 1998). By 2010, the number exceeded 335,000 (DEEWR, 2011). By 2018, the number had increased to 548,000 interna-tional students (UNSW Human Rights Clinic, 2019). This rate of increase is 3.5 times higher than that of domestic students (Calderon, 2020). Higher education in Australia—made up of 37 public universities, two private universities, and 130 other institutions that offer tertiary education—is an important section of the edu-cation export business, sometimes said to constitute Australia's third largest export industry (Bradley et al., 2008, p. xv; Calderon, 2020). How this situation has arisen requires further analysis.

The history of international students in Australia is recounted in detail by Maria Elena Indelicato (2018, pp. 21–45), but only a brief summary of her work is warranted here. International education before the 1980s was regarded in Australia as humanitarian aid. Global deregulation and emphasis by the international development agencies on obtaining human capital, along with local deregulation and conditions such as the Tianaman Square protests and political-economic problems in Hong Kong, increasingly made education an export commodity in Australia. There were local concerns about increasing the number of foreigners in Australia, which forced the authorities to try to reregulate the so-called influx. What is notable is that market-based systems were preferable.

Thus, the cost of international education was increased, at one stage by making international education 10% higher than its real cost (Indelicato, 2018, pp. 31–32). While the aid-cum-diplomatic functions of international education were not entirely abandoned because a relatively small amount of international education still served this purpose, the commodification of education became a key feature of Australian higher education. Indelicato (2018, pp. 1–15, 21–45, 180–183) argues strongly that the entire history of Australian higher education is one that shows a commitment to colonizing and civilizing international students.

But there is also plenty of evidence—such as the results of the 2010 survey by Australian Education International AEI (AEI, 2010a) and the 2017 survey by Elizabeth Broderick and Co. (Broderick and Co., 2017)—that international students are satisfied with their overall educational experience in Australia. The characteristic reasons for choosing Australian higher education are quality of education, the credibility of the qualifications, and the reputation of the institutions. Apart from such self-reported satisfaction levels, most Australian and overseas employers report high satisfaction levels with the output of overseas students who study at Australian universities (AEI, 2010b).

Satisfactory experience is not the only driver of increasing international student migration around the round. Among the key drivers are specific state support by sending countries and the activities of world development agencies such as the World Bank. The World Bank promotes the internationalization and standardization of higher education, which it is prepared to fund through loans. Moreover, the global movement of capital and the popular and media perception that transnational corporations recruit purely on merit defined in terms of international education are also considered significant factors in driving up international student migration (Kajanus, 2015, pp. 46–72). Other reasons are the deliberate and systematically implemented programmes by universities in Australia to recruit overseas students; the activities of private educational agents and promoters; the effect of exchange programmes; the teaching of English as a second language (see Kajanus, 2015, pp. 13–14); and the Westernization of education. Australia has increasingly become a haven for international students because it has been a place for international students in the past.

The forces at work here constitute circular, cumulative, and combined effects (Myrdal, 1944).Through the agency of international students themselves in going to Australia, and the nudge by families of international students, Australia has become a destination of choice for international students (Ramia, 2017; McCrohon and Nyland, 2018; Tran and Vu, 2018; Zhou and Jordan, 2019). While the substantial number of students from China, contributing about 33% in 2018 (an increase from 4.6% in 2000), is often discussed (Calderon, 2020), students travel from all over the world to Australia. In 2010, for example, international students came from Europe (4.4%), the Americas (4.9%), Asia (80.2%), Africa and the Middle East (8.4%), Oceania (0.8%), and elsewhere or not known (1.2%) to study in Australia (DEEWR, 2011, DEEWR Table 7.4). Australian universities, therefore, are major destinations for migrants.

The Australian government and Australian universities are paying particular attention to postgraduate education, among other things through internationalization of the curricula and revising immigration policies to make it possible for research degree holders to apply for a temporary visa that entitles them to work in Australia for eighteen months (Bradley et al., 2008, p. 99; Carrington et al., 2007). In turn, the population of international students pursuing postgraduate education has increased over the years. Between 2000 and 2008, the number of international postgraduate students in Australia increased by 83% (DEEWR, 2011). Postgraduate students are enrolled in doctorate, master's, and postgraduate certificate programmes.

Across the board, international students have become a major source of income for Australian universities and other institutions of higher education. Since 2000, international students alone have contributed more than $A90 billion to these institutions. The Australian government supports higher education, but the rate by which international students have contributed to the finances of these institutions has been five times higher than government contributions since 1995 (Calderon, 2020). Hence, international students have become the financial lifeline for Australian higher education providers. Table 8.1 provides an overview of the substantial contribution by international students to five major universities in Australia in 2017.

The figures in the table have generally kept increasing in terms of total student population, the share of international students, total revenue, and the share of revenue from international students. Consider, for example, the University of Melbourne. It received A$879.3 million from international students in 2018 compared to AS$756 million (29% share of total revenue) from international students in 2017 and A$23.6 million (4.5% of total revenue) in 1995 (Calderon, 2020). As of 2012, the share of revenue from international students in the total revenue of the University of Sydney was only 16.3%, increasing to 28.1 in 2016

Table 8.1 International students in selected Australian universities, 2017

University	Total student population	Share of international students	Total revenue	Share of revenue from international students
UNSW	59,781	20,204 (34%)	A$2.119 billion	A$708 m (33%)
Melbourne	50,270	19,903 (39%)	A$2.578 billion	A$756 m (29%)
Sydney	60,000	19,000 (32%)	A$2.345 billion	A$752 m (32%)
RMIT	49,408	22,034 (45%)	A$1.306 billion	A$487 m (37%)
Monash	62,400	27,800 (45%)	A$2.401 billion	A$810 m (34%)

Source: adapted from Shelton et al., 2019.

(Birrell and Betts, 2018) and then to 32% in 2017 (Table 8.1). Together with their research contributions and innovation, the footprint of international students in the Australian (knowledge) economy is large and increasing.

The contribution of international students to the Australian economy more broadly is also substantial. As of 2019, '[i]n full-year full-time equivalent terms, international students add up to 1.3% to the working age population in Australia' (OECD, 2019, p. 137). Together with their research contributions and innovation, the footprint of international students in the Australian (knowledge) economy is large and increasing.

There has been significant dissatisfaction among Australian educationists about the Australian economy's strong reliance on international students and wider issues of internationalization (e.g., Ramia, 2017, p. 208; Calderon, 2020; Hill, 2020). The COVID-19 pandemic has brought the fragility of this system into sharp perspective. As the Australian universities struggle to find sufficient number of international students to balance their accounts, it seems many universities have tried to cut cost by reducing the size of their faculty (Carnegie et al., 2021). Such 'voluntary' redundancies also signal some dissatisfaction among Australian academics and researchers. However, in general, international students have been quite satisfied with the quality of education they get. Harman's (2003) work, for example, suggests that most international students enrolled on Ph.D. courses in Australia are 'satisfied' or 'very satisfied' with the quality of their research training, particularly in relation to the quality of supervision, library facilities, working space, and general intellectual environment. The housing needs of international students, however, require particular attention. International students access one of six types of accommodation, namely rental properties (such as shared houses, flats, units or apartments, boarding houses, or hostels); on-campus accommodation colleges; off-campus, purpose-built accommodation; home stay; backpackers' residences; and rooming accommodation in family houses (National Liaison Committee for International Students in Australia, 2007).

Although it is widely recognized that housing is important in influencing the quality of international students' experience in Australia, research about international student housing is often lacking. Instead, general comments about housing, often subsumed under broader issues about education for overseas students, are commonplace (see, e.g., Adams, 2007). The Residential Tenancies Authority and Queensland Education and Training International commissioned a study on the housing situation of international students in 2005 for this reason (Consumer Affairs Victoria, 2007, p. 16). Other studies have been conducted, but most of them look at the accommodation of international students on a 'home stay' basis. This is an arrangement in which international students sojourn with a family in Australia, as opposed to acquiring rental units themselves (Richardson, 2003). It does not, however, reflect the housing experience as a whole, and it is thus important to dig much deeper into broader housing issues. The rest of this chapter attempts to do so by focusing on the situation at the University of Sydney.

International Students at the University of Sydney: Characteristics and Housing Experience

The University of Sydney had over 47,000 students and more than 6,000 members of staff in about 16 faculties and schools in 2012. In 2019, it had more than 73,000 students,[1] a dramatic increase, and more than 8,000 members of staff (University of Sydney, 2019). International students constituted about 22.8% of the population of students in 2012. By 2016, the share of international students had increased to 39.2% (Birrell and Betts, 2018). International students at the University of Sydney are from a diverse pool. In 2010, for example, students from around 134 countries studied at the university (ISSU, 2011, p. 69). Most (77%) of the international students come from Asia, although there are students from Africa and the Middle East (4%), the Americas (12%), Europe (7%), and other areas (1%) (University of Sydney, 2011b, p. 2).

There are as many female international students as male. In 2009, women constituted more than 48% of international postgraduate research students, 61% of postgraduate coursework students, and 58% of international undergraduate students (Strategic Planning Office, 2009, p. 13). Table 8.2 gives other descriptive statistics about international students at the University of Sydney.

Table 8.2 shows that the proportion of postgraduate coursework students is higher than that of the other three categories. Across the board, the share of international students has increased substantially from 2005 to 2019. In most cases, the share of international students has doubled. The total number of international students, amounting to 25,541 in 2019, is much higher than any single

[1] www.sydney.edu.au/about-us.html.

university in both the US and the UK, where New York University (19,605) and University College London (19,635) are the universities with the highest number of such students (*The Economist*, 2020q, pp. 15, 7, 14, 16). These trends shape how we address the remaining research questions.

What Is the Nature of the Accommodation of International Students?

The University of Sydney has a number of accommodation facilities that it manages or that are managed on its behalf. The Camperdown campus contains International House, the University of Sydney Residential Colleges, the Sydney University Village, the University of Sydney Terraces, Darlington House, and the University of Sydney Low Cost Housing. The university also has catered accommodation called Yannadah at the Cumberland campus and Nepean Lodge and Nepean Hall provide accommodation at the Camden campus. Apart from International House, the other accommodation facilities are open to both domestic and international students, with accommodation restricted to health science students at Yannada (Students Representative Council [SRC], 2010, pp. 30–31; University of Sydney AIS, 2010b). Table 8.3 sheds further light on the nature of university accommodation. Apart from the Sancta Sophia Residential College, which is exclusively for postgraduate students, all the other facilities can be used by undergraduate and postgraduate students.

Table 8.2 International students at the University of Sydney, 2005–2019

Level of study	2005	2006	2007	2008	2009	2019
International students postgraduate (research)	428	479	525	590	678	982
Total postgraduate research students	3,466	3,544	3,647	3,740	3,905	4,516
Proportion of total	12.4%	13.5%	14.4%	15.8%	17.4%	21.7%
International students postgraduate (coursework)	3,381	3,340	3,697	4,326	4,498	12,034
Total coursework students	11,135	10,649	10,809	11,609	12,236	21,940
Proportion of total	30.4%	31.4%	34.2%	37.3%	36.8%	54.8%
International students undergraduate	4,999	4,868	4,806	5,001	5,305	12,525
Total	31,337	30,846	30,726	30,705	31,634	37,146
Proportion of total	16.0%	15.8%	15.6%	16.3%	16.8%	33.7%

Source: Adapted from University of Sydney Strategic Planning Office, 2009, p.19; Office of the Vice-Chancellor and Principal, 2020, pp. 12–13.

Table 8.3 shows that university accommodation has the capacity to house only 2,582 students. Given that there are about 47,000 at the university, it follows that some 95% of the students live in non-university accommodation. The nature of international students' accommodation facilities varies. The results of the ISSU (2010) survey showed that most students live in shared houses (63%), flats or apartments (11%), and with other families in home stay arrangements. Of these accommodation facilities, 57% have two or three rooms. Most students live within 6 km of the university and only 21% of international students live more than 12 km away from their campus. Not surprisingly, for most of the students (53%), walking is the main means of commuting to the university (ISSU, 2010). That said, campus accommodation is dominated by domestic students. A survey conducted in 2017 (Broderick and Co., 2017, p. 20) showed that only 14% of the residents of the University of Sydney colleges are international students, whereas international students made up 43.33% of the University of Sydney student population in that year (Office of the Vice-Chancellor and Principal, 2018, p. 2).

Most international students live elsewhere. As shown by the survey by Ruming and Dowling (2017), even students who live in private rental accommodation in Parramatta strive for proximity. Ph.D. students who work at the University of Sydney Westmead Hospital tend to live in university-provided housing in the hospital block or in private rental accommodation close to the hospital.

Laurie Berg and Bassina Farbenblum's (2019) more recent survey is useful. It was conducted in 2019 among international students at various universities. Overall, a total of 2,440 answered questions about their housing experiences. We know that 64% of respondents live in the Greater Sydney area. The respondents described their housing of first occupation as follows: boarding (2%), other (2%), commercial student housing (7%), university housing (11%), private rental (14%), home stay

Table 8.3 Student accommodation in Sydney, 2008–2020

	Total places	Median weekly rental payments	
		2008/2011*	2017/2020
University-owned residence	2,223	157–273	220–571
Residential colleges	1,713	388–441	397–687
Independently run rental housing near campus	3,896	–	Up to 700
Open market rental housing	13,447	150–400	265–488

Source: adapted from City of Sydney, 2011, p. 10; the University of Sydney, 2008, pp. 31–32), 2011, p. 9; 2020, pp. 14–16; University of Sydney Accommodation Information Service (AIS), 2010a; Anglicare Australia, 2017; UNSW Human Rights Clinic, 2019.
* Figures are adopted from sources when readily available or, if unavailable, the means of upper and lower limits are taken for the various rental bands.

(18%) and shared housing (36%). These responses broadly reflect the findings of the ISSU survey for only University of Sydney students. What this means is that the housing experience of international students has been broadly similar across Australia, a finding corroborated by two large-scale surveys conducted in Sydney and Melbourne in 2020 (Morris et al., 2020): private rental housing is the most common type of student accommodation in Australia.

How Do International Students Locate Accommodation?

The university provides a range of services to assist international students to find accommodation, such as the University of Sydney Accommodation Information Service (AIS) database, which contains information about vacancies in university-managed housing and off-campus private housing. The officers at ISSU, SUPRA (especially the international students officer), and the SRC are also sometimes a source of accommodation-related information.

Outside these levels of support, international students consult friends, sections of newspapers, and various adverts informally displayed at popular spots for information. According to Bridge (2001) and the more recent survey by Morris et al. (2020), estate agents in Sydney provide another source of support, particularly because they act as financial and social intermediaries and know which accommodation may be suitable for students.

Table 8.4 shows that, of the 1,891 international students who were surveyed by ISSU, only 7% found their accommodation through the accommodation service provided by the university. In practice, which sources are used by international students is contingent on factors such as how long they have lived in Australia

Table 8.4 How international students locate accommodation, 2009–2019

Source of accommodation information	Proportion of respondents (%)		
	ISSU (2010)	Yinghui (2009)[*]	Berg and Farbenblum (2019)[*]
Housing website and social media	34	37	51
Friends	26	28	32
Estate agents	15	11	2
Newspapers	7	–	–
Accommodation service	7	40	2
Noticeboards and signs on posts	3	–	–
International Housing Officer	2	–	–
Other (e.g., previous accommodation, faculty email, university booklet)	7	–	4

[*] Percentages do not add up to 100 because of approximation.

and whether they attended the information sessions organized by the university. Table 8.4 shows that, while only 7% of international students found their accommodation through the university accommodation service, according to the ISSU survey, 40% of the students in Yinghui's (2009) survey used the service. What factors account for this disparity? Yinghui's (2009) survey involved 1,100 freshmen who were undergoing orientation.

ISSU's (2010) survey, on the other hand, involved some students who had been living in Australia for more than a year and some of them had previously stayed temporarily with friends. In addition, while only 25% of the students who were surveyed by the ISSU (2010) attended the daily information sessions organized by the university, a large share (42%) of the students in Yinghui's (2009) study had attended the information sessions. This evidence suggests that the longer students stay in Australia, the more likely they are to use friends and other sources of information to obtain accommodation. Also, the more students attend the university information sessions, the higher the chances are that they would find accommodation through the University AIS database, which is advertised during the sessions.

Similar comments apply to the Berg and Farbenblum (2019) survey. More fundamentally, that survey is much wider than the responses of the University of Sydney students. While respondents most likely include such students, they are not all at the university. Yet, as its findings are consistent with the two University of Sydney surveys, the conclusion is likely that over time the sources of information have not changed. Social media now provides more active sources of information. In the Berg and Farbenblum (2019) survey, 23% of accommodation was found in this way, which increases the website share (28%) to an overall share of 51%. Ruming and Dowling's (2017) survey confirms these findings. International students rely on friends or other students. Sometimes, they live with their friends for a while and, during that time, act on the advice and information of friends to obtain housing information. Supervisors who have other Ph.D. students who are international students tend to match new students with existing ones who, in turn, provide information or sublet their own rented places. Agents can help, too, as can the university itself. For the most part, however, international students actually obtain their housing from information provided by their friends.

How Much Do International Students Pay for Accommodation?

Table 8.3 provides an overview of prevailing rents for accommodation in Sydney. Open market rent seems to have been the lowest in the 2008–2011 period. However, that was no longer the case in the 2017–2020 period. University-owned residence was the most affordable for students, while residential colleges and other independently-run private rental housing constituted the mid-range, but was mostly unaffordable to international students. Anglicare Australia (2017) considers rent of around A$224 per week as affordable. Going by this measure, affordable housing can be found in only the university-owned residence. In practice, international students mostly find housing in the private rental market, not because prevailing rents are low, but because of 'flexible' shared renting arrangements. University accommodation was once the most expensive (ISSU, 2011, pp. 36, 46; SRC, 2010, p. 30). Although this is no longer the case, rent in the university-affiliated residential colleges in 2017–2020, as shown in Table 8.3, was usually in excess of A$300 per week.

Estimates of how much students actually pay provide additional information. The ISSU (2010) survey showed that 50% of the respondents paid less than A$100, 32% paid between A$150 and A$200, 25% paid between A$100 and A$150, 20% paid between A$200 and A$250, and 20% paid more than A$250. These rents included payment for internet, furnishing, and utilities and vary according to location and the number of rooms. Ruming and Dowling's (2017) survey updated these findings. Carried out in 2013, but published much later, in 2017, the survey is quite revealing. It showed that many University of Sydney students, notably Ph.D. candidates working at Westmead Hospital, lived in Parramatta. They either lived in student accommodation provided within the hospital's block of apartments or in private rental housing. If in the former, single rooms went for A$95 per week for single students. Family units cost more: they ranged from A$280 to A$310 to A$380 per week, depending on, among others, the number of rooms. According to the survey, private rental accommodation cost students about A$410 per week for two-bedroomed units. According to the survey, that would be about 89% of their income. The income of international students, therefore, needs further discussion.

Anglicare's 2017 survey suggests that international students face a very restricted market of affordable housing. Of the total of 13,447 rental properties available, international students could only afford 625 properties, 524 of which were within close proximity of the university of Sydney. The rest were in what Anglicare considered to be 'the outer ring'; that is, quite far away from the city centre. Affordability in the Anglicare survey meant that the going rent would be 30% of the minimum wage at the time (A$34,980 per annum). Around this time, international students who were on general doctoral scholarships at the University of Sydney received between A$30,003 (or A$30,0855.20 in a leap year, Australian Awards) and A$35,000 per annum (University of Sydney International Strategic Scholarship).[2] The figure is around A$35,000 because, even in the case of the Australian awards, a one-time payment of A$5,000 is made to international students upon arrival, so that they can pay for their rental bonds and books, among other essentials.

[2] University of Sydney, 2020, 'General Scholarships', University of Sydney, www.sydney.edu.au/scholarships/international/postgraduate-research/general.html.

With these figures, international students can be regarded as low-income earn-ers in the same bracket as minimum wage earners. The rest of the rental properties were not affordable, but students nevertheless still had to find money to pay for them somehow. Consequently, of the 7,084 international students surveyed by Alan Morris's team in early December 2019 (Morris et al., 2020), 36% regularly worried about how to pay their weekly rent.

How Do International Students Finance Their Accommodation?

A related issue to affordability is how international students find the money to pay their rent. A significant number of international students do not have scholarships. Indeed, 70% of international Ph.D. students are not on any scholarship (SUPRA, 2010b). The University of Sydney Financial Assistance Office may, however, give a loan of up to A$1,000 to international students. Unlike a grant, it has to be repaid. International students, in turn, are cautious about taking up this offer. According to the Financial Assistance Officer (whom I interviewed), only 129 international students used this facility in 2009.

The present situation necessitates that international students work while study-ing. In fact, 80% of all University of Sydney students work part-time to meet their financial needs (Sydney Talent, 2010, p. 2). For international students, visa restrictions mean that they can work no more than twenty hours a week. It follows that family support, especially for Asian students (some of whom are the only off-spring of their parents), is common. These reverse remittances from the Global South to the Global North are rarely discussed even in the limited research on re-verse remittances (Adiku, 2022). In theory, students pay rent from their stipends, loans, income from part-time work, or remittances from family members. In prac-tice, international students simultaneously obtain money from multiple sources. According to Marginson's team, which employed face-to face interviews with 200 students in nine universities in Australia, it is not uncommon to have a funding plan that is made up of familial support (61%), scholarship (34.5%), paid work (32.5%), and other miscellaneous sources (7%) (Forbes-Mewett et al., 2011). The disproportionate share of familial support in this plan brings to the fore the cur-rency volatility problem and how that, in turn, creates a burden for both students and their sponsors. To overcome these problems, one popular coping strategy is to invite friends to share rooms—originally intended for fewer people—in order to reduce per capita rent (as suggested by Gao and Liu, 1998 and Morris et al., 2020, p. xiii; Morris et al., 2021).

Ruming and Dowling (2017) provide recent examples of these sources, high-lighting the role of previously underemphasized sources, namely past savings and partners' savings. As one of their interviewees, an international student, pointed out, 'I have to bring money from my country sometimes to live here' (Ruming and Dowling, 2017, p. 818). Another noted, 'I couldn't have afforded it but my husband is working' (Ruming and Dowling, 2017, p. 818). Community support, in the form of crowdsourcing money from entire villages, is also quite common.[3] These sources bring with them attendant expectations, including the idea that successful completion would mean the end of material long-term poverty, as the student is expected to send remittances (for further discussion, see Shelton et al., 2019 and Morris et al., 2020). Many kinds of such adjustments have to be made—and all for quite problematic accommodation.

What Problems Do International Students Face and How Do They Solve Them?

As with many migrants around the world (for a review, see Kemper, 1998; White, 1998), accommodation issues pose a serious challenge to international students, whose knowledge of the housing market in Sydney is not, on average, as good as that of local students. Indeed, not many of them are familiar with the real estate terms in Australia (International Student Development Taskforce, 2009, pp. 3–4; Nguyen and Bretag, 2021). Also, the pressure of living in a new country, coupled with limited financial means, implies that they do not have as much time to explore the different options available to them. Furthermore, they are usually under pressure to settle quickly to begin their academic work. In turn, finding accommodation is difficult. Of the 1,100 international students surveyed in 2009 at the University of Sydney, 50% could not find permanent accommodation before the semester began (International Student Development Taskforce, 2009, p. 3; Yinghui, 2009). Searching for accommodation is not the only problem. After obtaining a place, there are other challenges.

Consider the findings from the two major surveys (UNSW Human Rights Clinic, 2019; Berg and Farbenblum, 2019) about international students experiences with housing, for example. These surveys did not involve only University of Sydney students, but their results reflect the issues uncovered in the University of Sydney-specific surveys. For instance, the UNSW Human Rights Clinic (2019) survey showed that rental scams (38%) led the complaints by international students to the Kingsford Legal Centre. This problem was followed by challenges with reclaiming rental bonds (25%), poor living conditions (11%), no written agreements (9%), and other problems (8%). Students also complained about forced terminations and evictions (3%), as well as harassment and assault (6%).

---

[3] This was mentioned to me in a discussion with two scholarship officers.

This outcome means that, while other students, family, and friends may be the source of stress to international students, most housing problems faced by international students relate to landlords. Although landlords create or condone flexible rental arrangements which, on face value, ease the affordability problem, their actions and inactions directly increase the stress of housing for international students. These conclusions are also consistent with the Berg and Farbenblum (2019) survey outcomes. Landlords tend to bring in more and more tenants without prior notice to existing tenants. They confiscate part of the bond paid by students. They usually give no receipts. They charge significant upfront bond payments, in violation of Australian rental housing laws. They flout laws about giving formal tenancy. They arbitrarily increase rent. Both surveys (UNSW Human Rights Clinic, 2019; Berg and Farbenblum, 2019) show that these problems are more common in shared rental arrangements.

These conditions could, in fact, worsen with time. Like international evidence elsewhere in the Netherlands (Fang and van Liempt, 2021), the surveys show that these problems recur and worsen with time. They are neither frictional nor fickle. There is clearly no evidence that housing careers systematically improve over time. Instead, the surveys (Berg and Farbenblum, 2019) suggest that some international students move into less and less secure housing and more and more dangerous neighbourhoods as the cost of living becomes unbearable.

With this 'race to the bottom', international students in Australia become exposed to typical hate crimes that intersect with systemic racial abuse. Such were evidently the well-known cases of the attacks on Indian students living in large numbers in crime-prone areas in Australian cities (Forbes-Mewett and Wickes, 2018; Indelicato, 2018, pp. 91–125). Universities focus largely on milking so-called 'cash cows', as international students are often called, in a process in which the Australian government is complicit (Forbes-Mewett and Wickes, 2018). Australian authorities have initiated programmes to remedy these social problems (see, e.g., Ramia, 2017). However, they assume that racist attacks are mere urban crimes that can be redressed by making racial minorities invisible, controlling their presence in the public space, and offering lectures on not travelling alone, not carrying mobile phones and ipods, not working or walking late at night, and not living in risky places. These suggestions by the authorities amount to blaming victims and considering the students to be at fault (Indelicato, 2018, pp. 93–94). So, the prevailing attempt to correct deficient behaviour overlooks the structural nature of the problem.

For instance, landlords continue to subdivide their properties to appropriate more rental windfalls as rents increase through social investments, landlord monopoly of rental property, and general speculation in Australian housing development. According to the Berg and Farbenblum survey:

Participants may have experienced problems multiple times in the multiple accommodations. Others may have had problem-free first housing but moved

on to one or more problematic housing situations. Indeed, 61% of participants moved from first housing to other housing ... and ... each problem was similarly common in first housing and subsequent housing.

(Berg and Farbenblum, 2019, p. 30, bold in original)

Landlords often take advantage of the vulnerability of international students. During national economic, environmental, or health crises, international students are particularly vulnerable. For instance, of the 817 international students in Sydney and Melbourne who were surveyed by Alan Morris's team during the COVID-19 pandemic of 2020, 8% had been evicted from their homes (Morris et al., 2020, p. xii). Many more were at risk of becoming homeless because 61% of those who were working before the pandemic had lost their jobs during the pandemic (Morris et al., 2020, p. xv). Landlords continued to demand the same amount of rent from 78% of the 817 international students who were specifically surveyed by Morris's team to ascertain the impacts of COVID-19 on international student (Morris et al., 2020, p. xv; Morris et al., 2021). Even if landlords eventually grant requests to postpone the payment of rent, international students risk becoming quite heavily indebted. Although such crisis-related effects might be short-term, student indebtedness is a well-known, long-term problem (Baum, 2017), which is often aggravated by the housing question. Both are strongly related to land and landlords.

This evidence shows that the problems faced by international students are neither simply the result of their ignorance, nor merely the problems of big-city urban violence that affects everyone, as the authorities and mainstream Australia have sought to portray it (Indelicato, 2018, pp. 91–121). The fact that problems experienced by international students were similar whether they found housing prior to or after moving to Australia (Berg and Farbenblum, 2019, p. 37) suggests that ignorance or misinformation was not the key problem. The root causes are more systemic, many arising from discrimination in the private rental market. They can be found elsewhere, too. For example, *The Red Zone Report* (End Rape on Campus Australia, 2018, pp. 75–76) suggests that sexual harassment appears to be more common in the residential colleges at the University of Sydney and other Australian university residential colleges. A detailed analysis of the nature of sexual harassment specifically at the University of Sydney residential colleges can be found in the Broderick and Co. (2017) report.

So, how problems are experienced depends on whether students live in university, university-affiliated, or private rental accommodation. Consequently, one of the demands by Indian students after attacks on them was to be given access to campus accommodation to prevent encounters with problematic landlords, along with diversifying the Australian police force, making crime statistics public, and addressing the exploitation of international students (Indelicato, 2018, p. 93). Numeric evidence of the problems of international students residing in university accommodation was difficult to find because the dataset was not disaggregated to make it possible to know which complaints are made by international students, as distinct from domestic students.

Furthermore, different subunits of the university housing service (e.g., plumbing, electrical) deal with specialised complaints. In addition, some housing managers regard such information as confidential. Informal conversations with some students, property, and security officers, as well as the case officer of the SRC, however, showed that problems with university accommodation are few, minor, and experienced similarly by local and international students. The problems span personal conflicts and noise-making (from other students and vehicles or other programmes on campus) to homesickness and bad natural lighting in a few parts of the residences. There is also the problem of rationing places, namely occupying for only a year in order to make it possible for all international students to experience life in university accommodation. Some university housing (see Table 8.1), is quite old, and susceptible to problems of repair, such as broken fittings.

However, typically these residences have processes in place to take and resolve disputes and problems. The University Village has in-house professional staff members responsible for taking care of residents, while Darlington House and the University Terraces have the professional staff of the Accommodation Services Department, Student Housing, and Campus Security as managers. Students who occupy these facilities have formal contracts, which seem to be working well (according to those interviewed). The environment in university accommodation is communal and the managers make an effort to provide extra care, including appointing students to act as representatives to liaise between management and resident students. The facilities, being on campus, enable students to have sufficient rest before going to classes. As one international student resident of International House put it:

> I love living at International House, and moving here was probably the best choice I made .... I love that the community is so tightly woven with so many individuals from all over, just sitting down to lunch is like taking a trip around the world! You can literally sleep until 10 minutes before your class, because everything is just five minutes away.
>
> (International House, 2011, p. 2, exclamation in original)

The experience with living in private accommodation is rather different. Some students are wrongfully ejected, forced to pay for costs such as repairs, for which they are not legally responsible, or asked to fulfil onerous responsibilities in their tenancy agreements. Some suffer from invasion of privacy, while for others the rent is arbitrarily increased or no receipt is given them for rental payment. Most international students are not given tenancy contracts and some are victims of internet scams, while others do not get their rental bonds refunded (SRC, 2010; SUPRA, 2010a, 2010b; UNSW Human Rights Clinic, 2019; Berg and Farbenblum, 2019). Research on domestic students in Australia (e.g., Abbey, 1994; Carson,

2010; James et al., 2007; Rizvi and Lingard, 2011) shows that they can also face similar problems.

However, the scale is nowhere near that of international students (Marginson, 2011). The reasons are legion, but the principal ones are that most local students live at home with their parents (Khawaja and Dempsey, 2008), and private rental housing is mostly targeted at international students (Fincher and Shaw, 2009). Also, local students are more familiar with the housing market, and are not under the pressure of settling down in a foreign country. In turn, they are able to obtain better-quality housing at competitive rents (Fincher and Shaw, 2011). Additionally, local students usually enjoy price concessions for public transport, so they can choose to live further away from the university in social networks that they value and where accommodation is cheaper (Fincher and Shaw, 2009; UNSW Human Rights Clinic, 2019). Finally, white, local students usually enjoy 'property interest in whiteness', shielding them from discrimination and propelling them ahead with privileges (Harris, 1993). Accordingly, white international students, similar in skin colour and race to the dominant racial group in Australia, are, in general, much better off than non-white and, particularly, darker and different international students who look more like the oppressed Indigenous people of Australia. While international students who hold Australian government scholarships typically benefit from concessions too, only a few international students have these scholarships.

According to AusAID (2010, p. 2), only 2,082 international students across Australia were given short-term Australian government scholarships in 2010, around which time there were over 335,000 international students studying at Australian universities (DEEWR, 2011). It is not correct to infer from the analysis that international students suffer accommodation problems solely because they are international students. Accommodation is a major problem for all tertiary students—local and international. However, a combination of factors, including information asymmetry, public policy, structural discrimination and the inability of the university to regulate private housing providers for its students, makes the incidence of housing problems higher for international students than for domestic students. Not surprisingly, although the share of international postgraduate students at the University of Sydney averaged only 31% between 2007 and 2009 (Strategic Planning Office, 2009, p. 19), according to SUPRA (2010b, p. 7), about 80% of the accommodation complaints it received from postgraduate students within that period were from international students.

It follows that for every complaint lodged by a local student there are four complaints from international students, especially those with darker skin colour or non-white international students generally. The net result is that international students regularly change houses. Of the students surveyed by ISSU (2010), 51% were no longer living in their first accommodation since they arrived in Sydney and, according to SUPRA (2010, p. 11), some students changed accommodation about five times in a semester. It is even possible that the situation is worse than has been reported, given that more than 70% of international students do not know about SUPRA (Yinghui, 2009, p. 18), have little knowledge about where to report the problem, believe that nothing can be done, or simply consider problems to be the result of cultural differences (National Liaison Committee for International Students in Australia, 2007, p. 4; see also UNSW Human Rights Clinic, 2019; Berg and Farbenblum, 2019).

Domestic students face challenges, too. Notably, female students appear to be disproportionately affected by widespread sexual harassment problems in residential colleges (Broderick and Co., 2017; End Rape in Australia, 2018). However, in general, domestic students have strong social support. For example, in the Ruming and Dowling (2017, p. 818) survey, one domestic student noted, 'I didn't actually feel the pressure because we're very lucky, my parents and my partner's parents they're always willing to help' (Ruming and Dowling, 2017, p. 819). The incidence of problems also varies between international students who occupy university accommodation and the rest. An interview with the Student Advisor of SUPRA, who was also in charge of accommodation issues, revealed that SUPRA did not have records of the proportion of complaints that come from international students who lived in private rental or university accommodation.

However, given that international students in university houses normally report problems to a resident housing manager, the Accommodation Services Department, Campus Security, or Student Housing Department, the officer believed that most of the complaints that SUPRA receives are those from international students who live in private accommodation. Overall, the evidence suggests that international students, especially non-white students who live in private rental units—constituting the biggest share of international students—bear a disproportionate share of accommodation problems.

How Satisfied Are International Students with Their Housing Experience?

Peck and Stewart (1985) have long established that there are several ways to measure housing satisfaction levels, including making inferences from general satisfaction with life to looking at the quality of accommodation and examining neighbourhood characteristics. In Australia, following the history of home stay and the concern for expensive housing for international students (Richardson, 2003), it is often suggested that the lack of affordable housing implies discontent with one's accommodation (Harman, 2003; Khawaja and Dempsey, 2007). However, a survey of international students from China (Gao and Liu, 1998) shows a more complex picture.

Table 8.5 How international students perceive the amount of rent they pay: is it 'close to their expected budget of accommodation'?

Response	Share of students (%)
1 Agree	16
2	24
3	20
4	16
5	16
6 Disagree	8

Source: International Student Support Unit (ISSU), 2010.

The students typically rent a place, invite friends to share the unit, and thereby reduce the cost of rental payment. Although Western standards may regard such practices as 'overcrowding', the Chinese students were satisfied with the quality of their accommodation (Gao and Liu, 1998). Outcomes of this nature may explain why housing scholars have turned to the use of student residential satisfaction surveys as a more direct approach to studying housing satisfaction (Nurul et al., 2011). The closest the ISSU (2010) came to measuring satisfaction levels was when it asked respondents whether the rent they paid was 'close to [their] expected budget for accommodation'. Only 16% 'agreed' it did. Interestingly, even fewer (8%) 'disagreed'.

Table 8.5 shows the full range of the answers provided by the students on a Likert scale of 1–6, where 1 means 'agree' and 6 means 'disagree'. The results in Table 8.5 are open to various interpretations. One may ascribe degrees of agreement to the answers, such as 'strongly agree' [1], 'agree' [2], and 'moderately agree' [3]. If that approach is accepted, it can be said that 60% of international students moderately agree, agree, or strongly agree that the rent they pay is 'close to their expected budget for accommodation', so they are satisfied. Whether the respondents analysed the question in this way is not clear, however.

What *is* clear is that 'close to budget' is not the same as 'within budget'. Since only 16% agreed that the rent they pay is 'close to their expected budget', it is fair to say that, for the majority of students, the rent they pay is only close to, but not within, their budget. Compared to the global average of 62% satisfaction level or 60% satisfaction level among international students in Australia as a whole (AEI, 2010a, p. 10), the situation at the University of Sydney suggests that 84% of international students are not satisfied with their housing experience. More recent surveys uphold these findings. Anglicare Australia (2017) found that a rental value of A$224 per week is an affordable rent in Sydney. However, '[f]ocus group participants indicated that international students believe affordable rent to be ap-proximately $150 per week for a shared bedroom, or $200 for a private room', according to the UNSW Human Rights Clinic (2019, p. 9) survey.

Whether the disconnect between international students' expectation of the amount of rent that they should pay and what they actually pay is a reflection of 'unrealistic expectations' is hard to say. However, given that international students recurrently mention high rental cost as a downside of their housing experience (Fincher and Shaw, 2009, 2011), that disconnect itself may be taken as evidence of housing dissatisfaction. Yinghui's (2009) survey contained a more direct ques-tion about housing satisfaction, to which 38% of the respondents rated 'hunting for accommodation' as their most unsatisfying experience at the university (In-ternational Student Development Taskforce, 2009, p. 3; Yinghui, 2009, p. 19). The problem appears to be deeper than offering supply-side remedies:

> Although there has been growth in the suppy of purpose-built accommodation with good facilities, many dwellings are not affordable to students whose parents cannot subsidize their rent. This is particularly so for mature-age and postgrad-uate students. Student housing advisors reported rents were typically around $300–$400 per week for purpose-built room accommodation, with the bond and upfront living costs in the order of $1,200–$3,000.
>
> (Parkinson et al., 2018, p. 56)

So, it is not only rents, but also bonds or advance lump sum payments that create stress. This is worse with rental history: international students typically have no Australian experience to provide on rental-housing application forms (Berg and Farbenblum, 2019; UNSW Human Rights Clinic, 2019). These stresses do not end with students. They affect entire families and communities. Research (McCrohon and Nyland, 2018;Zhou et al., 2019) shows that many parents take loans to finance their children's education. Others sell their property or work extra hours. Often, families combine all these strategies. So, even though it is the better-off families, those of a much higher social class, caste, and position, who are able to support their children, international students, abroad, the decision to do so comes with serious costs. It follows that the higher the cost of living, particularly increasing rents, the more pressure is brought to bear both on international students and the communities, both home and abroad, who support them. Housing problems for international students in Australia, therefore, are social problems for the Global South, where most international students come from. The Global South subsidises the luxury and leisure of the wealthy and dominant groups in the Global North.

Overseas education is clearly important. International students in Australia do quite well, according to the results of Australian Council for Educational Research survey (Matthews et al., 2019):

Over 10,000 international students who graduated from an Australian university in the last decade ('international graduates') were asked a range of questions about their current employment status and their opinions on their Australian qualification. In brief the results indicate that: 90 per cent of graduates who are available for employment are currently employed—incorporating 93 per cent who returned home and 85 per cent who were still in Australia; 77 per cent of respondents said that they would recommend Australia as a study destination; 67 per cent of respondents consider their qualification was worth the financial investment; 43 per cent of respondents were currently living in Australia, gaining work experience or undertaking further study, while 47 per cent have returned to their country of origin. The likelihood of employment was time-dependent, where 97 per cent of those who graduated prior to 2014 were employed. For graduates who completed their qualification in 2017 or later, 80 per cent were employed, with most of the remainder pursuing further study.

(Matthews et al., 2019, p. 7)

The growing Westernization of local higher education is similar in its effect. Characterized by the diffusion of more and more universities, particularly in China, and the spread of Western ideas of education for individualized human capital rather than for public good, this boom in the education market has expanded access for women and the marginalized (Fan et al., 2017). However, as the Chinese case shows, it has neither become an avenue for inclusive transformation nor a way to generate employment for all. These models neither alleviate poverty nor address inequality. They can worsen both. Consider the effect of international education on Chinese female students, for example. Such students return to China greatly aware of uneven gendered relations and parents in the West investing similarly for their female and male children. However, structural gendered relations, including expectations of different genders in the marriage relationship, have not been transformed (Kajanus, 2015). Although some are even based overseas, prompting commentators to call them 'privileged daughters', their so-called 'left-behind' parents continue to influence their life choices (Tu and Xie, 2020, p. 74). Structures of inequality serve as barriers to the upward mobility of returnee children of the poor, just as they impede the mobility of those who have graduated from Westernized higher education locally (Fan et al., 2017). Class and position continue to be much stronger drivers. The unfettered power of human capital to break these chains is clearly questionable.

The stronger social and class positions of the wealthy enhance the value of their children's international education when they return from overseas (Zhou et al., 2019). In this sense, the so-called 'human capital' obtained by the children of the poor could impoverish them in a number of ways. Some realize that their international education teaches skills that are incompatible with Chinese job positions. Others obtain much less cutting-edge skills than the market requires. There is no certainty or guarantee about obtaining jobs (Tu and Nehring, 2020).

More fundamentally, because the process of education piles debt on poor families, if they had to sell off their properties, take loans, or work more to finance the international education of their children, the process of obtaining international education is, indeed, saddled with problems both during the educational journey and for years after. Research on student debt in the US (Baum, 2017) shows that default rate is much higher among postgraduates from poor families, typically black but also Hispanic. It is these poor students who also risk not completing their courses of study, particularly if enrolled at for-profit universities. Seeking employment as a buffer to the conditions of the indebted student sounds like common sense. In Australia, however, when such vulnerable students gain employment, they also procure a pact to endure systemic discrimination and exploitation(McCrohon and Nyland, 2018). As Ly Thi Tran (2017, p. 390) concluded from a survey of 169,700 international students: 'The research highlights forms of injustice including non-recognition of skills due to skin colour, disadvantage with regard to employment opportunities, being positioned as deficient in the classroom and workplace, unjust stereotypes and violation of rights.'

International students can exercise agency. Some organize and present petitions. According to Tran (2017, p. 390), '[t]he research also reports international students' specific strategies in exercising both individual and collective agency to seek a "space" for comfort, mutual support and communal strength and to confront injustices'. Others may decide to exit. The trouble is that those international students from poorer families cannot envisage returning until they have made enough money. Some continue to be exploited. Many develop serious mental health problems and others commit suicide (Shelton et al., 2019). Whatever they do, whether overtly or covertly, research (Cubas, 2020) shows that, globally, international students are not passive. They make valuable and vital contribution to the knowledge of nations, cities, and regions.

These issues raise fundamental questions about the housing question for international students: In what ways could it be addressed? Why has the University of Sydney approach yielded so few results? The next section discusses these policy issues before turning to my conclusions.

Policy Recommendations and Conclusion

There are several reasons why the housing situation for international students must be improved. From the report of the National Liaison Committee for International

Students in Australia (2007, p. 4) and many other surveys of international students' experiences in Australia and elsewhere (UNSW Human Rights Clinic, 2019; Berg and Farbenblum, 2019), it would seem that the situation at the University of Sydney is not unique. Indeed, the International Student Survey (AEI, 2010a, p. 3) notes that with regard to accommodation, international students have relatively low levels of satisfaction.

Given that the housing question is faced by a large section of international students at other universities in Australia, it follows that it is a national, rather than a local, University of Sydney problem. As migrants, international students make major contributions to Australia's vibrant scholarly, economic, and social experiences. These migrants are, for the most part, a major lifeline for Australia's best-known universities (Schreuder and Bowman, 2010; Marginson, 2010b; Calderon, 2020). 'Doing nothing' about the housing question is not an option. The University of Sydney has recognized the need to act quickly and has set up several committees to look at the issue (e.g., Schreuder and Bowman, 2010; Broderick and Co., 2017). So has the Australian government (Matthews et al., 2019), which is also keen to understand the wider levels of student satisfaction. These committees have recommended several policies (see, e.g., the International Student Development Taskforce, 2009; Berg and Farbenblum, 2019; UNSW Human Rights Clinic, 2019). They include allocating designated beds to first-year students, enabling some university staff or alumni to provide temporary accommodation, improving the laws about housing to make them deter problematic behaviours, and giving more information to international students.

Many of these policies seem appropriate. They are much broader than others proposed elsewhere (see, for e.g., Amole, 2009; Khozaei et al., 2010). The University of Sydney also does better than other universities in Australia in terms of providing international students with information to assist them in settling (Forbes-Mewett et al., 2011). But, as succinctly noted in the *2011–2015 Green Paper* (University of Sydney, 2011a, p. 5), 'The University of Sydney ... cannot be complacent. The higher education sector in particular, and the broader social, political, institutional and economic climate more generally, is changing rapidly.' The university is seeking ideas to improve its position as an institution which is welcoming to international students, who, among other things, enrich the experience of both the staff and domestic students of the university (University of Sydney, 2011b, pp. 16–17).

It is useful to think through the existing recommendations, most of which tend to look for answers in terms of 'cheap' accommodation, a view that is pervasive in Australia. Marginson (2010a; 2010b), for example, notes that his team sees 'subsidised, affordable student accommodation as a circuit breaker. On-campus and near-campus housing shared by international and local students could tackle several problems at once—housing shortages, high rents, unsafe conditions.' It is a reasonable proposition, given that 90% of students in the ISSU (2010) survey named cost as the most important consideration when choosing accommodation. However, most of these recommendations are not sensitive to the different needs of international students. At the very basic level, the disproportionate share of students from certain regions in the total population of international students suggests that some international students have more support—including information on housing—than others.

In addition, not all international students are incapable of paying for unaffordable accommodation. White and wealthy international students are better off. Furthermore, research students have needs that are different to coursework master's or undergraduate students (Ruming et al., 2017). At the University of Sydney, there are few facilities designated solely for research students, even though, as shown in Table 8.2, their rate of increase between 2005 and 2009 (12.7%) was higher than postgraduate coursework (9.9%) and undergraduate (1.0%) students. By not accounting for the variety in the needs of different international students, including the different costs of information asymmetry, it is hard to see how the existing one-size-fits-all proposals can provide a sustainable remedy to the housing question.

A more serious weakness in the prevailing policies on solving the housing question for international students is the thinking that it is only a 'shortage of accommodation issue', solutions to which require the provision of more accommodation. Holton and Mouat (2021) have detailed a boom in high-rise, purpose-built student accommodation in Australia. A spatial commodity, this attempt to redress the housing question redraws it. Clearly, providing more affordable university-owned and strictly regulated private rental accommodation would be welcome. However, underpinning the housing question is the economic question; a more desirable and important aim is to improve the economic conditions of international students. The problem of accommodation is not only a contributor to the financial hardship of international students, but it is also a symptom of their low-income status. An analysis of the number of cases reported to SUPRA between 2008 and 2009 is revealing.

Table 8.6 shows that, in terms of percentage, complaints about tenancy are one of the least. The most pervasive is the consumer/credit/debt problem, which arises mainly because students are unable to amortize their loans. In order to shore up their low incomes, some students end up taking part-time jobs, some of which are not regulated, and may have problems with employers (SUPRA, 2010b, p. 23). However, as shown in Table 8.6, this latter problem is not pervasive, although it might be that it *is*, but students are so desperate that they tolerate whatever treatment they receive for fear of losing their jobs.

Framing the housing problem *solely* as a shortage of accommodation issue misses the point, as does regarding the housing problem as 'the leading 'social issue', from which many other problematic issues then flow' (Schreuder and Bowman, 2010, p. 45). It is the 'land-housing-economic development' nexus which

Table 8.6 Complaints lodged at SUPRA, 2008–2009

Case (N = 225)	Percentage of total number of cases (%)
Consumer/credit/debt	19
Traffic offence/fine	13
Intellectual property/contracts	13
Crime	11
Motor vehicle accidents	9
Tenancy	9
Employment	7
Other	19

Source: Sydney University Postgraduate Representative Union (SUPRA), 2010a, p. 23.

is at the root of the issue. Looking at the housing problem as a land-based, socio-economic issue, rather than as a solely accommodation issue, turns attention away from regarding the housing question as a symptom or cause to looking at it as both a symptom *and* a cause of economic disadvantage. A similar argument may be made for financially stressed domestic students. However, as argued in this chapter, the differences between the two categories of students are not trivial. Local students have many advantages over international students, such as rent subsidies and reduction in the cost of public transportation. Transport cost is an important economic disadvantage, especially if housing affordability is measured in terms of general living costs (Burke and Hulse, 2010; UNSW Human Rights Clinic, 2019). Therefore, a housing policy for international students that neglects issues such as transport concessions is too narrow.

More fundamentally, the housing question for international students is a reflection of the wider housing question in Australia. Although usually analysed within a framework of supply and demand or as a crisis of capitalism (see, e.g., Milligan et al., 2015; Ferreira, 2016), and most fundamentally as a reflection of increasing immigration (*The Economist*, 2017, pp. 42–43), it is, perhaps, more accurate to regard it as a land problem that morphs into a wider capitalist crisis (Stilwell, 1993; Obeng-Odoom, 2017b, Chapter 7; Cashmore, 2017). Increasing housing costs can more accurately be described as a problem of increasing housing prices. These prices are not on the rise merely because demand exceeds supply or because of neoliberal capitalism in general.

Rather, institutions that support speculation on land prices, such as negative gearing, rental assistance schemes, zoning laws, and various policies that subsidize private property development, need re-examination. The difficulty in carrying out such reforms is that about half of the country's federal MPs own investment property (*The Economist*, 2017, pp. 42–43) and, hence, are complicit in the systemic transfer of value from society and producers to absentee owners, bankers, financiers, and rentiers. Similar comments apply to the transport sector, where structural reforms would need to tackle the institutional influence of what the Finnish urban economist, Anne Haila (2016, Chapter 6), called 'the property lobby'. Doing so, however, would be crucial in addressing the housing question.

Caution must be exercised in making suggestions to improve the economic status of international students. They are in Australia to study, not to enrich themselves. Like local students who receive government support, some international students have financial support. The *2011–2015 Green Paper* (University of Sydney, 2011a) notes the increase in the number of scholarships awarded to international students over the years. What ought to be considered is the adequacy of existing scholarships and other financial arrangements. Most students on doctoral research scholarships are entitled to hold them for three years, with the possibility of obtaining an extension of six months. But is this sufficient? Not many people will accept that they have 'adequate income', particularly so in Australia where, according to Hamilton and Denniss (2005), there is an 'affluenza' epidemic (a never-ending desire to have more, see also Stilwell, 2019, pp. 159–173), so asking students about the adequacy of their scholarship can produce questionable outcomes. An alternative approach is to ascertain how long, on average, students at the university take to finish their doctorates and juxtapose that period with the tenure of scholarships awarded to international students. According to SUPRA (2010a, p. 4), on average, it takes four years to finish a Ph.D. degree. If so, the scholarships of most international students are inadequate, in that the scholarships do not cover the entire duration of their study.

Another way to verify the adequacy of scholarships to international students is to compare the value of the typical Australian scholarship to the national minimum wage. While the value of Australian scholarships is around A$30–35,000 per annum,[4] as of 2020, the Australian national minimum wage is much higher: 39,197.6.[5] A similar gap existed in 2008, when the value of the University of Sydney International Scholarship (USydiS) was A$20,007, while the federal minimum wage was A$28,276.56.[6] So international students constitute a lower class in Australian society. This precarity is worsened by long periods of no payment: the fallow period between 'first submission', obtaining examination results, and the termination of scholarships, which constitutes a third indicator of the inadequacy

---

[4] E.g., The Lambert Initiative for Cannabinoid Therapeutics advertised a Ph.D. scholarship in August, 2020 at www.seek.com.au/ valued at A$30,000 for three years. The scholarship is to be held at the University of Sydney. As discussed in this chapter, the University of Sydney International Strategic Scholarship and other Australian awards are valued in the range of A$30–35,000.

[5] Fair Work Ombudsman, 2020, 'Minimum Wages', *Fair Work Ombudsman* official website, www.fairwork.gov.au/how-we-will-help/templates-and-guides/fact-sheets/minimum-workplace-entitlements/minimum-wages.

[6] Fair Work Commission, 2008, 'AFPC 2008 Wage-Setting Review', Fair Work Commission official website, www.fwc.gov.au/awards-agreements/minimum-wages-conditions/annual-wage-reviews/afpc-airc-reviews/afpc-2008-wage.

of scholarships. Research scholarships, such as University of Sydney international scholarships, would usually run out as soon as students submit their theses for examination. However, the practice in Australia is to send the submitted thesis out for external review, which may take 'up to five months or longer'. For 75% of the time, the reviewers/examiners require some correction (Faculty of Arts and Social Sciences, 2010, p. 1), which may take between one and twelve months to finish. In the meanwhile, students who are awaiting their results have to do without any financial support. Could they not depend on funds saved during the period when they had their scholarships? Not really. The work of Forbes-Mewett et al. (2011) shows that, after paying for their living costs and books from their scholarships, international students have nothing left for savings.

To solve the housing problems of international students, more broad-ranging policies need to be considered. It may be argued that the value and duration of international scholarships need to be increased or that financial support must be given for the periods during which students wait for examination results or do emendations. It might even be argued that the visa restrictions about work be modified or that international students be regarded as local students for the purpose of paying tuition fees. Whether these measures can remedy the problem of accommodation and enhance the experience of students at the University of Sydney, in particular, or in Australia generally, would require a more systematic analysis that is beyond the scope of this chapter. However, there is growing global evidence (e.g., Laferrère and Le Blanc, 2004; Tibaijuka, 2009; Wallace and Quilgars, 2005; Haila, 2016; Yu and Cheung, 2021) that housing problems are usually a function of socio-economic stress and wider problems about private property in land.

This finding has major analytical implications for the Becker–Bourdieu debates. The experiences analysed in this chapter show that international students are quite diverse, even at the point of entering Australia to commence their studies. Yet, upon entry, it appears that the stratification among the students hardens through various institutions related to both their education and housing and, in particular, to their educational housing. Apart from the stratification among international students, there is also stratification between international students and domestic students and between international students who are non-white and wealthy white international students from the Global North. Neither education nor housing addresses these issues. Housing choices are clearly constrained by what Bourdieu (2005) calls 'the social structures of the economy', rather than free choice. 'Human capital' does not address systemic inequalities, whether in the labour or housing spaces in Australia. Bourdieu's claims are clearly borne out by the Australian experience. That said, Bourdieu's contentions need to be more solidly grounded on the land question which, in the case of Australia at least, is quite central to addressing the housing question. These findings also raise questions about the Marxian analytical framework presented by Frederich Engels. In this classic 'housing question', the emphasis is entirely on workers. Questions of race, education, status, gender, and class, conceived of as broad-based power dynamics, are not analysed, nor are institutions that drive and shape migration examined.

Analytically, therefore, this chapter further develops how Georgist political economy, institutional economics, and stratification economics (GIS), especially institutions ranging from land and property rights interacting with wider social relations, shape education outcomes, temporary migration, housing, social, and economic change and disadvantage.

9

Remittances and Return

Introduction

Migrants hold hopes of return. They also take concrete steps to return. Working to obtain their own housing is, perhaps, the most important step towards realizing the dream of return. Africans, Asians, and South Americans have been well documented as sending remittances for this purpose. 'Between 1990 and 2015' notes Deborah Bryceson (2019, p. 3,051), 'remittances increased more than 10-fold while aid transfers merely doubled in monetary value.' In this process, Ghana is a standout. Newspaper accounts and interviews with housing professionals indicate that a major driver of Ghana's housing development is remittances from Ghanaians living abroad (Buckley and Mathema, 2007). Many studies (e.g., Aryeetey and Ackah, 2009; Vasta and Kandilege, 2007; Kuuire et al., 2016) have established that there is a large flow of remittances to Ghana, but the share, amount, and nature of these remittances to the housing sector remain understudied. A few studies have tried to fill this gap. Diko and Tipple (1992) were among the first to take up the challenge.

They considered the mode of transfer of remittances from Ghanaians living in London, the house-building process, and the characteristics of the houses built in Ghana. Margaret Peil published her work three years later (see Peil, 1995). Since then, other studies (e.g., Henry and Mohan, 2003; Mazzucato, 2006a, 2006b; Poeze, 2019) have briefly examined remittances from Ghanaians in the Netherlands to various sectors in Ghana, including housing. A relatively thorough study of the housing remittances nexus has been undertaken by Kabki et al. (2004), examining the economic and socio-cultural effects of remittances from Ghanaians in the Netherlands on rural life in Ghana.

However, even this latter study did not explore the housing question in as much depth as Diko and Tipple (1992) because it had a broad scope (looking at, among other aspects, health care and funerals). In any case, Kabki et al. (2004) interviewed the recipients of remittances in Ghana, whereas Diko and Tipple (1992) interviewed the givers (of remittances) in London (abroad). In addition, while Diko and Tipple focused on cities, Kabki et al. (2004) focused on rural areas. This makes Diko and Tipple's work quite unique, because even Poel's (2005) more recent work, which examines the house construction process in some detail, still differs from Diko and Tipple in terms of methodology and scope. Poel's work draws on responses by the caretakers in Ghana, not the migrants abroad. Therefore, there is still some dearth of information about the 'long distance building process' (Diko and Tipple, 1992) from the perspective of the migrants themselves.

As has long been noted, Accra's housing market appears to be a focal point for the investment of remittances. However, we need to know more about the dimensions or scale of these flows. Hence, an important first step is to develop this sort of information (Buckley and Mathema, 2007, p.19; Kuuire et al., 2016; Ehwi et. al., 2021). Grant (2007, 2009), one of the leading writers on urban economic development in Ghana, has also called for more studies on remittances in the housing sector, especially from places outside the US, Europe, and Scandinavia (particularly the Netherlands), where most of the other studies on housing and remittances in Ghana have been carried out.

Crucially, such a study must take the question of return seriously, in terms of what it means both in theory and in practice. This chapter responds to these calls. It is similar to the pioneering work by Diko and Tipple (1992) focusing specifically on housing-related remittances and the more recent and yet more general work by Ehwi and his collaborators (Ehwi et al., 2021) in terms of the socio-economic characteristics of the migrants studied and the methodology, examining the building process in cities from the perspective of the migrants. However, the present study differs from their work in three respects. First, whereas Diko and Tipple (1992) only examined the process of building per se and the effect of this building process on housing conditions of migrants (Ehwi et al., 2021), this chapter is even more comprehensive. For example, I explore the post-building experience in order to examine concerns about absentee ownership and speculation by migrants. Second, the research for this chapter was undertaken in Sydney, Australia, a relatively understudied continent in the remittances–housing literature on Ghanaian migrants. Indeed, to the best of my knowledge, the present study is the first of its type in Australia.

Third, in contrast to previous studies that have only focused on transnational families, class, and gender dynamics (e.g., Wong, 2000, 2014), or not probed family structures systematically (e.g., Diko and Tipple, 1992; Ehwi et al., 2021), this chapter uses transnational family life cycle analysis (Bryceson, 2019). The emphasis is not on one family, but several, and how their structures change over time. Instead of looking at the families in isolation, the chapter considers them in relation to one another within a multi-scalar space, from local to global, probing how their characteristics are shaped by institutions such as the state and property rights. Hence, this chapter emphasizes intergenerational dynamics about decision making related to exit, voice, and loyalty (Hirschman, 1970) to countries or places.

These are shaped by evolutionary changes in family structures across space and time in ways mediated by global economic forces, state policies, and wider institutions of land and property rights. Such regulations about retirement and diverse policies of citizenship and residency as local and global families change in age, size, and composition are also crucial. Bryceson (2019) offers a detailed theoretical exposition of this transnational family life cycle analysis, while the work of others, notably Poeze's (2019), throws light on how such an analysis can be applied to Ghanaian men with parental responsibilities to children who have been left behind. Where this chapter extends this life cycle analysis is in linking it to housing, still a relatively neglected theme in global migration research (see Chapter 9).

In this chapter, housing in Ghana is investigated, the role of remittances is established, the research in Sydney is described, and the case for 'return migration' in development economics is revisited. In all these processes, the evidence challenges existing orthodoxies and their alternatives.

Housing in Africa

The housing problem in Africa today arises from the commodification of land.

One way to demonstrate this fundamental cause is to analyse the urban-economic transformation of Accra (Yeboah, 2000, 2003, 2005; Grant, 2007, 2009; UN-HABITAT, 2011), the capital city of Ghana, and Africa's leading 'globalizing city' (Grant, 2009). It is a useful case study for another reason: many in Accra have expressed significant interest in the promises and prospects of commodifying land (Ehwi et al., 2021; Ehwi and Mawuli, 2021). Indeed, the annual demand for registration of land rose about ten-fold between 1988 and 2013 and outstripped supply by an average factor of four (Abusah, 2004; Ehwi and Asante, 2016).

One reason for this widespread interest is that formally registered land is usually valued at 10% higher than non-titled land (Obeng-Odoom and McDermont, 2018). Another is the perceived security that formalization is supposed to confer (Obeng-Odoom and Stilwell, 2013; Ehwi et al., 2021). A third is statutory: in Accra, designated as a 'registration area', it is compulsory for newly purchased land to be registered (Ehwi and Asante, 2016). Prestige and a certain desire for modernity (Obeng-Odoom et al., 2014) constitute additional incentives. Shading into all of these is the widespread and sustained promotion of registration as central to home ownership. Not only is registration advocated as a route for potential homeowners to access housing finance for potential homeowners, but it is also marketed to property developers as such (Ehwi et al., 2021; Ehwi and Mawuli, 2021). Whether these representations are borne out by social reality, however, needs more careful assessment.

Insecurity of tenure in Accra, if narrowly conceived as the absence of conflict about land (Obeng-Odoom and Stilwell, 2013), is becoming more, rather than less widespread (Obeng-Odoom, 2014; Ehwi and Mawuli, 2021). The attempt to mark out collectively held land as privately owned individual land has been associated with growing conflict (Obeng-Odoom, 2016b; Grajales, 2020; Ehwi and Mawuli, 2021). As Ghanaian courts have not automatically ruled in favour of registered land when they determine questions of land ownership, financializing land through registration has created even more uncertainty (Obeng-Odoom and McDermott, 2018). It follows that individual choices cannot be the primary basis for policy, especially when it is well known in both theory (Bourdieu, 2005) and practice (Obeng-Odoom, 2011a, 2016a) that such so-called *free* choices are *socially* constructed.

The number of transactions in Accra's 'luxury real estate' has, however, been substantial. 'There are more than 85,000 transactions per year in luxury real estate alone, with an estimated value of USD 1.7 billion.' Indeed, 'With approximately 30,000 new expatriates expected over the next 10 to 15 years, demand for luxury residential real estate is expected to increase' (Ghana Home Loans plc, 2015, p. 19). Within this class of housing, also called 'luxury real estate', the number of gated communities increased from twenty-four to sixty-three between 2004 and 2011 (Obeng-Odoom et al., 2014, p. 550). Apart from their numbers, the exchange value of these gated properties is also on the rise. Two-bedroomed houses in the gated neighbourhoods of the Airport residential area, which sold for some $96,000 in 2004, could only be purchased for $290,000 in 2011. By 2017, gated property prices could be up to $450,000 (Obeng-Odoom, 2011b, Ehwi et al., 2021; Ehwi, 2021). A fortified space for the wealthy classes of the city, gated estates vary in their degrees of luxury and value over space and time (Obeng-Odoom, 2018a), such that over time, the superwealthy classes now build additional walls within the walled and gated estates to protect their properties (Ehwi, 2021). Rents are similarly high.

Rental values in Accra in non-gated estates have been increasing, too. In 2008 alone, they increased by 180% (Owusu-Ansah et al., 2018). Such increases affect the housing situation of the 67% of residents who are renters, and, hence, might face the possibility of paying an estimated rent of $5,000 per month, instead of the prevailing $4 paid as rent by those in lower-income brackets (Obeng-Odoom, 2011b). This spectre of housing crisis raises important socio-spatial questions in the light of increasing urban land values.

Between the 1950s and the 1990s, the value of land in some parts of the city increased by over 300% (Obeng-Odoom et al., 2014, p. 554). This increase has generated serious social problems: lower middle-income groups have been evicted to poor and marginalized neighbourhoods and, hence, have experienced a sharp decline in the quality of their housing, while still spending more of their income and time to commute in a process which puts pressure on the poor to pay more rents because landlords seek to cash in on new low-income renters who compete for housing.

The moderately rich, on the other hand, have had to seek new types of gated communities. Located at the urban frontier, they increase rental values in the urban core, while contributing to urban ecological crisis because residents have to commute over longer periods and distances in private cars, usually fuelled by dirty oil (Obeng-Odoom et al., 2014; Obeng-Odoom, 2018b, 2018c). The resulting urban pollution, sprawl, and biodiversity loss as property developers remove urban green spaces to provide exclusive housing (Obeng-Odoom, 2018b, 2018c), raise additional questions. How can these two trends be analytically explained? What is the effect of their interlocking links on housing, household debt, inequality, uncertainty, and the urban socio-ecological crises? Could these ramifications shape the urban form in the future, and if so, why and how?

Most people in Accra are crowded into, and transact in, small parcels of urban land. Only a small class of absentee landowners is involved in large-scale, high-value land transactions (Grant, 2009; Obeng-Odoom, 2013). Thus, the transformation in urban land can be understood as restructuring urban society in favour of the wealthy. They make a living through rents, as has been established both theoretically (Haila, 1988, 2016) and empirically (Asante and Ehwi, 2020). These speculators, many of them based in the Global North, finance the purchase of land in the Global South. They hold on to this land, build on it speculatively in what is often called 'development looking for consumers', and sell when they find willing and able buyers.

Major transnational real estate companies, located in London, New York, and Chicago, have become particularly vibrant in buying land in the South (Liberti, 2013; Watson, 2014; Leon, 2015). This urban land development is usually designed by international architects with little or no consultation with local planners and citizens and is usually executed by international property developers engaged in building speculatively (Watson, 2014). In Accra, the Rendeavour Company, whose shareholders live in the US, New Zealand, Norway, and the UK, have built Appolonia City, regarded as an 'urban oasis' (Lutter, 2018). This descriptor calls attention to the exclusive nature of this wealthy suburb.

At the local level, a wide range of institutions collaborate to facilitate this speculation (Obeng-Odoom, 2011b; Arku et al., 2012; Akaabre et al., 2018). Although it is believed in mainstream urban economics that private banks mainly give credit to finance 'real' urban development through industrialization, in practice, they create money to finance speculative urban development by lending against landed property. While the literature on 'financialization' is growing (see Bonizzi, 2013), much less research has been done on the transformation of land, a process which, although it has long been sketched theoretically in the literature (e.g., Haila, 1988, 2016; Ryan-Collins, 2021; Sclar, 2021), is quite historically specific and, hence, ought to be untangled both contextually and empirically (Bourdieu, 2005).

A useful starting point is to consider the trends in the asset/debt profile of Ghana Home Loans (GHL), which is the largest single mortgagor in Ghana. Not only does it hold 50% of existing mortgages in Ghana, but it also generates 75% of all new mortgage facilities with very rapid growth in the 2010s (Ghana Home Loans plc, 2015). So, analysing the trends in the size of its assets and debtors can shed some light on the mortgage market. With the potential to become owners through foreclosure, GHL is often interested in maintaining the value of land. Hence, it sets higher interest rates. Although such rates can deter borrowing, GHL as a monopolist is in a position to impose them without consumer backlash. Others, such as the Republic Bank, also charge similar rates of interest.

The effects of this dynamic on property values are wide-ranging (Obeng-Odoom, 2011b; 2013; Arku et al., 2012; Akaabre et al., 2018; Ehwi et al., 2021; Asante and Ehwi, 2020). To obtain such private bank loans, potential credit seekers—whether they are aspirant investors, homeowners, or property developers—tend to talk up their property values. Professional valuers are caught in between the banks (which seek to give out more credit for higher rates of interests), and potential debtors (who try to access such loans). Indeed, the valuers grapple with the additional conflict of interest dilemma that arises because their professional fee is charged as a percentage of property value and, hence, the higher the property value, the more professional fees valuers earn. In practice (Owusu-Ansah et al., 2018), the resulting vibrant property market is characterized by cumulatively higher land values, even if valuers do not make value themselves. Landlords do and, as the class that stands the most to benefit, they tend to determine rents in a property market that they monopolize.

These resulting increases create the impression that property values increase ad infinitum which, in turn, encourages the process of speculation. As demonstrated by Hyman Minsky (1992), more banks are built when opportunities for private money creation and enrichment abound (Bezemer and Hudson, 2016, pp. 27–32). So, banks transform themselves from simply extending hedge financial credit to giving out speculative credit which, in a race to the bottom, turns into a grand Ponzi scheme. Some of these 'absentee owners' (Veblen, 1923/2009) are shareholders of transnational property development companies. Others are shareholders of banks in Accra, most of which are foreign-owned (Sulemana et al., 2018). One effect is colonial uneven urban development.

Another is the increase in household debt. Often neglected in urban research in Ghana, indebtedness is a major feature of urban households in Accra. Successive surveys showed that between 2006 and 2013, the share of indebted households in Accra had increased from 14% to 41%. Crucially, most people in 2013 were taking loans for land acquisition and housing, not for business (cf. Ghana Statistical Service [GSS], 2013, Round 6, p.165; 2008, and GSS, 2008, Round 5, p. 113).

Increasing household debt has several implications (for a detailed analysis, see Montgomerie, 2019). The direct cost of the debt in the form of compound interest is often the focus of discussion for mainstream urban economists, as is often the case in sterile discussions about what is and what is not a good debt among mainstream accountants. Anxiety and uncertainty are additional outcomes. Of far more importance for Georgist political economists, however, is the *opportunity cost* of servicing a growing household debt. Such costs relate to health, education, and other family expenditures that have to be neglected in order to amortize escalating loans. Servicing such debts, therefore, prevents the economic ripple effects often called 'the Keynesian multiplier'. Clearly, the money which could have been injected into the economy to trigger *additional multiplier effects* and investment into capital goods such as factories is (mis)directed into the payment of speculative ventures, including further speculative land adventures (Gaffney, 2015). Over the long haul, therefore, land-based debt, fuelled by speculation, can throw the entire economy into multiple crises.

At the individual level, the effect is most felt by the defaulting mortgagee. Often, this spectre of default is increased because of the largely inflated nature of the property prices and, for that reason too, the high-risk interest that is attached to loans. The banks do not have the security or certainty to be able to recoup their investment through foreclosure, however. That is not just because Ghanaian laws make foreclosures difficult, but mostly because such inflated properties stand little chance of being sold in the open market, even when advertised at the reserve price. Consequently, not only the households, but also the banks in Accra, have become risky ventures. They could undermine themselves, throw households into multiple crises, including saddling them with debts which become albatrosses around their necks even in their old age, and drawing the entire Ghanaian economy into depression.

Sensing these risks, the Ghanaian state has taken so-called remedial steps. Not only has the Bank of Ghana revoked the licences of banks, but it has also amalgamated several others into one grand bank overseen by the state. Subsequently, it has increased the minimum payment required to start and maintain banks (Addison, 2018). The Bank of Ghana is also to be more stringent in its supervisory activities to detect risky behaviour.

The Ministry of Finance, for its part, is to cooperate with the Central Bank, while the Government of Ghana has sought to absorb the debt of the private banks by paying off debtors (Ministry of Finance, 2018). State officials have justified socializing private bank problems on the grounds of restoring confidence in the market, trying to prevent joblessness, maintaining economic growth, and avoiding economic crises. Nevertheless, this bailout package is problematic. The direct cost is often the easiest to pinpoint in the form of money lost to the state These state resources are themselves generated from debt contracted from overseas sources which impose harsh terms and increasing indirect taxation, which, unlike direct taxation, which the majority of people in the urban informal economy escape (Obeng-Odoom, 2011a), is paid by both formal and informal workers, rich and poor, wealthy and wealth-poor labourers, workers, and other residents. Indirect taxation on essential goods and services penalizes the poor, as it falls more heavily on them. Direct taxes penalize workers for doing productive work, while neglecting rents. In turn, such taxes encourage speculative behaviour (George, 1935/2006, pp. 226–235). Servicing the growing public debt, itself securitized by landed resources such as oil, is diverting resources away from strategic urban and national investments.

Clearly, increasing the current public debt by bailing out private banks cannot be a sustainable strategy. At a deeper level, the misdiagnosis of these social problems is even more problematic. Identified as a 'banking crisis', the attempts to address them have centred almost exclusively on the banking sector, to the neglect of the root cause, namely the commodification of land and the private appropriation of socially created land rent.

I have illustrated this process with the experience of Accra, Ghana, but it is common more generally, especially in South Africa and Uganda, as I have shown elsewhere (Obeng-Odoom, 2013, pp. 175–198). The details differ. South Africa, with a housing loan penetration rate of 5.4 and a much more advanced banking system, would align more closely with Ghana, whose housing loan penetration rate is 2.8, with additional racial makeovers. On the other hand, Kampala in Uganda, with a less advanced mortgage system and a housing loan penetration rate of 1.2, differs in its experiences of indebtedness (Badev et al., 2014, pp. 45–46). With a total population of 40 million and a mortgage market of only 5,000 mortgages, in Uganda it is mainly microcredit institutions that securitize land (*The Economist*, 2019b, pp. 58–59). They may not insist on formal land titles, but land is still the required collateral security.

The repayment period, between one and three years, is much shorter in Kampala than in Accra's financialized mortgage market, but the microcredit institutions would foreclose mortgages that are not amortized anyway. In this environment, stress levels are particularly high, as entire families work under harsh conditions to repay their loans. Recent surveys in East Africa show that, although taking such microcredit loans helps in improving the quality of housing, the stress levels of the mortgagees have remained unchanged, even with a decent home (*The Economist*, 2019b, pp. 58–59). If anything, the rise of microfinance institutions engaged in fraudulent lending practices has heightened uncertainty and anxiety (Wiegratz, 2016, pp. 278–279).

The wider political-economic ramifications of transferring money from real work to pay absentee owners create fundamental problems. Henry George himself considered these issues (George, 1883/1966, pp.161–170). Public debt, often contracted under usurious terms, he argued, could be put to public improvement purposes, but it could also be put to war making, extravagant spending, and tyrannous purposes. Even public uses of debt tend to be characterized by inefficiencies and corrupted tendencies, given the loose accountabilities between the public and the debt-contracting state. If so, 'public debt' is particularly problematic because it tends to be put to private purposes, while still being securitized by land, which is common property.

Such debt also binds future generations to pay for the wastefulness of the present generation. 'It is not', George wrote, 'the case of asking a man to pay a debt contracted by his great-grandfather; it is asking him to pay for the rope with which his great-grandfather was hanged, or the fagots with which he was burned' (George, 1883/1966, p. 165). Not only does it advantage the present over the future, but debt also makes the wealthy wealthier, as they are able to privately appropriate debt for their own uses, while socializing its payment. Not only does this process entail creating cumulatively escalating debt-driven inter-group inequality between Africa and the rest of the world, it also transfers socially created rents into the hands of absentee private landlords.

It is crucial to place this position on public debt within current debates in economics. The dominant view is the neoclassical economic thesis that public debt must be only a small percentage of GDP. Although clearly the orthodox position, this economic determinism is questionable. According to the widely discussed Modern Monetary Theory (MMT), the fetish about fixed quantities should be dropped. Instead, MMT posits that there should be no filters nor fetters on the ability of a sovereign monetary power to obtain public debt, a position which is quite distinct from the Keynesian argument to use public debt for public purpose. What is being canvassed here is that, as a country with subordinate status in the global system, Ghana's public debt profile can generate social costs for both the present and future generations of Ghanaians. As discussed by Vidal and Marshall (2021), for countries of such marginalised status, they must contend with the forces of unequal exchange and the tyranny of private rating agencies. More fundamentally, creating more and more debt does not address social problems, nor attenuate socio-ecological, nor fundamentally change the institutions of political-economic crises.

If land commodification, advocated by mainstream economists and *The Economist* (2020r) newspaper as a panacea, is malign, not benign as claimed, is rent control the answer? Popular across the world, this alternative is often hurriedly imposed to defuse potential uprising resulting from worsening social problems. That was evidently the case when, on 18 June 2019, legislators in Berlin voted to impose a freeze on rents for five years after residents of Karl-Marx-Allee demanded liberation from their urban economic crisis, central to which was the housing problem. Rent controls are in force in Spain, Barcelona, and Amsterdam (*The Economist*, 2019a, pp. 21–22), as they are in Accra, where, in addition, there is even a Rent Control Department. However, as the evidence considered in this chapter suggests, rent control is no panacea. Rent control can simply be ignored by a powerful landlord class, as it was recently in San Francisco (*The Economist*, 2019a, p. 22) where, city-wide rents rose by 5%. Georgists (George, 1935/2006, 1883/1966; Stilwell and Jordan, 2004a, 2014b; Gaffney, 2015; Harrison, 2021) propose to address social problems by institutionalizing the single tax, entailing the implementation of equal right to land and guaranteed rights to the fruits of one's labour, along with rewarding invisibilised 'others' who labour to sustain more visibilised workers. Designing and demanding a robust reparations programme is a complementary strategy, as I discuss more carefully elsewhere (Obeng-Odoom, 2020b, 2021b) right to land. Neoclassical economists and humanists, some of them Marxists, propose to use migration and remittances instead.

A Spatial Fix?

The neoclassical case for migration and remittances is well known. Some have considered remittances as holding the same position as aid. Others contend that promoting remittances is superior to giving aid because it is better administered and it is much larger (e.g., World Bank, 2019). Some Western Marxists (e.g., Withers, 2019) tend to suggest that Marxist analysis is anti-remittances. That might be accurate in theory, but not in practice. Certainly, not among black Marxists. Consider John Arthur's well-known Marxist analysis of migration published as *Class Formations and Inequality Structures in Contemporary African Migration* (Arthur, 2014). Arthur's analysis of remittances is dialectical. While recognizing that they can deepen the class divide in Africa, particularly Ghana, which is the focus of his book, he also considers the possible liberation that might arise from leveraging the use of remittances for independent development and global migration. Humanists (e.g., Gollerkeri and Chhabra, 2016) make such pro-migration, pro-remittances case, too.

So, the possibility of using migration as a spatial fix requires serious attention. Generally, emigrants from Ghana typically go to Europe, North America, the Middle East, and Asia. Others migrate to other African countries, especially Nigeria, South Africa, Namibia, Botswana, Lesotho, and Côte d'Ivoire (Higazi, 2005; Tonah, 2007, 2021). It is difficult to estimate the total number of Ghanaians living abroad, and much more difficult to disaggregate the numbers by destination, because these figures exclude 'informal emigrants' and they vary with time and space. Existing research (UN-HABITAT, 2011, p. 168) suggests that some 10–20% of Ghanaians live abroad, mostly in North America, the most usual destination for Ghanaians who travel outside Africa (Anarfi et al., 2003; Oppong, 2004; UN-HABITAT, 2011; Yeboah, 2008, 2018); and Europe, the second most popular destination for Ghanaian migrants. Portugal, Italy, France, Spain, and the Netherlands are common destinations for such emigrants, as are the UK and Germany (Anarfi et al., 2003; Higazi, 2005; Oppong, 2004; Oppong, 2004; Burgess, 2019; Tonah, 2007, 2021).

The present chapter focuses on remittances from Ghanaians abroad and their role in the process of house building in Ghana. The particular country of origin that is studied is Australia, a country with which Ghana has had diplomatic relations since 1957,[1] but where the activities of Ghanaian migrants are poorly understood.

Compared to other migrant destinations, such as Europe and North America, Australia is relatively less popular as a destination. However, as Table 9.1 shows, it is becoming increasingly popular as a destination for Ghanaians. The number of Ghanaians living in Australia has more than quadrupled since 1996. It is now higher than the number of migrants from Sub-Saharan Africa, which has increased 3.3 times.

---

[1] The Australian Government Department of Foreign Affairs and Trade maintains a web pages for of Australia–Ghana relations.

Table 9.1 Ghanaians and other migrants in Australia, 1996–2019

Region of birth	1996	2001	2006	2011	2016	2019
Oceania and Antarctica	14,391,270	15,320,260	15,979,750	17,010,040	18,014,720	18,580,770
North-West Europe	1,520,880	1,477,490	1,503,770	1,594,560	1,598,170	1,567,970
Southern and Eastern Europe	883,950	846,080	842,270	805,630	778,100	742,700
North Africa and the Middle East	215,360	241,370	295,800	355,250	428,790	483,020
South-East Asia	494,820	537,530	632,810	798,460	950,990	1,066,030
North-East Asia	272,100	318,590	453,340	637,790	875,660	1,013,490
Southern and Central Asia	159,300	200,060	311,050	572,000	857,110	1,146,730
Americas	168,020	178,740	212,280	260,260	322,830	366,450
Sub-Saharan Africa	119,070	154,590	219,900	306,040	364,550	398,420
Total overseas-born	**4,240,050**	**4,452,360**	**5,031,630**	**6,018,180**	**6,912,110**	**7,529,570**
Australian-born	**13,984,720**	**14,822,350**	**15,419,340**	**16,321,840**	**17,278,800**	**17,836,000**
Total Australian population	**18,224,770**	**19,274,710**	**20,450,970**	**22,340,020**	**24,190,910**	**25,365,570**
Ghanaian-born Australian population	1,680	2,250	3,150	4,440	6,300	7,320

Source: adapted from Australian Bureau of Statistics (ABS), 2020.

My own participant observation of Australian money transfer organizations show that migrants remit a considerable amount of money home. According to the Government of Australia (2015, p. 2), 'An estimated AUD 21 billion in remittances is sent from Australia a year globally, more than five times the amount of Australia's Official Development Assistance of AUD 4 billion (2015–16 estimates).' Australian authorities recognize that remittances from Australia are poverty-reducing, much like the international development agencies, such as the World Bank: 'Remittances ... are a proven way of sharing prosperity. Were it not for remittances, the share of the poor in the population would have been ... 5 percentage points higher in Ghana' (World Bank, 2019, p. 15). To amplify this effect, the Australian authorities have been committed to reducing the cost of money transfer. 'Since 2011, Australia's average cost of transferring remittances has fallen by 38% from 14.8 to 9.2%' (Government of Australia, 2015, p. 2). The Australian Government is committed to the G20 National Remittance Plan of reducing the cost of money transfer to 5% (Government of Australia, 2015, p. 2).

Exempting remittances from taxes, ensuring competitiveness among monetary transfer organizations, and leveraging the power of technology are the central pillars of the Australian National Remittance Plan. Like the Australian authorities, Australian researchers (e.g., Withers, 2019; Brickenstein, 2020) who have investigated remittances tend to focus on Asia and the Pacific, Australia's regional neighbours. Further, the emphasis tends to be on capital and labour interactions, analysed using a Marxist structuralist framework of dependency and underdevelopment as a challenge to the argument that remittances create a triple win: to the migrants, to the sending countries, and to the receiving countries. This literature, instead, argues that the benefits to migrants and to the sending countries are minuscule. Western countries are the real winners.

The approach in this chapter extends this body of work in three respects. First, the methodology centres on the transnational building process itself, so this work sheds greater light on questions of class across scales. Second, the GPE, institutional, and stratification economics (GIS) approach utilized in this chapter also helps to reveal racial, social, and spatial segregation, along with trying to untangle the complexities of rentierism. Third, the focus of the chapter is Africa, starting with Ghana as the point of departure. The overall argument is that the remittances are substantial; their effects are similarly substantial for the migrants, the receiving countries, and the sending countries. The social costs of this triple win, however, are disproportionately borne by migrants, particularly those of darker skin colour, and tenants, particularly blacks. The rents are significantly skewed in favour of landlords, some of whom also double as the owners of capital, disproportionately controlled by whites. Return becomes a complex process not only because of institutional forces that shape transnational family life, rules about obtaining real estate finance, and the norms of social services in Australia.

Table 9.2 Characteristics of respondents

	Percentage of respondents
a. Gender	
Male	70
Female	30
b. Age	
20–30	8
31–40	40
41–50	22
51–60	22
60+	8
c. Hometown in Ghana	
Kumasi	40
Accra	18
Cape Coast	4
Koforidua	8
Sekondi-Takoradi	4
Other	26
d. Length of stay in Australia	
1–5 years	8
6–10 years	22
11–15 years	18
16–20 years	30
20+ years	22

Source: Field Survey October 2008–February 2009.

The Research in Sydney

Between October 2008 and February 2009, I conducted interviews with Ghanaians living in Sydney. Because of the variations in working hours and different schedules of work by Ghanaians in Sydney, coupled with the fact that the research problem was one that required information from only those who are building, or have built, homes in Ghana, I had to rely on information provided by some executives of the Ghana Association of New South Wales on whom to contact and how. It turned out that the best approach was to visit Ghanaian churches, shops, markets, and restaurants. Doing so resulted in interviewing people with a diverse range of characteristics, as shown in Table 9.2.

During the month of December, the interviews were also carried out at Ghanaian Christmas parties. The rest of the interviews were carried out in Michael's, a Chinese and Malaysian restaurant in Redfern, Sydney, where some Ghanaian taxi drivers would meet for lunch or dinner. The interviews were structured and conducted face-to-face. Ten interviewees felt it would be more convenient to take the questionnaires home and return them later, mainly because of lack of time. They were all literate and could understand the questions. However, of these ten, only four returned the questionnaires. Added to forty-six questionnaires completed during face-to-face interviews, this gave a total of fifty responses.

At the time of my interviews, the sample constituted 3.33% of the population of Ghanaians in New South Wales (1,500), the state where Sydney is located. Of the respondents, 80% were between the ages of 31 and 40, which compares quite favourably with 36.9, which was the median age of Ghanaians in New South Wales as a whole. Men constituted 70% of the sample, creating a gender ratio of 233.33 men per every 100 women, which is bigger than the gender ratio of Ghanaians (114.5 men per every 100 women) in New South Wales. Although the sample is not fully representative, it is a useful starting point to understand housing-related remittances from Ghanaians in Australia. In this methodology, the overall gender question also probes the relationship between women and men as well as the intersectionality of gender, race, class, and migrant status (Manuh, 2021), not simply 'women'. This relationship has been the focus of much scrutiny in the courts of Ghana. According to the Supreme Court of Ghana (see, for example, *Boateng vs Serwah, Nyamekye, and Prempeh, Jnr.,* 2021; *Serwaa vs Gariba Hashimu and Issaka Hashimu,* 2021. For further discussion of the cases, see Manuh, 2021), women make significant contributions to the migrant house building process. They could do so indirectly, for example, by giving up their own work in order to support their husbands as homemakers *(Obeng vs Obeng,* 2015). Often, though, women make direct financial contributions to property development by husbands *(Boateng vs Serwah, Nyamekye, and Prempeh, Jnr.,* 2021). So, even when the names of wives are excluded from title deeds and other property documents, the courts in Ghana should presume that husbands hold resulting property from marriage in trust. The beneficial interest is for both wives and husbands *(Boateng vs Serwah, Nyamekye, and Prempeh, Jnr.,* 2021, p. 16). The question of relative contribution is a matter of detail to be deduced from, among others, the property development process. In order to discuss the findings of the study, the house construction process in Ghana was divided into three phases: land acquisition, the building process, and post-building phases (cf. Ratcliffe and Stubbs, 1996). Table 9.3 shows the interview questions.

As can be seen in Table 9.3, my interviews did not carefully engage the issue of return. So, between 2019 and 2021, I followed up on these interviews with specific interviewees. I was particularly interested in asking about what had happened during the so-called 'post-building phase'. More than ten years on, some

Table 9.3 Interview questions

Land acquisition
1. Where is your land/house located?
2. From whom did you purchase land?
3. Did you use an agent?
4. What problems did you encounter?
Housing finance
5. About how much in total have you spent on your house?
6. Approximately how many jobs have you had to keep building this house?
7. About what percentage of your income per month goes/went into this house?
8. How do/did you send this money home?
9. Were there any problems with any of the aspects of housing finance (see questions   5–9)?
Building process
10. Who is building the house on your behalf?
11. How long has the housing project taken/did it take?
12. Please explain your choice of developer.
13. Any problems encountered?
Post-building phase
14. Who is currently occupying it/will occupy it once it is finished?
15. Who manages the house (rent, repairs, etc.)?
16. Have you encountered any problems in managing your completed house?
17. Which was the most challenging of all the phases of the building of your house?

---

of the migrants I interviewed in 2009 have finished building. Others were in a position to pass comments about their parents, who have now finished building their houses in Ghana. Have they returned? Will they return? What is the meaning of return? These and other questions, such as what are the ramifications of remittances on migrants' ability to build or buy a house in Australia, were unstructured. Also, at a time of a pandemic with restrictions on travel to Australia and the imposition of strict curfews in the country, Facebook and telephone conversations became substitutes. I also did several hours of intensive interviews with one Ghanaian building professional in Ghana. In addition, I interviewed two Ghanaian women and one Ghanaian man who lived in Australia. My questions ranged from remittances, retirement, and home ownership in Sydney, or Australia more broadly, to their children and experiences with racism and building in Ghana. Because all of them but one (the building professional) were also involved in my earlier study, I could also ask them to reflect on their earlier answers.

In what follows, I analyse my findings. First, I consider the questions I asked in 2009, which are arranged under themes that require additional elaboration. Next, I analyse the complexities of return, drawing on my 2019–2021 unstructured interviews. Then, I conclude.

Land Acquisition Process

Building a house and/or starting a business in Ghana is the goal of most Ghanaians who migrate overseas (Mazzucato, 2005). Most do not migrate solely because they want to build a house in Ghana, but, more broadly, for a variety of reasons, including to improve their economic well-being and that of their families (Kabki et al., 2004). However, building a house is frequently an important aim (Henry and Mohan, 2003) and could be called the 'Ghanaian dream' (Yeboah, 2001, p. 82). Therefore, as with the Ghanaians living in London interviewed by Diko and Tipple (1992), the Ghanaians in Sydney start house building back home as soon as possible, beginning with the purchase of land.

Although most of the respondents come from Kumasi (see Table 9.3), the majority of them (52%) bought land in Accra, and the rest bought land in Kumasi (26%) and other urban areas (22%). This pattern was also observed by Diko and Tipple (1992). This may be the result of the 'capital city' bias, which makes Accra the location of many businesses, government offices, and good hotels, among others.

However, unlike Ghanaian migrants in London, who predominantly bought land from chiefs and family heads (Diko and Tipple, 1992), a majority of the Ghanaians in Sydney bought land from private individuals (46%), although stool lands[2] obtained from chiefs were also popular among them (34%). Only a few bought land from the state (8%) or inherited land (4%). A total of 74% of these migrants did not experience problems associated with land acquisition in Ghana, which may have been because they had been more vigilant (via their caretakers) or just lucky to have obtained land which was not subject to litigation. However, the rest (26%) were not as fortunate, as they ended up buying land which was the subject of litigation.

Housing Finance

The prices of houses in the most expensive communities in Accra ranged from US$30,000 to US$460,000 (Grant, 2009). Taking account of inflation, the average migrant spent approximately US$100,000 on a house. Some spent more (up to US$200,000) or less (as low as US$42,000), depending on location, type of finish and whether land was purchased or inherited. Put together, the

---

[2] [the stool/skin is] the seat of a chief of an indigenous state (sometimes of a head of family) which represents the source of authority of the chief (or head of family). It is a symbol of unity and its responsibilities devolve upon its living representative, the chief and his councillors. Land owned by such a state is referred to as stool land.

(Ministry of Lands and Forestry, 1999, p. 26)

total amount of money spent by migrants is in the region of US$10 million, approximately 0.1% of the total remittances from Ghanaians in Australia (US$7 billion) in 2007 (Sekyiamah, 2006), and about 0.2% of all remittances received through the banks in Ghana (US$6.4 billion) in 2007 (Dogbevi, 2009).

Unlike Ghanaians in London, who usually sent money on a regular basis (Diko and Tipple, 1992; see also Ehwi et al., 2021), remittances from the migrants in Sydney were largely irregular. Thus, there could be some months during which no money was sent at all. This erratic pattern was not because the migrants received irregular incomes, but mainly because of the fluctuations in the exchange rate and the timing of requests for money by the caretakers of the housing project. More money would be sent when the exchange rate was better. Some migrants had developed so much mastery of the relationship between the Ghanaian cedi and the Australian dollar that, at the time of the interview, they were known informally by names such as 'Finance Minister' and 'Finance Expert'. However, such financial rationality may be suspended when caretakers requested money for a housing project. In this case, money would be remitted regardless of how favourable or unfavourable the exchange rate was. This dynamism makes it rather more difficult to estimate how much the migrants remit on a regular basis.

However, a relatively clear pattern emerges regarding how many jobs they must have in order to remit money. It is not easy for the migrants to remit an average of approximately US$100,000 to build a house in Ghana when the average Ghanaian migrant earned about US$454 a week and had to meet the high cost of living in Sydney. For this reason, 66% had to have two jobs to be able to make this investment. Of these, 26% had just one job, 4% had three jobs, and 4% had four or more jobs. In total, 48% of the interviewees contributed one-third (33.33%) of their monthly income to their houses, 26% invested half of their monthly income to build at home, and the remaining 26% (usually those with more stable jobs or financially supported by their spouses) committed one-quarter of their monthly incomes (of between US$1,000 and US$166,416) to their houses in Ghana.

Unlike Ghanaians in the UK (Diko and Tipple, 1992) and the Netherlands (Mazzucato, 2006a, 2006b), who mostly financed their houses by sending money through other Ghanaians going to Ghana[3], nearly all of the Ghanaians in Sydney used money transfer (88%) or banks (8%) to send money for the housing project. Only 4% relied on intermediaries, who were sometimes accused of diverting funds. The most popular money transfer was Ria Financial Services Ltd., which, according to the interviewees, had lower charges. To remit US$87, Western Union Money Transfer charged US$19[4] and the Commonwealth Bank of Australia charged US$28, whereas Ria Financial Services Ltd. charged

---

[3] It seems that, more recently, Ghanaians in the UK also increasingly rely on money transform systems (Ehwi et al., 2021), so the difference here might simply be temporal rather than spatial.
[4] Original measurement in Australian dollars (AU$22).

only US$5.20. This shift from global giant money transfer systems to relatively small ones provides an opportunity to analyse this system of finance in more detail.

All the respondents who used the formal modus operandi to remit money were satisfied with the system (74%). The only problem was occasional cases of misappropriation and embezzlement of funds when the money arrived in Ghana (26%). It could be said that, by remitting money more formally, the migrants in Sydney were saved the delays associated with the informal method of using intermediaries (see Diko and Tipple, 1992). It is also useful to consider the effect of the 2008 global economic crisis on how much money was remitted. The economic meltdown that began in September 2008 could have affected the migrants during the duration of the study (November–December 2008 and February 2009). However, an interview with officials at a Sydney agency of Ria Financial Services Ltd. revealed that remittances from Ghanaians during this period did not decrease in quantity, but rather increased.

This finding is consistent with the general trend in remittances to Ghana around the time. According to the Governor of the (Central) Bank of Ghana, the global economic downturn did not affect the inflow of remittances to Ghana. In fact, remittances increased by 26.8% between 2007 and 2009, and in January 2009, inward transfers amounted to US$660,500,000 compared to US$654,900,000 in January 2007 (Dogbevi, 2009).

The House-Building Process

Houses financed by the Sydney migrants are completed much more quickly than the houses built by Ghanaians in London. According to Diko and Tipple (1992), Ghanaian migrants in London took between five and seven years to finish their houses after about 25% of them suffered 'long delays and the consequent problem of inflation' (Diko and Tipple, 1992, p. 291). Because of the use of more formal sources to remit money, such delays were not usually suffered by the Sydney migrants; 48% finished their houses within three years, 34% finished within five years, and the rest (18%) completed their houses within six years.

To guard against the inflationary conditions in Ghana, all the migrants in Sydney built as they earned, rather than saving the money to build later. Money set aside for the house was usually—but not always—sent to a caretaker. As with the Ghanaians in London, these caretakers were mostly family members. However, unlike the caretakers for the houses by the Ghanaians in London, who had the power to act as '... the contractor on the building site; engaging building tradesmen, supervising their work, ordering materials, and dealing with the building authorities' (Diko and Tipple, 1992, p. 292), the caretakers for the houses of the Sydney migrants helped the migrant to find an 'all knowing contractor', who was then supervised by the caretaker (for a more detailed analysis of the activities of caretakers, see Poel, 2005).

These informal builders are called 'contractors' in Ghana because they sub-contract various parts of the building process to the various artisans, such as carpenters, electricians, and plumbers, as and when they are needed and serve as the migrants' representative on the building site. The 'contractor' is typically a mason and is often selected based on the recommendation of a family member or a friend who could vouch for the contractor's skill and service. None of the Ghanaians interviewed contracted a fully qualified estate developer. They gave two reasons why they preferred 'contractors' to estate developers: the estate developers were more expensive and their mode of operation required a large initial capital outlay for the housing project. However, the interviewees said they did not have lump sums committed to the housing project. The 'contractors', on the other hand, were cheaper and more convenient, since the workers (subcontractors) could go back to their 'private' work and reconvene when there was money. In addition, because of the camaraderie relationship between the 'contractors' and the Ghanaians in Sydney, the contractors were sometimes able to prefinance some building work, something estate developers were perceived not to do. Only 14% had problems with the 'contractors' and the problem could be anything from inflating cost estimates to failing to build to specification.

Those who did not engage contractors managed the building projects themselves. These migrants would work and accumulate much larger sums of money than those who engaged 'contractors'. When they have saved enough money, they would arrange with their employers in Sydney to take a short period of time off work, then travel to Ghana to supervise the building of their house themselves. Playing the role of 'owner contractor', they hire and supervise members of the building team themselves, along with contributing their labour on site as well.

These two building models need not be alternatives. Even for those who rely on contractors to do the hiring and supervision, whenever they are in Ghana to visit, to attend funerals, or to to fulfil other obligations, they temporarily work as 'contractors', too. Those who distrust the reliance on local contractors might rely more on themselves as contractors when they visit Ghana, but they need to deal with the problem of encroachment during the time when the building process stalls. Perhaps this risk, and the flexibility of sending money in bits rather than bulk, make hiring contractors or family members as contractors a more promising option. Even if that latter option carries risks of embezzlement and misappropriation, as my interviews show, such risks are quite low.

In general, among a small elite of middle- and high-class Ghanaians, there are other options open to them. Hiring a professional estate developer affiliated with the Ghana Real Estate Developers' Association is one option. Professional fees here could inflate building costs, as could professional bureaucracy, reflecting drawn-out processes of planning and building in Ghana (UN-HABITAT, 2011). Payment here takes the form of a series of lump sums made into formal bank accounts over a much shorter period of time. The building process can take a much shorter period of time, with much fewer risks, albeit at a much higher cost. On the other end of the professional spectrum are 'formal' building professionals, who act as contractors. Although the payments (also placed in formal accounts) required by such professionals are much less, and the risks a bit higher, the building takes much less time to be completed. Such building professionals do not necessarily comply with all formal requirements for building, but they are reliable professionals and, hence, appear to be quite attractive to middle-income Ghanaian migrants who can afford to remit larger lump sums regularly.

Post-Building Phase

Many studies (e.g., Berger, 2002; Grant, 2007, 2009; Wijburg et al., 2020) suggest some investment motive for houses built by migrants. However, consistent with Poel (2005), 86% of the interviewees did not rent out their houses upon completion. Neither did they leave the houses vacant on a speculative basis to earn unearned rent, contrary to findings of speculative behaviour by Arku (2009). The houses were mostly occupied by family members, who paid no rent. The few (14%) who rented out their houses faced the problem of mismanagement of rent or simply the failure of the tenants to keep the premises in a fair and tenantable state. This situation raises the question of owner occupation, especially when the migrants would wish to occupy their houses upon return. Diko and Tipple (1992) investigated this question and found that the migrants in London intended to return about a year after completion.

Unlike Diko and Tipple (1992), in my 2009 study, I did not investigate when or whether the migrants would return at all. That study assumed that the respondents were building because they would eventually relocate to Ghana. This assumption was confirmed by some respondents in random comments made during the interviews. However, towards the end of this study, one 'potential respondent' was encountered, 'potential' because he had started a building project in Ghana, but sold it midway through the project. The author was interested in knowing why he had changed his mind about building a house for his return home. He simply explained that he had sold his house because, upon introspection, he knew he would not return to Ghana to live in the house.

He said he was 'building just for the sake of prestige … just because everyone else was doing it. The people back home [Ghana] expect us to build when we travel overseas.' A previous study by Tipple and Willis (1992) throws some light on the issue of motivation. It revealed that people in Ghana build in urban areas for three main reasons: status/symbol of prestige, family obligations and security for later generations (dependants and successors), and rental income. The present study does not find evidence of rental income as a motive for building. However, following Tipple and Willis (1992), it might be concluded that the 'potential respondent' was right in claiming that houses built through the long-distance building process are mainly for prestige and security for dependants. However, fieldwork in Accra by Richard Grant (2009, p. 80) shows that 'Non-resident Ghanaians own 22% of new houses, returnees 25%, and others 9%.'

Then, I concluded that combining these insights, it may be that some of the respondents could build for the sake of prestige and the security of their dependants or because of family obligations, but there is also a frequent intention to return to occupy their houses. This notion of 'return' might either be temporary (e.g., living in Australia and going to Ghana for holidays) or permanent, that is returning to Ghana—probably, the latter. While most of the respondents have lived in Australia for more than ten years (see Table 9.3) and have formed new networks in Australia, the prospect of living in nursing homes after retirement, as is common in Western nations, may be difficult to contemplate by Ghanaian migrants because in Ghana the social network in terms of family support for elders is presumed to be strong. I revisit this assumption in the section on 'The Complexities of Returning Home'.

As such, I argued that these migrants may return to Ghana when they are nearing retirement. It seemed that this conclusion was founded at the time. Indeed, research that had been published around the time by Anarfi and Jagare (2005) showed that the less skilled a migrant was, the more likely they were to return home later in life. Yeboah (2001) has also suggested that people build in cities in Ghana in order to retire there. Such analysis may explain why only 2.5% of Ghanaians in Australia are aged sixty-five and over.[5]

According to one Ghanaian migrant in New York:

> When you look at it, it doesn't make sense. I'm not living there and with the kind of money I put in there, if I used it here I could have tripled the size of my store. But when I go to Ghana I have a place to live. I wouldn't like to bother my relatives or live in a hotel there. That would be a let down. After all those years here, I would go back to Ghana and it would be like being homeless. So with that kind of pride, anybody who makes a little money here will buy a house in Ghana.
>
> (Berger, 2002)

A related issue is whether the family members who helped to build and continue to manage these houses in Ghana would continue to live with the respondents

---

[5] This figure is taken from the 2006 census in Australia conducted by the Australian government and reported by the Department of Immigration and Citizenship, Australia in its publication, 'Community Information Summary: Ghana-Born'.

if they returned to Ghana. The respondents in the 2009 study were not asked this question. Diko and Tipple (1992) suggest that such 'caretakers' would eventually be allowed to live in much smaller detached houses on the same estate or compound, when the migrants returned to occupy their houses, perhaps out of gratitude to the 'caretakers', but also because of some extended familial pressure to accommodate such people (Henry and Mohan, 2003). Living in such houses, albeit less grand than the main house, is prestigious for the 'caretakers' because migrant houses are in the 'higher echelons of the current Ghanaian housing stock, both in the space provided for one household and the standards of finish'(Diko and Tipple, 1992, p. 292).

The houses built by migrants, therefore, stand in striking contrast to traditional family and compound houses, with the latter typified by characteristics such as high density and lack of privacy, since they tend to be occupied by many members of the extended family (Grant, 2009). I investigated these claims between 2019 and 2021, leading me to additional findings which I present later (see 'The Complexities of Returning Home'). For now, it is important to close the 2009 study with a discussion of how my interviewees, on reflection, saw the house-building process.

Reflections on the House-Building Process

When they were asked to reflect on the most challenging of the processes they had to endure to build a house in Ghana, 34% of the respondents felt the building process per se was the most stressful. This was because prices for building materials were often increased as a result of the high rate of inflation in Ghana. In addition, according to the interviewees, co-ordinating the process of building from abroad was difficult.

In total, 32% of respondents felt that the housing finance stage was the most challenging. According to them, there was no support by the Government of Ghana to help them build more quickly. While generic statements of intent about reducing the cost of remittances are in the *National Migration Policy for Ghana* (Government of Ghana, 2016, pp. 69–72), specifics are lacking and no reference is made to the house-building process. Also largely unavailable or inaccessible were private-sector loan schemes. Respondents said they had to hold down two or three jobs and work long hours in order to be able to pay their bills in Sydney and still send some money to Ghana to build at home. To quote one respondent, who had lived in Australia for twenty years, 'it is not easy to save the money from the wages to complete the house'. Another respondent lamented that he 'wanted to obtain finance from Ghana but the terms and rates were outside of our commitments [means]'.

Of the respondents, 26% complained about the multiple sale and purchase of land. This group had had bad experiences with the insecurity of tenure in the land market in Ghana. According to one respondent, 'it has been tough to get all the documentation on the lease prepared'. Another respondent, who had lived in Australia for 24 years complained that '... after purchased [sic] the land somebody was also claiming ownership ... the landowners are not trustworthy'. Only 8% of the respondents considered the post-building process to be the most problematic. This finding is significant because, although most of the completed houses were managed by family members or friends, namely non-professionals, they managed the completed houses to the satisfaction of the house builders.

The Complexities of Returning Home

Returning home is a function of multiple complexities. Migrant status is one of them. The effect of remittances on the long-term house acquisition in the destination settlement is a second. A third relates to class, networks, and broader questions of identity. Consider how undocumented migrants partake in this highly formalized process. Some anthropologists (see, for example, Meagher, 2010) suggest that these undocumented migrants have special arrangements, such as different informal systems to enable them to remit. This line of analysis has been developed by dualists within development economics. I have consistently argued that a more institutional and structuralist interpretation of informality is better borne out by the evidence (Obeng-Odoom, 2011a, 2013, 2016b, 2020b). Indeed, my own 2019–2021 interviews with Sydney migrants and observations show far more complexities that could enhance institutional and stratification economic analysis.

Usually, the undocumented migrant uses the personal information of friends or hosts to remit. The 'identity' of the friend might be used in one of three ways. First, the migrant could go with the friend to do the remitting. Second, the migrant could go to the friend's remitting shop and simply mention the name of the friend, which is already in the computerised system, and, hence, no additional identification is needed. Third, migrants could simply use their passports because only the biographical data are used for transfer, not the visa status. However, as many migrants do not want to draw attention to themselves, they rarely use their own data or documents. Employers of undocumented migrants may also help in sending money overseas. Generally, wives send remittances to Ghana through husbands when they are visiting Ghana (Manuh, 2021). Also, wives send remittances to husbands through relatives in highly informal processes. These practices, though not typically covered by documentation and receipts, are recognised by the Supreme Court of Ghana (see, for example, *Serwaa vs Hashimu and Hashimu,* 2021, p. 38; *Berima vs Nanor, Opoku, and Cator,* 2021 cited in Manuh, 2021).

How remittances are sent to Ghana has changed considerably over the years. In the very early days, Ghanaians would send money through friends who were returning home. For example, X amount of money to be given to Y in

Table 9.4 Housing tenure of Ghanaians and others in Australia, 2016

Tenure type	Born in Ghana	%	All overseas born	%	Australian born	%	Total	%
Owned	276	9.2	970,425	29.4	2,013,505	30.5	2,565,695	31.0
Mortgage	936	31.2	1,122,252	34.0	2,474,999	37.5	2,855,222	34.5
Rental	1,673	55.7	1,099,840	33.3	1,907,007	28.9	2,561,302	30.9
Other tenure type	11	0.4	25,380	0.8	59,681	0.9	78,994	1.0
Tenure type not stated	107	3.6	81,928	2.5	144,494	2.2	224,869	2.7
Median monthly mortgage repayment	2,167	–	1,950	–	1,742	–	1,755	–
Median weekly rent paid	360	–	370	–	330	–	335	–

Source: adapted from Australian Bureau of Statistics (ABS), 2016b.

Ghana, or money would be hidden in shoes, clothing, and other articles and an accompanying cassette would tell the intended recipient where the money was hidden.

So, there are elements of time, class, race/ethnicity, gender, and space in remitting. Migrant remittance behaviour exerts a significant toll on migrants' quality of living in the host countries. As systematic research (Kuuire et al., 2016) has shown, Ghanaian migrants take less rest, work longer days, do more jobs, and eat less nutritiously than the average migrant and Australian-born people. They live in poorer neighbourhoods, endure more overcrowding, and put themselves under considerably more stress to accomplish the tasks of building housing back in Ghana. The pressure on fellow Ghanaians, both in the host countries and in Ghana, as well as the anxieties of having no savings to rely on should accidents and emergencies occur are additional stresses. The lack of migrant home ownership in the host countries is also well known (Kuuire et al., 2016). In Australia, as Table 9.4 shows, only 9.2% of Ghanaians own their homes, a number significantly lower than the situation with all overseas-born migrants (29.4%) and Australian-born people (30.5%).

Three explanations tend to be offered for the low rate of migrant homeownership (e.g., Kuuire et al., 2016; Andersen, 2019; Wijburg et al., 2020; Ehwi et al., 2021). First, the long-distance building process is said to substantially reduce migrant resources such that migrants have no extra resources for obtaining homes. In this view, remitting is inversely related to quality of life at least after a certain point. In the UK, for instance, recent work (Ehwi et al., 2021) puts the point of dis-equilibrium of diminishing returns at 150 Pounds Sterling a month, which leads to 19.8 per cent decline in quality of living. A second, closely related reason is that migrants are, indeed, capitalists, or they become capitalists, driving the financial-ization of housing from afar and rationally deciding not to invest in housing in the Global North. After all, the returns in the Global South are much higher. A third set of reasons, according to existing research (e.g., Kuuire et al., 2016; Andersen, 2019; Wijburg et al., 2020), could be described as related to culture and human capital. They range from anything from religious objection to paying interest rates, lack of assimilation, to a lack of knowledge and experience with the mortgage market in Australia. Such reasons appear consistent with claims by Sydney-based mortgage and finance providers.

The sorting of housing into ethnic and non-ethnic enclaves and the creation of spatial segregation, on the other hand, can be explained by a set of different but interrelated factors. Hans Skifter Andersen names three:

> Deviant preferences for housing and neighbourhoods among eth-nic minorities that influence their choice of residence, 2. The strong influence of the locational preferences and moving behaviour among the native majority, who for different reasons often prefer to avoid living in neighbourhoods with ethnic minorities (*white flight and avoidance*), and 3. The options available for ethnic minorities on the housing markets, and the spatial disruption of different kinds of housing in cities.
>
> (Andersen, 2019, p. 4)

This line of analysis stresses individual and household choices, preferences, and behaviour as driving segregation. State intervention in housing markets wors-ens the problem because so-called public housing is located in such a way that it concentrates and isolates migrants. Accordingly, as research (Andersen, 2019, pp. 1–33) shows, free housing markets, assimilation, and education programmes are recommended as the most effective ways to address both social and spatial segregation.

These interpretations of the lack of home ownership among Ghanaian migrants and socio-spatial stratification are, however, partial and quite problematic. They reflect the symptoms of a much deeper structural problem of class and race. As Table 9.6 shows, many Ghanaians are from the lower classes, working far more hours than other migrants and Australian-born people. Table 9.6 shows that they earn more income, too.

Table 9.5 Conditions of work for Ghanaians and others in Australia, 2016

Hours worked in a week	Born in Ghana	%	All over-seas born	%	Australian born	%	Total	%
1–15	352	11.1	313,561	9.7	890,779	12.2	1,218,823	11.4
16–24	317	10.0	358,890	11.1	706,291	9.7	1,079,236	10.1
25–34	418	13.2	352,748	10.9	824,331	11.3	1,193,445	11.2
35–39	750	23.6	705,848	21.8	1,300,092	17.8	2,031,263	19.0
40 or more	1,143	36.0	1,346,985	41.6	3,191,643	43.7	4,591,801	43.0

Source: adapted from ABS, 2016b.

Table 9.6 Median Weekly Income of Ghanaians and others in Australia, 2016

Median weekly income	Born in Ghana	%	All over-seas born	%	Australian born	%	Total	%
Personal	733	–	615	–	688	–	662	–
Family	1,844	–	1,725	–	1,834	–	1,734	–
Household	1,671	–	1,562	–	1,539	–	1,438	–

Source: ABS, 2016b.

Nevertheless, their conditions tend to be worse than Australian-born workers in Australia. Ghanaian migrants are, in general, a *lower* class people, with much less access to quality work and considerably lower share of total assets. According to the 2016 Australian census (Australian Bureau of Statistics, 2016a, 2016b), 53.1% of Ghanaians in Australia worked full time, less than all overseas born (58%) and Australian-born people (57.5%). The rest can be classified as casual (part-time), away from work, or unemployed. As a community, the Ghanaians hardly have any savings for 'precautionary motive' which, according to J.M. Keynes (1953/1964, p. 170) is 'the desire for security as to the future cash equivalent of a certain proportion of total resources.' Many are temporary migrants, so they receive no state support. Even the 61.5% of Ghanaians who are citizens do not automatically have a much easier life. Consider the share of Ghanaians with mortgages: a mere 31.2%, again lower than other nationals (34.0%) and Australian-born people (37.5%), as Table 9.4 shows. Ghanaians are often forced to work in dirty, demeaning, and dangerous jobs. Racial discrimination is not only encountered in the banking or housing system (Galster et al., 2018), it is also found in the labour market. Ghanaians make much less professional progress than other groups, white workers, for example, often telling the supervisors among Ghanaian workers directly that they do not take orders from them. The competence of Ghanaian professionals tends to be doubted. Lack of acknowledgment is more common. Recurrent reference is made to their poor English or their accent to deny them recognition or promotion. They are excluded from professional networks and are treated as 'different' (Kwansah-Aidoo and Mapedzahama, 2018). Consequently, these interconnections between race and class stand in the way of getting formal mortgage facilities. When they are given mortgages, their repayments are higher, as they are considered a risk (see Matsebula and Yu, 2020; Table 9.4), a discriminatory banking practice widely deployed against black people around the world. Together with the rising property prices in Australia, itself a reflection of property speculation, building in Ghana becomes the only option.

Coupled with institutional discrimination against minorities in the rental markets in Sydney, Ghanaian migrants have to pay a high price for participating in a global economy of remittances. Without any sustained institutional support from the Australian state, migrants rely on their community for social protection. The conundrum is that this vibrant economy of remittances contributes to reducing the pressure on the state to provide social protection (Mina, 2019). So, part of the reasons for the failure of of the Ghanaian state is to provide affordable, enduring housing and other public and merit goods tends to be paradoxically the regime of remittances itself. So, in many cases, the Ghanaian state, relieved of the pressure that could have been brought to bear on it, instead encourages more remitting practices.

A major social problem, therefore, has become individualized. Left on their own, migrants tend to rely on each other. For instance, in the case of the Ghanaians in Sydney, they have pooled their resources to invest in a real estate complex called the Ghana House Trust. While innovative, it is a stretch to regard this facility as a panacea, especially when the trust has received less funding from its members than its full potential (Obeng-Odoom, 2012). This evidence shows that the process of preparing to return is complex. The evidence also raises questions about migration and remittances as a so-called spatial solution to a social problem.

Migrants are not the *homo economicus* that mainstream economists frame them uniformly to be. Characteristically, they are likely to work hard and think about their families, about their country of origin, about the host country, and about one another. Neither are migrants generally opportunists, as some anti-returnees argue, nor do they contribute to or exhibit hallmarks of possessive individualism, as recent scholarship (e.g., Bromley, 2016, 2019) suggests. Even though migrants live overseas, they make contributions back home. There are class spaces and time dimensions that need to be untangled here. While a small class of migrants can afford to buy property up front, most are not property investors.

Even those who buy housing in gated communities can hardly be regarded as a rentier class. My follow-up interviews of the Sydney migrants in 2020 show that, for those who have completed their housing, when they have rented them out, the rent is used by the caretakers to maintain the houses, not to enhance their standards of living in Sydney. Clearly, then, migrants are not really absentee owners who live off rent. They are not the ones primarily causing property prices in Ghana and Africa to increase more widely, although their activities sometimes do feed into this dynamic. Most build from equity, so they are not contributing to the speculative increases and, because their houses are often occupied by relatives and caretakers, they are not really simply speculating.

As fundamental to the discussion is the question of ageing and how it complicates 'return', remittances, and life in the migrants' original home in Ghana. In this respect, too, transnational family life cycle analysis is important (Bryceson, 2019). Migrants have long helped to provide the missing labour needed as Australians increasingly become an ageing people (Australian Institute of Health and Welfare, 2018). However, the demographics of migrants raises the question about their own retirement. The question is doubly important, first because of the growing ageing population of Australia and second because of the growing ageing migrant population in the country. These points have been made by the Australian Institute of Health and Welfare (2018). 'In 2016', notes the Australian Institute of Healthcare and Welfare (2018, n.p.), 'just over 3 in 10 (33%) people aged 65 and over were born overseas, up from 25% in 1981.' Table 9.7 summarizes the various theoretical positions about 'return'.

Neoclassical economics contends that return is definite. With a decline in wage income, living in the country of origin is more rational. Even if migrants receive their pension in the destination country, it is much more rational to definitely return because the value of this money is increased in the point of origin. For this reason, too, remittances are theorized to cease, while the quality of life back in the country of origin is dramatically enhanced, partly because of the investments made in physical capital, partly because of the value of the pension, and partly

Table 9.7 The meaning of return in diverse schools of economic thought

	Neoclassical	NELM	Structuralist	Institutional
Return	Definite return	Depends on household conditions	No return	Circular migration
Remittance	Ceases	Can cease	Continues ad infinitum	Transforms
Origin life	Wealthy life	N/A or wealthy life	Stronger class position	Complex life of class improvement and alienation

Source: adapted from Hunter (2018).

because after accumulating so much human capital, migrants would be in strong demand in their home country. This train of thought feeds into the perception of higher quality living or earnings in the country of origin.

New institutional economics or the new economics of labour migration is rather different. From this perspective, family members composed of migrants who make a new home in the destination countries find it difficult to return to their home country. Indeed, for those migrants who receive permanent residency status to enable them to keep living in the destination country, return is not anticipated. Similar comments apply to migrants with homes in the country of destination. Therefore, compelling ties prevent return. Remittances will accordingly cease when all members of the household move in to live with the migrants. Life back in the origin country is not anticipated much but, if a return is made, then, like neoclassical economics, it is assumed that the lives of returnees will be much better.

Structuralism takes a rather rigid position. No permanent return is envisaged because the structures of capitalism force migrants to continue a cycle of living precariously. Remittances continue, as more remittances create more dependency. If the migrants are ever to return home, however, their class position is assumed to have been enhanced. After all, they were also the dominant class that migrated. Years away and the mechanism of remittances only strengthens class position.

None of these positions, however, reflects the reality of Ghanaian migrants fully. Nor do these positions reflect the research that has been done on migrants from other African countries. Demographic changes are important. Whether these Ghanaians have married Australians or other nationals, whether they have Australian-born children, and in what ways their Australian-born grandchildren are close to them are all important. So is their class. Ghanaians who are professionals develop life-long professional attachments and friendships, alumni connections, and networks which make Australia home, too. Ghanaian professionals—including researchers—working with black Australians appear particularly connected to Australia, in spite of ongoing challenges with black, but particularly white, Australian society.

In this sense, it is not so much the remoteness of Australia or the great distance of Ghana from Australia that forges the binding connections that obviate 'return', but the possible connection to networks. For non-professionals, such class connections and formations do not necessarily exist. So, from a class perspective, they are more likely to return on completion of their housing projects. Yet, even for them, other institutions can make their experiences non-conforming to existing theoretical positions.

Consider the strong pan-African community that exists in Australia, to which many Ghanaians fondly contribute and belong. Historically, Ghanaians have intermarried black Australians, strongly contributed to the black power movement in Australia, and strongly feel part of black Australia (Foley, 2001, Aboagye, 2018). The children resulting from such interactions—according to research by such offspring themselves (Aboagye, 2018)—do not only provide a static glue, but they also start a wider community, society-wide black community on their own, replicating and expanding what they saw while growing up with their black parents.

Institutions are, therefore, crucially important in explaining these complexities. With the Ghanaian migrants whom I interviewed, those who have retired are now involved in circular migration. They still go to Ghana, although many have the required residency permit to live in Australia permanently. Remittances change their form, but they continue. The migrants appear to have 'returned' to Ghana, but they are still 'away'. Migrant housing is evidence of returnees' presence in Ghana, even though they might go back to Australia to be with their children and grandchildren. Sometimes, a wife goes to Ghana to take care of migrant family investments, while her husband stays behind in Australia. The reverse is also common: the husband goes to Ghana to work on some investments, while his wife stays behind to work in Australia. Either way, the partners who go to Ghana do not live there permanently. They may well sometimes visit, and if children are taken with them to Ghana they normally return to Australia. However, whether 'return' is circular or permanent, the Supreme Court of Ghana has consistently recognised that transnational migrant families typically build a return plan around jointly or solely owned landed property (see, for example, *Boateng vs Phyllis Serwah, Nyamekye, and Prempeh, Jnr.*, 2021; *Serwaa vs Hashimu and Hashimu*, 2021). Partners may plan their return by building solely, jointly, or both (build their own housing and also contribute to housing by both partners). This plan seems quite sound because even if the marriage fails, the Supreme Court of Ghana has held that the contributions of both wives and husbands to the property are secure. So, when housing plans are executed this way, transnational migrants can return home.

A number of factors shape the form of return. For one thing, pension rules in Australia differ widely. Although state pensions for seniors are generally seen as universal, in practice, questions of access often determine the real state of affairs. The Australian Institute of Health and Welfare puts the case succinctly: 'Many overseas-born Australians face substantial barriers in accessing and engaging with the essential supports and services that contribute to good outcomes' (Australian Institute of Health and Welfare, 2018, n.p.). Even for those Ghanaian seniors who might be entitled to an age pension, the housing experience of such beneficiaries is sobering.

Granted an age pension amount of A$425 (individuals living alone) or A$642 (couples living together), Table 9.8 shows that the surplus living amount after the mean national weekly housing cost (a–d) is deducted is quite modest. In the case of mortgage owners, the cost of housing is so high and the age pension amount so low that, for individuals living alone, they have to find other sources of income to pay for housing. In other cases, notably instances of private rental housing, individuals living alone must live on A$26 per week.

Sociological research (Morris and Verdasco, 2020) shows that such people are particularly lonely, anxious, and depressed. Private renters and mortgage owners stress about their limited financial resources, which cut them off from opportunities for socializing, but they also feel depressed because of the insecurity of tenure and social isolation. Seniors who live in public housing are much better off. Even if, they too feel bored socially and spatially estranged from their friends and family because of the form and nature of public housing, they have much more surplus finance for living and socializing. They enjoy security of tenure and much more certainty of income. That public housing is limited to only 3% of the housing stock in Australia (Morris and Verdasco, 2020) suggests that looking elsewhere is a necessity, especially when it is carefully established (Herro et al., 2021), organisations of older persons in Australian and elsewhere in the world are so poorly organized, are divisive, focused entirely on the interests of dominant groups, and there are issues that are tangential to the deeper questions related to the rights of the elderly.

Hence, relocating to Ghana for a while is a possibility, but it is dependent on both how the elderly are treated in Ghana and on their return. In contrast to the assumption that the elderly are well cared for in Ghana (see my own analysis in the subsection on the 'Post-Building Phase'), recent research (Malmedal and Anyan, 2020) unearths widespread and systemic abuse of the elderly by people closest to them in Ghana. So, the issue of return is complex, in part shaped by schemes and regimes of 'return'. For example, programmes arranged by specific companies with different rules could shape alternative paths. These rules mould how long, when, and how some Ghanaian seniors 'return' to Ghana. For many other seniors, too, the

Table 9.8 Age pension and housing cost in Australia, 2017–2018

		A$	Individual (A$425)	Couple (A$642)
			Surplus living amount (A$)	
Mean national weekly housing cost for:			Individuals	Couples
(a)	Homeowners	53	372	589
(b)	Mortgage owners	484	−59	158
(c)	Public housing renters	158	267	484
(d)	Private housing renters	399	26	243

Source: author's estimates, based on Morris and Verdasco, 2020.

health provision in Australia is valuable, but they do not rely only on the Australian health system.

Even in Ghana, they also consult other health providers. Ultimately, the complexity of being both in Ghana and in Australia shows that social and health policies matter. Institutions of protection and support, both formal and informal, are of great value. These institutions include support for transport, such as reduced bus, train, and tram fares. Ghanaian conditions change, too. Deaths of relatives in Ghana, for example, could transform migrant ties. So could the relocation of migrant families to Australia to join migrants.

Structural elements are significant, but they are underpinned by institutions. This is not only the case in Australia, but elsewhere in locations popular for Ghanaians and other Africans. Consider the pension system in France, for example. While the country is facing a crisis of ageing population, its attempt to reform the pension system by increasing the pension age has made little progress. With one of the earliest retirement ages among industrialized countries, French seniors also enjoy one of the highest life expectancies in the Organisation for Economic Co-operation and Development (OECD). Retirees receive 61% of their gross earnings before retirement when they retire (cf. 83% in Italy and 38% in Germany). In France, 14% of the gross domestic product (GDP) is spent on pensions (cf. 16% in Italy and 10% in Germany), almost twice as high as the OECD average of 8%. The minimum retirement age was increased from sixty years to sixty-two years in 2010, but increasing this minimum retirement age further to sixty-four years (*The Economist*, 2019c, pp. 25–26) is causing what *The Economist* (2019c, p. 25) has called 'risking the rage of the aged'. But what *The Economist* leaves out is, perhaps, even more intriguing: the continuing contributions by aged African migrants to the vitality of French society, which continues a long history (for a discussion, see Obeng-Odoom, 2020b, pp. 165–170), in which African resources have shored up the good life for French people and French society.

Questions about retirement, return, and home, therefore, are socially constructed. Retirement is not just about a legal retirement age, for many work while still 'retired'. Return is not definite; it is, instead, a series of comings and goings. Nor is 'home' just one place. It is multiple; Ghanaian migrants develop multiple identities. All these flexibilities and uncertainties shape the process of return. In 2019–2021, when I followed up on those I interviewed in 2009, some had finished building. The caretaker had her own place throughout the process of building. The situation has remained the same, but the house itself has now been leased out at a peppercorn rent to church ministers, with the caretaker managing the rental housing, too. To this extent, Ghanaian migrants are rightly described by Mazzucato (2005) as 'transnational' for engaging simultaneously (or at different stages of their lives) in the economies of two or even more countries.

Other more recent studies (e.g., Burgess, 2019) also appear to support my data. Alistair Hunter's (2018) is, perhaps, the better known and is more directly relevant to the present discussion. His investigations of West and North African migrants who live in migrant worker hostels built by the French government in France have culminated in a highly recommended book, *Retirement Home? Ageing Migrant Workers in France and the Question of Return* (Hunter, 2018). Yet, there are other studies, too. Consider Lisa Åkesson and Maria Eriksson Baaz's *Africa's Return Migrants: The New Developers?* (2015). This book is principally devoted to analysing the idea that Africa can use the collective experiences of its migrants to enhance the continent's development and socio-economic transformation. The countries discussed in the book are the Democratic Republic of Congo (Chapter 2), Somalia (Chapter 3), Ghana (Chapter 4), Senegal (Chapter 5), Burundi (Chapter 6), South Sudan (Chapter 7), and Cape Verde (Chapter 8).

There are many reasons for the continuing emphasis on this notion of return migration for development. The economic crisis in Europe might shape decisions to migrate, but whether migration actually takes place is contingent on other, wider processes and institutions, while recent progress in Africa could attract the diaspora to return, but, again, institutions such as explicit programmes and laws about return play a role. A grand assumption in this process is that migrants possess what it takes for them to make an impact. A more fundamental issue is the assumption in the West and among Western policymakers that Africans who have been enlightened by their experiences in the West can carry that torch of enlightenment to the (still) 'Dark Continent'. While this is sometimes a guise for encouraging migrants to exit the West, this view is colonialism reincarnated, a subtle, but more toxic neocolonialism.

The fact that it is the basis of policy in many African countries (e.g., *National Migration Policy for Ghana*, Government of Ghana, 2016), regions (e.g., *ECOWAS Common Approach on Migration*, Economic Community of West African States Commission, 2008), and the continent as a whole *(Migration Policy Framework for Africa and Plan of Action, 2018–2030*, African Union (AU) Commission and AU Department of Social Affairs, 2018) is questionable. That this frame of thought conditions the actions of many return migrants, who see themselves as superior to their fellow country people when they return, shows the persistence of the neocolonial moment and the compartmentalized view that Frantz Fanon discusses in *The Wretched of the Earth* (1961/2004) or the colonial mentality that is carefully analysed in *Black Skin; White Masks* (1925/2008). It is particularly correct in the sense that the policy space for return targets Africans in the West, not those in other African countries.

Lisa Åkesson and Maria Eriksson Baaz's book, *Africa's Return Migrants: The New Developers?*, is critical in the sense that it seeks to problematize the idea that migrants are the new agents of development (Åkesson and Baaz, 2015, pp. 1–3).

Based on rich ethnographic data and longitudinal study, this book provides the real experiences of return migrants.

Many assumptions about the idea of return migrants as development agents are shown by the book to be flawed and, hence, inapplicable to the countries of return. For instance, many migrants will have worked in low-skilled jobs, for which the skills they acquired abroad are not needed in the country of origin and, in many cases, those return migrants that worked in professional areas have to learn that the home country has dramatically different rules of engagement. Even those return migrants who appreciate the different institutions in their home countries must learn that they need different social networks to be able to drive the ideas and skills they have acquired overseas. In fact, it is not always the case that those who stayed behind welcome or work well with professional returnees. Sometimes, too, the institutional challenges in the return country—problematic service provision (e.g., unreliable electricity), major bottlenecks, and infrastructure can stifle any transformative initiatives that a well-intentioned returnee may propose or undertake. Just as fundamentally, existing laws might prevent returnees from making civic contributions. The reasons for such exclusion usually relate to the question of allegiance, if the returnee is a dual citizen. While such returnees are, indeed, citizens of the country to which they return, the fact that they also took, or continue to hold the citizenship status of the other country where they lived could prevent them from holding certain sensitive positions in the country to which they return (see, for example, *Asare vs Attorney General*, 2011/2012; *Ankomah-Nimfah vs Quayson*, 2021; *Quayson vs Ankomah-Nimfah and the Electoral Commission*, 2021). Still, a few returnees become quite successful.

The point, then, is not that migrants cannot be part of a professional cadre to move a country forward, but actually doing so is contingent on a number of factors. Are the returnees persons with skills who worked in their field while overseas? What was their social class in the country of origin, for this is likely to have shaped the migration experience in the first place? Have the returnees built links in the country of return while in the diaspora? Are the returnees well versed in the changing political economy of the country of return and the local conditions, and how readily are local staff prepared to work with and share in their vision of transformation? A major contradiction, even if all the conditions are met, is that returnee professionals have the dual identity of being an outsider and considering themselves superior to the rest, hence re-establishing inequality and class structures that propelled the migration in the first place.

Åkesson's and Baaz's *Return Migrants* (2015), on the other hand, is centred more strongly on migrants. Three areas could have been better developed. First, certainly, its non-class analysis limits the ability of the contributors and editors to offer a systematic explanation of why some migrants continue to work in low-skilled jobs even when they are qualified. Indeed, second, the same analysis of social capital, or the lack of it in the return country, might be inflected to analyse migrant experiences in the host countries and the two experiences could be understood dialectically. Third, the idea of 'development' is not really taken seriously. The spatio-temporal meaning of development in the form of evolving in country and regional variations is not carefully analysed either, nor is the continuing emphasis on growth and its deleterious implications for equity (for a discussion, see Obeng-Odoom, 2015c). The book itself ends abruptly. There is an introduction to set the scene, but no conclusion to show how we might proceed in the future.

It is regrettable that the book focuses almost entirely on returnees from the West, ultimately leading to the neglect of the experiences of returnees from other African countries (see the chapter on migration to Kenya as an exception). More work is needed on such returnees disaggregated according to their various class positions. Western thought is still wedded to the idea that African migrants are all headed to Europe or, even if they are not doing so directly, they are only transiting in some African country or another. In fact, a special issue of *African Review of Economics and Finance* on 'temporary migration in the Global South' (Özkul & Obeng-Odoom, 2013) showed that much African migration is south–south. The failure to understand this leads the West to pressurize African leaders to tighten their borders, as was the case in Libya under Gaddafi (Bob-Milliar and Bob-Milliar, 2013). In turn, the contributions of these migrants are devalued and policy focus centres not on social protection for the precarious work conditions of some of the migrants, but on getting the migrants out of Europe.

Like the undervaluation of Africa-to-Australasia migration, all the books I have discussed in this section of the chapter founder in not relating their analysis back to the global economic system. The books succeed in considering the migration process as part of social processes of change, but they tend to isolate Africa from the economic engine of the global system. In *Africa in the World* (2014), New York University Professor of History, Frederick Cooper shows why it is crucial to consider the way in which one studies Africa. Africa must be studied as a major part of the story of capitalism. Moreover, it is not sufficient to study capitalism without paying serious attention to how Africa experienced it, shaped it, and contributed to it as a world system. Africa has been central to the development of global capitalism and its story cannot be fully told without adopting this kind of focus, migration and return being a major point of departure.

Conclusions and Policy Implications

Remittances cannot provide a solution to the housing problem. Housing-related remittances do not guarantee fixed 'return' either. Return, even if it means circular migration, instead of the neoclassical dualist notion of 'remain-or-return', is made doubly difficult when rent which is socially created by migrants and others is privately appropriated, both in the origin and the destination of migrants. In this sense, migration is not at all a spatial fix to a social problem.

Four additional insights can be drawn from this chapter. First, Ghanaian migrants in Australia build houses for residential reasons, not for investment. Second, the formal medium for remitting money through money transfer schemes (not traditional banks) has helped to prevent the delays and despairs that informal transfers often involve (as noted by Diko and Tipple, 1992). However, the more crucial point is that the migrants' use of formal transfers might be because they are reliable. While the transaction costs seem quite high, the opportunity cost of transfer is higher. Still, informal remittances are not entirely eliminated from the process. Some migrants still rely on certain informal social relations to remit money formally. Third, migrants do not want credit per se. The reference to credit is a preference for expedited processes of building to escape the problems of inflation. Fourth, it follows that the housing problem in Ghana can be linked to the private appropriation of socially created rent, a dynamic worsened by the prevalence of certain institutions. Therefore, providing well-paid and sustainable jobs—through which people can save and still have a decent life without debt—can only be a partial solution.

Migrating to a more affluent nation and, hence, becoming relatively rich enables a person to complete a house more quickly, in between five and seven years in the case of London-based Ghanaians (Diko and Tipple, 1992) or, as my study has shown in the case of Ghanaian migrants in Sydney, between three and six years. These findings have implications for the current supply-side housing policy of liberalization that ignores the direct empowerment of people and the land question.

How can a low-income group, made up of a huge number of people in Ghana, buy the expensive houses supplied by the private sector? The successful experience of these migrants suggests that the housing problem is only a symptom of more structural causes, such as no or low-paid work in Ghana. Housing problems, inequality, and poverty are mutually reinforcing, and the experience of migrants suggests that it is time for a radical change from supply-side, the demand-side housing policies, and the land question. As such, poverty reduction strategies, such as provision of sustainable jobs and the redistribution of wealth, must be made an integral part of housing policy.

As far as inflation is concerned, policies could directly tackle both supply- and demand-induced inflation, rather than trying to suppress their characteristics by providing housing credit. Unfortunately, the current land title registration regime is more preoccupied with issuing title certificates, which invariably provide little or no security (Abdulai, 2006; Obeng-Odoom, 2020b). Registration creates more problems than it addresses.

Seeking the institutionalisation of the 'single tax' is a long-term, more fundamental alternative. This alternative is much deeper than the legal pursuit of the 'right to housing'. This 'single tax' comes in three forms: first, the right to the fruits of one's labour; second, the common rights to socially created rents which, in Georgist political economy, can only be put to public and common uses; and third, and the most fundamental of these rights, the equal right to land.

To guarantee the right to land, Henry George taught that public debt, obtained under the usurious and unscrupulous conditions offered by lenders and securitized by land, should be repudiated. Thus, he provided early insights into what contemporary debates refer to as odious debt (Ndikumana and Boyce, 2011). Hence, taking inspiration from Thomas Jefferson, George noted that 'one generation should not hold itself bound by the laws or the debts of its predecessors ... measures which would give practical effect to this principle will appear the more salutary the more they are considered' (George, 1883/1966, p. 167). Clearly, controlling the value of land makes the wages of the labourer hostage to the wishes of landlords because land rent reduces the size of wages. Incentives for hard work can be destroyed in this process too. War, hunger, disease, crime, and grime stem from the drive to control land. Finally, the power of rent, or the power of landlords to extract rent, makes them masters over the poor, indeed over all. Economic interests would appear to underpin the problem of persistent racism in Australian society, so fixing attitudes cannot address the structural racism faced by non-White migrants. But a single tax alone might not go far enough even when implemented at all scales in the migration process. Perhaps, the distribution of the socially created rents could be done in such a way as to give migrants an equal playing field.

From this diagnosis, housing problems can be addressed in another way. By guaranteeing that the fruits of labour are not taxed or taken away by capitalists; and by taxing land rents or land value, the situation can be addressed. So, What is socially created should be returned to the public, and these returns should be put to public purposes. In this way, the problem of reproducing inequality is confronted, and existing and intergeneration poverty, inequality, and uncertainty can be addressed, too. Beyond offering analysis and policy solutions for present problems, these lines of analyses could make the urban economy more prosperous. Through the provision of incentives for self-employment, quality wage employment, and comprehensive social protection programmes in which urban housing is framed as a merit good, this political economy provides avenues for a new research agenda.

Notes

1 Figures do not add up to 100% due to rounding up.
2 As will be seen later, this deficit or shortfall, worsened by other factors, leads to overcrowding in housing, homelessness, and general slum conditions.
3 Made up of self-employed artisans, who would work as general labourers (such as plumbers, carpenters, masons, tilers, and so on) or specialists like electricians.
4 That is, a low-income person (defined in the Ghana Living Standard Survey in 1999 as one who earns US$172 or 2,500,000 old Ghana cedis per year) needs to save all

that money for fifty-four years in order to buy a two-bedroomed house that sells for US$9226 or 134 million old Ghana cedis (Obeng-Odoom, 2008, p. 77).

5 According to UN-HABITAT, these are settlements with poor access to improved water, sanitation, security of tenure, structural quality of dwellings and sufficient living area (UN-HABITAT, 2003). This definition broadly corresponds to the definition of slums in the National Housing Strategy of Ghana (see Jack and Braimah, 2004, pp. 14–15). For that reason, housing studies in Ghana (e.g., Grant, 2009) adopt the UN-HABITAT definition and statistics.

6 For more information about this figure and other figures related to it, see the statistics page of the official website of the Ghana Statistical Service, www.statsghana.gov.gh/.

7. The data here is taken from the 2006 census in Australia conducted by the Australian government and reported by the Department of Immigration and Citizenship, Australia in its publication, 'Community Information Summary: Ghana-Born'.

8 The population of Ghana is 23,416,518.

9 At the time, 140 people lived in Australian Capital Territory, which, unlike other territories, is not a state in Australia.

10 Original measurement in Australian dollars (AU$520).

11 The good response rate in this study is fairly significant compared to a previous study during which Professor Richard Grant lamented his frustrations as follows:

> these are sensitive questions in any housing environment, and particularly so in Ghana because of cultural norms. 25% of respondents ... did not provide answers to the questions, and one-third of respondents were nonresponsive to the same questions. Non-respondents also included two heads of households who credited the Grace of God ... and a Foreign Aunty as a source of funds but would not elaborate ...
>
> (Grant, 2009, p. 83)

Perhaps, the fact that the current survey was conducted by a Ghanaian played a part in making the respondents feel more comfortable about taking part in the study. However, even here, copious assurances had to be given that respondents would not be identified and that the survey was for research—not tax—purposes.

12 These figures are deduced from the 2006 census in Australia conducted by the Australian government and reported by the Department of Immigration and Citizenship, Australia in its publication, 'Community Information Summary: Ghana-Born'.

13 Original measurement in Australian dollars (AU$100).

14 Reduced to US$24 (or the original amount, AU$28, in Australian dollars) for customers of the Commonwealth Bank.

15 Original measurement in Australian dollars (AU$6).

16 Particularly if it is democratically controlled.

10

The Promised Land

A View from Nowhere

Migration has become one of the central questions in political economy. What is often called 'the migration crisis' is challenging to analyse, let alone to resolve. This book set out to address the three most common questions about migration. First, what is the nature of global migration? Second, why does global migration occur? And third, what are the ramifications of migration for economy, society, and the environment?

Existing empirical approaches to addressing these questions are many, but what they have in common is that they are problematic. They range from neoclassical development economics and new institutional economics approaches to Marxian analyses, from conservative and liberal to humanistic approaches. Is the solution to turn to deontological methodologies that dismiss empirical approaches as consequentialist (see, e.g., Wellman and Cole, 2011; Carens, 2013; Bertram, 2018) and, hence, contend that answers need to be given in vacuo, without probing ecological, economic, and political-economic considerations as this book has done? This is the wrong question. 'The question' should be 'whether it is possible to exclude ... on these 'legitimate' grounds without relying on 'illegitimate' invidious distinctions' (Champlin and Knoeder, 2020, p. 38) on consequentialist terrain. So, these two philosophical approaches are, in essence, interlinked. The bases for their analyses are merely different parts of the same coin.

Both positions—consequentialism and deontologies—separate the indivisible interactions of ecology, economy, and society. Both underestimate the power of holistic social science research. As Jacobsen and Landau once pointed out, 'refugee studies, and humanitarian studies in general, reveal a paucity of good social science, rooted in a lack of rigorous conceptualization and research design, weak methods, and a general failure to address the ethical problems of researching vulnerable communities' (2003, p. 187). Indeed:

> much of the work on forced migration is weakened by the fact that key components of the research design and methodology are never revealed. Researchers are seldom told how many people were interviewed, who did the interviews, where the interviews took place, how the subjects were identified and selected and how translation or local security issues were handled.
>
> (Jacobsen and Landau, 2003, p. 186)

There is much to praise about existing consequentialist analysis, too, but the trilemma of how to make research change the lives of migrants, directly influence policy, and still be academically rigorous, continues to raise serious method-ological and ethical questions about many of the existing studies on migration policy (Jacobsen and Landau, 2003, p. 186). Historically, Marxist political econ-omy provided an excellent framework and basis to grapple dialectically with these challenges, but its typically narrow focus on labour migrants, among others, limits its analytical power.

A View from Somewhere

Theorizing about migration should not be from Thomas Nagel's *The View from Nowhere* (1986). Instead, it should, as Nagel (1986, p. 3) famously argued, 'combine the perspective of a particular person inside the world with an objective view of that same world'. Born in Ghana, where I grew up, I have also lived in England, the US, South Korea, France, Switzerland and Australia. Not only have I been to and stayed in other places, too, including the Middle East and South America, I have also worked in many of these countries. I now teach in Finland, from where I have written this book based on a Georgist (G), institutional (I), and stratification (S) political-economic analysis of the world. Fundamentally, I have tried to extend the theorizing of migration beyond (a) existing consequentialist approaches; (b) the view from nowhere; and (c) the individual schools in GIS.

Based on my more holistic approach, this book has provided new explanations of the forms, drivers, and consequences of global migration for society, economy, and nature. Migration is clearly a local process, an urban process, and a global process in which various types of migrants and migration processes transform along the way. Temporary migrants, like international students, become labour migrants. Refugees become international students. Regular and irregular statuses are interlinked, as are temporary and permanent and various notions of 'formal', 'informal', and 'return'. Still, some identities—migrant status, race, gender, and class, to name a few—remain largely persistent, even if they transform by in-termingling with others and various institutions in defining migrants and their relationships with hosts or local residents. These considerations are also impor-tant in addressing questions about why and how they migrate (see, for example, chapters 5, 7 and 8).

The book has also shown that in terms of consequences, migrants have con-tributed mightily to local vitality and global prosperity (see, for example, chapters 6, 7 and 8). Nevertheless, migrants generally tend to be at the bottom of the wellbeing ladder. They usually struggle, not win out—as is typically claimed by conservatives, neoliberals, and humanists. This struggle is quite different from what radicals contend it is (see, for example, chapters 5, 8 and 9). Some migrants are forced into degrading livelihoods that corrode the land (see, for example, chapter 4), but these practices have nothing to do with migration per se. They are the direct consequences of a rentier capitalism in which socially created rent is privately appropriated. If at all, in general, the actions of migrants who ensure local food sovereignty around the world (see, for example, chapters 4 and 6) suggest that migrants support processes of food self-sufficiency, sovereignty, and sustainability. Universal claims that migration harms the environment made by nativists and even progressives (e.g., Boulding, 1964; Meadows et al., 1972, 2004; Daly, 2019) are often based on overpopulation arising out of a certain consequentialism. In this view, socio-ecological problems arise from *growth*. Overpopulation, which, in turn, leads to more births is a practice that drives growth. The link to migration is not simply that when there is a population explosion, people will be *pushed* to move. It is also that if more people are allowed to migrate, others would be incentivised to breed more. This view dovetails with the excessive economic growth critique: more people generate more economic activities and as there are limits to the carrying capacity of the earth, migration and population growth are pathways to environmental destruction.

But these arguments are fundamentally flawed (see, for example, chapter 2). What undermines ecological health is neither migration, over population, nor their interconnections. Rather, as I have demonstrated elsewhere (Obeng-Odoom, 2021a, 2021b) and discussed in chapters 3, land rent-based, long-term inequalities and social stratification generate the conditions that drive, produce, and reproduce socio-ecological crises. These same processes of private appropriation of socially created rent produce and reproduce the so-called global migration crises. So, migration crises, like socio-ecological crises, arise from the same ecological political-economic forces.

But these processes are also interlinked. How migrants are treated, where they work, and what rights they have cannot be delinked from their identities nor global inequalities. However, these forms and consequences are not fortuitous. Nor does the evidence show that migration in and of itself offers a 'spatial fix'. Institutions shape them all (see, for example, chapter 3). Formal rules about who can migrate, to where, when, and how are crucial, so are informal rules, norms, practices, and networks. They all mould the migration experience. Schools and what they transmit in the curricula, but also in the compounds and surrounds of the school, shape and reinforce identities (see, for example, chapters 6 and 8). So do housing, state policies about retirement, and the nature of work, in the local and national economies, if not in the global economy itself (see, for example, chapters 7 and 9).

Yet, as this book has shown, of all the institutions discussed here, land is the most important (see chapters 1–9). Land is critical in answering all three research questions, from the form and forces of migration to the consequences of migration. So, considering land rights as inherent to the global migration debate is critical. Doing so is only in terms of rural to urban migration, but in all forms of migration, across all scales and times. I have tried to illustrate these issues by demonstrating the practical consequences of taking away such rights to land and land rights throughout this book. Even the labour question is strongly linked to the land question (see, for example, chapters 4 and 7), as is the question of education and experience or what is problematically called 'human capital' (see, for example, chapter 8). In all these cases in which land is deemed central, we have also seen the nested relationships between labour and capital with respect to land. Thus, it can be said that land, labour, capital, and the state closely interact in creating and recreating the migration question. Addressing the migration question, must, accordingly be about resolving the land question and the institutions which produce and reproduce the land question.

A View from Everywhere

For this purpose, it is important to revisit the story in the preface of this book about how Landen became the Democratic Land. From this perspective, a major immediate step is to address both inequality and stratification centred on land. As a major impulse to migrate is *inherent* in private property-based capitalism, resisting to transform the remaining commons to commodities can be a key step at all scales for settlements of origin, transit, and destination. Some migrant activities already point in this direction, albeit in non-systematic ways (see, for example, chapter 5). Similarly, taxing the rent from existing value of enclosed land would make it possible to return socially created rent to the public, and rewarding labouring workers their surpluses would provide incentives and create some of the conditions for shared and sustainable prosperity (see, e.g., George, 1883/1981; Beck, 2012; Obeng-Odoom, 2017b), self-employment, and public employment. The resulting revenues from this commons-based economic model can be invested for collective socio-economic, public, and ecological purposes.

For migrants who are already settled, comprehensive and quality social protection and decent permanent employment in quality self-employment, in decent public service, and in various nourishing social sectors are needed. More fundamentally, this can help to prevent speculations-based crises that characterize the sites and systems of migration discussed in this book, whether internal migration, economic crises, the migrant town, education, or remittances and return.

Historical reparations would be pivotal. They are broad-ranging. They can be from the aggressors to the rest. Reparations from the nation states to people who have lost their homes and loved ones through war could be another. The lifting of sanctions, the resumption of the right to self-determination over decisions of the government and the economy, and the freedom of nations to protect their natural resources could be complementary. Using the resulting resources for the benefit of the common people are core elements that Keynes advocated and which are still valid in our time. But having said that, Keynesian reparations do not go far enough: rentiers must also pay reparations, as Thorstein Veblen (1920) taught. Rentiers must pay back the socially created rents they have privately pocketed, especially to minorities, as both Georgists and stratification economists (Darity and Mullen, 2020; Obeng-Odoom, 2021a) have argued. This commons-based strategy, then, could help to rebuild the whole world, to make the world more peaceful, more inclusive, cleaner, and greener.

These analyses prepare the grounds for additional investigations. What this final chapter has tried to do is not to address, but to illustrate the intra-connections, intersections, and interstices between socio-economic cycles, economic crises, resource grabs, and global migration.

To emphasise, I have argued that much of the crisis of migration—if it can so be called—can be seen as simultaneously local and global. Either way, migration can be understood as driven by the crisis of the commons, to wit, inequality, social stratification, and social problems arising from unequal access to land institutionalized in ways that further frustrate groups with minority identities.

The argument is not that all migration arises from the rules that institutionalise unequal access to land. Other inequality and social stratification producing institutions are crucially important, too. Yet, the evidence clearly shows that the myriad of social problems and policies driving the mass migration of people cannot be satisfactorily resolved or fully understood without addressing the class-based land question. There is clearly a *temporal* aspect to the role of land: the nature of the land question varies at different times. Unequal access to land may be the primary driver of migration, as dispossession was in colonial times, or it may be complementary to other social forces such as the rules about labour and capital, looking at how lack of land rights merge with other forces to shape, for instance, the *spatial* aspects of migration in terms of what it leads to and how.

If so, mere migration—whether it is of the conservative, neoliberal, or a humanistic hue (see, for example, chapters 1 and 2) —is neither a problem, nor a panacea. It is not migration that drives socio-ecological and political-economic problems, nor is it migration that will save the world. The case of opening borders is justified, but mainly on the grounds that the earth belongs to all. A borderless world is not a solution to world problems, especially when the destination settlements have similarly monopolistic—indeed oligopolistic—land ownership structures as many 'source' countries, counties, and cities. The conservative and nationalist stance is worse because erecting borders is another form of monopolizing the commons and land and, hence, is likely to intensify the inequality and social problems that underpin the global migration crisis.

Creating equal access to land in both origin and destination settlements is crucial. Granting social protection and permanent and citizenship status to migrants on grounds that we are *all*—regardless of identities—citizens of the earth is complementary. According migrants their contribution to common wealth is fundamental. A willing social state and similarly supportive institutions committed to inclusive cosmopolitan societies and reparations are fundamental, too. True economic freedom comes from deinstitutionalizing inequalities and social stratifications (among others, to nourish the earth), giving unto labour what belongs to labour, and commoning the land for ecology, economy, and society.

This much is pretty clear. A major contribution to how global migration is studied, the approach developed in this book trumps existing approaches, be they conservative, mainstream, humanist, or radical. Whether this approach displaces the existing order is, however, a different issue (see, for example, de Vroey, 1975; Reich, 1980; Chibber, 2013; Bromley, 2019; Stilwell, 2019). Karl Popper's (1959/2014) argument that theories rise and fall merely due to their scientific power is not only questionable but also misleading, as I show more systematically elsewhere (Obeng-Odoom, 2020b, 2021a). Thomas Kuhn's (1967) alternative explanation about the persistence of problematic theories even in the face of overwhelming evidence is more illuminating. In *Decolonizing Methodologies*, Linda Tuhiwai Smith (1999) shows that approaches to studying society, economy, and environment are shaped by particular interests and ideologies. Thus, the insistence of one approach over the other is neither random nor 'objective'. Certainly, Marxists, Ricardians, and Feminists have all pointed to these interested tendencies as obstacles to the progress of their theorising.

The approach I have canvassed in this book faces even more impediments. Historically, any approach that prioritises land, rent, and power has been targeted (see, for example, Haila, 2016, 2017). When that is done within the Black Radical Tradition (Robinson, 1983) as I have approached global migration with my GIS methodology, even so-called radicals have cringed at the resulting theoretical insights and political power, as the approach cuts both ways, not just orthodoxy, but also heterodoxy, and indeed radical thinking itself. 'Minority reports' are deemed powerless but paradoxically, as they speak truth to power, they cause foundations to quaver. Precisely because of that, as I have argued elsewhere (Obeng-Odoom, 2021c), obstacles are likely to be thrown into the spokes. Smokescreens will be raised. Caricature will surface and resurface. These will come from various quarters, covert and overt. Propertied interests are, indeed, omnipresent. They cut across the board, from capitalist interests, through humanist interests, to radical interests.

While these considerations often lead to a post-modern, post-truth exercise in which anything goes, a dystopian view of science and scholarship is clearly ineffective. It takes us nowhere, especially when it is evident that some theorists also change their minds. Others do not, but the rest may nuance their positions, both theoretically and politically. That is all the more reason why a dystopian view of science should not be taken. There are prospects for change, even if little. To this end, three sets of reflections and lessons are warranted. First, engaged theorising is fundamental. Abduction is key. Second, the purpose of theorising is not simply to comprehend or to contest the world, but also to change it, transforming its society and economy, but fundamentally the planet itself, the environment. That inevitably leads to the third and most fundamental lesson: studying global migration could be done in such a way that under all our reconstruction of theories is the land.

Bibliography

A Submission to a Committee. 2007. 'Submission to Residential Accommodation Issues Paper. Consumer Affairs', Victoria, 6 September 2007.

Abbey, B. 1994. 'Student Housing: A Retrospect and Some Prospects', *Journal of Tertiary Education Administration*, 16 (2), 195–204.

Abdul-Korah, G.B. 2006. '"Where Is Not Home?": Dagaaba Migrants in the Brong Ahafo Region, 1980 to the Present', *African Affairs*, 106 (422), 71–94.

Abdulai, R. T. 2006. "Is land title registration the answer to insecure and uncertain property rights in Sub-Saharan Africa?" *RICS Research paper series*, 6 (6), 1–27.

Aboagye, K. 2018. 'Australian Blackness, the African Diaspora and Afro/Indigenous Connections in the Global South', *Transition*, 126, 72–85.

Abreu, A. 2012. 'The New Economics of Neoclassicals Bearing Gifts', *Forum for Social Economics*, 41 (1), 46–67.

Abusah, S. 2004. *Access to Land for Housing Development: A Review of Land Title Registration in Accra, Ghana* (M.Sc. thesis). Department of Infrastructure, KTH Royal Institute of Technology, Stockholm.

Achenbach, R., Beek J., Kargia J.N., Mageza-Barthel R., and Schulze-Engler F., 2020, 'Afrasian Transformations: An Introduction', in *Afrasian Transformations: Transregional Perspectives on Development Cooperation, Social Mobility, and Cultural Change*, eds. R. Achenbach, J. Beek, J.N. Kargia, R. Mageza-Barthel, and F. Schulze-Engler. Leiden and Boston: Brill, pp. 1–20.

Adaawen, S. and Jørgensen, H.S. 2012. 'Eking Out a Living: The Livelihood Implications of Urban Space Regulation on Street Hawking in Accra, Ghana', *African Review of Economics and Finance*, 3 (2), 49–93.

Adams, T. 2007. 'The Development of International Education in Australia: A Framework for the Future', *Journal of Studies in International Education*, 11 (3 & 4), 410–420.

Adawen, S. and Owusu, B., 2013. 'North-South Migration and Remittances in Ghana', *African Review of Economics and Finance*, 5 (1), 29–45.

Adiku, G. A. 2022. Reverse Remittances in Obeng-Odoom F, ed., *Handbook on Alternative Global Development*. Cheltenham: Edward Elgar Publishing.

Addison, E. 2018. Address by the Governor of the Bank of Ghana, given at the Annual Dinner of the Chartered Institute of Bankers, Accra Marriot Hotel, 1 December.

Adomako, E.B. and Baffour, F.D. 2019. 'Suffering in the Hands of a Loved One: The Endemic to Intimate Partner Violence and Consequences on Migrant Female Head-Load Carriers in Ghana', *Journal of Interpersonal Violence*, 1–28, doi: 10.1177/0886260519888547.

African Union (AU) Commission and AU Department of Social Affairs, 2018, Migration Policy Framework for Africa and Plan of Action, 2018–2030, Addis Ababa, AU.

Afriyie K, Abass K, and Adjei P.O.-W. 2020. 'Urban Sprawl and Agricultural Livelihood Response in Peri-Urban Ghana', *International Journal of Urban Sustainable Development*, 12 (2), 202–218.

Afutu-Kotey, R.L., Gough, K.V., and Yankson, P.W.K. 2017. 'Transitions to Adulthood among Young Entrepreneurs in the Informal Mobile Telephony Sector in Accra, Ghana', *Geoforum 85* (October), 290–298.

Agarwal, S., Attah, M., Apt, N., Grieco, M., Kwakye, E., and Turner, J. 1997. 'Bearing the Weight : The Kayayoo, Ghana's Working Girl Child', *International Social Work*, *40* (3), 245–263.

Agyei, Y.A., Kumi, E., and Yeboah, T. 2016. 'Is Better To Be a *Kayayei* Than To Be Unemployed: Reflecting on the Role of Head Portering in Ghana's Informal Economy', *GeoJournal*, *81* (April), 293–318.

Agyeman, J. and Giacalone, S. (eds). 2020. *The Immigrant–Food Nexus: Borders, Labor, and Identity in North America*, Cambridge, MA: The MIT Press.

Aidoo, R. 2010. *China–Ghana Engagement: An Alternative Economic Liberalization in Sub-Saharan Africa* (Ph.D. dissertation). Miami University, Ohio, Oxford.

Akaabre, P.B., Poku-Boansi, M., and Adarkwa, K.K. 2018. 'The Growing Activities of Informal Rental Agents in the Urban Housing Market of Kumasi, Ghana', *Cities*, *83* (December), 34–43.

Åkesson, L. and Baaz, M.E. 2015. *Africa's Return Migrants: The New Developers?* London: Zed.

Akorsu, A.D. 2010. *Labour Standards Application in Ghana: Influences, Patterns and Solutions* (Ph.D. thesis). University of Manchester.

Akyeampong, E. 2011. 'Africa, the Arabian Gulf, and Asia: Changing Dynamics in Contemporary West Africa's Political Economy', *Journal of African Development*, *13* (1), 85–116.

Alatinga, K.A. 2019. 'Internal Migration, Socio-Economic Status and Remittances: Experiences of Migrant Adolescent Girl Head Porters in Ghana', *African Human Mobility Review*, *5* (3), 1717–1748.

Alden, C., and Large, D. 2018. 'Studying Africa and China', in *New directions in Africa-China studies*, eds. C. Alden and D. Large, London: Routledge. pp. 3–35.

Aleinikoff, T.A. and Klusmeyer, D, eds., 2000, *From Migrants to Citizens: Membership in a Changing World*. Washington, D.C: Carnegie Endowment for International Peace.

Amankwaa, E.F., Esson, J., and Gough, K. 2020. 'Geographies of Youth, Mobile Phones, and the Urban Hustle', *The Geographical Journal*, *186* (4), 362–374.

Amankwaa, E.F., Esson, J., Gough, K.F., 2020. 'Geographies of Youth, Mobile Phones, and the Urban Hustle', vol. 186, issue 4, pp. 362-374

Amantana, V. 2012. *A Sociological Study of Street Children in Ghana: Victims of Kinship Breakdown and Rural–Urban Migration*. Lewiston, ME: The Edwin Mellen Press.

Amin, S. 1977. *Imperialism and Unequal Development*. New York: Monthly Review Press.

Amoah, L.G.A. 2016. 'China, Architecture and Ghana's Spaces: Concrete Signs of a Soft Chinese Imperium?', *Journal of Asian and African Affairs*, *51* (2), 238–255.

Amoah, L.G.A. 2019. 'Six Decades of Ghanaian Statecraft and Asia Relations: Strategies, Strains and Successes', in *Politics, Governance, and Development in Ghana*, ed. J.R.A. Aryee. Lanham, MD: Lexington Books, pp. 147–164.

Amole, D. 2009. 'Residential Satisfaction in Students' Housing', *Journal of Environmental Psychology*, *29*, 76–85.

Ananat, E., Shihi, F., and Ross, L.S. 2018. 'Race-Specific Urban Wage Premia and the Black–White Wage Gap', *Journal of Urban Economics*, *108* (November), 141–153.

Anarfi, J. and Jagare, S. 2005. 'Towards the Sustainable Return of West African Transnational Migrants: What Are the Options?', paper presented at the Arusha Conference, New Frontiers of Social Policy, 12–15 December.

Anarfi, J., Kwankye, S., Ofuso-Mensah, A., and Tiemoko, R. 2003. 'Migration from and to Ghana: A Background Paper', Working paper C4 issued by the Development Research Centre on Migration, Globalisation and Poverty.

Ancharaz, V.D. 2011. 'China's Challenge to India's Economic Hegemony over Mauritius: A Tale of Two Giants and a Pigmy', *Journal of African Development*, 13 (2), 197–222.

Anderson, B. 2013. *Us and Them? The Dangerous Politics of Immigration Control*. Oxford: Oxford University Press.

Anderson, B. 2020. *The City in Transgression: Human Mobility and Resistance in the 21st Century*. London: Routledge.

Anderson, T. 2015. 'The Dirty War on Syria: Washington, Regime Change and Resistance', www.globalresearch.ca/the-dirty-war-on-syria-washington-supports-the-islamic-state-isis/5494957.

Anderson, T. 2016. *The Dirty War on Syria*. Canada: Global Research Publishers.

Anderson, T. 2017. 'The War in Syria and Europe's Refugee Crisis', in *Crossing Borders Conference Proceedings*, eds M. Nikolakaki, S. Georgoulas, and A. Grubacic. Lesvos: Cooperative Institute for Transnational Studies, pp. 5–37.

Andersen, H.S., 2019, *Ethnic Spatial Segregation in European Cities*. London: Routledge.

Anglicare Australia. 2017. *Anglicare Australia Rental Affordability Snapshot*, Canberra.

Ankomah-Nimfah vs Quayson, 2021, CRP/E/3/21, Dennis Law repository. https://www.dennislawgh.com/case-preview?dl_citation_no=[2021]DLHC10756&srb= (acccessed 8.09.2021).

Anyidoho, N.A. and Steel, W.F. 2016. 'Informal–Formal Linkages in Market and Street Trading in Accra', *African Review of Economics and Finance*, 8 (2), 171–200.

Appiah, K.A. 2020. 'The Importance of Elsewhere', *Foreign Affairs*, 98 (2), 20–26.

Arenas, A. 2021. 'Human Capital Portability and International Student Migration', *Journal of Economic Geography*, 21 (2), 195–229.

Arezki, R., Deininger, K., and Selod, H. 2015. 'What Drives the Global "Land Rush"?', *The World Bank Economic Review*, 29 (2), 207–233.

Arku, G. 2009. 'Housing policy changes in Ghana in the 1990s', *Housing Studies*, 24 (2), 261–272.

Arku, G., Luginaah, I., and Mkandawire, P. 2012. 'You Either Pay More Advance Rent or You Move Out: Landlords and Tenants Dilemma in the Low Housing Market in Accra, Ghana', *Urban Studies*, 49 (14), 3177–3193.

Armar-Klemesu, M. and Maxwell, D. 1999. 'Accra: Urban Agriculture as an Asset Strategy, Supplementing Income and Diets', in *Growing Cities, Growing Food: Urban Agriculture on the Policy Agenda: A Reader on Urban Agriculture*, eds N. Bakker, M. Dubbeling, S. Gündel, U. Sabel-Koschella, and H. de Zeeuw. Feldafing, Allemagne: DSE.

Arrighi, G. 2008. *Adam Smith in Beijing: Lineages of the Twenty-First Century*. London: Verso.

Arthur, J. 2014. *Class Formations and Inequality Structures in Contemporary African Migration*. London and New York: Lexington Books.

Aryeetey, E. and Ackah, C. 2009. The global credit crunch—implications for Ghana, in: Voices from the South, the Impact of the Financial Crisis on Developing Countries. Report compiled and analysed by the Globalisation Team at the Institute of Development Studies, pp. 29–30.

Asante, L.A. and Ehwi, R.J. 2020. 'Housing Transformation, Rent Gap and Gentrification in Ghana's Traditional Houses: Insight from Compound Houses in Bantama, Kumasi', *Housing Studies*, doi: 10.1080/02673037.2020.1823331.

Asante, L.A. and Helbrecht, I. 2020. 'Urban Regeneration and Politically Induced Displacement in a Secondary African City: A Case of the Kotokuraba Market Project, Cape Coast, Ghana', *Geoforum*, 115, 21–33.

Asare vs Attorney General (J1 / 6 / 2011) [2012] GHASC 31 (22 May 2012), Available via https://ghalii.org/gh/judgment/supreme-court/2012/31 (accessed 3.09.2021), Ghana Legal Information Institute (GhaLII) repository, Accra

Ashton, P. 2008. 'Suburban Sydney', *Sydney Journal*, *1* (3), 36–50.

Asiedu, A. and Agyei-Mensah, S. 2008. 'Traders on the Run: Activities of Street Vendors in the Accra Metropolitan Area, Ghana', *Norwegian Journal of Geography*, *62* (3), 191–202.

Attride-Stirling, J. 2001. 'Thematic Networks: An Analytic Tool for Qualitative Research', *Qualitative Research*, *1* (3), 385–405.

Auburn City Council. 2012. 'Economic Profile: Business Counts (Staff)—Auburn City', www.economicprofile.com.au.

Auburn City Council. 2013a. *Auburn Crime Prevention Plan, 2013–2016*. Auburn.

Auburn City Council. 2013b. 'Community Profile', http://profile.id.com.au/auburn.

Auburn City Council. 2015a. 'Community Profile, Auburn City: Birthplace—Auburn City', http://profile.id.com.au/auburn/birthplace.

Auburn City Council. 2015b. 'Community Profile, Auburn City: Populations, dwellings, and ethnicity—Auburn City', http://profile.id.com.au/auburn/population.

Auburn City Council. 2015c. 'Community Profile, Auburn City: Employment Status—Auburn City', http://profile.id.com.au/auburn/employment-status.

Auburn City Council. 2015d. 'Community Profile, Auburn City: Occupation of Employment—Auburn City', http://profile.id.com.au/auburn/occupations.

Auburn City Council. 2015e. 'Community Profile, Auburn City: Household Income Quartiles—Auburn City, http://profile.id.com.au/auburn/household-income-quartiles.

Auburn City Council. 2015f. 'Community Profile, Auburn City: Household Income Quartiles—Auburn City', http://profile.id.com.au/auburn/household-income-quartiles?WebID=210.

Auburn Review. 1988. 'Let Lidcombe Live Again!' *Auburn Review*, 20 July 1988.

Auburn Review. 2014. 'Hunt on for Local Work'. *Auburn Review*, 7 October 2014.

Aubry, C., J. Ramamonjisoab, M. H. Dabat, J. Rakotoarisoad, J. Rakotondraibee, J. Rabeharisoa. 2012. Urban agriculture and land use in cities: An approach with the multifunctionality and sustainability concepts in the case of Antananarivo (Madagascar). *Land Use Policy 29*: 429–439. DOI: 10.1016/j.landusepol.2011.08.009

AusAID. 2010. *Annual Scholarship Update 2010*. Canberra: Australian Government.

Austin, G. 2005. *Labour, Land and Capital in Ghana: From Slavery to Free Labour in Asante, 1807–1956*. New York: University of Rochester Press.

Austin, G. 2007. 'Labour and Land in Ghana, 1874–1939: A Shifting Ratio and an Institutional Revolution', *Australian Economic History Review, 47* (1), 95–120.

Australian Bureau of Statistics (ABS). 2016a. '2016 Census Report', Canberra, ABS, https://quickstats.censusdata.abs.gov.au/census_services/getproduct/census/2016/quickstat/SSC12316.

ABS. 2016b. '2016 Census QuickStats Country of Birth', Canberra, ABS, https://quickstats.censusdata.abs.gov.au/census_services/getproduct/census/2016/quickstat/9115_036.

ABS. 2020. 'Estimated Resident Population, Country of Birth—As at 30 June, 1996 to 2019', Canberra, ABS, www.abs.gov.au/AUSSTATS/abs@.nsf/DetailsPage/3412.02018-19?OpenDocument.

Australian Education International (AEI). 2010a. *International Students Survey*. Canberra: Australian Government.

AEI. 2010b. *International Graduate Outcomes and Employer Perceptions*. Canberra: Australian Government.

Australian Institute of Health and Welfare (AIHW). 2018. 'Older Australia at a Glance. Cat. No. AGE 87', Canberra: AIHW, www.aihw.gov.au/reports/older-people/older-australia-at-a-glance.

Awumbila, M. and Ardayfio-Schandorf, E. 2008. 'Gendered Poverty, Migration and Livelihood Strategies of Female Porters in Accra, Ghana', *Norwegian Journal of Geography*, *62* (3), 171–179.

Axelsson, L. 2012. Making Borders: Engaging the Threat of Chinese Textiles in Ghana (Ph.D. thesis). Stockholm University, Sweden, Stockholm Studies in Human Geography No. 22.

Ayers, A.J. 2010. 'Sudan's Uncivil War: "The Global–Historical Constitution of Political Violence"', *Review of African Political Economy*, *37* (124), 153–171.

Baada, M.J., Baruah, B., and Luginaah, I. 2019, '"What We Were Running from Is What We're Facing Again": Examining the Paradox of Migration as a Livelihood Improvement Strategy Among Migrant Women Farmers in the Brong-Ahafo Region of Ghana', *Migration and Development*, *8* (3), 448–471.

Baah-Boateng, W., Twum, E., and Baffour, P.T. 2019. '"Whom You Know" and Labour Market Outcomes: An Empirical Investigation in Ghana', *Ghanaian Journal of Economics*, *7* (1), 24–43.

Badev, A., Beck, T., Vado, L., and Walley, S. 2014. 'Housing Finance across Countries: New Data and Analysis', World Bank Policy Research Working Paper 6756.

Balce, J. 2015. 'The Land of Ozy and Lam', *Good Government: A Journal of Political, Social and Economic Comment*, October, *1029* (October), 7–9.

Ballerini, V. and Feldblum, M., 2021, 'Immigration Status and Postsecondary Opportunity: Barriers to Affordability, Access, and Success for Undocumented Students, and Policy Solutions', *American Journal of Economics and Sociology*, *80* (1), 161–186.

Bangura, Y. (ed.) 2006. *Ethnic Inequalities and Public Sector Governance*. New York/Geneva: UNRISD/Palgrave Macmillan.

Bangura, Y. and Stavenhagen, R. (eds). 2005. *Racism and Public Policy*. Geneva/New York: UNRISD/Palgrave Macmillan.

Bara, A., Mugano, G., and Roux, P.L. 2017. 'Spatial Externalities, Openness and Financial Development in the SADC', *African Review of Economics and Finance*, *9* (1), 245–271.

Battersby, J. and Watson, V. 2018. 'Improving Urban Food Security in African Cities: Critically Assessing the Role of Informal Retailers', in *Integrating Food into Urban Planning*, eds Y. Cabannes and C. Marocchino. London: UCL Press/Rome: FAO, pp. 186–208.

Bauder, H. 2017. 'Sanctuary Cities: Policies and Practices in International Perspective', *International Migration*, *55* (2), 174–187.

Baum, S. 2017. 'Student Debt: Rhetoric and Reality', *Forum for Social Economics*, *46* (2), 206–220.

Bayat, A. 2009. *Life as Politics: How Ordinary People Change the Middle East*. Stanford, CA: Stanford University Press.

Beasley B.A., 2019. 'The Strange Career of Donald Rumsfeld: Military Logistics and the Routes from Vietnam to Iraq', *Radical History Review*, *133* (Januray), 56–77.

Beck, J.H. 2012. 'Henry George and Immigration', *American Journal of Economics and Sociology*, *71* (4), 966–987.

Becker, G.S. 1962. 'Investment in Human Capital: A Theoretical Analysis', *Journal of Political Economy*, *70* (5), 9–49.

Becker, G.S. 1974. 'A Theory of Marriage', in *Economics of the Family: Marriage, Children, and Human Capital*, ed. T.W. Schultz. Chicago, IL: University of Chicago Press, pp. 299–351.

Bellwood-Howard, I., Kranjac-Berisavljevic, G., Nchanji, E., Shakya, M., and van Veen-huizen, R. 2018. *Participatory Planning for Food Production at City Scale: Experiences from a Stakeholder Dialogue Process in Tamale, Northern Ghana*. London: UCL Press/Rome: FAO, pp. 292–311.

Benjamin, Chris. 2007. 'The Relocation and Reinvention of Old Fadama', *The Statesman*, 15 January 2007.

Berg, L. and Farbenblum, B. 2019. 'Living Precariously: Understanding International Students' Housing Experiences in Australia', *MWJI* (4 December), https://papers.ssrn.com/sol3/papers.cfm?abstract_id=3550890.

Berger, J. 2002. 'American Dream Is a Ghana Home; Mark of Immigrant Success To the Folks Back in Accra', *The New York Times*, 21 August.

Bermudez, L.G., Sensoy Bahar, O., Dako-Gyeke, M., Boateng, A., Ibrahim, A., Ssewamala, F., and McKay, M. 2020. 'Understanding Migrant Child Labor within a Cumulative Risk Framework: The Case for Combined Interventions in Ghana', *International Social Work*, 63 (2), 147–163.

Berry, M. 2013. *The Affluent Society Revisited*. Oxford: Oxford University Press.

Bertini R. and Zouache A, 2021, 'Agricultural Land Issues in the Middle East and North Africa', *American Journal of Economics and Sociology*, 80 (2), 449–583.

Bertram, C. 2018. *Do States Have the Right to Exclude Immigrants?* Cambridge, UK: Polity Press.

Betts, A., Bloom, L., Kaplan, J., & Omata, N. 2016. *Refugee Economies: Forced Displacement and Development*. Oxford: Oxford University Press.

Betts, A. 2019. 'Nowhere To Go: How Governments in the Americas Are Bungling the Migration Crisis', *Foreign Affairs*, 98 (6), 122–133.

Betts, A., Bloom, L., Kaplan, J., and Omata, N. 2017. *Refugee Economies: Forced Displacement and Development*. Oxford: Oxford University Press.

Bezemer, D. and Hudson, M. 2016. 'Finance Is Not the Economy', *Progress*, Winter, 5–10, 27–32.

Bieler, A. and Lee, C.-Y. 2017. 'Chinese Labour in the Global Economy: An Introduction', in *Chinese Labour in the Global Economy: Capitalist Exploitation and Strategies of Resistance*, eds A. Bieler and C.-Y. Lee. London: Routledge, pp. 1–10.

Birrell, B. and Betts, K. 2018. *Australia's Higher Education Overseas Student Industry: In a Precarious State*. The Australian Population Research Institute, Middle Camberwell, Victoria 3124, Australia.

Blaauw, D, Pretorius, A, and Schenck, R, 2019, 'The Economics of Urban Waste Picking in Pretoria', *African Review of Economics and Finance*, 11 (2), 129–164.

Boakye-Boaten, Agya. 2008. 'Street Children: Experiences from the Streets of Accra', *Research Journal of International Studies 8* (November), 76–84.

Boateng vs Serwah and Others (J4/08/2020) [2021] GHASC 19 (14 April 2021), https://ghalii.org/gh/judgment/supreme-court/2021/19 (accessed on 4.10.2021).

Bob-Milliar, G.M and Bob-Milliar, G.K. 2013. 'The Politics of Trans-Saharan Transit Migration in the Maghreb: Ghanaian Migrants in Libya, c. 1980–2012', *African Review of Economics and Finance*, 5 (1), 60–73.

Bodomo, A.B. 2012. *Africans in China: A Socio-Cultural Study and Its Implications on Africa–China Relations*. New York: Cambria Press.

Bodomo, A.B. and Ma, G. 2010. 'From Guangzhou to Yiwu: Emerging Facets of the African Diaspora in China', *International Journal of African Renaissace Studies—Multi-, Inter- and Transdisciplinarity*, 5 (2), 283–289.

Bonizzi, B. 2013. 'Financialization in Developing and Emerging Countries: A Survey', *International Journal of Political Economy*, 42 (4), 83–107.

Book, J. 2021. 'Voting with Your Feet', American Institute for Economic Research, www.aier.org/article/voting-with-your-feet/.

Borjas, G. 1994. 'The Economics of Immigration', *Journal of Economic Literature*, 32 (4), 1667–1717.

Borjas, G. 2002. 'Rethinking Foreign Students', *National Review*, 17 June, pp. 38–41.

Borjas, G. 2007. 'Do Foreign Students Crowd Out Native Students from Graduate Programs?', in *Science and the University*, eds P.E. Stephan and R.G. Ehrenberg. Madison, WI: University of Wisconsin Press, pp. 134–149.

Borjas, G. 2009. 'Immigration in High-Skill Labor Markets: The Impact of Foreign Students on the Earnings of Doctorates', in *Science and Engineering Careers in the United States*, eds R.B. Freeman and D.L. Goroff. Chicago, IL: University of Chicago Press, pp. 131–161.

Borjas, G.J., Doran, K.B., and Shen, Y. 2018. 'Ethnic Complementarities after the Opening of China: How Chinese Graduate Students Affected the Productivity of Their Advisors', *Journal of Human Resources*, 53 (1), 1–31.

Botchwey, G., Crawford, G., Loubere, N., and Lu, J. 2019. 'South–South Irregular Migration: The Impacts of China's Informal Gold Rush in Ghana', *International Migration*, 57 (4), 310–328.

Boulder, K.E. 1964. *The Meaning of the Twentieth Century: The Good Transition*. New York: Harper & Row.

Boulding, K, 1964, *The Meaning of the Twentieth Century: The Greal Transition*. (World Perspectives Volume 34). New York: Harper & Row.

Bourdieu, P. 1988. *Homo Academicus*. London: Polity Press.

Bourdieu, P. 2005. *The Social Structures of the Economy*. London: Polity Press.

Bradley, D., Noonan, P., Nugent, H., and Scales, B. 2008. *Final Report: Review of Australian Higher Education*. Canberra: Australian Government.

Brautigam, D. 2009. *The Dragon's Gift: The Real Story of China in Africa*. Oxford: Oxford University Press.

Brautigam, D. 2015. *Will Africa Feed China?* Oxford: Oxford University Press.

Brautigam, D. 2019. 'Review of 'The Specter of Global China: Politics, Labor and Foreign Investment in Africa', *The China Quarterly, Cambridge*, 238 (June), 534–535.

Brennan, E.M. 1984. 'Irregular Migration: Policy Responses in Africa and Asia', *The International Migration Review*, 18, 409–425.

Brickenstein, C. 2020. 'Review of *Sri Lanka's Remittance Economy: A Multiscalar Analysis of Migration-Underdevelopment*', *Journal of Australian Political Economy*, 84 (Summer), 221–223.

Bridge, G. 2001. 'Estate Agents as Interpreters of Economic and Cultural Capital: The Gentrification Premium in the Sydney Housing Market', *International Journal of Urban and Regional Research*, 25 (1), 87–101.

Brisard, J-C., Dasquie, G., and Shashikumar, V.K. 2001. *Bin Laden: The Forbidden Truth*. Winnipeg: Peace Research.

Broderick E. and Co. 2017. *Cultural Renewal at University of Sydney Residential Colleges Report*. Sydney: Elizabeth Broderick & Co.

Bromley, D.W. 2016. 'The 2016 Veblen-Commons Award Recipient: Daniel W. Bromley: Institutional Economics', *Journal of Economic Issues, 50* (2), 309–325.

Bromley, D.W. 2019. *Possessive Individualism*. Oxford: Oxford University Press.

Bromley, D.W. and Anderson, G.D. 2012. *Vulnerable People, Vulnerable States: Redefining the Development Challenge*. London: Routledge.

Broomhill, R. 2008. 'Australian Economic Booms in Historical Pperspective', *Journal of Australian Political Economy, 61* (June), 12–29.

Brown v. Board of Education, 347 U.S. 483 (1954), Library of Congress, https://tile.loc.gov/storage-services/service/ll/usrep/usrep347/usrep347483/usrep347483.pdf (accessed 8.09.2021)

Brown, A., Lyons, M., and Dankoco, I. 2010. 'Street Traders and the Emerging Spaces for Urban Voice and Citizenship in African Cities', *Urban Studies, 47* (3), 666–683.

Brown, L.C. 1989. 'The Duke of Damthes: ASAD The Struggle for the Middle East by Patrick Seale with the Assistance of Maureen McConville', *Los Angeles Times*, 18 June.

Browne, I., Tigges, L., and Press, J. 2003. 'Inequality through labor markets, firms, and families: The intersection of gender and race-ethnicity across three cities', in A. O'Connor, C. Tilly, & L. Bobo, eds., *Urban Inequality: Evidence from Four Cities*. New York: The Russell Sage Foundation, pp. 372–406.

Browne, I, Reingold, B., and Kronberg, A. 2018. 'Race Relations, Black Elites and Immigration Politics: Conflict, Commonalities and Context', *Social Forces, 96* (4), 1691–1720.

Browne I and Sullivan A, 2022. 'Human Capital, Gender, and Intersectionality', in Obeng-Odoom F, ed, *Handbook on Alternative Global Development*. Cheltenham: Edward Elgar Publishing.

Bryceson D. and MacKinnon D. 2012. 'Eureka and Beyond: Mining's Impact on African Urbanisation', *Journal of Contemporary African Studies, 30* (4), 513–537.

Bryceson D.F, Jamal V, 2020, Farewell to Farms: De-Agrarianisation and Employment in Africa, Routledge, London.

Bryceson, D.F. 2019. 'Transnational Families Negotiating Migration and Care Life Cycles across Nation-State Borders', *Journal of Ethnic and Migration Studies, 45* (16), 3042–3064.

Bryceson, D.F. and Jamal, V. (eds). 2019. *Farewell to Farms: De-Agrarianisation and Employment in Africa*. London: Routledge.

Bryceson, D.F. and Mbara, T. 2003. 'Petrol Pumps and Economic Slumps: Rural–Urban Linkages in Zimbabwe's Globalisation Process', *Tijdschrift voor Economische en Sociale Geografie, 94* (3), 335–349.

Bryson, P.J. 2011. *The Economics of Henry George: History's Rehabilitation of America's Greatest Early Economist*. New York: Palgrave Macmillan.

Buchanan, J.M. 1993. *Property as a Guarantor of Liberty*. Cheltenham: Edward Elgar.

Buchanan, J.M. and Tullock, G. 1962. *The Calculus of Consent: Logical Foundations of Constitutional Democracy*. Ann Arbor, MI: University of Michigan Press.

Buckley, R. and Mathema, S. 2007. 'Is Accra a Superstar City?', Policy Research Working Paper 4453, The World Bank Finance Economics and Urban Department.

Burgess, G. 2019. *Refugees and the Promise of Asylum in Postwar France*. London: Palgrave Macmillan.

Burke, T. and Hulse, K. 2010. The Institutional Structure of Housing and the Sub-Prime Crisis: An Australian Case Study. *Housing Studies, 25* (6), 821–838.

Burnazoglu, M. 2020. 'Built-in Normativity in Tailoring Identity: The Case of the EU Skills Profile Tool for Integrating Refugees', *Journal of Economic Methodology, 27* (2), 117–129.

Burnazoglu, M. 2021, 'An Identity-Based Matching Theory Approach to Integration', *Forum for Social Economics, 50* (1), 108–123.

Burnley, I. 2006. 'Sydney's Changing Peoples: Local Expressions of Diversity and Difference', in *Talking about Sydney: Population, Community and Culture in Contemporary Sydney*, eds R. Freestone, B. Randolf, and C. Butler-Bowdon. Sydney: UNSW Press Ltd. and Historic Houses Trust, pp. 37–50.

Cabannes, Y. 2012. 'Financing Urban Agriculture'. *Environment and Urbanization, 24* (2), 665–683.

Cabannes, Y. and Marocchino, C. (eds). 2018. *Integrating Food into Urban Planning.* London: UCL Press/Rome: FAO.

Carnegie, G.D., Guthrie, J. and Martin-Sardesai, A. (2021), 'Public universities and impacts of COVID-19 in Australia: risk disclosures and organisational change', Accounting, Auditing & Accountability Journal, Vol. ahead-of-print No. ahead-of-print. https://doi.org/10.1108/AAAJ-09-2020-4906

Cobb, C, 2021, 'Foreword', *American Journal of Economics and Sociology, 80* (2), 279–289

Çaglar, A. and Schiller, N.G. 2018. *Migrants and City-Making: Dispossession, Displacement, and Urban Regeneration.* Durham and London: Duke University Press.

Cain, A. 2014. 'African Urban Fantasies: Past Lessons and Emerging Realities', *Environment & Urbanization, 26*, 561–567.

Calderon, A. 2020. 'What Will Follow the International Student Boom? Future Directions for Australian Higher Education', *Australian Universities' Review, 62* (1), 18–26.

Caldwell, J. 1969. *African Rural–Urban Migration: The Movement to Ghana's Towns.* Canberra: Australian National University Press.

Carens, J. 2013. *The Ethics of Immigration.* New York: Oxford University Press.

Carpi, E. and Boano, C. 2018. 'Border Towns: Humanitarian Assistance in Peri-Urban Areas', *Humanitarian Exchange, 71* (March), 39–41.

Carpi, E. and Glioti, A. 2018. 'Toward an Alternative "Time of the Revolution"? Beyond State Contestation in the Struggle for a New Syrian Everyday', *Middle East Critique, 27* (3), 231–246.

Carrington, R., Meek, L., and Wood, F. 2007. 'The Role of Further Government Intervention in Australian International Education', *Higher Education, 53*, 561–577.

Carson, T. 2010. 'Overcoming Student Hardship at Swinburne University, Australia: An Insight into the Impact of Equity Scholarships on Financially Disadvantaged University Students', *Widening Participation and Lifelong Learning, 12* (12), 36–59.

Cashmore, C. 2017. 'Speculative Vacancies in Melbourne: 2015 Report', *Progress, 116* (Summer), 6–12.

Castles, S. 1987. 'Multiculturalism', Occasional Working Paper 4, Centre for Multicultural Studies, University of Wollongong, 30, https://ro.uow.edu.au/cmsocpapers/4.

Castles, S. 2008 International migration at the beginning of the twenty- first century: Global trends and issues. *International Social Science Journal, 52* (165), 269–281.

Castles, S. 2011. 'Migration, Crisis and the Global Labour Market', *Globalizations, 8* (3), 311–324.

Castles, S. 2012. 'Migration, Crisis, and the Global Labour Market', in *Migration, Work and Citizenship in the New Global Order*, eds R. Munck, C.U. Schierup, and R.D. Wise. New York: Routledge, pp. 63–76.

Castles, S. 2015. 'Migration, Precarious Work, and Rights: Historical and Current Perspectives', in *Migration, Precarity, and Global Governance: Challenges and Opportunities for Labour*, eds C.-U. Schierup, R. Munck, B. Likic-Brboric, and A. Neegaard. Oxford: Oxford University Press, pp. 46–67.

Castles, S. 2017. *Migration, Citizenship and Identity: Selected Essays*. Cheltenham: Edward Elgar Publishing.

Castles, S. and Miller, M. 2011. *The Age of Migration: International Population Movements in the Modern World*. Nagoya: Nagoya University Press.

Castles, S., Arias Cubas, M., Kim, C. and Özkul, D. 2012. 'Irregular Migration: Causes, Patterns, and Strategies', in *Global Perspectives on Migration and Development: GFMD Puerto Vallarta and Beyond*, ed. I. Omelaniuk. Dordrecht: Springer Science+Business Media, pp. 117–152.

Castles, S., De Haas H., and Miller, M. 2014. *The Age of Migration: International Population Movements in the Modern World*. Fifth edition. New York: Guilford Press.

Catholic Action for Street Children. 2010. 'Statistics', www.casghana.com/street_statistics.php.

Champlin, D.P. and Knoedler J.T. 2020. 'Dualistic Discourse and Immigration Policy', *Journal of Economic Issues, LIV* (1), 38–53.

Chandra, Ramesh (2021). Allyn Young on Henry George and the Single Tax, *Review of Political Economy*, DOI: 10.1080/09538259.2021.1920715

Chang, H.J. 2015. 'Is Industrial Policy Necessary and Feasible in Africa? Theoretical Considerations and Historical Lessons', in *Industrial Policy and Economic Transformation in Africa*, eds A. Noman and J.E. Stiglitz. New York: Columbia University Press, pp. 30–52.

Chang, L. 2008. *Factory Girls*. New York: Spiegel and Grau.

Chan-Hoong, L. and Soon, D. 2011. 'A Study on Emigration Attitudes of Young Singaporeans (2010)', IPS Working Paper No. 19.

Chasse, J.D. 2017. *A Worker's Economist: John R. Commons and His Legacy from Progressivism to the War on Poverty*. London: Routledge.

Chen, Y. 2019. 'The Myth of *Hukou*: Re-Examining *Hukou*'s Implications for China's Development Model', *Review of Radical Political Economics, 51* (2), 282–297.

Chen, Y.-W. and Duggan, N. 2016. 'Soft Power and Tourism: A Study of Chinese Outbou'd Tourism to Africa', *Journal of China and International Relations, 4* (1), 45–66

Chen, Y. 2018. 'The Myth of Hukou: Re-examining Hukou's Implications for China's Development Model', *Review of Radical Political Economics, 51* (2), 282–297

Cheru, F. and Calais, M. 2010. 'Countering "New Imperialisms": What Role for the New Partnership for Africa's Development?', in *The Rise of China and India in Africa*, eds F. Cheru and C. Obi. London: Zed, pp. 221–237.

Cheru, F. and Obi, C. 2010. 'Introduction—Africa in the Twenty-First Century: Strategic and Development Challenges', in *The Rise of China and India in Africa*, eds F. Cheru and C. Obi. London: Zed, pp. 1–9.

CHF International. 2004. *Strategic Assessment of the Affordable Housing Sector in Ghana*. Accra: CHF International.

Chibber, V. 2013. *Postcolonial Theory and the Specter of Capital*, London: Verso.

Chigudu, D. 2019. Demystifying the Root Causes of Conflict in Old "Greater" Sudan: Ethnicity and Tribalism? *Journal of Developing Societies, 35* (2), 303–318.

Chowdhury, K. 2017. '(En)countering the Refugee: Capital, Oscar Martinez's *The Beast*, and the "Problem" of the Surplus Population', *Postcolonial Text, 12* (3 and 4), 1–20.

Christoforou, A. 2018. 'Special Issue: Alternative Research Methods for Social Economists: Engaging Pierre Bourdieu's Methdology', *Forum for Social Economics, 47* (3-4), 278–287.

Chung, P. 2019. 'From Korea to Vietnam: Local Labor, Multinational Capital, and the Evolution of US Military Logistics, 1950–97', *Radical History Review*, *133* (Januray), 31–55.

Cissé, D. 2013. 'South–South Migration and Sino-African Small Traders: A Comparative Study of Chinese in Senegal and Africans in China', *African Review of Economics and Finance*, *5* (1), 21–35.

Cissé, D. 2015. 'African Traders in Yiwu: Their Trade Networks and Their Role in the Distribution of "Made in China" Products in Africa', *Journal of Pan-African Studies*, *7* (10), 44–64.

City of Sydney. 2011. Education Sydney. City of Sydney.

Clausing, K. 2019a. *Open: The Progressive Case for Free Trade, Immigration, and Global Capital*. Cambridge, MA: Harvard University Press.

Clausing, K. 2019b. 'The Progressive Case against Protectionism: How Trade and Immigration Help American Workers', *Foreign Affairs*, *98* (6), 109–121.

Cleveland, M. (2020) 'Homelessness and Inequality', *American Journal of Economics and Sociology*, *79* (2), 559–590.

Coles, R. 1971. *Migrants, Sharecroppers, Mountaineers: Vol. II of Children of Crisis*. Boston, MA and Toronto: Little, Brown and Company.

Coles, R. 2003. *Children of Crisis*. Boston, MA and Toronto: Little, Brown and Company.

Ćolić-Peisker, V. 2004. 'Australian Croatians at the Beginning of the Twenty-First Century: A Changing Profile of the Community and its Public Representation', *Croatian Studies Review*, *3–4* (1), 1–26.

Coll, S. 2004. *Ghost Wars: The Secret History of the CIA, Afghanistan, and Bin Laden, from the Soviet Invasion to September 10, 2001*. London: Penguin Books.

Collier, P. 2009a. *The Bottom Billion: Why the Poorest Countries Are Failing and What Can Be Done about It*. New York: Oxford University Press.

Collier, P., 2008. *The Bottom Billion: Why the Poorest Countries Are Failing and What Can Be Done About It*. Oxford University Press, New York.

Collier, P. 2009a. *The Bottom Billion: Why the Poorest Countries Are Failing and What Can Be Done about It*. New York: Oxford University Press.

Collier, P. 2009b. *Wars, Guns, and Votes: Democracy in Dangerous Places*. London: The Bodley Head.

Collier, P. 2013. *Exodus: How Migration is Changing Our World*. Oxford and New York: Oxford University Press.

Collins, J. 2008. 'Globalisation, Immigration and the Second Long Post-War Boom in Australia', *Journal of Australian Political Economy*, *61* (June), 244–266.

Collins, J. 2013. 'Rethinking Australian Immigration and Immigrant Settlement Policy', *Journal of Intercultural Studies*, *34* (2), 160–177.

Collins, J. 2016. *From Refugee to Entrepreneur in Sydney in Less Than Three Years*. Sydney: UTS Business School.

Collins J., 2021. 'Immigrant Entrepreneurship in Sydney: Australia's Leading Global City', in *Immigrant Entrepreneurship in Cities, The Urban Book Series*, ed. C.Y. Liu. Cham: Springer, pp. 47–65.

Collins, J., Gibson, K., Alcorso, C., Castles, S., and Tait, D. 1995. *A Shop Full of Dreams: Ethnic Small Business in Australia*. Sydney: Pluto Press Australia.

Collins J., Krivokapic-Skoko, B., Jordan, K., Babacan, H., and Gopalkrishnan, N., 2020. *Cosmopolitan Place Making in Australia: Immigrant Minorities and the Built Environment in Cities, Regional and Rural Areas*. Singapore: Palgrave Macmillan.

Collins, J. and Reid, C Fabiansson, C, 2011, 'Identities, Aspirations and Belonging of Cosmopolitan Youth in Australia', *Cosmopolitan Civil Societies: An Interdisciplinary Journal*,
2011, *3* (3), 92–107

Collins, J. and Norman, H. 2018. 'Indigenous Entrepreneurship and Indigenous Employment in Australia', *Journal of Australian Political Economy*, *82* (December),
149–70.

Collins, J. and Reid C., 2012, 'Immigrant Teachers in Australia', *Cosmopolitan Civil Societies
Journal*, *4* (2), 38–61

Collins, J. and Shin, J. 2012. *Korean Immigrant Entrepreneurs in the Sydney Restaurant
Industry*. Sydney: UTS Cosmopolitan Civil Societies Research Centre.

Collins, J.H. and Shin, J. 2014. 'Korean Immigrant Entrepreneurs in the Sydney Restaurant
Industry', *Labour and Management in Development*, *15*, 1–25.

Commons, J.R. 1907. *Races and Immigrants in America*. New York: The MacMillan Company.

Commons, J.R. 1924. *Legal Foundations of Capitalism*. New York: The Macmillan Company.

Commons, J.R. 1934a/2009. *Institutional Economics: Its Place in Political Economy* (Vol. 1).
Piscataway, NJ: Transaction Publishers.

Commons, J.R. 1934b/2009. *Institutional Economics: Its Place in Political Economy* (Vol. 2).
Piscataway, NJ: Transaction Publishers.

Commons, J.R. 1934c/1964. *Myself*. Madison, WI: University of Wisconsin Press.

Consumer Affairs Victoria (CAV). 2007. *Residential Accommodation Issues Paper, Stakeholder Consultation*. State of Victoria: CAV.

Cooper, F. 2014. *Africa in the World: Capitalism, Empire, Nation-State*. Cambridge, MA:
Harvard University Press.

Cox, O. C. 1945. 'An American Dilemma: A Mystical Approach to the Study of Race
Relations', *Journal of Negro Education*, *14* (2), 132–148.

Crenshaw, K. 1989. 'Demarginalizing the Intersection of Race and Sex: A Black Feminist Critique of Antidiscrimination Doctrine, Feminist Theory, and Antiracist
Politics', *University of Chicago Legal Forum*, *1* (Article 8), 139–167, https://
chicagounbound.uchicago.edu/uclf/vol1989/iss1/8.

Crenshaw, K. 1991. 'Mapping the Margins: Intersectionality, Identity Politics, and Violence
against Women of Color', *Stanford Law Review*, *43* (July), 1241–1299.

Crossman, J. and Clark, M. 2010. 'International Experience and Graduate Employa-
bility: Stakeholder Perceptions on the Connection', *Higher Education*, *59* (August),
599–613.

Cubas, M.A. 2020. 'Migrants as Knowledge Producers: Participatory Photography as a
[Limited] Tool for Inclusion', *Migration Letters*, *17* (2), 265.

Currie, L, 1976, *Taming the Megalpolis: A Design for Urban Growth*, Pergamon Press Ltd.,
Oxford

Daly, H. 2019. 'A Country of Immigrants', *Steady State Herald*, 4 February, https://
steadystate.org/a-country-of-immigrants/.

Darity, W. Jr 2009. 'Stratification Economics: Context Versus Culture and the Reparations
Controversy', *Kansas Law Review*, *57* (4), 795–811.

Darity, W.A. 2021. 'Reconsidering the Economics of Identity: Position, Power, and Property', T.W. Schultz Memorial Lecture, Agricultural and Applied Economics Association,
Virtual, 3 January.

Darity, W.A. Jr, Hamilton D., and Stewart, J. 2015. 'A Tour de Force in Understanding In-
tergroup Inequality: An Introduction to Stratification Economics', *The Review of Black
Political Economy*, *42* (1–2), 1–6.

Darity Jr., W, 1995, 'The Undesirables, America's Underclass in the Managerial Age: Beyond the Myrdal Theory of Racial Inequality', *Daedalus, 124* (1), 145–165.

Darity Jr., W, 1982, "Review of 'Alas, Alas, Kongo': A Social History of Indentured African Immigration into Jamaica, 1841-1865 by Monica Schuler", *Canadian Journal of African Studies*, vol. 16, no. 1, pp. 145-150.

Darity, W.A. Jr and Mason, P.L. 1998. 'Evidence on Discrimination in Employment: Codes of Color, Codes of Gender', *Journal of Economic Perspectives, 12* (2), 63–90.

Darity, W.A. Jr and Mullen, K. 2020. *From Here to Equality: Reparations for Black Americans in the Twenty-First Century*. Chapel Hill, NC: The University of North Carolina Press.

Darkwah, A.K. 2019. 'Book Review: *The Twilight of Cutting: African Activism and Life after NGOs*', *African Review of Economics and Finance, 11* (1), 240–244.

Date-Bah, S.K. 2015. *Reflections on the Supreme Court of Ghana*. London: Wildy, Simmonds and Hill Publishing.

Date-Bah, S.K. 2021. *Selected Papers and Lectures on Ghanaian Law*. Tema: DigiBooks Ghana Ltd.

Davidson, K. and Gleeson, B. 2013. 'The Urban Revolution That Isn't: The Political Economy of the "New Urbanology"', *Journal of Australian Political Economy, 72* (Summer), 52–79.

Davis, J.B. 2015. 'Stratification Economics and Identity Economics', *Cambridge Journal of Economics, 39* (5), 1215–1229.

Davis, J.B. 2019. 'Stratification Economics as an Economics of Exclusion', *Journal of Economics, Race, and Policy, 2*, 163–172.

De Genova, N. (ed.). 2017. *The Borders of 'Europe': Autonomy of Migration, Tactics of Bordering*. NC and London: Duke University Press.

De Graft-Johnson, K.T. 1974. 'Population Growth and Rural–Urban Migration, with Special Reference to Ghana', *International Labour Review, 109* (5–6), 471–485.

Debrah, E. and Asante, R. 2019. 'Sino-Ghana Bilateral Relations and Chinese Migrants' Illegal Gold Mining in Ghana', *Asian Journal of Political Science, 27* (3), 286–307.

Debrah, Y. 2007. 'Promoting the Informal Sector as a Source of Gainful Employment in Developing Countries: Insights from Ghana', *The International Journal of Human Resource Management, 18* (6), 1063–1084.

Deninger, K. 2003. *Land Policies for Growth and Poverty Reduction*. New York: World Bank and Oxford University Press.

DeParle, J. 2019. *A Good Provider Is One Who Leaves: One Family and Migration in the 21st Century*. New York: Viking.

Department of Education, Employment and Workplace Relations (DEEWR). 2011. *Selected Higher Education Statistics: Overseas Students 2010, Canberra*. DEEWR.

Department of Employment, Education, Training and Youth Affairs (DEETYA). 1998. *Higher Education Students Time Series Tables, Canberra*. DEETYA.

Department of Immigration and Citizenship (DIAC). 2006. *Community Information Summary: Ghana-Born*. Canberra: Department of Immigration and Citizenship.

Department of Infrastructure and Transport. 2011. *State of Australian Cities 2011*, Canberra: Department of Infrastructure and Transport.

Department of Infrastructure and Transport. 2013. *State of Australian Cities Report 2013*. Canberra: Major Cities Unit, Government of Department of Infrastructure and Transport.

Desmarais, A.A. 2007. *Globalization and the Power of Peasants: La Vía Campesina*. London: Pluto Press.

de Vroey, M. 1975. 'The transition from classical to neoclassical economics: A scientific revolution', *Journal of Economic Issues, 9* (3), 415–439.

Dickson, K.B. 1966. 'Trade Patterns in Ghana at the Beginning of the Eighteenth Century', *Geographical Review, 56* (3), 417–431.

Dickson, K.B. 1968. 'Background to the Problem of Economic Development in Northern Ghana', *Annals of the Association of American Geographers, 58* (4), 686–696.

Djaba O.A, 2017, Statement Delivered by Hon. Otiko Afisah Djaba to The Press on The 'Operation Get Off The Street Now, for A Better Life' Programme on 3rd August, 2017 at The Ministry Premises, Accra. Available online at https://www.peacefmonline.com/pages/local/news/201708/322625.php (accessed 24.06.2021).

Diko, J. and Tipple, A.G. 1992. 'Migrants Build at Home: Long Distance Housing Development by Ghanaians in London', *Cities, 9* (4 November), 288–294.

Division of Local Government, Department of Premier and Cabinet. 2013. 'Local Council Boundaries Sydney Outer (SO)', Sydney: New South Wales Government, www.dlg.nsw.gov.au.

Dodson, J. and Sipe, N. 2010. 'A Suburban Crisis? Housing, Credit, Energy and Transport', *Journal of Australian Political Economy, 64* (Summer), 199–210.

Dogbevi, E. 2009. 'Remittances into Ghana Increase Despite Global Financial Crunch', *Ghana Business News*, http://ghanabusinessnews.com.

Doran, C. 2007. 'A Militarised Neo-Liberalism: Australia's Economic Policies in Iraq', *Journal of Australian Political Economy, 59* (June), 48–73.

Drakakis-Smith, D. 1987. *The Third World City*. First edition. London: Methuen and Co. Ltd.

Drakakis-Smith, D. 2000. *The Third World City*. Second edition. London: Routledge.

Dubbeling, M., de Zeeuw, H., and van Veenhuizen, R. 2010. *Cities, Poverty and Food: Multi-Stakeholder Policy and Planning in Urban Agriculture*. Leusden: RUAF.

Duncan, B. 2010. 'Cocoa, Marriage, Labour and Land in Ghana: Some Matrilineal and Patrilineal Perspectives', *Africa: The Journal of the International African Institute, 80* (2), 301–321.

Dunn, B. 2017. 'Class, Capital and the Global Unfree Market: Resituating Theories of Monopoly Capitalism and Unequal Exchange', *Science and Society, 81* (3), 348–374.

Economic Community of West African States (ECOWAS), 2008. ECOWAS Common Approach on Migration, 33rd Ordinary Session of the Head of State and Government, January 18, Ougadougou, ECOWAS.

ECPAT International. 2008. *Global Monitoring Report on the Status of Action Against Commercial Sexual Exploitation of Children*. Bangkok: ECPAT International.

Eder, M. and Özkul, D. 2016. 'Editors' Introduction: Precarious Lives and Syrian Refugees in Turkey', *New Perspectives on Turkey, 54* (May), 1–8.

Edwards, H.S. 2019. 'Beyond Walls: Why the Forces of Global Migration Can't Be Stopped', *Time* (4 and 11 February), 24–46.

Ehrlich, P.R. 1968. *The Population Bomb*. New York: Ballantine Books.

Ehwi, R.J. 2021. 'Walls within walls: examining the variegated purposes for walling in Ghanaian gated communities', *Housing Studies*, DOI: 10.1080/02673037.2021. 1900795

Ehwi, R.J. and Asante, L.A. 2016. 'Ex-Post Analysis of Land Title Registration in Ghana since 2008 Merger: Accra Lands Commission in Perspective', *Sage Open, 6* (2),1–17.

Ehwi, R.J. and Mawuli, D.A. 2021. "Landguardism' in Ghana: Examining public perceptions about the driving Factors', *Land Use Policy, 109*, October, 105630, 1–13

Ehwi, R.J., Morrison, N., and Tyler, P. 2021. 'Gated Communities and Land Administration Challenges in Ghana: Reappraising the Reasons Why People Move into Gated Communities', *Housing Studies, 36* (3), 307–335.

Ehwi, R.J., Maslova, S. & Asante, L.A. 2021, 'Flipping the page: exploring the connection between Ghanaian migrants' remittances and their living conditions in the UK', *Journal of Ethnic and Migration Studies*, doi: 10.1080/1369183X.2021.1945915

El-Gamal, M.A., and Jaffe, A.M. 2010. *Oil, Dollars, Debt, and Crises: The Global Curse of Black Gold*. Cambridge, UK: Cambridge University Press.

Ely, R.T. 1914. *Property and Contract in their Relations to The Distribution of Wealth.* London: Macmillan and Co. Limited.

Emerson, A. 2001. *Historical Dictionary of Sydney*. Lanham, MD and London: Scarecrow Press.

Emser, M. 2017. 'Review of *Migrant, Refugee, Smuggler Saviour', Transformation: Critical Perspectives on Southern Africa*, 95, 140–144.

End Rape on Campus Australia, 2018, Red Zone Report: An investigation into sexual violence and hazing in Australian university residential colleges. End Rape on Campus Australia 2018, End Rape on Campus Australia, Sydney.

Engelen, E., Froud, J., Johal, S., Salento, A. and Williams, K. November 2017. The grounded city: from competitivity to the foundational economy, *Cambridge Journal of Regions, Economy and Society, 10* (3), 407–423.

Engels, F., 1872, 'The Housing Question', Marxists.org Archives, www.marxists.org/ archive/marx/works/download/Marx_The_Housing_Question.pdf.

England, C.W. 2015. *Land and Liberty: Henry George, the Single Tax Movement, and the Origins of 20th Century Liberalism* (D.Phil. thesis). Faculty of the Graduate School of Arts and Sciences of Georgetown University.

Fabini, G. 2015. 'Review of Us and Them? The Dangerous Politics of Immigration Control', *Punishment and Society, 18* (2), 249–253.

Faculty of Arts and Social Sciences. 2010. *Submission of Higher Degree Theses*. Sydney: The University of Sydney.

Fan, H. and Lee, F.L.F. 2019. 'Judicial Visibility under Responsive Authoritarianism: A Study of the Live Broadcasting of Court Trials in China', *Media, Culture and Society, 41* (8), 1088–1106.

Fan, M., Wen, H., Yang, L., and He, J. 2017. 'Exploring a New Kind of Higher Education with Chinese Characteristics', *American Journal of Economics and Sociology, 76* (3), 731–790.

Fang, C. and Van Liempt, I. 2021. '"We Prefer *Our* Dutch": International Students' Housing Experiences in the Netherlands', *Housing Studies, 36* (6), 822–842.

Fanon, F. 1925 [2008]. *Black Skin; White Masks*, New York: Grove Press.

Fanon, F. 1961 [2004]. *The Wretched of the Earth*, New York: Grove Press.

Ferreira, R.R. 2016. 'Stepping Stones to an Exclusionary Model of Home Ownership in Australia', *Journal of Australian Political Economy, 77* (Winter), 79–109.

Fincher, R. and Shaw, K. 2009. 'The Unintended Segregation of Transnational Students in Central Melbourne', *Environment and Planning A, 41*, 1884–1902.

Fincher, R. and Shaw, K. 2011. 'Enacting Separate Social Worlds: 'International' and 'Local' Students in Public Space in Central Melbourne', *Geoforum, 42* (5), 539–549.

Fincher, R., Carter, P., Tombesi, P., Shaw, K., and Martel, A. 2009. *Transnational and Temporary: Students, Community and Place-Making in Central Melbourne, Final Report 2009.* Melbourne: University of Melbourne.

Fincher, R., Iveson, K., Leitner, H., and Preston, V. 2019. *Everyday Equalities: Making Multicultures in Settler Colonial Cities.* Minneapolis, MN: University of Minnesota Press.

Fine, B. 1989. *Marx's Capital*. Houndmills and London: Macmillan Education Ltd.

Firmin-Sellers K. (1996) *The transformation of property rights in the Gold Coast*, Cambridge University Press, New York.

Fisher, M.H. 2014. *Migration: A World History*. Oxford: Oxford University Press.

Florida, R. 2003. 'Cities and the Rise of the Creative Class', *City and Community*, 2 (1), 3–19.

Florida, R. and Mellander, C. 2020. 'The Creative Class and National Economic Performance', in *Development Studies in Regional Science: New Frontiers in Regional Science: Asian Perspectives*, eds Z. Chen, W. Bowen, and D. Whittington (Vol. 42). Singapore: Springer, pp. 553–575.

Foley, G. 2001. 'Black Power in Redfern 1968–1972', Victoria University Repository online, ahttp://vuir.vu.edu.au/27009/1/Black%20power%20in%20Redfern%201968-1972.pdf.

Foley, G. 2011. 'Black Power, Land Rights and Academic History', *Griffith Law Review*, 20 (3), 608–681.

Foley, G., Schaap, A., and Howell, E. (eds). 2014. *The Aboriginal Tent Embassy: Sovereignty, Black Power, Land Rights and the State*. London: Routledge.

Forbes-Mewett, H. and Wickes R. 2018. 'The Neighbourhood Context of Crime against International Students', *Journal of Sociology*, 54 (4), 609–626.

Forbes-Mewett, H., Marginson, S., Nyland, C., Ramia, G., and Sawir, E. 2011. 'Australian University International Student Finances', unpublished manuscript. Clayton, Australia: Monash University.

Foreign Affairs. 2001. 'Review of *Bin Laden: The Forbidden Truth*', *Foreign Affairs*, 33 (2), 102–104.

Foubert, J., Tepper, R., and Morrison, D. 1998. 'Predictors of Student Satisfaction in University Residence Halls', *Journal of College and University Student Housing*, 27 (1), 41–46.

Frank A. G. (1966). *The development of underdevelopment*. In K. Rajani Paradigms in Economic Development: Classic Perspectives, Critiques and Reflections, London: M.E.Sharpe, pp. 99–106.

Freeman, L. 2017. 'Environmental Change, Migration, and Conflict in Africa: A Critical Examination of the Interconnections', *Journal of Environment and Development*, 26 (4), 351–374.

French, H.W. 2014. *China's Second Continent: How a Million Migrants are Building a New Empire in Africa*. Vintage Books, New York.

Fukuyama, F. 1992. *The End of History and the Last Man*. New York: The Free Press.

Fuseini I, 2016, 'Urban Governance and Spatial Planning for Sustainable Urban Development in Tamale, Ghana' (Ph.D. thesis). University of Stellenbosch, http://scholar.sun.ac.za/handle/10019.1/98655.

Gaffney, M. 1994. 'Neo-Classical Economics as a Strategem against Henry George', in *The Corruption of Economics*, ed. F. Harrison. London: Shepheard-Walwyn Publishing Co., pp. 29–163.

Gaffney, M. 2015. 'A Real-Assets Model of Economic Crises: Will China Crash in 2015?', *American Journal of Economics and Sociology*, 74 (2), 325–360.

Gaffney, M. 2018. 'Corporate Power and Expansive US Military Policy', *American Journal of Economics and Sociology*, 77 (2), 331–417.

Galbraith, J.K. 1956. *American Capitalism: The Concept of Countervailing Rower*. Revised edition. Cambridge, MA: The Riverside Press.

Galbraith, J.K. 1958/1998. *The Affluent Society*. New York: Houghton Mifflin Harcourt Publishing Co.

Galbraith, J.K. 1967. *The New Industrial State*. Boston: Houghton Mifflin.

Galbraith, J.K. 1973. *Economics and the Public Purpose*. Boston, MA: Houghton Mifflin Co.

Galbraith, J.K. 1977. *The Age of Uncertainty: A History of Economic Ideas and their Conse-quences*. Boston, MA and New York: Houghton Mifflin Co.

Galbraith, J.K. 1979. *The Nature of Mass Poverty*, Cambridge, MA and London: Harvard University Press.

Galbraith, J.K. 2004. 'A Cloud over Civilisation', *The Guardian*, July 14. https://www.theguardian.com/world/2004/jul/15/usa.iraq (accessed 1.10. 2021)

Galster, G., MacDonald, H., and Nelson, J. 2018. 'What Explains the Differential Treatment of Renters Based on Ethnicity? New Evidence From Sydney', *Urban Affairs Review*, *54* (1), 107–136.

Gao, M. and Liu, X. 1998. 'From Student to Citizen: A Survey of Students from the People's Republic of China in Australia', *International Migration*, *36* (1), 28–48.

George, H. 1881. 'The Irish Land Question: What It Involves and How Alone It Can Be Settled', www.wealthandwant.com/HG/irish_land_question.html.

George, H. 1883/1966. *Social Problems*. New York: Robert Schalkenbach Foundation.

George, H. 1883/1981. *Social Problems*. New York: Robert Schalkenbach Foundation.

George, H. 1884. *Moses*. London: The United Committee for Taxation of Land Values.

George, H. 1885. 'The Crime of Poverty', Robert Schalkenbach Foundation, accessed 14.6.2021 at http://schalkenbach.org/library/henry-george/hg-speeches/the-crime-of-poverty.html.

George, H. 1886/1991. *Protection or Free Trade: An Examination of the Tariff Question, with Especial Regard to the Interests of Labor*. New York: Robert Schalkenbach Foundation, http://schalkenbach.org/library/henrygeorge/protection-or-free-trade/preface-index.html

George, H. 1891. *The Condition of Labor: An Open Letter to Pope Leo XIII*. New York: United States Book Company.

George, H. 1892/1981. *A Perplexed Philosopher*. New York: Robert Schalkenbach Founda-tion, www.schalkenbach.org/library/henry-george/.

George, H. 1897/1935. *Progress and Poverty*. Fiftieth anniversary edition. New York: Robert Schalkenbach Foundation.

George, H. 1935/2006. *Progress and Poverty*. Fiftieth anniversary edition. New York: Robert Schalkenbach Foundation.

George, H. 1898/1992. *The Science of Political Economy*. London: Kegan Paul, Trench, Trübner and Co.

George, H. and Hyndman, H.M. [1885] 1914. 'Socialism and Rent-Appropriation', *Land Value*, May, pp. 530–534.

Ghana Home Loans plc. 2015. *Ghana Home Loans plc—Programme Memorandum*. Accra: Ghana Home Loans plc.

Ghana Statistical Service (GSS). 1995. *Ghana Living Standards Survey (Third Round)*. Accra: GSS.

GSS. 2007. *Pattern and Trends of Poverty in Ghana 1991–2006*. Accra: GSS.

GSS. 2008. *Ghana Living Standards Survey (Fifth Round)*. Accra: GSS.

GSS. 2010. 'Revised GDP Estimates for 2009', *GSS Statistical Newsletter*, No. B 12-20 03.

GSS. 2018. *Ghana Living Standards Survey: Report of the Seventh Round*. Accra: GSS.

Gibson-Graham, J.K. 1996/2006. *The End of Capitalism (As We Knew It): A Feminist Critique of Political Economy*. Minneapolis, MN and London: Minnesota University Press.

Giles, R.L. 2019. *An Exploration of the Growth of Economic Insanity: An Indictment of the Economics Profession*. Sydney: Association for Good Government.

Gitau, L.W. 2018. *Trauma-Sensitivity and Peacebuilding: Considering the Case of South Sudanese Refugees in Kakuma Refugee Camp*. New York: Springer International Publishing.

Glaeser, E. 2011. *Triumph of the City: How Urban Spaces Make Us Human*. London: Pan Books.

Gollerkeri, G., Chhabra, N. 2016. *Migration Matters: Mobility in a Globalizing World*. New Delhi: Oxford University Press.

Gonzalez, B., Collingwood, L., and El-Khatib, S.O. 2017. 'The Politics of Refuge: Sanctuary Cities, Crime, and Undocumented Immigration', https://journals.sagepub.com/doi/abs/10.1177/1078087417704974?journalCode=uarb.

Gordon, L. 2008. 'Berala', *Sydney Journal, 1* (3), 110–112.

Gordon, M. 1964. *Assimilation in American Life*. New York: Oxford University Press.

Gordon, M.M. 1961. 'Ethnic Groups in American Life', *Daedalus, 90*, 263–285.

Gore, C. (1997). 'Irreducibly Social Goods and The Informational Basis of Amartya Sen's Capability Approach'. *Journal of International Development, 9* (2), 232–250.

Gottlieb, A. 2019, 'Review of Liberalism at Large: The Id According to The Economist', *The Economist* (16–22 November), pp. 77–78.

Gough, K.V. 2008. 'Geographies of Children and Youth', *Geografiska Annaler 90B* (3), 217–303.

Gough, K.V. and Langevang, T. (eds). 2016. *Young Entrepreneurs in Sub-Saharan Africa*. London and New York: Routledge.

Government of Australia. 2015. 'National Remittance Plan 2015 Australia', Government of Australia, Canberra and The Global Partnership for Financial Inclusion (GPFI), www.gpfi.org/sites/gpfi/files/Australia_0.pdf.

Government of Ghana.1998. *The Children's Act, 1998*. Accra: Ministry of Women and Children.

Government of Ghana. 2010a. *National Urban Policy (Draft)*. Accra: Ministry of Local Government and Rural Development.

Government of Ghana. 2010b. *National Youth Policy*. Accra: Ministry of Youth and Sports.

Government of Ghana. 2012. *National Urban Policy Framework*. Accra: Ministry of Local Government and Rural Development.

Government of Ghana, 2016. *National Migration Policy for Ghana*, Accra: Ministry of the Interior.

Graham-Harrison, E. and Garside, J. 2019. 'Complete Control', *The Guardian Weekly, 201* (25), 10–11.

Grajales, J. 2020. 'From War to Wealth? Land Policies and the Peace Economy in Côte d'Ivoire', *Review of African Political Economy, 47* (163), 78–94.

Grant, R. 2007 'Geographies of investment: how do the wealthy build new houses in Accra, Ghana?' *Urban Forum, 18* (1), 31–59.

Grant, R. 2009. *Globalizing City: The Urban and Economic Transformation of Accra, Ghana*. New York: Syracuse University Press.

Green, S.F. 2018. 'Lines, traces, and tidemarks: further reflections on forms of border'. in O Demetriou & R Dimova (eds), *The political materialities of borders: new theoretical directions*. 1 edn, vol. 2, *Rethinking Borders*. Manchester: Manchester University Press, 67–83.

Grieco, M., Turner, J., and Kwakye, E. 1995. 'Informal Public Transport and the Woman Trader in Accra, Ghana', Presented at the Seventh World Conference on Transport Research, Sydney, 16–21 July 1995.

Griethuysen, P.V. 2012. 'Bona Diagnosis, Bona Curatio: How Property Economics Clarifies the Degrowth Debate', *Ecological Economics, 84* (December), 262–269.

Grieves, V. 2003. 'Windschuttle's Fabrication of Aboriginal History: A View from the Other Side', *Labour History, 85* (November), 194–199.

Grieves, V. 2009. 'Aboriginal Spirituality: Aboriginal Philosophy, The Basis of Aboriginal Social and Emotional Wellbeing', Discussion Paper No. 9, Cooperative Research Centre for Aboriginal Health, Darwin.

Gyami, G.O. 2019. *Victimization and Vulnerability of Migrants in the Streets: Case Study of Street Children in Agbobloshie, Accra* (M.A. thesis). Centre for Migration Studies, University of Ghana, Accra.

Haifang, L. 2010. 'China's Development Cooperation with Africa: Historical and Cultural Perspectives', in *The Rise of China and India in Africa*, eds F. Cheru and C. Obi. London: Zed, pp. 53–62.

Haila, A. 1988. 'Land as a Financial Asset: The Theory of Urban Rent as a Mirror of Economic Transformation', *Antipode, 20* (2), 79–101.

Haila, A. 2016. *Urban Land Rent: Singapore as a Property State*. Chichester: Wiley-Blackwell.

Haila, A. 2017. 'Institutionalizing "The Property Mind"'. *International Journal of Urban and Regional Research 41* (3): 500–507.

Haila, A. 2020. 'Financialization and Real Estate', in *Companion to Urban and Regional Studies*, eds A. Orum,. J. Ruiz-Tagle, and S. Vicari. Hoboken, NJ: Wiley-Blackwell.

Hall, R., Scoones, I., and Tsikata, D. 2017. 'Plantations, Outgrowers and Commercial Farming in Africa: Agricultural Commercialisation and Implications for Agrarian Change', *The Journal of Peasant Studies, 44* (3), 515–537.

Hamilton, C. and Denniss, R. 2005. *Affluenza: When Too Much Is Never Enough*. Sydney: Allen and Unwin.

Hamilton, D. 2020. 'The Moral Burden on Economists: Darrick Himiton's 2017 NEA Presidential Address', *The Review of Black Political Economy, 47* (4), 331–342.

Hamilton, T.G. 2018. *Immigration and the Remaking of Black America*. New York: Russell Sage Foundation.

Hampwaye, G. 2008. *Decentralisation, Local Economic Development and Urban Agriculture in Zambia* (Ph.D. thesis). University of Witwatersrand, Johannesburg.

Han, J.J. and Han, G.-S. 2010. 'The Koreans in Sydney'. *Sydney Journal, 2* (2), 25–35.

Handmer, J.W. 1995. 'Managing Vulnerability in Sydney: Planning or Providence', *GeoJournal, 37* (3), 355–368.

Hardin, G. 1968. 'The Tragedy of the Commons', *Science, 162* (3859), 1243–1248.

Hardin, G. 1974. 'Lifeboat Ethics: The Case against Helping the Poor', *Psychology Today* (September), 800–812.

Hardin, G. 1991. 'How Diversity Should Be Nurtured', *The Social Contract*, (Spring), 137–139.

Hardin, G. 1993. *Living within Limits: Ecology, Economics and Population Taboos*. Oxford and New York: Oxford University Press.

Harman, G. 2003. 'International PhD Students in Australian Universities: Financial Support, Course Experience and Career Plans', *International Journal of Educational Development, 23* (3), 339–351.

Harris, C. 1993. 'Whiteness as Property', *Harvard Law Review, 106* (8), 1707–1791.

Harrison, F. (ed.). 2016. *Rent Unmasked: How to Save the Global Economy and Build a Sustainable Future, Essays in Honour of Mason Gaffney*. London: Shepheard-Walwyn Ltd.

Harrison, F. (2020) 'Cyclical Housing Markets and Homelessness', *American Journal of Economics and Sociology*, 79 (2), 591-612.

Harrison, F. (2021). *We Are Rent: Book 1 - Capitalism Cannibalism, and How We Must Outlaw Free Riding.* London: Land Research Trust.

Hart, K. (1973). 'Informal Income Opportunities and Urban Employment in Ghana', *Journal of Modern African Studies*, 11 (1), 61–89.

Hartley L.K., Baker, S., Fleay, C., and Burke, R. 2019. '"My Study Is the Purpose of Continuing my Life": The Experience of Accessing University for People Seeking Asylum in Australia', *Australian Universities' Review*, 61 (2), 4–13.

Harvey, D. 1973. *Social Justice and the City.* Baltimore, MD: Johns Hopkins University Press/London: Edward Arnold.

Harvey, D. 1978. 'The Urban Process under Capitalism', *International Journal of Urban and Regional Research*, 2 (1–4), 101–131.

Harvey, D. 2003. *The New Imperialism.* Oxford: Oxford University Press.

Harvey, D. 2006. *Limits to Capital.* London: Verso.

Hedges, S.L. 1992. *Liberty Plains: A History of Auburn, NSW.* Sydney: George Lewis Group.

Henry, L. and Mohan, G. 2003. 'Making Homes: The Ghanaian Diaspora, Institutions and Development', *Journal of International Development*, 15 (5), 611–622.

Herro A, Lee KY, Withall A, Peisah C, Chappell L, Sinclair C, 2021. 'Elder Mediation Services among Diverse Older Adult Communities in Australia: Practitioner Perspectives on Accessibility', *Gerontologist*, 61 (7), 1141–1152.

Herro, A., Lambourne W., and Penklis, D. 2009. 'Peacekeeping and Peace Enforcement in Africa: The Potential Contribution of a UN Emergency Peace Service', *African Security Review*, 18 (1), 49–62.

Higazi, A. 2005. 'Ghana Country Study', Paper submitted as part of the Report on Informal Remittance Systems in Africa, Caribbean and Pacific Countries, Reference No. RO2CS008.

Hill, P. 1963. *The Migrant Cocoa-Farmers of Southern Ghana: A Study in Rural Capitalism.* Cambridge, UK: Cambridge University Press.

Hill, R. 2020. 'Watch Out! The Great University Implosion Is On Its Way', *Australian Universities' Review*, 62 (1), 51–53.

Hilson, G., Hilson, A., and Adu-Darko, E. 2014. 'Chinese Participation in Ghana's Informal Gold Mining Economy: Drivers, Implications and Clarifications', *Journal of Rural Studies*, 34 (April), 292–303.

Hirschman, A.O. 1970. *Exit, Voice, and Loyalty: Responses to Decline in Firms, Organizations, and States.* Cambridge, MA: Harvard University Press.

Ho, C.G.-Y. 2012. *Living in Liminality: Chinese Migrancy in Ghana* (Ph.D. thesis). University of California, Santa Cruz.

Ho, K.C. 2021. Land and Housing in Singapore: Three Conversations with Anne Haila *American Journal of Economics and Sociology* (Ph.D. thesis). University of California, Santa Cruz. 80 (2), 325–351.

Hobson, J.M. 2004. *The Eastern Origins of Western Civilisation.* Cambridge, UK: Cambridge University Press.

Hodzi, O., and Chen, J.Y.-W. 2020. 'Complexities of Representation: Chinese Outbound Tourists as De Facto Ambassadors in Southern Africa', *Journal of China and International Relations*, 1–21, https://journals.aau.dk/index.php/jcir/article/view/4427.

Hodzic, S. 2017. *The Twilight of Cutting: African Activism and Life after NGOs.* Berkeley, CA: University of California Press.

Holsti, O.R. 1969. *Content Analysis for the Social Sciences and Humanities*. Reading: Addison-Wesley Publishing Co.

Holton, M. and Mouat, C.M. 2021. 'The Rise (and Rise) of Vertical Studentification: Exploring the Drivers of Studentification in Australia', *Urban Studies*, 58 (9), 1866–1884.

Howard, R. (1978) *Colonialism and underdevelopment in Ghana*, Croom Helm, London.

Howard, R. (1980) 'Formation and stratification of the peasantry in colonial Ghana', *Journal of Peasant Studies*, 8 (1), 61–80.

Hubbert, M.K. 1974. 'M. King Hubbert on the Nature of Growth', Published in National Energy Conservation Policy Act of 1974, Hearings before the Subcommittee on the Environment of the Committee on Interior and Insular Affairs House of Representatives, USA, 6 June.

Hudson, M. 2008. 'Henry George and his Critics', *American Journal of Economics and Sociology*, 67 (1), 1–45.

Hugo, G.J. 2008. 'In and Out of Australia: Rethinking Indian and Chinese Skilled Migration to Australia', *Asian Population Studies*, 3 (4), 267–291.

Hujo, K. 2013. 'Linking Social Policy, Migration, and Development in a Regional Context: The Case of Sub-Saharan Africa', *Regions* and *Cohesion*, 3 (3), 30–55.

Hujo, K. 2019. 'A Global Social Contract: New Steps towards a Rights-Based Approach to Migration Ggovernance?', *Global Social Policy*, 19 (1-2) 25-28.

Hunter, A. 2018. *Retirement Home? Ageing Migrant Workers in France and the Question of Return*. IMISCOE Research Series. Cham: Springer.

Huntington, S. 1996. *The Clash of Civilizations and the Remaking of World Order*. New York: Simon & Schuster.

Hutchinson, Kenneth. 2003. 'There Is No Word for Cousin: Understanding Ghanaian Homelessness from an American Context', *African Diaspora ISPs*. Paper 49, http://digfricanlections.sit.edu/african_diaspora_isp/49.

Ike, N., Baldwin, C., and Lathouras, A. 2016. 'Student Accommodation: Who Cares?', *Planning for Higher Education Journal*, 44 (3) (April–June), 46–60.

Indelicato, M.E. 2018. *Australia's New Migrants: International Students' History of Affective Encounters with the Border*. London: Routledge.

International Labour Organization (ILO). 2010. *Joining Forces against Child Labour Inter-Agency Report for The Hague Global Child Labour Conference*. Geneva: ILO.

International Centre for Migration Policy Development (ICMPD) and the International Organization for Migration (IOM). 2015. *A Survey on Migration Policies in West Africa*, Vienna and Dakar: ICMPD and IOM.

International House. 2011. *Living the World … Share the World*. Sydney: International House.

International Organization for Migration (IOM). 2015. *World Migration Report 2015*. Geneva: IOM.

IOM. 2020. World Migration Report 2020. Geneva: IOM.

International Student Development Taskforce. 2009. *Final Report of the International Student Development Taskforce*, August, 2009. Sydney: University of Sydney.

International Student Support Unit (ISSU). 2010. ISSU Accommodation Survey 2009. The University of Sydney: ISSU.

ISSU. 2011. International Student Guide: Your Road to Success. Sydney: The University of Sydney ISSU.

IRIN (The Integrated Regional Information Networks now called The New Humanitarian). 2007. 'What Hope for Thousands of Street Children?', 6 March, www.irinnews.org/Report.aspx?ReportId=70530/.

Ismael, T.Y. 1989. 'Review of *Asad: The Struggle for the Middle East*', *Canadian Journal of Political Science*, 22 (4), 889–891.

Iveson, K. 2007. *Publics and the City*. Oxford: Blackwell.

Jack, M. and Braimah, R. 2004. 'Feasibility Study for the Application of Community-Led Infrastructure Finance Facility Operations in Ghana', Report prepared for UN-HABITAT, www.homeless-international.org/doc_docs/GhanaReportFinal_30Sep04.pdf.

Jacobs, J. 1969. *The Economy of Cities*. London: Jonathan Cape.

Jacobsen, K. and Landau, L.B. 2003. 'The Dual Imperative in Refugee Research: Some Methodological and Ethical Considerations in Social Science Research on Forced Migration', *Disasters*, 27 (3), 185–206.

James, R., Bexley, E., Devlin, M., and Marginson, S. 2007. *Australian University Student Finances 2006: Final Report of a National Survey of Students in Public Universities*. Canberra: Australian Vice-Chancellors Committee.

Jang, H.S. 2015. *Social Identities of Young Indigenous People in Contemporary Australia: Neo-Colonial North, Yarrabah*. Cham: Springer.

Jaynes, G.D. 2007. 'Migration and Social Stratification: Bipluralism and the Western Democratic State', *Du Bois Review*, 4 (1), 5–17.

Johnson, J. 2009. 'Croydon', *Sydney Journal*, 2 (1), 92–97.

Johnson, L.C. 2015. 'Governing Suburban Australia', in *Suburban Governance: A Global View*, eds P. Hamel and R. Keil. Toronto: University of Toronto Press, pp. 110–129.

Jones, R. 2016. *Violent Borders: Refugees and the Right to Move*, London: Verso.

Jones, S. 2021. 'Atlantic route exacts a deadly toll from hope', *The Guardian Weekly*, 13th August, pp. 10–14.

Jorgensen, E.O. 1925. *False Education in Our Colleges and Universities*, Chicago, IL: Manufactures and Merchants Federal Tax League.

Kabki, M., Mazzucato, V., and Appiah, E. 2004. '"Wotheane a eye bebree": The Economic Impact of Remittances of Netherlands-Based Ghanaian Migrants on Rural Ashanti', *Population, Space and Place*, 10, 85–97.

Kahn M. E., 2021, Adapting to Climate Change: Markets and the Management of an Uncertain Future, Yale University Press, New Haven and London.

Kajanus, A. 2015. *Chinese Student Migration, Gender and Family*. New York: Palgrave Macmillan.

Kaldor, N. (1956), 'Alternative Theories of Distribution', *Review of Economic Studies*, 23 (2), 83–100.

Kang S.K., DeCelles, K.A., Tilcsik, A., and Jun, S. 2016. 'Whitened Résumés: Race and Self-Presentation in the Labor Market', *Administrative Science Quarterly*, 61 (3), 469–502.

Kansangbata, C. 2008. 'Streetism and Child Labour in the Wa Municipality of Ghana: A Gender Analysis of Drivers', *Studies in Gender and Development in Africa*, 1 (September), 14–33.

Kapp, K.W. 1950/1971. *The Social Costs of Private Enterprise*. New York: Schocken Books.

Karg H.L., 2016, *The Role of Locality in Feeding Cities: Spatial Analysis of Agriculture, Markets and Food Flows in West African Urban Food Systems* (Ph.D. thesis). Faculty of Environment and Natural Resources, Albert-Ludwigs-Universität Freiburg im Breisgau, Germany.

Kass, T. 2008. 'Lidcombe', in *Dictionary of Sydney*, http://dictionaryofsydney.org/entry/lidcombe.

Keller, E., Hilton, D., and Twumasi-Ankrah, K. 1999. 'Teenage Pregnancy and Motherhood in a Ghanaian Community', *Journal of Social Development in Africa*, 14 (1), 69–84.

Kemper, F. 1998. 'Restructuring of Housing and Ethnic Segregation: Recent Developments in Berlin', *Urban Studies, 35* (10), 1765–1789.

Kerr, W.R. 2018. *The Gift of Global Talent: How Migration Shapes Business, Economy and Society.* Stanford, CA: Stanford Business Books.

Keynes, J.M. 1953/1964. *The General Theory of Employment, Interest, and Money.* San Diego, CA: Harvest Books/Harcourt, Inc.

Kahn M. E. 2021. *Adapting to Climate Change: Markets and the Management of an Uncertain Future.* New Haven and London: Yale University Press.

Khawaja, N. and Dempsey, J. 2007. 'Psychological Distress in International University Students: An Australian Study', *Australian Journal of Guidance and Counselling, 17* (1), 13–27.

Khawaja, N. and Dempsey, J. 2008. 'A Comparison of International and Domestic Tertiary Students in Australia', *Australian Journal of Guidance and Counseling, 18* (1), 30–46.

Khozaei, F., Ayub, N., Hassan, A., and Khozaei, Z. 2010. 'The Factors Predicting Students' Satisfaction with University Hostels, Case Study, Universiti Sains Malaysia', *Asian Culture and History, 2* (2), 148–158.

Kim, H.H.-S. 2014. 'Immigrant Network Structure and Perceived Social Capital: A Study of the Korean Ethnic Enclave in Uzbekistan', *Development and Society, 43* (2), 351–379.

Kinané, L.M., Tougma, A., Ouédraogo, D., and Sonou, M. 2008. 'Urban Farmers' Irrigation Practices in Burkina Faso', *Urban Agriculture Magazine, 20,* 25–26.

Klare, M.T. 2001a. *Resource Wars: The New Landscape of Global Conflict.* New York: Owl Books.

Klare, M.T. 2001b. 'New Geography of Conflict', *Foreign Affairs, 80* (May/June), 49–61.

Klare, M.T. 2003. 'For Oil and Empire? Rethinking War with Iraq', *Current History 102* (662), 129–135.

Klein, N. 2007. *The Shock Doctrine: The Rise of Disaster Capitalism.* New York: Penguin Books.

Klimina A, 2018, 'Rethinking the Role of the State', in *The Routledge Handbook of Heterodox Economics: Theorizing, Analyzing and Transforming Capitalism*, eds T.-H. Jo, L. Chester, and C. D'lppoliti. London: Routledge, pp. 458–470.

Koido A, 2021, 'Migration: Diversifying Transnational Flows Under Neoliberal Transformation', *International Sociology Reviews, 36* (2), 265–277.

Kotze, N. 2013. 'A Community in Trouble? The Impact of Gentrification on the Bo-Kaap, Cape Town', *Urbani izziv, 24* (2), 124–132.

Kpienbaareh, D, Kansanga, M.M., Konkor I, and Luginaah I, 2021, 'The Rise of the Fourth Estate: The Media, Environmental Policy, and the Fight against Illegal Mining in Ghana', *Environmental Communication,* vol. 15, no. 1, pp. 69-84.

Krivokapic-Skoko, B and Collins, J. 2014, "Looking for Rural Idyll 'Down Under': International Immigrants in Rural Australia", *International Migration 54* (1), 167–179.

Kuhn, T. 1967. *The Structure of Scientific Revolutions.* Chicago: University of Chicago Press.

Kuuire, V.Z., Arku, G., Luginaah, I., Abada, T., and Buzzelli, M. 2016. 'Impact of Remittance Behaviour on Immigrant Housing Ownership Trajectories: An Analysis of the Longitudinal Survey of Immigrants in Canada from 2001 to 2005', *Social Indicators Research, 127* (3), 1135–1156.

Kuuire, V.Z., Arku, G., Luginaah, I., Buzzelli, M., and Abada, T. 2016. 'Obligations and Expectations: Perceived Relationship between Transnational Housing Investment and Housing Consumption Decisions among Ghanaian Immigrants in Canada', *Housing, Theory and Society, 33* (4), 445–468.

Kwansah-Aidoo, K. and Mapedzahama, V. 2018. "'There Is Really Discrimination Everywhere": Experiences and Consequences of Everyday Racism among the New Black African Diaspora in Australia', *The Australian Review of African Studies*, *39* (1), 81–109.

Kwok, E. 2015, 'Agency In Appropriation: The Informal Territory of Foreign Domestic Helpers in Hong Kong', *IDEA Journal Urban + Interior*, *15* (1), 102–117.

Kwok, E. 2017, Foreign Domestic Helpers in Hong Kong : Occupation, Resistance, Autonomy', PhD Thesis, University of Technology, Sydney, Sydney, Australia.

Kwoyiga, L. 2019. 'Institutional Analysis of Groundwater Irrigation in Northeast Ghana', *African Review of Economics and Finance*, *11* (2), 389–419.

Lebailly, P., and D. Muteba. 2011. Characteristics of urban food insecurity: The case of Kinshasa. *African Review of Economics and Finance 3* (1): 58–68.

Laferrère, A. and Le Blanc, D. 2004. 'Gone with the Windfall: How Do Housing Allowances Affect Student Co-Residence?', *CESifo Economic Studies*, *50* (3), 451–477.

Lalich, W.F. 2004. 'The Development of Croatian Communal Places in Sydney', *Croatian Studies Review*, *3–4* (1), 95–124.

Lambourne, W. and Herro, A. 2008. 'Peacebuilding Theory and the United Nations Peace Building Commission: Implications for Non-UN Interventions', *Global Change, Peace & Security*, *20* (3), 275–289.

Lammensalo, L. 2021. *Integrating Sexual and Reproductive Health and Rights and Climate Action: A Pathway for Win–Win Solutions?* (ECGS M.A. thesis). University of Helsinki, Finland.

Lan, S. 2015. 'State Regulation of Undocumented African Migrants in China: A Multi-Scalar Analysis', *Journal of Asian and African Studies*, *50* (3), 289–304.

Landis, J. 2012. 'The Syrian Uprising of 2011: Why the Asad Regime Is Likely to Survive to 2013', *Middle East Policy*, *XIX* (1), 72–84.

Larson, D.F., Otsuka, K., Matsumoto, T., and Kilic, T. 2012. 'Should African Rural Development Strategies Depend on Smallholder Farms? An Exploration of the Inverse Productivity Hypothesis', World Bank Policy Research Working Paper, WPS6190.

Le, D. 2016. 'Environmental and Social Risks of Chinese Official Development Finance in Africa: The Case of the Lamu Port Project, Kenya', *African Review of Economics and Finance*, *8* (1), 106–129.

Lee, C.K. 2017. *The Specter of Global China: Politics, Labor, and Foreign Investment in Africa*, Chicago, IL: The University of Chicago Press.

Lee, E.S. 1966. 'A Theory of Migration', *Demography*, *3* (1), 47–57.

Lee, M.C. 2014. *Africa's World Trade: Informal Economies and Globalization*. London: Zed.

Lefebvre, H. 1974/1991. *The Production of Space*. Trans. D. Nicholson-Smith. Oxford: Blackwell.

Lemberg-Pedersen, M. 2016. 'Review of *Violent Borders: Refugees and the Right to Move*', *Torture*, *28* (3), 139–141.

Lenner, K. and Turner, L. 2019. 'Making Refugees Work? The Politics of Integrating Syrian Refugees into the Labor Market in Jordan', *Middle East Critique*, *28* (1), 65–95.

Lentz, C, 2013, *Land, Mobility, and Belonging in West Africa*, Indiana University Press, Bloomington and Indianapolis.

Leon, J.K. 2015. 'The Role of Global Cities in Land Grabs', *Third World Quarterly 36* (2), 257–273.

Leonard, T.C. 2016. *Illiberal Reformers: Race, Eugenics and American Economics in the Progressive Era*. Princeton, NJ and Oxford: Princeton University Press.

Leung, J.K.-S. and James, K. 2010. *Sydney's Construction Union Strategy and Immigrant Worker Issues: A Roman Catholic-Marxist Perspective*. Toronto: Spire Publishing.

Leung, J.K.-S. and James, K., 2010, *Sydney's Construction Union Strategy and Immigrant Worker Issues: A Roman Catholic-Marxist perspective*, Spire Publishing, Toronto, Canada.

Levin, C. E., M. T. Ruel, S. S. Morris, D. G. Maxwell, M. Armar-Klemesu, and C. Ahiadeke. 1999. Working Women in an Urban Setting: Traders, Vendors and Food Security in Accra. *World Development 27* (11), 1977–1991.

Liberti, S. 2013. *Land Grabbing: Journeys in the New Colonialism*. London and New York: Verso.

Lowe, M. 2010. 'Contemporary Rural–Urban Migration in Alaska', *Alaska Journal of Anthropology*, 8 (2), 75–92.

Lubell, J. and Brennan, M. 2007. 'Framing the Issues—the Positive Impacts of Affordable Housing on Education', Centre for Housing Policy paper, July.

Ludovic, A. and Lebailly, P. 2011. 'Peri-Urban Agriculture: The Case of Market Gardening in Niamey, Niger', *African Review of Economics and Finance*, 3 (1), 68–79.

Lutter, M. 2018. Rendeavour: an interview with Preston Mendenhall, the Head of Corporate Affairs for Rendeavour, https://www.chartercitiesinstitute.org/post/rendeavour, accessed 30 June 2021.

Lynch, K., Maconachie, R., Binns, T., Tengbe, P., and Bangura, K. 2013. 'Meeting the Urban Challenge? Urban Agriculture and Food Security in Post-Conflict Freetown, Sierra Leone', *Applied Geography*, 36 (3), 31–39.

Mabo vs Queensland (No 2) ("Mabo case") [1992] HCA 23; (1992) 175 CLR 1 (3 June 1992), High Court of Australia, http://www6.austlii.edu.au/cgi-bin/viewdoc/au/cases/cth/HCA/1992/23.html (accessed 8.09.2021).

MacLean, N. 2017. *Democracy in Chains: The Deep History of the Radical Right's Stealth Plan for America*. New York: Penguin Books.

Malmedal, W. and Anyan, C. 2020. 'Elder Abuse in Ghana—a Qualitative Exploratory Study', *Journal of Adult Protection*, 22 (5), 299–313.

Malthus, T.R. 1798/2004. *An Essay on the Principle of Population*. New York: Oxford University Press.

Manatschal, A., Wisthaler, V., and Zuber, C.I. 2020. 'Making Regional Citizens? The Political Drivers and Effects of Subnational Immigrant Integration Policies in Europe and North America', *Regional Studies*, 54 (11), 1475–1485.

Manby, B. 2018. *Citizenship in Africa: The Law of Belonging*. Oxford, London, New York, New Delhi, and Sydney: Hart.

Manuh, T. 2021. 'Gender, Migration, Property and the Law in Ghana: A Discussion of Some Recent Decisions by the Supreme Court of Ghana', Zoom Seminar, Centre for Migration, University of Ghana, Accra, September 29.

Marais, L., Burger, P., Campbell, M., van Rooyen, D., Denoon-Stevens, S., 2022. *Coal and energy in Emalahleni, South Africa: Considering a Just transition*, Edinburgh University Press, Edinburgh.

Marcus, E. 2017. *Guangzhou Dream Factory*, www.kanopystreaming.com/product/guangzhou-dream-factory.

Marginson, S. 2010a. International Student Security. Asia-Pacific Association for International Education Conference, Australia, Gold Coast, 14 April.

Marginson, S. 2010b. 'International Students Left in the Shadows', *Sydney Morning Herald*, 28 May.

Marginson, S. 2011. 'It's a Long Way Down: The Underlying Tensions in the Education Export Industry', *Australian Universities' Review*, 53 (2), 21–33.

Markaki, Y. and Longhi, S. 2013. 'What Determines Attitudes to Immigration in European Countries? An Analysis at the Regional Level', *Migration Studies*, *1*(3), 311–337.

Markusen, A. (2006). Urban Development and the Politics of a Creative Class: Evidence from a Study of Artists. Environment and Planning A: Economy and Space, *38* (10), 1921–1940.

Masri, E.Y. 2019. 'The Complexity and Contradictions of Humanitarian Neutrality: Observing the Challenges of UNRWA and Palestinian Refugees in Lebanon', Corso di Laurea Magistrale in Local Development, Universita' degli Studi di Padova—Dipartimento di Scienze Storiche, Geografiche e dell'Antichità.

Mathews, G., Lin, L.D., and Yang, Y. 2017. *The World in Guangzhou.* Chicago, IL and London: University of Chicago Press.

Matsebula, V. and Yu, D. 2020. 'An analysis of financial inclusion in South Africa', *African Review of Economics and Finance, 12* (1), 171–202.

Matthews, D., Radloff, A., Doyle, J., and Clarke, L. 2019. *International Graduate Outcomes Survey—2018, Final Report.* Adelaide: Australian Council for Educational Research.

Maxwell, D. 1999. 'The Political Economy of Urban Food Security in Sub-Saharan Africa', *World Development, 27*, 1939–1953.

Maxwell, D., Larbi, W.O., Lamptey, G.M., Zakariah, S., and Armar-Klemesu, M. 1998. Farming in the Shadow of the City: Changes in Land Rights and Livelihoods in Peri-Urban Accra. Cities Feeding People Series Report 23. Washington, DC: IFPRI.

Maxwell, D., Levin, C., Armar-Klemesu, M., Ruel, M., Morris, S., and Ahiadeke, C. 2000. *Urban Livelihoods and Food and Nutrition Security in Greater Accra, Ghana.* Washington, DC: FPRI, NMIMR, and WHO.

Mazzucato, V. 2005. 'Ghanaian Migrants' Double Engagement: A Transnational View of Development and Integration Policies', *Global Migration Perspectives, 48* (October), 1–17.

Mazzucato, V. 2006a. 'Informal Insurance Arrangements in a Transnational Context: The Case of Ghanaian Migrants' Networks', paper presented at the Centre for the Study of African Economies Conference on Reducing Poverty and Inequality: How Can Africa Be Included? Oxford University, 19–21 March.

Mazzucato, V. 2006b. Migrant Transnationalism: Two-Way Flows, Changing Institutions and Community Development between Ghana and the Netherlands', *Economic Sociology—The European Electronic Newsletter, 7* (3), 8–16.

McCrohon, M. and Nyland, B. 2018. 'The Perceptions of Commoditisation and Internationalisation of Higher Education in Australia: An Interview of Chinese International Students and Their Lecturers', *Asia Pacific Education Review, 19* (March) , 17–26.

McGrath-Champ, S., Rosewarne, S., and Rittau, Y. 2011. 'From One Skill Shortage to the Next: The Australian Construction Industry and Geographies of a Global Labour Market', *Journal of Industrial Relations, 53* (4), 467–485.

McVeigh, K. and Dzradosi, N. 2019. 'Ghana: Missing Fishermen', *The Guardian Weekly, 201* (25), 26–27.

Min, P. G. and Park, S.S. (2014) Twice-migrant Chinese and Indians in the United States: Their origins and attachment to their original homeland. *Development and Society, 43* (2), pp. 381–401.

Meadows, D.H., Meadows, D.L., Randers, J., and Bahrens, III. W.W. 1972. *Limits to Growth.* Washington,DC: Potomac Associates.

Meadows, D.H., Meadows, D.L., Randers, J., and Bahrens III. W.W. 2004. *Limits to Growth: The 30-Year Update.* White River Junction,VT: Chelsea Green Publishing.

Meagher, K., 2010, *Identity Economics: Social Networks and the Informal Economy in Nigeria*, Ibadan: James Currey, New York and Hebn Publishers PLC

Meagher, K., 2020, 'Deciphering African informal economies' in *The Informal Economy Revisited: Examining the Past, Envisioning the Future*, eds, M. Chen and F. Carré, London: Routledge, pp. 233–238.

Mealing K. 1988. *The Roof Over Our Heads*. Sydney: Auburn District Historical Society.

Melguizo, C. and Royuela, V. 2020. 'What Drives Migration Moves to Urban Areas in Spain? Evidence from the Great Recession', *Regional Studies*, 54 (12), 1680–1693.

Mendoza C, 2020, 'Southern Europe Skilled Migration into Mexico: The Impact of the Economic Crisis', *Regional Studies*, 54 (4), 495–504.

Mezzadra, S. 2013. *Border as Method, or, The Multiplication of Labor*. Durham, NC and London: Duke University Press.

Michael, G. 2003. 'Review of *Resource Wars: The New Landscape of Global Conflict*', *Population and Environment* 24 (4), 359–364.

Milligan, V., Pawson, H., Williams, P., and Yates, J. 2015. *Next Moves? Expanding Affordable Rental Housing in Australia through Institutional Investment*. City Futures Research Centre, University of New South Wales, March 2015.

Mina, W. 2019. 'Diaspora and Government Welfare Spending: Do Migrant Remittances Increase Public Social Protection?', *Economic Notes*, 48 (3), 1–18, https://doi.org/10.1111/ecno.12141.

Ministry of Finance. 2018. 2019 Financial Year Presented to Parliament on Thursday, 15th November 2018. Ministry of Finance, Accra.

Ministry of Lands and Forestry 1999. National Land Policy (Accra: Ministry of Lands and Forestry).

Minsky, H.P. 1992. *The Financial Instability Hypothesis*, Levy Economics Institute of Bard College Working Paper No. 74.

Mishan, E.J. 1967. *The Costs of Economic Growth*. New York: Praeger Publishers.

Mitchell, J. 2008. 'John Joseph Therry—His Lidcombe Property', *Australian Railway History*, September, 308–310.

Mohan, G. and Lampert, B. 2013. 'Negotiating China: reinserting African agency into China-Africa relations', *African Affairs*, 112 (446), 92–110.

Mohan, G., Lampert, B., Tan-Mullins, M., and Chang, D. 2014. *Chinese Migrants and Africa's Development: New Imperialists or Agents of Change?* London: Zed.

Molero-Simarro, R. 2017. 'Is China Reaching the Lewis Turning Point? Agricultural Prices, Rural–Urban Migration and the Labour Share', *Journal of Australian Political Economy*, 78 (Summer), 48–86.

Molho, I. 2013. 'Theories of Migration: A Review', *Scottish Journal of Political Economy*, 60 (5), 526–556.

Molotch, H. 1976. 'The City as a Growth Machine: Toward a Political Economy of Place', *American Journal of Sociology*, 82 (2), 309–332.

Monare, P.T., Kotze, N., and McKay, T.M. 2014. 'A Second Wave of Gentrification: The Case of Parkhurst, Johannesburg, South Africa', *Urbani izziv*, 25 (supplement), S108–S121.

Montgomerie, J. 2019. *Should We Abolish Household Debts?* Cambridge: Polity Press.

Morales, R. and Ong, P. 1991. 'Immigrant Women in Los Angeles', *Economic and Industrial Democracy*, 12 (1), 65–81.

Moras, A. 2011. 'Immigrants in Alaska—Authorized and Unauthorized', *Alaska Justice Forum*, 28 (2–3), 1–12.

Morris, A. and Verdasco, A. 2020. 'Loneliness and Housing Tenure: Older Private Renters and Social Housing Tenants in Australia', *Journal of Sociology*, doi: 10.1177/14407833209 60527.

Morris, A., Hastings, C., Wilson, S., Mitchell, E., Ramia, G., and Overgaard, C. 2020. *The Experience of International Students Before and During COVID-19: Housing, Work, Study and Wellbeing.* Sydney: University of Technology Sydney

Morris, A., Wilson, S., Mitchell, E., Ramia, G., and Hastings, C. (2021). *International students struggling in the private rental sector in Australia prior to and during the pandemic, Housing Studies,* doi: 10.1080/02673037.2021.1961695.

Morrison, J., Merrick, B., Higgs, S., and Metais, J. 2005. 'Researching the Performance of International Students in the UK', *Studies in Higher Education,* 30 (3), 327–337.

Mourad, H. 2009. *The Development and Land Use Impacts of Local Mosques* (Batchelor of Planning thesis). Faculty of the Built Environment, University of New South Wales, Sydney.

Moustafine, M. 2011. 'Russians', *Sydney Journal,* 3 (2), 55–64.

Moyo, S. and Yeros, P. (eds). 2005. *Reclaiming the Land: The Resurgence of Rural Movements in Africa, Asia and Latin America.* London: Zed.

Mulcahy, K. and Kollamparambil, U. 2016. 'The Impact of Rural–Urban Migration on Subjective Well-Being in South Africa', *The Journal of Development Studies,* 52 (9), 1357–1371.

Mung, E.M. 2008. 'Chinese Migration and China's Foreign Policy in Africa', *Journal of Chinese Overseas,* 4, 91–109.

Murray, L. 2016. *Sydney Cemeteries: A Field Guide.* Sydney: NewSouth Publishing.

Mutethya, E. 2018. 'Bloom of Youth', *China Daily, Africa Weekly,* 7 (November), 23–29.

Myrdal, G. 1944. *An American Dilemma: The Negro Problem and Modern Democracy.* New York: Harper and Brothers Publishers.

Myrdal, G. 1968. *Asian Drama: An Inquiry into the Poverty of Nations* (Vol. III). New York: Pantheon.

Nagel, T. 1986. *The View from Nowhere.* Oxford and New York: Oxford University Press,.

Ndikumana, L. and Boyce J.K. 2011. *Africa's Odious Debts: How Foreign Loans and Capital Flight Bled the Continent.* London and New York: Zed.

Ndjio, B. 2009. '"Shanghai Beauties" and African Desires: Migration, Trade and Chinese Prostitution in Cameroon', *European Journal of Development Research,* 21 (September), 606–621.

Ndjio, B. 2014. '"Magic Body" and "Cursed Sex": Chinese Sex Workers as "Bitchwitches" in Cameroon', *African Affairs,* 113 (452), 370–386.

Nelson, J. 2016. 'Male is a Gender, Too: A Review of Why Gender Matters in Economics by Mukesh Eswaran', *Journal of Economic Literature,* 54 (4), 1362–1376.

Netto, G. 2011. 'Identity Negotiation, Pathways to Housing and "Place": The Experience of Refugees in Glasgow', *Housing, Theory and Society,* 28 (2), 123–143.

Nevins, J. 2019. 'Migration as Reparations', in *Open Borders: In Defense of Free Movement,* ed. Reece Jones. Athens: University of Georgia Press, pp. 129–140.

New African Magazine. 2015. 'China's Long History in Africa', New African Magazine, 11 March, http://newafricanmagazine.com/chinas-long-history-africa/.

New South Wales Government. 2020. *Lidcombe Public School 2019 Annual Report.* Sydney: NSW Government.

New South Wales Government. 2021. *Lidcombe Public School 2020 Annual Report. Sydney: NSW Government.*

Ngai, P. 2016. *Migrant Labor in China.* London: Polity.

Nguepjouo, D. 2020, 'Dealing with Chinese Investors in Cameroon's Mines: African Agency and Participation' in *Afrasian Transformations: Transregional Perspectives on Development Cooperation, Social Mobility, and Cultural Change*, eds. R. Achenbach, J. Beek, J. N. Kargia, R. Mageza-Barthel, and F. Schulze-Engler, Leiden and Boston: Brill, pp. 134–154

Nguyen, K.H. and Bretag, T. 2021. 'Socio-cultural and Settlement Support Services for International Students: A 'Home Away from Home' Approach', In: Huijser H., Kek M., Padró F.F. (eds). *Student Support Services*. Singapore: University Development and Administration. Springer. https://doi.org/10.1007/978-981-13-3364-4_28-1

Niemi, S. 2018. *Theory of Control Tuning: The Processing of Control in Migration-Related Place Coping*. Helsinki: University of Helsinki.

Nine (9)/11 Commission. 2004. *9/11 Commission Report: Final Report of the National Commission on Terrorist Attacks upon the United States*. Washington, DC: US Government Printing Office.

Nour, S.S.O.M. 2011. 'Assessment of the Impact of Oil: Opportunities and Challenges for Economic Development in Sudan', *African Review of Economics and Finance 2* (2), 122–148.

Nour, S.S.O.M. 2019. 'Migration of Higher Education Students from the North Africa Region', Maastricht Economic and Social Research Institute on Innovation and Technology Working Paper Series, 2019–010.

Nowotny, K. 2019. 'Review of *The Gift of Global Talent: How Migration Shapes Business, Economy and Society*', *Regional Studies, 53* (11), 1646.

Nurul, N., Nor, Y., and Nazirah, A. 2011. 'Student Residential Satisfaction in Research Universities', *Journal of Facilities Management, 9* (3), 200–212.

Nyantakyi-Frimpong, H. 2020. 'Unmasking Difference: Intersectionality and Smallholder Farmers' Vulnerability to Climate Extremes in Northern Ghana', *Gender, Place and Culture, 27* (11), 1536–1554.

Nyantakyi-Frimpong, H., Arku, G., and Inkoom, D.K.B. 2016. 'Urban Agriculture and Political Ecology of Health in Municipal Ashaiman, Ghana', *Geoforum, 72* (June), 38–48.

O'Donnell, E.T. 2015. *Henry George and the Crisis of Inequality*. New York: Columbia University Press.

O'Hara, P.A. and Sherman, H.J. 2004. 'Veblen and Sweezy on Monopoly Capital, Crises, Conflict, and the State', *Journal of Economic Issues, 38* (4), 969–987.

O'Sullivan, A. 2006. *Urban Economics*. Eighth edition. Boston, MA. McGraw-Hill

Obeng, M.K.M. 2019. 'Journey to the East: A Study of Ghanaian Migrants in Guangzhou, China', *Canadian Journal of African Studies, 53* (1), 67–87.

Obeng v Obeng (J4/37/2015) [2015] GHASC 112 (09 December 2015) https://ghalii.org/gh/judgment/supreme-court/2015/112 (accessed 4.10.2021)

Obeng-Odoom, F. 2008. 'Has the Habitat for Humanity Housing Scheme achieved its goals? A Ghanaian case study', *Journal of Housing and the Built Environment, 24* (1), 67–84.

Obeng-Odoom, F. 2009. 'The Future of Our Cities', *Cities: The International Journal of Urban Policy and Planning, 26* (1), 49–53.

Obeng-Odoom, F. 2010a. 'Abnormal Urbanisation in Africa: A Dissenting View', *African Geographical Review, 29* (2), 13–40.

Obeng-Odoom, F. 2010b. 'Is Decentralisation in Ghana Pro-Poor?', *Commonwealth Journal of Local Governance, 6* (July), 120–126.

Obeng-Odoom, F. 2011a. 'The Informal Sector in Ghana under Siege', *Journal of Developing Societies, 27* (3 and 4), 355–392.

Obeng-Odoom, F. 2011b. 'Private Rental Housing in Ghana: Reform or Renounce?', *Journal of International Real Estate and Construction Studies, 1* (1), 71–90.

Obeng-Odoom, F. 2012. 'The Ghana House Trust: An Innovation by Migrants?', *Global Built Environment Review*, 8 (1), 37–44.

Obeng-Odoom, F. 2013. *Governance for Pro-Poor Urban Development: Lessons from Ghana*. London: Routledge.

Obeng-Odoom, F. 2014. *Oiling the Urban Economy: Land, Labour, Capital, and the State in Sekondi-Takoradi*. London: Routledge.

Obeng-Odoom, F. 2015a. 'Review of *A Sociological Study of Street Children in Ghana: Victims of Kingship Breakdown and Rural–Urban Migration*', *City*, 19 (6), 879–881.

Obeng-Odoom, F. 2015b. 'Oil Rent, Policy, and Social Development: Lessons from the Ghana Controversy', Research Paper 2, United Nations Research Institute for Social Development (UNRISD).

Obeng-Odoom, F. 2015c. 'The Social, Spatial, and Economic Roots of Urban Inequality in Africa: Contextualizing Jane Jacobs and Henry George', *The American Journal of Economics and Sociology*, 74, 550–586.

Obeng-Odoom, F. 2016a. 'Migration, African Migrants, and the World: Towards a Radical Political Economy', *African Identities*, 14 (4), 1–13.

Obeng-Odoom, F. 2016b. *Reconstructing Urban Economics: Towards a Political Economy of the Built Environment*. London: Zed.

Obeng-Odoom, F. 2017a. 'Teaching Property Economics Students Political Economy: Mission Impossible?', *International Journal of Pluralism and Economics Education*, 8 (4), 359–377.

Obeng-Odoom, F. 2017b. 'Unequal Access to Land and the Current Migration Crisis', *Land Use Policy*, 74, 159–171.

Obeng-Odoom, F. 2017c. 'Urban Governance in Africa Today: Conceptualisation, Trends, and Innovation', *Growth and Change*, 48 (1), 4–21.

Obeng-Odoom, F, 2018a. 'The Contribution of J.R. Commons to Migration Analysis', *Evolutionary and Institutional Economics Review*, 15 (1), 73–88.

Obeng-Odoom, F. 2018b. 'The Gated Housing Hierarchy', in *Property, Place and Piracy*, eds M. Fredriksson and J. Arvanitakis. London: Routledge, pp. 187–201.

Obeng-Odoom, F. 2018c. 'Transnational Corporations and Urban Development', *American Journal of Economics and Sociology*, 77 (2), 447–510.

Obeng-Odoom, F. 2020a. 'COVID-19, Inequality, and Social Stratification in Africa', *African Review of Economics and Finance*, 12 (1), 3–37.

Obeng-Odoom, F. 2020b. *Property, Institutions, and Social Stratification in Africa*. Cambridge, UK: Cambridge University Press.

Obeng-Odoom, F. 2020c. 'The African Continental Free Trade Area', *American Journal of Economics and Sociology*, 79 (1), 167–197.

Obeng-Odoom F, 2020d, 'Urban Political Economy', in Dunn B, editor, *Research Agenda for Critical Political Economy*, Edward Elgar, London, 181–193.

Obeng-Odoom, F. 2021a. *The Commons in an Age of Uncertainty: Decolonizing Nature, Economy, and Society*. Toronto: University of Toronto Press.

Obeng-Odoom, F., 2021b, 'Oil Cities in Africa: Beyond Just Transition', *American Journal of Economics and Sociology*, 80 (2), 777-821.

Obeng-Odoom, F., 2021c, 'Rethinking Development Economics: Problems and Prospects of Georgist Political Economy', Review of Political Economy.

Obeng-Odoom, F. and Gyampo, R.E.V. 2017. 'Land Grabbing, Land Rights, and the Role of the Courts', *Geography Research Forum*, 37, 127–147.

Obeng-Odoom, F. and Jang, H.S. 2016. 'Immigrants and the Transformation of Local Towns: A Study of Socio-Economic Transformation of Lidcombe, Australia', *Urbani izziv*, *27* (1), 132–148.

Obeng-Odoom, F. and McDermott, M. 2018. *Valuing Unregistered Land*. London: RICS.

Obeng-Odoom, F. and Stilwell, F. 2013. 'Security of Tenure in International Development Discourse', *International Development Planning Review*, *35* (4), 315–333.

Obeng-Odoom, F., Elhadary Y.A., and Jang H.S. 2014. 'Living behind the Wall and Socio-Economic Implications for Those Outside the Wall: Gated Communities in Malaysia and Ghana', *Journal of Asian and African Studies*, *49* (5), 544–558.

Obi, C. 2009. 'Nigeria's Niger Delta: Understanding the Complex Drivers of Violent Oil-Related Conflict', *Africa Development*, *34* (2), 103–128.

Obi, C. 2019. 'The Changing Dynamics of Chinese Oil and Gas Engagements in Africa', in *China–Africa and an Economic Transformation*, eds A. Oqubay and J. Yifu Lin. Oxford: Oxford University Press, pp. 173–191.

Obosu-Mensah, K. 1999. *Food Production in Urban Areas a Study of Urban Agriculture in Accra, Ghana*. Aldershot, UK: Ashgate.

Obosu-Mensah, K. 2002. 'Changes in Official Attitudes towards Urban Agriculture in Accra', *African Studies Quarterly 6* (3), 19–32.

Obour, P.B., Owusu, K., and Teye, J.K. 2017. 'From Seasonal Migrants to Settlers: Climate Change and Permanent Migration to the Transitional Zone of Ghana', in *Migration and Development in Africa: Trends, Challenges, and Policy Implications*, eds S. Tonah, M.B. Setrana, and J.A. Arthur. Lanham, MD, Boulder, Co, New York, and London: Lexington Books.

Odabaş, M. and Adaman, F. 2018. 'Engaging with Social Networks: The Bourdieu-Becker Encounter Revisited', *Forum for Social Economics*, *47* (3–4), 305–321.

Office of the Vice-Chancellor and Principal. 2018. *Annual Report 2017*. Office of the Vice-Chancellor and Principal, University of Sydney, Sydney.

Office of the Vice-Chancellor and Principal. 2020. *Annual Report 2019*. Office of the Vice-Chancellor and Principal, University of Sydney, Sydney.

Ojong, N. 2011. 'Livelihood Strategies in African Cities: The Case of Residents in Bamenda, Cameroon', *African Review of Economics and Finance*, *3* (1), 8–25.

Ojong, N. 2020. *The Everyday Life of the Poor in Cameroon: The Role of Social Networks in Meeting Needs*. London: Routledge.

Oka, R. 2011. 'Unlikely Cities in the Desert: The Informal Economy as a Causal Agent for Permanent "Urban" Sustainability in Kakuma Refugee Camp, Kenya', *Urban Anthropology and Studies of Cultural Systems and World Economic Development*, *40* (3–4), 223–262.

Olarinde, O. S, 2021, The Spatial Distribution of African Migrants In Selected Global North Destinations, PhD Thesis, University of Ibadan, Nigeria.

Oliveri, F. 2014. 'Review of *Us and Them? The Dangerous Politics of Immigration Control*', *Space and Polity*, *18* (3), 306–309.

Oppong, R. 2004. 'Ghana: Internal, International, and Transnational Migration', in *Migration and Immigration: A Global View*, eds M. Toro-Morn and M. Alicea. Westport, CT: Greenwood Press, pp. 81–94.

Organisation for Economic Co-operation and Development (OECD). 2019. *International Migration Outlook 2019*. Paris: OECD Publishing.

O'Sullivan, A. 2012, *Urban Economics*, McGraw-Hill Irwin, Boston.

Ouma, S. 2020. *Land and Finance Farming as Financial Asset: Global Finance and the Making of Institutional Landscapes*. Newcastle upon Tyne: Agenda Publishing.

Overa, R. 2007. 'When Men Do Women's Work: Structural Adjustment, Underemployment and Changing Gender Relations in the Informal Economy of Accra, Ghana', *Journal of Modern African Studies 45* (4), 539–563.

Owoo, N.S., Lambon-Quayefio, M.P., and Onuoha, N.A. 2020. 'Effects of Higher Spousal Earnings on Women's Social Empowerment in Ghana', *Forum for Social Economics, 49* (2), 139–165.

Owusu, G. 2010. 'Social Effects of Poor Sanitation and Waste Management on Poor Urban Communities: A Neighbourhood-Specific Study of Sabon Zongo, Accra', *Journal of Urbanism: International Research on Placemaking and Urban Sustainability, 3* (2), 145–160.

Owusu, G., Agyei-Mensah, S., and Lund, R. 2008. 'Slums of Hope and Slums of Despair: Mobility and Livelihoods in Nima, Accra', *Norwegian Journal of Geography, 62* (3), 180–190.

Owusu-Ansah, A., Ohemeng-Mensah, D., Talinbe, R., and Obeng-Odoom, F. 2018. 'Public Choice Theory and Rental Housing: An Examination of Rental Housing Contracts in Ghana', *Housing Studies, 33* (6), 938–959.

Özkul, D. 2019. 'The Making of a Transnational Religion: Alevi Movement in Germany and the World Alevi Union', *British Journal of Middle Eastern Studies, 46* (2), 259–273.

Özkul, D. and Obeng-Odoom, F. 2013. 'Temporary Migration in Africa: Views from the Global South', *African Review of Economics and Finance, 5* (1), 2–8.

Palmer, R. 2007. 'Skills for Work?: From Skills Development to Decent Livelihoods in Ghana's Rural Informal Economy', *International Journal of Educational Development, 27* (4), 397–420.

Paltridge, T., Mayson, S., and Schapper, J. 2010. 'The Contribution of University Accommodation to International Student Security', *Journal of Higher Education Policy and Management, 32* (4), 353–364.

Pantuliano, S. 2010. 'Oil, Land and Conflict: The Decline of Misseriyya Pastoralism in Sudan', *Review of African Political Economy, 37* (123), 7–23.

Paquet, M. and Xhardez, C. 2020. 'Immigrant Integration Policies when Regions Decide "Who Comes In": The Case of Canadian Provinces', *Regional Studies, 54* (11), 1519–1534.

Park, J.P., Lampert, B., and Robertson, W. 2016. 'Editorial: China's Impacts on Africa's Development', *African Review of Economics and Finance, 8* (1), 3–11.

Park, J.Z. 2013. 'Ethnic Insularity among 1.5- and Second-Generation Korean-American Christians', *Development and Society, 42* (1), 113–136.

Park, Y.J. 2019. 'Early Chinese Migrants in Sub-Saharan Africa: Contract Labourers and Traders' Chinese and African Entrepreneurs', in *Chinese and African Entrepreneurs Social Impacts of Interpersonal Encounters*, eds K. Giese and L. Marfaing. Leiden: Brill, pp. 84–99.

Parker, J. 2000. *Making the Town: Ga State and Society in Early Colonial Accra*. Portsmouth, NH, Oxford, and Cape Town: Heinemann.

Parkinson, S., James, A., and Liu, E. 2018. *Navigating a Changing Private Rental Sector: Opportunities and Challenges for Low-Income Renters*. Sydney: Australian Housing and Urban Research Institute.

Pearce, F. 2012. *The Land Grabbers: The New Fight Over Who Owns the Earth*. Boston, MA: Beacon Press.

Peck, C. and Stewart, K. 1985. 'Satisfaction with Housing and Quality of Life', *Home Economics Research Journal*, 13 (4), 363–372.

Pécoud, A. 2018. 'What Do We Know about the International Organization for Migration?', *Journal of Ethnic and Migration Studies*, 44 (10), 1621–1638.

Peil, M. 1972. *The Ghanaian Factory Worker*. New York: Cambridge University Press.

Peil, M. 1995. 'Ghanaians Abroad', *African Affairs*, 94 (376), 345–367.

Pellow, D. 2002. *Landlords and Lodgers: Socio-Spatial Organization in an Accra Community*. Chicago, IL and London: University of Chicago Press.

Pemberton, S. and Phillimore, J. 2018. 'Migrant Place-Mmaking in Super-Diverse Neighbourhoods: Moving beyond Ethno-National Approaches', *Urban Studies*, 55 (4), 733–750.

Perdigao, Y.P. 2017. 'Review of *Migrant, Refugee, Smuggler, Saviour*', http://blogs.lse.ac.uk/africaatlse/2017/09/29/book-review-migrant-refugee-smuggler-savior-by-peter-tinti-and-tuesday-reitano/.

Peters, R. 2013. *Surabaya, 1945–2010: Neighbourhood, State and Economy in Indonesia's City of Struggle*. Singapore: National University of Singapore Press.

Petrella, F. 1984. 'Henry George's Theory of State's Agenda: The Origins of His Ideas on Economic Policy in Adam Smith's Moral Theory', *American Journal of Economics and Sociology*, 43 (3), 269–286.

Phibbs, P. and Young, P. 2009. 'Going Once, Going Twice: A Short History of Public Housing in Australia', in *Where the Other Half Lives: Lower Income Housing in a Neoliberal World*, ed. S. Glynn. New York: Pluto Press, pp. 217–231.

Pickering, J. 2001. 'Globalisation: A Threat to Australian Culture?', *Journal of Australian Political Economy*, 48 (December), 46–59.

Piketty, T. 2014. *Capital in the Twenty-First Century*. Cambridge, MA and London: The Belknap Press of Harvard University Press.

Ping, W. 2010. 'A Case Study of an In-Class Silent Postgraduate Chinese Student in London Metropolitan University: A Journey of Learning', *TESOL Journal*, 2, 207–214.

Piper, N., Rosewarne, S., and Withers, M. 2016. 'Redefining a Rights-Based Approach in the Context of Temporary Labour Migration in Asia', *UNRISD* Working Paper, 2016–11, Geneva.

Piper, N., Rosewarne, S., and Withers, M. 2017. 'Migrant Precarity in Asia: "Networks of Labour Activism" for a Rights-Based Governance of Migration', *Development and Change*, 48 (5), 1089–1110.

Pishé, V. 2013. 'Contemporary Migration Theories as Reflected in Their Founding Texts', *Population-E*, 68 (1), 141–164.

Poel, P. 2005. *Informal Institutions, Transaction Costs and Trust: A Case Study on Housing Construction by Migrants in Ashanti-Mampong, Ghana* (M.A. thesis). University of Amsterdam.

Poeze, M. 2019. 'Beyond Breadwinning: Ghanaian Transnational Fathering in the Netherlands', *Journal of Ethnic and Migration Studies*, 45 (16), 3065–3084.

Polanyi, K. 1944/2001. *The Great Transformation: The Political and Economic Origins of Our Time*. Boston, MA: Beacon Press.

Polanyi, K. 1957. 'The Economy as Instituted Process', in *Trade and Market in the Early Empires: Economies in History and Theory*, eds K. Polanyi, C.M. Arensberg, and H.W. Pearson. Glencose, IL: The Free Press, pp. 243–270.

Pollen, F. 1988. *The Book of Sydney Suburbs*. Auckland: Angus & Robertson.

Pope Francis. 2016. *Post-Synodal Apostolic Exhortation—Amoris Laetitia—of the Holy Father Francis to Bishops, Priests and Deacons, Consecrated Persons, Christian Married Couples, and All the Lay Faithful: On Love in the Family*. Rome: Vatican Press.

Pope Francis. 2020. *Post-Synodal Apostolic Exhortation: Querida Amazonia of the Holy Father Francis to the People of God and to All Persons of Good Will*. Rome: Vatican Press.

Popper, K.R., 1959/2014, *The Logic of Scientific Discovery*, Martino Publishing Mansfield Centre, CT.

Portes, A. and Yiu, J. 2013. 'Entrepreneurship, Transnationalism, and Development', *Migration Studies*, 3 (1), 75–95.

Potter, A.B. 2015. 'The Economic Consequences of the Peace, John Maynard Keynes (1919)', www.classicsofstrategy.com/Potter-Keynes-Economic-Consequences.pdf.

Potts, D. 2009. 'The Slowing of Sub-Saharan Africa's Urbanization: Evidence and Implications for Urban Livelihoods', *Environment and Urbanization 21* (1), 253–259.

Powell, J. (2021). 'The Non-evolutionary and non-benign character of stylised facts', *Journal of Economic Issues*, LV (2), 349–358.

Prain, G., Karanja, N., and Lee-Smith, D. 2010. *African Urban Harvest: Agriculture in the Cities of Cameroon, Kenya and Uganda*. Ottawa: Springer.

Priest, N., Chong, S., Truong. M., Sharif, M., Dunn, K., Paradies, Y., Nelson, J., Alam, O., Ward, A., and Kavanagh, A. 2019. 'Findings from the 2017 Speak Out Against Racism (SOAR) Student and Staff Surveys', Centre for Social Research and Methods (CSRM) Working Paper No. 3/2019, Australian National University, Canberra.

Pritchett, L. 2006. *Let Their People Come*. Washington, DC: Center for GlobalDevelopment.

Pullen, J. 2014. *Nature's Gifts: The Australian Lectures of Henry George on the Ownership of Land and Other Natural Resources*. Sydney: Desert Pea Press.

Quayson, A. 2014. *Oxford Street, Accra: City Life and the Itineraries of Transnationalism*. Durham, NC and London: Duke University Press.

Quayson vs Ankomah-Nimfah and the Electoral Commission, 2021, Court of Appeal, https://www.graphic.com.gh/images/pdfs/STAY_OF_EXECUTION_PENDING_APPEAL_-_James_Quayson.pdf (acccessed 8.09.2021)

Ramamurti, R. and Hillemann, J. 2018. 'What is "Chinese" about Chinese Multinationals?', *Journal of International Business Studies*, 49 (November), 43–44.

Ramazzotti, P., Frigato, P., and Elsner, W. 2012. *Social Costs Today: Institutional Analyses of the Present Crisis*. London: Routledge.

Ramia, G. 2017. 'Higher Education Institutions and the Administration of International Student Rights: A Law and Policy Analysis', *Studies in Higher Education*, 42 (5), 911–924.

Ramia, G. 2018. 'The Development of Policy on International Student Welfare and the Question of Crisis Response', *Australian Journal of Social Issues*, 53 (1), 71–82.

Randolph, B., Holloway, D., and Ruming K. 2005. *Social Outcomes of Residential Development, Sydney Olympic Park Stage 1: Local Area Analysis*. Sydney: City Futures Research Centre Publication, University of New South Wales.

Ratcliffe, J. and Stubbs, M. 1996. *Urban Planning and Real Estate Development*. London: UCL Press.

Ravenstein, E.G. 1885. 'The Laws of Migration', *Journal of the Royal Statistical Society*, 48, 167–235. Series: Economics and Organization, 8 (4), 345–356.

Ravenstein, E.G. 1889. 'The Laws of Migration', *Journal of the Royal Statistical Society*, 52, 241–305.

Ray White Lidcombe. 2018. *Market Review: March Quarter*. Sydney: Ray White Lidcombe.

Reich, M. 1980. 'Empirical and Ideological Elements in the Decline of Ricardian Economics', *Review of Radical Political Economics, 12* (3), 1–14.

Remoff, H. 2016. 'Malthus, Darwin, and the Descent of Economics', *American Journal of Economics and Sociology, 75* (4), 862–903.

Ricardo, D. (1817/2001) *The Principles of Political Economy and Taxation*, Ontario: Batoche Books.

Richardson, K. 2003. 'International Education: The Quality of Homestay Services', 17th IDP Australian International Education Conference, 21–24 October 2003, Melbourne, Australia.

Riddell, J. 2009. '"World Farmers" Alliance Challenges Food Profiteers', *Socialist Voice Pamphlet*, May, 3–11.

Riley, R. and Weale, M. 2006. 'Commentary: Immigration and Its Effects', *National Institute Economic Review, 198* (October), 4–9.

Rizvi, F. and Lingard, B. 2011. 'Social Equity and the Assemblage of Values in Australian Higher Education', *Cambridge Journal of Education, 41* (1), 5–22.

Robertson, W. 2016. 'Review of China's Superbank: Debt, Oil and Influence—How China Development Bank Is Rewriting the Rules of Finance', *African Review of Economics and Finance, 8*, 164–167.

Robinson, C.J. 1983. *Black Marxism: The Making of the Black Radical Tradition*. Chapel Hill, NC and London: The University of North Carolina Press.

Robinson, J. 1979/2009. *Aspects of Development and Underdevelopment*. Cambridge, UK: Cambridge University Press.

Rodney, W. 1972/2011. *How Europe Underdeveloped Africa*. Baltimore, MD: Black Classic Press.

Roose, J., Karolewski, I.P., Pawel, I., and Sata, R. 2020. 'Introduction: Patterns and Implications of Migration and Rebordering; introduction', in *Migration and Border-Making: Reshaping Policies and Identities*, eds R. Sata, J. Roose, and I.P. Karolewski. Edinburgh: Edinburgh University Press. 52–75

Rosewarne, S. 2010. 'Globalisation and the Commodification of Labour: Temporary Labour Migration', *The Economic and Labour Relations Review, 20* (2), 99–110.

Rosewarne, S. 2012. 'Temporary International Labor Migration and Development in South and Southeast Asia', *Feminist Economics, 18* (1), 63–90.

Rosewarne, S. 2014. 'Migrant Domestic Work: From Precarious to Precarisation', *Journal fuer Entwicklungspolitik (Austrian Journal of Development Studies), 30* (4), 133–154.

Rosewarne, S. 2016. 'Transnationalization and the Capitalization of Labor: Female Foreign Domestic Workers', in *Women Migrant Workers: Ethical, Political and Legal Problems*, ed. Z. Meghani. New York & London: Routledge, pp. 199–223.

Rosewarne, S. 2020a. 'Editorial: The Making of the Agricultural Industry's Temporary Migrant Workforce: Beyond Exploitative Experiences?', *Journal of Australian Political Economy, 84* (Summer), 5–12.

Rosewarne, S. 2020b. 'The Structural Transformation of Australian Agriculture: Globalisation, Corporatisation and the Devalorisation of Labour', *Journal of Australian Political Economy, 84* (Summer), 175–218.

Ruming, K., Dowling, R. 2017. 'PhD students' housing experiences in suburban Sydney, Australia', *Journal of Housing and the Built Environment 32* (April), 805–825.

Russell, J., Thomson, G., and Rosenthal, D. 2008. 'International Student Use of University Health and Counselling Services', *Higher Education, 56* (August), 59–75.

Ryan-Collins, R., 2021, 'Private Landed Property and Finance: A Checkered History', *American Journal of Economics and Sociology*, 80 (2), 465-502.

Ryan-Collins, J., Lloyd, T., and MacFarlane, L. 2017. *Rethinking the Economics of Land and Housing*. London: Zed.

Sackeyfio-Lenoch, N. 2014. *The Politics of Chieftaincy: Authority and Property in Colonial Ghana, 1920–1950*. Rochester, NY: University of Rochester Press.

Sager, A. 2016. 'Book Review: *Violent Borders: Refugees and the Right to Move* by Reece Jones', *LSE Review of Books blog*, 12 June, https://blogs.lse.ac.uk/lsereviewofbooks/2016/12/06/book-review-violent-borders-refugees-and-the-right-to-move-by-reece-jones/.

Saleeby, B. 2010. 'Anchorage, Alaska: City of Hope for International Refugees', *Alaska Journal of Anthropology*, 8 (2), 93–102.

Sandbrook, R. and Arn, J. 1977. *The Labouring Poor and Urban Class Formation: The Case of Greater Accra*. Montreal: McGill University.

Sanderson, H. and Forsythe, M. 2013. *China's Superbank: Debt, Oil and Influence—How China Development Bank is Rewriting the Rules of Finance*. Singapore: Wiley.

Sassen, S. 2014. *Expulsions: Brutality and Complexity in the Global Economy*. Cambridge, MA: Harvard University Press.

Sassen, S. 2020. 'When primitive accumulation inhabits advanced systems', in De Schutter O and Rajagopal B, eds., *Property Rights from Below: Commodification of Land and the Counter-Movement*, Routledge, London, pp. 23–27.

Sata, R., Roose, J., and Karolewski, I.P. (eds). 2020. *Migration and Border-Making: Reshaping Policies and Identities*. Edinburgh: Edinburgh University Press.

Saunavaara, J. 2017. 'The Role of International Development Strategies in Making Regional Development Policies: Hokkaido as a Case Study', *Urbani izziv*, 28, 122–135.

Saunders, D. 2012. *Arrival City: How the Largest Migration in History Is Reshaping our World*. New York: Vintage Books

Schreuder, D. and Bowman, D. 2010. *Review of Support Services for International Students at the University of Sydney*, Appendix 13, January, University of Sydney.

Schumpeter, J.A. 1947. 'The Creative Response in Economic History', *The Journal of Economic History*, 7, 149–159.

Sclar, E. 2021, 'The Infinite Elasticity of Air: New York City's Financialization of Transferable Development Rights', *American Journal of Economics and Sociology*, 80 (2),353–380.

Seale, P. 1965. *The Struggle for Syria: A Study of Post-War Arab Politics, 1945–1958*. New York: Oxford University Press.

Seale, P. 1988. *Asad: The Struggle for the Middle East*. Berkeley, CA: University of California Press.

Seale, P. and Butler, L. 1996. 'Asad's Regional Strategy and the Challenge from Netanyahu', *Journal of Palestine Studies* 26 (1), 27–41.

Searle, G. 2012. 'The Long-Term Urban Impacts of the Sydney Olympic Games', *Australian Planner*, 49 (3), 195–202.

Sekyiamah, K. 2006. Speech delivered by H.E. Mr. Kofi Sekyiamah, Ghana High Commissioner at the Cultural Night on Saturday 11 November, at the Theo Notaras Multicultural Centre.

Sen, A. 1999. *Development as Freedom*. New York: Oxford University Press.

Sen, A. 2006. *Identity and Violence: The Illusion of Destiny*. London: Penguin.

Serra, P. 2012. 'Global Businesses "from Below": Ethnic Entrepreneurs in Metropolitan Areas', *Urbani izziv*, 23 (2), S97–S106.

Serwaa vs Hashimu and Another (J4/31/2020) [2021] GHASC 3 (14 April 2021) https://ghalii.org/gh/judgment/supreme-court/2021/3?fbclid=IwAR3DxRatlqtpQsilVSqmCcR35E-2mCTWTqu5KDhcCKx65K4yd2iRTpThIDU (accessed 4. 10.2021)

Shelton T., Renaldi E., and Xiao, B. 2019. 'World Suicide Prevention Day: How International Students Are Vulnerable to Mental Health Issues', Australian Broadcasting Corporation, 9 September, www.abc.net.au/news/2019-09-10/suicide-prevention-day-pressures-facing-international-students/11476938.

Sheridan, D. 2016. 'Review: *China's Second Continent: How a Million Migrants are Building a New Empire in Africa*', *African Review of Economics and Finance*, 8 (1), 156–159.

Sherman, H. 2006. 'The Making of a Radical Economics', *Review of Radical Political Economics*, 38 (40), 519–538.

Sherman, H. 2011. 'Portrait of a Crisis', *Journal of Economic Issues*, 45 (3), 703–716.

Showers, K. 2014. 'Europe's Long History of Extracting African Renewable Energy: Contexts for African Scientists, Technologists, Innovators and Policy-Makers', *African Journal of Science, Technology, Innovation and Development*, 6 (4), 301–313.

Simonneau, D. 2017. 'Review: Reece Jones, *Violent Borders: Refugees and the Right to Move*', *European Review of International Studies*, 4 (1), 97–99.

Singerman, D.R. 2016. 'Keynesian Eugenics and the Goodness of the World', *Journal of British Studies*, 55 (3), 538–565.

Smit, J., Nasr, J., and Ratta, A. 2001. *Urban Agriculture: Food, Jobs and Sustainable Cities*. Washington, DC: The Urban Agriculture Network, Inc.

Smith, L.T. 1999. *Decolonizing Methodologies Research and Indigenous Peoples*. London: Zed/Dunedin: University of Otago Press.

Somin, I. 2020, *Free to Move: Foot Voting, Migration, and Political Freedom*. Oxford: Oxford University Press.

Soong H, 2018, 'Transnational Teachers in Australian Schools: Implications for Democratic Education', *Global Studies of Childhood*, 8 (4), 404-414.

Songsore, J. 2011. *Regional Development in Ghana: The Theory and the Reality*. Accra: Woeli Publishing Services.

Speak, S. 2004. 'Degrees of Destitution: A Typology of Homelessness in Developing Countries', *Housing Studies*, 19 (3), 465–482.

Speak, S. 2005. 'Relationship between Children's Homelessness in Developing Countries and the Failure of Women's Rights Legislation', *Housing, Theory and Society*, 22 (3), 129–146.

Speak, S. 2019. 'The State of Homelessness in Developing Countries Presented to the Expert Group Meeting on 'Affordable housing and social protection systems for all to address homelessness'', *United Nations Office at Nairobi*, https://www.un.org/development/desa/dspd/wp-content/uploads/sites/22/2019/05/SPEAK_Suzanne_Paper.pdf (accessed 3.09.2021)

Stache, C. 2019. 'Review of *Red–Green Revolution: The Politics and Technology of Ecosocialism* by Victor Walls', *International Critical Thought*, 9 (1), 142–147.

Stacey P, Grant R, Oteng-Ababio M, 2021, 'Food for thought: Urban market planning and entangled governance in Accra, Ghana', Habitat International,Volume 115, pp. 1-8.

Stafford, T. 1991. *Living in Liddy*. Sydney: Ettalong Beach.

Stewart, J.B. 2008. 'Stratification Economics', *International Encyclopedia of the Social Sciences*. Second edition, ed. W.A. Darity, Jr. Detroit: Macmillan Reference USA, pp. 530–531.

Stewart, J.B. and Coleman, M. 2005. 'The Black Political Economy Paradigm and the Dynamics of Racial Economic Inequality', in *African Americans in the U.S. Economy*, eds J. Whitehead, C. Conrad, P. Mason, and J. Stewart. Lanham, MD: Rowman & Littlefield, pp. 118–129.

Stilwell, F. 1993. *Reshaping Australia: Urban Problems and Policies*. Sydney: Pluto Press.

Stilwell, F. 1998. 'Globalization and Cities: An Australian Perspective', *Review of Radical Political Economics*, *30* (4), 139–167.

Stilwell, F. 2003. 'Refugees in a Region: Afghans in Young, NSW', *Urban Policy and Research*, *21* (3), 235–248.

Stilwell, F. 2006. *Political Economy: The Contest of Economic Ideas*. Second edition. Oxford: Oxford University Press.

Stilwell, F. 2011. 'The Condition of Labour, Capital and Land', paper presented at the Conference of the Association for Good Government, Sydney.

Stilwell, F. 2012. *Political Economy: The Contest of Economic Ideas*. Third edition. Melbourne: Oxford University Press.

Stilwell, F. 2016. 'The Science of Political Economy', *Conference of the Association for Good Government 2016*. Australia: Association for Good Government.

Stilwell, F. 2019. *The Political Economy of Inequality*. Cambridge, UK: Polity Press.

Stilwell, F. and Jordan, K. 2004a. 'Land Tax: A Green Policy Priority?', discussion paper prepared for the Greens Economic Policy Group, Sydney.

Stilwell, F. and Jordan, K. 2004b. 'The Political Economy of Land: Putting Henry George in His Place', *Journal of Australian Political Economy*, *54* (December), 119–134.

Stilwell, F., Jordan K., and Pearce, A. 2008. 'Crises, Interventions and Profits: A Political Economic Perspective', *Global Change, Peace and Security*, *20* (3), 263–274.

Stilwell F.J.B. 1974. *Australian Urban and Regional Development*. *Sydney* Australia and New Zealand Book Co.

Stilwell, F.J.B. 1979. 'Australian Urban and Regional Development in the Late 1970s: An Overview', *International Journal of Urban and Regional Research*, *3* (1–4), 527–541.

Stilwell, F.J.B. 1980. *Economic Crisis, Cities, and Regions*. Sydney: Pergamon Press.

Storper, M., Kemeny, T., Makarem, N., Makarem, N.P., and Osman, T. 2015. *The Rise and Fall of Urban Economies*. Stanford, CA: Stanford University Press.

Street Child Africa. 2010. 'The Street Children Project', www.streetchildafrica.org.uk/pages/ghana.html.

Students Representative Council (SRC). 2010. *International Students Handbook*. Sydney: Usyd SRC.

Subulwa A.G., 2019, 'Urban Refugees', in *The Wiley-Blackwell Encyclopedia of Urban and Regional Studies*, ed. A. Orum. London: John Wiley & Sons, pp. 1–10.

Sulemana, M., Dramani, J.B., and Oteng-Abayie, E.F. 2018. 'Foreign Bank Inflows: Implications for Bank Stability in Sub-Saharan Africa', *African Review of Economics and Finance*, *10* (1), 54–81.

Šutalo, I. 2004. *Croatians in Australia: Pioneers, Settlers and Their Descendants*. Kent Town, SA: Wakefield Press.

Sydney University Postgraduate Representative Union (SUPRA). 2010a. *Annual Report 2008–2009*. Sydney: SUPRA.

SUPRA. 2010b. 'SUPRA Green Paper Submission', SUPRA, Sydney.

Sydney Talent. 2010. *Business Brochure*. RGC Branding & Design Agency and the University of Sydney.

Tanis, K. 2020. 'Regional Distribution and Location Choices of Immigrants in Germany', *Regional Studies*, *54* (4), 483–494.

The Economist. 2016. 'A Plan for Europe's Refugees: How to Manage the Migrant Crisis and Keep Europe from Tearing Itself Apart', 6 February, pp. 9–10, 19–22.

The Economist. 2017. 'Macron's Mission', *The Economist*, 13–19 May, pp. 42–43.

The Economist. 2019a. 'The New Scramble for Africa and How Africans Can Win It', 9–15 March, pp. 9, 18–20.

The Economist. 2019b. 'The Next 50 Years in Space', 20–26 July, pp. 58–59.

The Economist. 2019c. 'Growing Barriers: Why Europe's Single Market Is at Risk', 14–20 September, pp. 13, 30–31, 35–36.

The Economist. 2019d. 'The $650bn Binge: Fear and Greed in the Entertainment Industry', 16–22 November, pp. 3–12 (special report: 'The Magic of Migration'), 1–12, and 15–16.

The Economist. 2019e. 'Inequality Illusions: Why Wealth and Income Gaps Are Now What They Appear', 30 November–6 December, pp. 53–54.

The Economist. 2019f. 'Christmas Double Issue', 21 December–3 January, pp. 81–82.

The Economist. 2020a. 'The Horrible Housing Blunder', 18–24 January, pp. 9, 3–12 (special report: 'Housing').

The Economist. 2020b. 'Big Tech's $2trn Bull Run', 22–28 February, pp. 7, 3–12 (special report: 'The Data Economy').

The Economist. 2020c. 'It's Going Global', 29 February–6 March, p. 7.

The Economist. 2020d. 'The Right Medicine for the World Economy', 7–13 March, p. 9.

The Economist. 2020e. 'The Politics of Pandemics', 14–20 March, p. 7.

The Economist. 2020f. 'Closed', 21–27 March, pp. 9–10, 14–17 (special report: 'The Pandemic').

The Economist. 2020g. 'The Next Calamity', *The Economist*, 28 March–3 April, pp. 9, 33–36.

The Economist. 2020h. 'A Grim Calculus', 4–10 April, pp. 39–40.

The Economist. 2020i. 'The Business of Survival: How COVID-19 Will Shape Global Commerce', 11–17 April, p. 7.

The Economist. 2020j. 'Your Country Needs Me: A Pandemic of Power Grabs', 25 April–1 May, pp. 25–26.

The Economist. 2020k. 'The 90% Economy', 2–8 May, p. 7.

The Economist. 2020l. 'Seize the Moment', 23–29 May, pp. 25–26.

The Economist. 2020m. 'The New World Disorder', 20–26 June, p. 44.

The Economist. 2020n. 'The New Ideology of Race. And What's Wrong with It', 11–17 July, pp. 7–8, 13–15, 48–50.

The Economist. 2020o. 'Free Money: When Government Spending Knows No Limits', 25–31 July, pp. 29–30, 36–38.

The Economist. 2020p. 'Locked Out: When and How to Let Migrants Move Again', 1–7 August, pp. 7, 41–42, 44–46.

The Economist. 2020q. 'The Absent Student', 8–14 August, pp. 7, 14–16.

The Economist. 2020r. 'Office Politics: The Fight Over the Future of Work', 12–18 September, pp. 31–33.

The Economist Intelligence Unit. 2016. *Measuring Well-Governed Migration. The 2016 Migration Governance Index*. London: The Economist Intelligence Unit.

The RUAF Foundation. 2008. *Urban Agriculture Magazine*, 20 September. Leusden: RUAF.

The RUAF Foundation. 2011. *Urban Agriculture Magazine*, 25 September. Leusden: RUAF.

Thornton, P. 2014. 'Chinese Miners and Ghana's Golden Reform Opportunity', *International Growth Centre*. London: London School of Economics and Political Science.

Tibaijuka, K. 2009. *Building Prosperity: Housing and Economic Development*. London and Sterling: Earthscan Publishing.

Tiebout, C. 1956. 'A Pure Theory of Local Expenditures', *The Journal of Political Economy*, 64 (5), 416–424.

Tinti, P. and Reitano, T. 2017. *Migrant, Refugee, Smuggler, Savior*. New York: Oxford University Press.

Tipple, A.G. and Korboe, D. 1998. 'Housing Policy in Ghana: Towards a Supply-Oriented Future', *Habitat International*, 22 (3), 245–257.

Tipple, A.G. and Speak, S. 2006. 'Who is Homeless in Developing Countries? Differentiating between Inadequately Housed and Homeless People', *International Development Planning Review*, 28 (1), 57–84.

Tipple, A.G. and Speak, S. 2009. *The Hidden Millions: Homelessness in Developing Countries*. London and New York: Routledge.

Tipple, A.G. and Willis, K.G. 1992. 'Why Should Ghanaians Build Houses in Urban Areas?', *Cities*, 9 (1), 60–74.

Todaro, M.P. 1969. 'A Model of Labor Migration and Urban Unemployment in Less Developed Countries', *American Economic Review*, 59 (1), 138–148.

Todaro, M.P. and Smith, S. 2006. *Economic Development*. London: Pearson Addison Wesley.

Tonah, S. 2005. *Fulani in Ghana: Migration History, Integration and Resistance*. Accra: The Research and Publication Unit.

Tonah, S. 2007. 'Ghanaians Abroad and Their Ties Home: Cultural and Religious Dimensions of Transnational Migration', paper no. 25, presented at the conference on 'Transnationalisation and Development(s): Towards a North–South Perspective', Center for Interdisciplinary Research, Bielefeld, Germany.

Tonah, S. 2021. 'The Origins And Consequences Of The Mass Migration From West Africa To Libya And Europe - A West African Perspective', Inaugural Lecture, Ghana Academy of Arts and Sciences, Accra, Mar 25.

Tonah, S., Setrana, M.B., and Arthur, J.A. 2018. *Migration and Development in Africa: Trends, Challenges, and Policy Implications*. New York: Lexington Books.

Tonah, Steve, 2021, 'The Origins and Consequences of The Mass Migration From West Africa to Libya and Europe - A West African Perspective', Inaugural Lecture, Ghana Academy of Arts and Sciences, March 25, Accra., https://www.youtube.com/watch?v=KhzSuS1LPTo

Tran, L.T. 2017. '"I Am Really Expecting People to Judge Me by My Skills": Ethnicity and Identity of International Students', *Journal of Vocational Education and Training*, 69 (3), 390–404.

Tran, L.T. and Vu, T.T.P. 2018. '"Agency in Mobility": Towards a Conceptualisation of International Student Agency in Transnational Mobility', *Educational Review*, 70 (2), 167–187.

Tremann, C. 2013. 'Temporary Chinese Migration to Madagascar: Local Perceptions, Economic Impacts, and Human Capital Flows', *African Review of Economics and Finance*, 5 (1), 9–20.

Tsenkova, S. 2014. 'The Housing Policy Nexus and People's Responses to Housing Challenges in Post-Communist Cities', *Urbani izziv*, 24 (2), 90–106.

Tu, M. and Nehring, D. 2020. 'Remain, Return, or Re-Migrate? The (Im)mobility Trajectory of Mainland Chinese Students after Completing Their Education in the UK', *International Migration, 58* (3), 43–57.

Tu, M. and Xie, K. 2020. 'Privileged Daughters? Gendered Mobility among Highly Educated Chinese Female Migrants in the UK', *Social Inclusion, 8* (2), 68–76.

Turner, J. and Kwakye, E. 1996. 'Transport and Survival Strategies in a Developing Economy: Evidence from Accra, Ghana', *Journal of Transport Geography, 4* (3),161–168.

Turner, J.F.C. 1976/1977. *Housing by People: Towards Autonomy in Building Environments.* New York: Pantheon Books.

UN-HABITAT 2000. *Street Children and Gangs in African Cities: Guidelines for Local Authorities.* New York and Nairobi: World Bank and UN-HABITAT.

United Nations Human Settlements Programme. 2008. *The state of African cities 2008. A framework for addressing urban challenges in Africa.* Nairobi, Kenya: UN-HABITAT.

United Nations Human Settlements Programme. 2010. *The state of African cities 2008: Urban land markets, inequality, and governance.* Nairobi, Kenya: UNHABITAT.

UN-Habitat. 2003. The Challenge of Slums. London: Earthscan.

UN-HABITAT. 2011. Housing Profile in Ghana. Nairobi: UN-HABITAT.

United Nations High Commissioner for Refugees (UNHCR). 2017a. *Global Trends: Forced Displacement in 2017.* Geneva: UNCHR, www.unhcr.org/5b27be547.pdf.

UNHCR. 2017b. Statistical Yearbook 2016. Geneva: UNCHR.

UNHCR. 2018. 'Figures at a Glance: Statistical Yearbooks', www.unhcr.org/en-au/figures-at-a-glance.html.

United Nations Human Settlements Programme. 2008. The State of African Cities 2008. A Framework for Addressing Urban Challenges in Africa. Nairobi, Kenya: UN-Habitat.

United Nations Human Settlements Programme. 2010. The State of African Cities 2008: Urban Land Markets, Inequality, and Governance. Nairobi, Kenya: UN-Habitat.

University of Sydney. 2008. *International Student Guide 2008: Your Road to Success.* Sydney: The University of Sydney.

University of Sydney. 2011a. *The University of Sydney 2011–2015 Green Paper.* Sydney: The University of Sydney.

University of Sydney. 2011b. *Your International Student Guide to Undergraduate Study and Life at the University of Sydney 2011.* Sydney: The University of Sydney.

University of Sydney, 2019, *Annual Report 2018,* The University of Sydney, Sydney.

University of Sydney. 2020. *International Guide.* Sydney: The University of Sydney.

University of Sydney Accommodation Information Service (AIS). 2010a. *Find a Place to Live.* AIS Brochure, produced by Marketing and Communications. Sydney: The University of Sydney.

University of Sydney AIS. 2010b. 'On Campus and University Owned Accommodation', http://sydney.edu.au/current_students/accommodation/on_campus.shtml#uniown.

University of Sydney Strategic Planning Office. 2009. *Statistics 2009.* The University of Sydney, Sydney.

UNSW Human Rights Clinic. 2019. No Place Like Home: Addressing Exploitation of International Students in Sydney's Housing Market. Sydney: UNSW Human Rights Clinic.

Vasta, E. and Kandilege, L. 2007. 'London the Leveller: Ghanaian Work Strategies and Community Solidarity' Working Paper No. 52, Centre on Migration, Policy and Society, University of Oxford.

Veblen, T. 1899/1979. *The Theory of the Leisure Class*. New York: Penguin Books.

Veblen, T. 1920. 'Review of *The Economic Consequences of the Peace*', *Political Science Quarterly*, 35 (3), 467–472.

Veblen, T. 1923/2009, *Absentee Ownership: Business Enterprise in Recent Times: The Case of America*. New Brunswick and London: Transaction Publishers.

Vickers, T. 2019. *Borders, Migration and Class in an Age of Crisis Producing Immigrants and Workers*, Bristol: Bristol University Press.

Vidal, G. and Marshall, W. 2021. 'When and Why Does Public Debt Become a Problem?', *Journal of Economic Issues*, 55 (2), 559–564.

Voeten, E. 2021. *Ideology and International Institutions*. Princeton and Oxford: Princeton University Press.

Walia, H. 2021. *Border and Rule: Global Migration, Capitalism, and the Rise of Racist Nationalism*, Chicago, IL: Haymarket Books.

Wallace, A. and Quilgars, D. 2005. *Homelessness and Financial Exclusion: A Literature Review*. York: University of York.

Wallis, V. 2018. *Red–Green Revolution: The Politics and Technology of Ecosocialism*. Toronto and Chicago, IL: Political Animal Press.

Wang, Y. and Warn, J. 2018. 'Chinese Immigrant Entrepreneurship: Embeddedness and the Interaction of Resources with the Wider Social and Economic Context', *International Small Business Journal: Researching Entrepreneurship*, 36 (2), 131–148.

Wang, Z. 2016. 'Cross-Culture Adaptation Norms and Mechanism, Expatriation and Repatriation (Competitive Paper)', *Academy of International Business Annual Meeting*, New Orleans, 26 July 2016.

Watson, V. 2014. 'African Urban Fantasies: Dreams or Nightmares?', *Environment and Urbanization*, 26 (1), 1–17.

Wellman, C.H. and Cole, P. 2011. *Debating the Ethics of Immigration: Is There a Right to Exclude?* Oxford: Oxford University Press.

Whitaker, B.E. 2017. 'Migration within Africa and Beyond', *Africa Studies Review*, 60 (2), 209–220.

White, P. 1998. 'The Settlement Patterns of Developed World Migrants in London', *Urban Studies*, 35 (10), 1725–1744.

Wickramaararchchi, N. and Burns, E. 2017. 'Local Newspaper Reporting Humanitarian Migrants' Settlement Experience in an Australian Country Town', *Rural Society*, 26 (2), 125–142.

Widerquist, K. and Howard, M.W. (eds). 2012a, *Alaska's Permanent Fund Dividend: Examining Its Suitability as a Model*. New York: Palgrave MacMillan.

Widerquist, K. and Howard, M.W. (eds). 2012b. *Exporting the Alaska Model: Adapting the Permanent Fund Dividend for Reform around the World*. New York: Palgrave Macmillan.

Wiegratz, J. 2016. *Neoliberal Moral Economy: Capitalism, Socio-Cultural Change and Fraud in Uganda*. London and New York: Rowman & Littlefield International.

Wijburg, G., Aalbers, M.B., and Bono, F. 2020. 'Cuban Migrants and the Making of Havana's Property Market', *Urban Geography*, doi: 10.1080/02723638.2020.1774150.

Wilkins, S. 2020, 'Student Experience at International Branch Campuses', *Australian Universities' Review*, 62 (2), 39–46.

Williams, G.J. 2010. 'Anchorage Migration: The Movement between Alaska's Major Native Areas and Anchorage', *Alaska Economic Trends*, February, 4–12.

Williamson, O.E. 2009. 'Transaction Cost Economics: The Natural Progression', Nobel Prize Lecture, 8 December, Stockholm.

Wilkerson I, 2020, *Caste: The origins of our discontents*. NY: Random House.

Wilson, J. 2015. 'The Village That Turned to Gold: A Parable of Philanthrocapitalism', *Development and Change*, *47* (1), 3–28.

Withers, M. 2019. *Sri Lanka's Remittance Economy: A Multiscalar Analysis of Migration-Underdevelopment*. London: Routledge.

Wong, M. 2014. 'Geographies and Strategies of care-giving among Skilled Ghanaian migrant women'. *Women's Studies International Forum*, *42*, 28–43.

Wong, M. 2000. 'Ghanaian Women in Toronto's Labor Market: Negotiating Gendered Work and Transnational Household Strategies'. *Canadian Ethnic Studies*, *32*, 45–77.

World Bank. 2003. *Land Policies for Growth and Poverty Reduction*. Washington, DC: World Bank.

World Bank. 2011. *Rising Global Interest in Farmland: Can It Yield Equitable and Sustainable Benefits?* Washington, DC: World Bank.

World Bank. 2017. *Migrating to Opportunity: Overcoming Barriers to Labor Mobility in Southeast Asia*. Washington, DC: World Bank.

World Bank. 2018. *World Development Report 2018: Learning to Realize Education's Promise*. Washington, DC: World Bank.

World Bank. 2019. *Leveraging Economic Migration for Development: A Briefing for the World Bank Board*. Washington, DC: World Bank.

Xu, Z. and Chen, Y. 2019. 'Spatial Shift in China's Labor Struggles: Evidence and Implication', *Journal of Labor and Society*, *22*, 129–138.

Yagi, K. 2020. 'From Reproduction to Evolutionary Governance', in *From Reproduction to Evolutionary Governance: Toward an Evolutionary Political Economy*, ed. K. Yagi. Tokyo: Springer, pp. 3–23.

Yahya, M. 2019. 'The Middle East's Lost Decades: Development, Dissent, and the Future of the Arab World', *Foreign Affairs*, *98* (6), 48–55.

Yaro, J. 2006. 'Is Deagrarianisation Real? A Study of Livelihood Activities in Rural Northern Ghana', *The Journal of Modern African Studies*, *44* (1), 125–156.

Yau, Y. and Cheung, T.C. 2021. 'Revisiting the Concept of Property State: The Role of Private Landowners in the Suburb Development of Hong Kong', *American Journal of Economics and Sociology*. *80* (2), 427–464.

Yazgan, P., Utku, E.E., and Sirkeci, I. 2015. 'Syrian Crisis and Migration', *Migration Letters*, *12* (3), 181–192.

Yeboah, I.E.A. 2000. 'Structural Adjustment and Emerging Urban Form in Accra, Ghana', *Africa Today*, *47* (2), 61–89.

Yeboah, I.E.A. 2001. 'Structural adjustment and emerging urban form in Accra, Ghana', *Africa Today*, *7*, 61–89.

Yeboah, I.E.A. 2003. 'Demographic and Housing Aspects of Structural Adjustment and Emerging Urban Form in Accra, Ghana', *Africa Today*, *50* (1), 106–119.

Yeboah, I.E.A. 2005. 'Housing the Urban Poor in Twenty-First Century Sub-Saharan Africa: Policy Mismatch and a Way Forward for Ghana', *GeoJournal*, *62* (1), 147–161.

Yeboah, I.E.A. 2008. *Black African Neo-Diaspora: Ghanaian Immigrant Experiences in the Greater Cincinnati Area*. Lanham, MD: Lexington Books.

Yeboah, I.E.A. 2018. 'Capitalism and Sub-Saharan African Human Capital', *African Identities*, *16* (1), 67–86.

Yeboah, I.E.A, Maingi, J.K., and Arku, G. (2021) 'World Trade Center, Accra': production of urban space for the continued peripheral linkage of Ghana under globalization, *African Geographical Review*, *40* (1), 19–32,

Yeboah, M.A. 2010. 'Urban Poverty, Livelihood, and Gender: Perceptions and Experiences of Porters in Accra, Ghana', *Africa Today*, 56 (3), 42–60.

Yeboah, M.A. and Appiah-Yeboah, K. 2009. 'An Examination of the Cultural and Socio-economic Profiles of Porters in Accra, Ghana', *Nordic Journal of African Studies*, 18 (1), 1–21.

Yeboah, T. 2020. 'Future Aspirations of Rural–Urban Young Migrants in Accra, Ghana', *Children Geographies*, doi: 10.1080/14733285.2020.1737643.

Yinghui, L. 2009. *New Arrival International Student Survey Report*. The University of Sydney Office of the Deputy Vice Chancellor (International).

Young, J. 2012. *The Fate of Sudan: The Origins and Consequences of a Flawed Peace Process*. London: Zed.

Yu, S. 2019, 'The Belt and Road Initiative: Modernity, Geopolitics, and the Developing Global Order', *Asian Affairs*, 50 (2), 187–201.

Zein-Elabdin, E.O. 2016. *Economics, Culture and Development*. New York: Routledge.

Zevin, A. 2019. *Liberalism at Large: The World According to the Economist*. London and New York: Verso.

Zezza, A. and Tasciotti, L. 2010. 'Urban Agriculture, Poverty, and Food Security: Empirical Evidence from a Sample of Developing Countries', *Food Policy*, 35 (4), 265–273.

Zhang, Y. and Elsner, W. 2017. 'A Social-Leverage Mechanism on the Silk Road: The Private Emergence of Institutions in Central Asia, from the 7th to the 9th Century', *Journal of Institutional Economics*, 13 (2), 379–400.

Zhao, Y. 2019. 'The Way to Understand the Nature and Extent of Judicial Independence in China', *Asian Journal of Law and Society*, 6 (1), 131–157.

Zhou, X., Li, J., and Jordan, L.P. 2019. 'Parental Intent for Children to Study Abroad: The Role of Educational Aspiration and Children's Characteristics', *Cambridge Journal of Education*, 49 (6), 789–807.

Zhou, Y., Jindal-Snape, D., Topping, K., and Todman, J. 2008. 'Theoretical Models of Culture Shock and Adaptation in International Students in Higher Education', *Studies in Higher Education*, 33 (1), 63–75.

Zouache A. 2017a. 'Institutions and Development in Saint-Simonian Political Economy', in *Economic Thought and Institutional Change in France and Italy*, ed. R. Soliani. Springer, Cham, pp. 1789–1914.

Zouache, A. 2017b. 'Race, Competition, and Institutional Change in J. R. Commons', *The European Journal of the History of Economic Thought*, 24 (1), 341–368.

Zouache, A. 2018. 'Institutions and the Colonisation of Africa: Some Lessons from French Colonial Economics', *Journal of Institutional Economics*, 14 (2), 373–391.

Zouache, A. 2020. 'From Inequality to Stratification: Obeng-Odoom's Contribution to the Study of Inequality in Africa—*Property, Institutions, and Social Stratification in Africa*', *African Review of Economics and Finance*, 12 (1), 299–306.

Zuber, Z.I. 2020. 'Explaining the Immigrant Integration Laws of German, Italian and Spanish Regions: Sub-State Nationalism and Multilevel Party Politics', *Regional Studies*, 54 (11), 1486–1497.

Index

Note: Tables, figures and notes are indicated by italic *t*, *f* and *n* following the page number.

9/11 Commission 92